Eros in Neoplatonism and Its Reception in Christian Philosophy

Eros in Neoplatonism and Its Reception in Christian Philosophy

Exploring Love in Plotinus, Proclus and Dionysius the Areopagite

Dimitrios A. Vasilakis

BLOOMSBURY ACADEMIC
LONDON • NEW YORK • OXFORD • NEW DELHI • SYDNEY

BLOOMSBURY ACADEMIC
Bloomsbury Publishing Plc
50 Bedford Square, London, WC1B 3DP, UK
1385 Broadway, New York, NY 10018, USA
29 Earlsfort Terrace, Dublin 2, Ireland

BLOOMSBURY, BLOOMSBURY ACADEMIC and the Diana logo
are trademarks of Bloomsbury Publishing Plc

First published in Great Britain 2021
This paperback edition published in 2022

Copyright © Dimitrios A. Vasilakis, 2021

Dimitrios A. Vasilakis has asserted his right under the Copyright,
Designs and Patents Act, 1988, to be identified as Author of this work.

For legal purposes the Acknowledgements on pp. ix–xi constitute
an extension of this copyright page.

Cover design by Charlotte Daniels
Cover image © El Greco, *The Concert of Angels*, painting, circa 1610,
incamerastock / Alamy Stock Photo.

All rights reserved. No part of this publication may be reproduced or transmitted in
any form or by any means, electronic or mechanical, including photocopying,
recording, or any information storage or retrieval system, without prior
permission in writing from the publishers.

Bloomsbury Publishing Plc does not have any control over, or responsibility for,
any third-party websites referred to or in this book. All internet addresses given in
this book were correct at the time of going to press. The author and publisher
regret any inconvenience caused if addresses have changed or sites have
ceased to exist, but can accept no responsibility for any such changes.

A catalogue record for this book is available from the British Library.

Library of Congress Cataloging-in-Publication Data
Names: Vasilakis, Dimitrios A., author.
Title: Eros in Neoplatonism and its reception in Christian philosophy : exploring love in Plotinus, Proclus and Dionysius the Areopagite / Dimitrios A. Vasilakis.
Description: London ; New York, NY : Bloomsbury Academic, 2020. | Revision of author's thesis (doctoral)–King's College London, 2014, titled Neoplatonic love : the metaphysics of Eros in Plotinus, Proclus and the Pseudo-Dionysius. | Includes bibliographical references and index.
Identifiers: LCCN 2020034412 (print) | LCCN 2020034413 (ebook) | ISBN 9781350163850 (hardback) | ISBN 9781472985217 (paperback) | ISBN 9781350163867 (ebook) | ISBN 9781350163874 (epub)
Subjects: LCSH: Plotinus. Enneads. III, 5 (50) | Proclus, approximately 410-485. Alcibiades I. | Pseudo-Dionysius, the Areopagite. | Neoplatonism. | Platonic love. | Love–Philosophy. | Erōs (The Greek word) | Christianity–Philosophy–History–To 1500.
Classification: LCC B645 .V38 2020 (print) | LCC B645 (ebook) | DDC 186/.4–dc23
LC record available at https://lccn.loc.gov/2020034412
LC ebook record available at https://lccn.loc.gov/2020034413

ISBN: HB: 978-1-3501-6385-0
PB: 978-1-4729-8521-7
ePDF: 978-1-3501-6386-7
eBook: 978-1-3501-6387-4

Typeset by Integra Software Services Pvt. Ltd.

To find out more about our authors and books visit www.bloomsbury.com
and sign up for our newsletters.

To Despina and Teresa Irini

Ἔρως ἀνίκατε μάχαν, ...
σ' οὔτ' ἀθανάτων φύξιμος οὐδεὶς
οὔθ' ἀμερίων σέ γ' ἀνθρώπων, ...

    Sophocles,
Antigone, 781 and 787–90

οὔτοι συνέχθειν,
ἀλλὰ συμφιλεῖν ἔφυν.

Ibid., 523

« ... Ἐν ἀρχῇ ἦν ἡ ἀγάπη ... »

Nikiforos Vrettakos (1912–91),
«Τα Δεκατέσσερα παιδιά», 1 (from the collection,
The time and the river, 1957)

Contents

Acknowledgements		ix
Third-party material		x
Introduction		1
1	Plotinus and *Enneads* III.5.[50]: 'On Love'	13
	1.1 The ontological status of Soul's Eros	13
	1.1.1 Synopsis of III.5	13
	1.1.2 The main issue	14
	1.1.3 Eros and myth	16
	1.1.4 Eros and vision	20
	1.1.5 Eros and tragedy	24
	1.1.6 Eros and vision, again	27
	1.2 Potential objections and answers	29
	1.2.1 Unity of theme	30
	1.2.2 On daimonology	31
	1.2.3 A daimonic counter-objection from within III.5?	33
	1.2.4 Eros and Soul: Who is first?	34
	1.3 Nous and Eros	37
	1.4 Conclusions	41
2	Proclus on the *First Alcibiades*	67
	2.1 Providential and Reversive Eros: Proclus versus Plotinus?	68
	2.1.1 From Alcibiades' reversive eros to Socratic love	68
	2.1.2 From eros to the Demiurge and the statesman	72
	2.1.3 From Platonic eros to Aristotelian friendship	75
	2.1.4 Limiting the scope: From eros to providential eros	78
	2.1.5 Qualifying love: From manic eros to undefiled eros	84
	2.2 Locating Eros in the intelligible hierarchy	90
	2.2.1 Divine Eros and its function	91
	2.2.2 Eros as a mediator	96
	2.2.3 After Eros	99

		2.2.4 Before Eros	102
		2.2.5 Eros and friendship	108
3	Dionysius and the *Divine Names*		141
	3.1 Divine Eros and its function		143
		3.1.1 God and Eros: Causally or existentially?	143
		3.1.2 After God: Eros by participation	151
	3.2 From Christian agape to the Christification of Eros		155

Epilogue	184
Bibliography	187
Index	215

Acknowledgements

One of my earliest interlocutors and teachers, with whom I still discuss a wide range of problems, has been my father, Adonis (son of a Corfiot priest). Certainly, to a great extent he has shaped my various research, philosophical and artistic interests. In his doctoral dissertation, which was edited by myself and was subsequently published (Vasilakis 2009), the topic of love was central. Another figure of great influence upon me from my school years (secondary high school) was my teacher of the 'Religion'-class, Petros Moustakas, who introduced me, along with my father, to the richness of the (Neo-)Patristic tradition, with love playing a pivotal role. During my undergraduate degree in the University of Athens, I was taught more than once Plato's *Symposium*, recalling especially the course given by Vasilis Lentakis (son of Andreas Lentakis, the author of Lentakis 1992), while Vana Nicolaidou-Kyrianidou's lectures on Plato's *Republic* made for an excellent complement. When I came to King's College London,[1] thanks especially to the seminars, classes and tutorials with Mary Margaret McCabe (our beloved MM, by now Emerita), Peter Adamson (already since years in LMU[2]), Raphael Woolf, Will Rasmussen (and later Shaul Tor), I got such a fresh view of Plato and the subsequent tradition that it was like meeting with their philosophy for the first time. In the beginning of my PhD I did not know what topic to select. My inspiring mentor, wise teacher (and friend), Peter Adamson gave me the idea of reading Plotinus' treatise on love. Immediately we found a topic that I got in love with and in a musical manner I could set as an antiphon against the work of two other figures I am enamoured with, Proclus and Dionysius, ending up writing a counterpoint for three voices. The outcome (as harmonic as I could), my PhD thesis (Vasilakis 2014), was approved without corrections by the examiners (John Dillon and Pavlos Kalligas, who nonetheless made helpful suggestions) and formed the basis for the present book, although I have implemented various modifications, corrections and additions. It was Georgios Steiris, an old and good teacher of mine from the University of Athens (School of Philosophy), who gave me the impulse to reengage with the thesis and submit it for publication, undertaken by an excellent publishing house, Bloomsbury, with a most helpful personnel, such as Jade Grogan and Viswasirasini Govindarajan, as well as reviewers that supplied me with encouraging comments I profited from.

I heartily thank all these persons and foundations mentioned above, as well as all those relatives (esp. my mother and sister), friends, colleagues, teachers and institutions that have helped me in every respect, but I have not had the chance to name here. While doing the PhD, friends (from Goodenough College) would make fun of me saying that I should also undertake some practical training on love as a consummation of my studies. Well, as PhD was in its last stages (in a concert of Alkinoos Ioannidis) I met the person who would accompany me for the next years in every up and down of life. While in the initial stages of the preparations for this publication, a cycle seemed to have been completed and a new one was rising. For all her love this book is dedicated to Despina and to this sweet angel we gave birth to, our most beloved daughter, Teresa Irini.

Third-party material

Having started presenting drafts of PhD-subchapters more than once in various conferences already as a PhD student, I had already used some basic material from the present book's subchapters in publications (i.e. arrangements and variations on these themes) that have already appeared in print or are forthcoming. In the cases of reproduction of a chunk of text, along with my publisher I gratefully acknowledge the permission granted to reproduce the copyright material in this book from:

1. *Diotima*, with regard to Vasilakis 2015 that has used some material from chapter 1.1.2 and 3 (with a remark from 1.4);
2. *Dia-noesis* regarding Vasilakis 2019c, which was based on the main thesis of chapter 2.1.3;
3. *Θεολογία*, regarding Vasilakis 2016, having drawn on parts of chapter 3.2;
4. Peeters Publishers (for *Studia Patristica*), regarding Vasilakis 2017b, having drawn on other parts of chapter 3.2 (and the same holds for a forthcoming paper I recently read at the Ecclesiastical Academy of Athens);
5. Walter de Gruyter Verlag with regard to Vasilakis 2017a, which exploited ideas from chapters 2.1.1 and 2.1.2;
6. The Greek Philosophical Society regarding Vasilakis 2018 (for which holds the same as both Vasilakis 2017a and a forthcoming paper I read at the 'Metochi' Study Centre of the Norwegian University of Agder in the island of Lesvos, back in 2015 -adding some material from chapter 2.1.5).

Generally speaking, every effort has been made to trace copyright holders and to obtain their permission for the use of copyright material. We apologize for any errors or omissions and we would be grateful if notified of any corrections that should be incorporated in future reprints or editions of this book.

Notes

1 For postgraduate studies (MA/MPhil and PhD), generously funded by the Lilian Voudouris Foundation and the Academy of Athens. I have also been the recipient of educational grants by the A.G. Leventis Foundation.
2 For my first academic visit of this institution (in Munich), I must especially thank the AHRC-scheme, having contributed through KCL.

Introduction

Nowadays many people talk about Platonic love; in this book I present how the Neoplatonists understood it. Given that Eros plays a central role in Plato's thought,[1] it is not surprising that the same is true for Neoplatonic philosophy. My treatment attempts to show this significance. I will be focusing on three key figures: Plotinus, the acknowledged founder of Neoplatonism; Proclus, a great systematizer of Platonic philosophy; and Dionysius the Areopagite, who has affinities with Neoplatonism even if (in my view at least) he is fundamentally a Christian thinker. By juxtaposing Dionysius with the two earlier Neoplatonists, I will be able to explore the question of how Platonic love interacted with Christian love and how ancient Greek and pagan conceptions of eros survived in the Christian and especially Byzantine tradition, of which Dionysius is a cornerstone.

Love has of course attracted attention not only in contemporary systematic philosophy,[2] but also in the field of the history of philosophy.[3] There have been several studies examining love especially in Plotinus, but also in Proclus and Dionysius. Regarding Plotinus, on the one hand, there are studies which examine specifically his treatise on Love (on which more below) of which the doctoral dissertation of Wolters (1984) is the longest and most impressive study.[4] On the other hand, there are discussions with wider scope in Plotinus' metaphysics. Among these one needs to take note especially of Lacrosse (1994), Pigler (2002) and the recent as well as very systematic PhD thesis by Bertozzi (2012).[5] In contradistinction to the number of studies devoted to Plotinus, Terezis (2002) stands alone for the field of Proclean studies,[6] although one needs to take note, of course, of a hitherto unpublished PhD by D'Andres (2010), which is very close, as will see, to the thematic of my chapter on Proclus.[7] Things are again better arithmetically, when one turns to Dionysius, since we possess older studies, such as the one by Horn (1925),[8] as well as recent ones, a very good example of which is Riggs (2009).[9] There have been also some short treatments which make a comparison between the aforementioned philosophers.[10] Armstrong (1961), who stands out as an early example, gives a brief portrait of love in Plato, Plotinus and Proclus (including the Neoplatonist Hierocles), as well as Christianity (without specifically referring to any Christian author, save for passing mentions of Origen), and my approach is similar to his spirit.[11] Among more recent contributions,[12] one needs to pay attention to Tornau (2006)[13] and Riggs (2010). The latter gives the most systematic approach between Proclus and Dionysius on love I have come across.[14] I would say that my conclusions are similar (but not identical) to his, although (or actually because) I use other means, owing to different methodology, as well as the specific primary texts and some secondary literature I employ.

To my knowledge, though, there do not exist treatments that present both a detailed discussion of love in each of the abovementioned philosophers and a comparative treatment that can give us a basis for understanding how from Plato we can get to, say, Yannaras, a contemporary thinker who grounds his philosophy on the Patristic notion of Eros.[15] An exception forms the most recent monograph by Corrigan (2018), which starts with Plato and Aristotle and continues within the Platonic tradition till he includes Dionysius, having also references or treatments (admittedly not very long ones) to less prominent figures, like Alcinous and Olympiodorus,[16] but also to the more famous Iamblichus (although his references to eros are scarce) and Ficino.[17] Once more, Corrigan's dense, interesting and informative approach can be seen as complementary to mine, since it has a totally different structure, dealing extensively with a group of problems, such as pleasure (in Plato and Aristotle), which do not interest me within the context of my argument. What is more, in the case of Plotinus, Corrigan does not use at all the principal tractate I will be using and interpreting,[18] while his treatment of Proclus and Dionysius is much shorter and narrower than mine.[19]

For my part, I must add a few words regarding my methodology. I do not purport to present or reconstruct a system. My approach takes off as a philological study, i.e. a textual interpretation with all the tools that Classics has bequeathed us, and culminates with the delineation of philosophical problems, as well as the philosophical (metaphysical, ethical and sometime aesthetic) consequences I constantly highlight or bring to light.[20] The philosophers themselves I consider, Plotinus and Dionysius, were not system-builders, although they did 'first philosophy' (or theology in the sense of Aristotle's *Metaphysics* 1026a18-21).[21] Even Proclus, who is regarded as a systematizer of Neoplatonic philosophy, due to being a sensitive interpreter foremost of Platonic texts, as we will see, can be found to have (at least seeming) 'contradictions' among several works or even within one work.²² As a result, I am implementing such a kind of philosophical hermeneutics that tries to make sense of concrete texts,²³ which I then put into a wider textual and philosophical context. Thus, I end up not only with satisfactory readings of various important texts, but also with an enticing – I hope – philosophical account.²⁴ Although each chapter has an interest in itself (for the individual philosopher I interpret), with my constant interconnections I give also a narrative that is worth attending across the various chapters.²⁵ So, let me give an overview of my general argument in the book.

The first chapter discusses a treatise of Plotinus that is devoted to Love. Given the importance ascribed to Love throughout the *Enneads*, various interpreters have been dissatisfied by the discussion Plotinus offers in III.5. However, the critics have neglected the narrower scope of the treatise's exegetical character. One of Plotinus' main aims is the defence of genuine Platonic love against the interpretations that other philosophical circles, e.g. the Gnostics, had given for key Platonic passages, such as the myth of the genealogy of Eros in the *Symposium* (203b1-c6).²⁶ Despite its dialectical character, though, III.5 does provide us with insights into the function of Eros within Plotinus' system as a whole.²⁷ My main thesis here will be that eros is identified with reversion, because it implies deficiency in need of fulfilment. For an entity (say Soul) to be/exist is to be erotic, i.e. be directed to the intelligible realm. If, then, reversion is necessary for the constitution of an entity *qua* entity, then Plotinus' entire ontology is erotic.

The second chapter deals with Proclus' *Commentary on the First Alcibiades*. The *Alcibiades* is not a straightforwardly erotic dialogue.²⁸ Yet its opening lines give Proclus the occasion to say so many things about love that this Commentary²⁹ winds up as the principal source for Proclus' ideas on love.³⁰ With Proclus we have a new association of love with procession and/or providence. In various sections I explain how this is the case. In the first part I examine the ethical aspects, whereas in the second I deal more with metaphysics. Although already in the conclusion of the first part I note that Proclus' divergence from Plotinus is much more verbal than substantial, I give the final answer of how Proclus can consistently combine ascending (-upwards) and descending (-downwards) eros in the second part.³¹ A by-product of my overall treatment is that Proclus emerges as an interpreter of Plato who has affinities with modern scholars, and who should be consulted especially in defence of Plato against his modern critics. On the one hand, I show the way in which Proclus could answer to Vlastos' famous accusation that Plato's erotic theory fails to capture genuine concern for others,³² even if I also emphasize the negative aspects and limitations of the Proclean lover. On the other hand, my discussion of Proclus' dependence on Platonic texts can do away with A. Nygren's proposal about Christian influences.[33]

Because I do not accept Nygren's portrayal of (pagan) «ἔρως» and (Christian) «ἀγάπη»[34] as two rigid categories that are in absolute conflict,[35] I also cannot accept the statement that these two are confused in Dionysius' treatment,[36] with the further suggestion that Dionysius is a plagiarizer of Proclus.[37] My last chapter, which draws mostly on the *Divine Names*, defies the old suggestion about Dionysius' uncritical reception of Neoplatonism and concludes the book by showing how the Proclean language can be transformed in light of Christianity. The main difference stems from a different conception of ecstasy, which neglects the (upwards or downwards) direction. I have structured the chapter following the metaphysical scheme I discussed in the second part of the treatment of Proclus.[38] I show that Dionysius' system is at least as erotic as the Proclean, though I emphasize the differences between them as well by drawing a contrast between the Neoplatonic hero Socrates, an embodied soul, and Christ, the incarnated person of the Holy Trinity.

I hope that my discussions to follow will prove to be relevant not only to readers interested in Neoplatonism, including its various forms and interaction with Christian philosophy, but also to students of classical philosophy, i.e. Plato and Aristotle (as well as the Presocratics and Hellenistic philosophy). Recent scholarship tends to remind us that apart from modern interpreters we would be largely benefitted from reading ancient Commentaries, too, say on Plato,[39] even if we will not be willing to agree with their late antique authors. Hence, the historical period relevant to the scope of this book is quite broad.

In systematic terms a note might be added with respect to the key terminology. As the title indicates, this monograph is concerned with the phenomenon indicated by the ancient Greek word ἔρως. I have already remarked that in the case of Dionysius a twin name taken into account is ἀγάπη. With regard to the two pagan Neoplatonists examined here, the twin name of eros in Proclus is «φιλία» (friendship), while in Plotinus' case the main bulk of evidence considers solely the term eros.[40] Contemporary philosophy might want to separate three different phenomena according to the aforementioned threefold terminological distinction.[41] Another characteristic of the present book, then, is that by situating the terms in specific philosophical contexts it not only draws distinctions, but also marks similarities,[42] which might not be surprising in the light of the Neoplatonic almost erotic strive for unity at any level.

Notes

1 Apart from works to be referred to in the following chapters two classic studies about Platonic love are Robin (1933) and Gould (1963), while for more recent scholarship see Price (1989: 1–102, 207–35). See also Kosman (1976), O'Connell (1981: esp. 11–17), Halperin (1985), Bernardete (2001), Rhodes (2003), Karfík (2007), the wide-ranging approach of Gordon (2012), the introductory piece by Kalfas (2008) and most recently Woolf (2017) and Hobbs (2017). Platonic love is related to death by Maraguianou (1990: 3–26, 49–69) (with Maraguianou-Dermousi 1994: 13–67), and compared to Freud by Christodoulidi-Mazaraki (1983) (along with the short Christodoulidi-Mazaraki 1980) and (independently) Santas (1988), as well as Kahn (1987: 95–102), from a wider perspective. Finally, for a recent and remarkable attempt to trace among else the roots of 'Platonic love', *qua* part of a modus vivendi, in the biography of the young Socrates, identifying the fictional Diotima (priestess from Mantineia) of the Platonic *Symposium* with the historical Aspasia (of Miletus, partner of Pericles and featuring in Plato's *Menexenus*), see D'Angour (2019).

2 See for instance the relevant entry and its Bibliography in the online *Stanford Encyclopedia of Philosophy* (SEP). To this add: Martin (2019), Badiou-Truong (2009), Tzavaras (1993) (examining eros along with war), Ricoeur (1995) (regarding the dialectics between love and justice), Rozanis (2012), Manos (2015), Schindler (2018) and May (2019). From the more remote and recent past one should not forget Kierkegaard (1995) [1847] (whether existentialism can be termed as systematic philosophy or not) and Ortega y Gasset (1957), respectively. Approaches from the field of theology (whether systematically or historically) and Patristics are also relevant to the matter; see e.g. Chartier (2007), Voulgarakis (2004), Stamoulis (2009) (examining love along with death), Boswell (2018), the concise study of Mavropoulos (2017) and infra in n. 41 (as well as some entries of n. 42). Von Hildebrand (2009) is one among numerous examples of authors working in the borderlines between philosophy and theology (in this case phenomenology and Roman-Catholicism). Finally, for an approach combining (continental) philosophy (of religion) and psychoanalysis, see Clemente (2020), while Rapport (2019) is more interdisciplinary.

3 See the diachronic accounts in May (2011), Rist (1964), Osborne (1994), Düsing (2009) and *Filosofein* (2018). Bradshaw (2008), following the direction of Byzantium's reception of classical philosophy, is very brief, but lucid, while Rinne (2018) is a case study on Kant. Finally, Dillon-O'Brien (forthcoming) treats specifically of Platonic love from Antiquity till the Renaissance.

4 See also Dillon (1969) and Smith (2007). I have not consulted Heidl (2008), because I do not read Hungarian. From what I can understand, it is an annotated Hungarian translation of *Enn*. III.5 with a short introduction.

5   Additionally, see Damaskos (2003) and Rist (1964: 56–112), as well as Michaelides (2018). Romano (1984), Kelessidou-Galanos (1972: 98–100) and Ucciani (1998) have more specific focus.
6   See also Terezis-Tsakoymaki (2014b).
7   I thank Prof P. Hoffmann, who had informed me back in 2012 of the subject of D'Andres (2010) (PhD thesis written under the supervision of A. Longo). What is more, M. Martijn had informed me that she intends to turn a lecture of hers entitled 'The Demon Lover. Inspired love in Proclus' In Alc.' (read at the 9th ISNS 2011 Conference in Atlanta and at the International Conference 'Ἀρχαί: Proclus Diadochus of Constantinople and his Abrahamic Interpreters', Istanbul, December 2012) into an article, an intention which, however, has not been fulfilled yet.
8   See also Rist (1966).
9   See also Heide (2019) and Terezis-Vgenopoulou (1999). Riggs (2009), who closely compares Proclus and Dionysius in 82–7, and Perl (2013) have similar scope as Terezis-Panagopoulos (2009). Two more articles that can serve as a helpful introduction to the topic of my chapter on Dionysius are Perl (1998) and Ivanović (2015). (Kranidiotis (2018) is shorter and for a wider audience, although still helpful.) See also the entries in Aertsen (2009: 193, n. 11), Rist (1999), having modified some of his earlier views, and some short remarks in Gavrilyuk (2012: 99–101). Another recent attempt (with rather hasty comparisons with Plotinus and later Neoplatonists) is that of Kupperman (2013), but it is quite short, while Marica (2015) is very well informed in terms of representative bibliography from many areas (hence, judging esp. from n. 9 in 184a-b, one is puzzled as to why the 'first century' in the title is not accompanied at least by a question mark). Finally, the PhD thesis by Ivanovic 2014 compares Dionysius with Maximus the Confessor on the basis of eros (and its correlate Beauty) and has just been published as Ivanovic (2019). (Ivanovic (2009) compares the chronological extremes of Plato and Maximus, whereas Douma (1999) in her short account of pedagogic eros dwells on Plato and Dionysius, while mentioning very briefly Plotinus and Proclus.)
10 A notable article comparing Plotinus with Saint Augustine (for whom see infra, n. 36 in Section 3.1.1) is Tornau (2005). Edwards (2009) compares Augustine with Proclus, but his main focus is Augustine, rather than the Neoplatonist.
11 On the other hand, de Vogel (1963) treats also Dionysius and Boethius, but avoids specific references to Plato (at least the *Phaedrus*), while she presents some Hellenistic and Middle Platonic dimensions, too (4–10). McGinn (1996) has the scope of both papers (i.e. by Armstrong and de Vogel), adding to the list engagement with Origen (189 and 195–7) and Thomas Aquinas (204ff. I am afraid, though, that in n. 25 of 198, where Nygren's procrustean attitude, to be seen, is criticized, the criticism against Armstrong (1961: 113) is unfair). Quispel (1979) begins with the same grounds as de Vogel (1963) (189–95, with

some criticism of her in 194), but then he departs to other fields: apart from curious speculations about the author and the content of the Fourth Gospel (of love: 201–5, which invert Nygren's thesis, as we will see), he stresses Proclus' indebtedness to the *Chaldean Oracles* for the role of Eros in cosmogony, tracing this back to the Orphic cosmogonies (196–201), although he, too, neglects to mention Plato (save for some passing mentions of the *Symposium* in 194 and 203), and especially the *Phaedrus*. De Vogel (1981) answered the challenges of Quispel by elaborating on the topics she had touched in 1963, and especially on the ontological position of eros in Proclus' hierarchy (64–9. This fact explains the loose structure of that paper).

12 Starting with Beierwaltes (1986), who in his condensed presentation of Plato, Plotinus, Proclus and Dionysius examines primarily the status of Beauty in relation to the Good, god and the divine, and secondarily the complement of Eros, while in my treatment I do the reverse. What is more, Esposito Buckley (1992) (which formed the basis for chapter 1 of her PhD thesis: Esposito 1997) gives a comparison only of Dionysius and Plotinus on the issue of God as Eros. She leaves aside Proclus (referring to him only in n. 57 of 55, and 60 with n. 64) and with regard to Plotinus she focuses on procession (35ff., although we should bear in mind that the 'self-contemplation' of the One is applied 'as if' to it) and his conception of the One as Eros (hence the absence of references to *Enn.* III.5, apart from a passing ref. to §4 in n. 3 of 44). See also Ghiţ (2015), who has short sections on the antecedents of Plato, Aristotle, Plotinus and Proclus (in 100–7, as well as of Bible and Patristic literature: 108–11 and 115–17) before (and after) he gets to Dionysius (on love: 107–8 and 111–13 with 113–15). Finally, Molodeţ-Jitea (2015) offers only one short introductory section on Plato in 89–90.

13 Like Beierwaltes, Tornau, too, is concerned with the relation of Beauty to Goodness (e.g. Tornau 2006: 203), albeit in a lesser degree, while mainly he compares Proclus with Plotinus, in terms of ascending eros (and of its varying scope in these two philosophers). While Tornau (2006: 220 with n. 85; cf. also 218) acknowledges the existence of descending (/providential) eros in Proclus, he does not really account for it (despite 212–13). The same is true for Markus (2016: 7), too.

14 Ivanović (2015) makes also some extensive references (see, e.g., 127, 130–1) to comparisons with Proclus (and Plotinus), which are however narrower than those of Riggs.

15 His seminal work is Yannaras (2007), whose first Modern Greek version dates back to 1970; see also my brief account in the Epilogue. For an introduction to Yannaras, see Andreopoulos-Harper (2019) and Mitralexis (2018).

16 Olympiodorus' lectures on the *First Alcibiades* in sixth-century Alexandria bear the seal of Proclus (and Damascius) and are available in English with excellent introductions and notes by Griffin (2015, 2016).

17 For Corrigan's relevant references see in the (entries of the) Indices at the back of his rich monograph. I myself have only passing references to these figures mainly in footnotes throughout the body of my book.
18 Save for a sole and passing reference to *Enn.* III.5 in Corrigan 2018: n. 80 in 74–5.
19 See also the last comment of n. 221 infra, Section 2.1.5.
20 In this sense my approach is a typical 'history-of-philosophy' one.
21 The term 'theology' in Dionysius has much richer connotations, as we will see in Chapter 3.
22 See e.g. infra, n. 128 in Chapter 2.
23 As to why I have chosen the specific texts I will be presenting shortly, the answer is that in the case of each philosopher these are the main texts, whose central theme (or at least one of the major issues) has been eros. It was natural to take these works as the basis for my study, and then add the rest of the material that the reader will find amply attested in the pages of each chapter.
24 To do that, i.e. in order to give interesting philosophical answers, one should first construct and pose the right questions. I think that one of the contributions of the present study is that it brings into question and problematizes concepts that in some of the literature might pass as a kind of obvious 'given' (for instance, the Neoplatonic idea of descending eros), while they should not.
25 The philosophers I examine do not form a group whose participants were randomly selected out of well-known thinkers of Late antiquity. As the reader will assure in the pages to come, each figure of this trio has an important, distinctive and highly influential position with regard specifically to the (history of) philosophical (and/or theological) approaches to love, and they have been (in a linear fashion) the main, as well as direct interlocutors not only within intra-school debates (as in the Neoplatonic case of Plotinus and Proclus), but especially within the dialogue of Paganism and Christianity (the case of Dionysius with Proclus).
26 Cf. Kalligas (2014: 503 with n. 6). Kalligas (2014: 504, n. 12) rightly criticizes Miller (1992: 232–4), because, apart from parallels in erotic imagery, she fails to note Plotinus' distance from Gnosticism with regard to the positive value of eros.
27 Thus, it is no wonder that III.5 merited a Renaissance *Commentary* by Marsilio Ficino. For a good guide in the erotic journey from Plato to Ficino through Plotinus, see Wurm (2008).
28 Still, it is included in the anthology of Reeve (2006), and Belfiore (2012) devotes her first chapter (31–67) to the *Alcibiades I*, focusing on the relation between love and self-knowledge (for the second part of this pair, see now Wasmuth 2016). See also Dillon (1994: 390, 391 with n. 14), the vindication in Corrigan (2018: 51–3) and Markus (2016: 24) (with n. 112 for bibliographical tip).
29 Its extant part finishes with incomplete comments on *Alc. I* 116, a3-b1.
30 Another source, but not treated in the book, is within the Essay (ΙΔ') of the *Republic Commentaries* (2,28–31), as: «Τί αἰνίττεται ἡ τοῦ Διὸς πρὸς τὴν Ἥραν συνουσία, καὶ

τίς ὁ τῆς Ἥρας κόσμος, καὶ τίς ὁ τόπος, ἐν ᾧ ἡ συνουσία, καὶ τίς ὁ ἔρως τοῦ Διός, καὶ τίς ὁ θεῖος ὕπνος, καὶ ἁπλῶς πάσης ἐκείνης τῆς μυθολογίας ἐξήγησις.»

31   Here a static approach towards Proclus' metaphysical system is combined with a dynamic one.

32   See Vlastos (1973) (which is a revised form of a talk given in 1969). Vlastos generated a host of articles and books by other scholars as a response. Some of them have already been referred to in n. 1, while others are to be found in Chapter 2 (nn. 71 and 73 in Sections 2.1.2 and 2.1.3, respectively). For now, as an example of the criticism Vlastos has received, see Osborne (1994: 223–6 with n. 17 in 57), whose book contains an abundance of remarks pertinent to my project.

33   See Nygren (1953: 569). This is even accepted by Rist (1964: 214), who however criticizes Nygren's presentation of Proclus' Platonic (and Plotinian) interpretation in Rist (1964: 215–16); cf. also Rist (1964: 219) and McGinn (1996: 198, n. 27). Rist retracted his former concession to Nygren already in Rist (1966: 243); cf. also Rist (1970: 168 and n. 37 in 407). One cannot deny the historical possibility that Pagans and Christians gave reasons to each other in order to exploit certain themes. Cf. e.g. Corrigan (2018: 107). However, as I purport to show, in the case of love, from a systematic point of view, pagan Neoplatonists could have said what they wrote about love with sole reference to Plato and the pagan tradition commenced by him, without ever having met Christianity. (Cf. Corrigan's relevant, but not identical, remark in 2018: 110.)

34   To be sure, Nygren's discussion is learned and has some merits, but it is too oversimplified and driven by an objectionable agenda. A useful synopsis of Nygren's overall project is given in: Ramfos (1999: 128–34), who criticizes it in Ramfos (1999: 134–8); Rist (1970: 156–61, 169, and n. 53 in 408) (especially the two columns of 160–1), presenting his Platonic and Scriptural counter-arguments in 161–73 (although de Vogel (1981: 61–2) talks about the disagreement with Nygren, I am afraid she is too harsh with Rist's approach in de Vogel (1981: 63–5 and n. 28 in 77–8)); Düsing (2009: 30–8), who dwells much on Augustine (34–8) and presents a Roman-Catholic response (38–40). (See also Cooper (2015: 96–9, with n. 13 in 98), who succinctly and perceptively presents the pros and cons of Nygren's approach from a Roman-Catholic perspective, too.) Edwards (2009: 197–8) gives a brief description of Nygren's enterprise, mentioning some critique that has been hurled against the latter, but, in order to 'acquit' Augustine from Nygren's accusations, Edwards goes on to present 'at most an annotation to Nygren, not a refutation of his main thesis' (Edwards 2009: 199; cf. also 209). In any case, the most systematic critical treatment of (the Lutheran Bishop of Lund in Sweden) Nygren has been given by an orthodox priest: Ghiț (2011: esp. 34–108). (Nygren, or at least Nygren's Luther, has received Protestant criticism, too, with special reference to the interpretation of both Dionysius and eros – especially of the ascending type; see Darley 2018: *passim*, e.g. 268.)

35 Also Osborne (now Rowett) conceives her whole book as a counter-argument against Nygren; see Osborne (1994: 222; cf. also, e.g. 3, 5, 6, 10ff (not always mentioning Nygren by name), 29 (with n. 18), 52–5, 57, 60–1, 65–6, 69, 71, 76, 85, 164–5 and 221). Another classic response has been given by Armstrong (1961: esp. 119–20) (with the complement of Armstrong (1964) against W. J. Verdenius' accusations of egocentricity found in the divine lover of the *Phaedrus* and the Demiurge of the *Timaeus*). For another prudent critique from an Orthodox Christian point of view, see Florovsky (1987: 20–5), taking issue with Nygren's general stance in many other places: see e.g. Florovsky (1987: 29; 120–1 (on St Antony), 145–8 (on St Gregory of Nyssa), and 249–52 (on St John Climacus)). See also Ivanović (2015: 123 and 124–6 with regard to Dionysius). Even Vlastos (1973: 6 with n. 13; 20 with n. 56; 30) is critical to Nygren (though both of them were Protestants. See also Tornau (2005: 272 with n. 6), although I do not quite agree with his assessment in Tornau (2005, n. 5)). An interesting criticism of both Socratic–Platonic justice and Christian love as ethical conducts has been launched by Williams (2007), although I am afraid that his, like Nygren's, knowledge of versions of Christianity is limited. The same may be said about Sykoutris (1949: 230*–46*), but for chronological rather than geographical reasons. Still, he includes some excellent observations, e.g. his point (5) in Sykoutris (1949: 238*–9*). Writing almost contemporaneously with Nygren, he gives a brief exposition of the differences between 'Platonic Love and Christian Agape', which in many places is similar to Nygren's approach; see e.g. 237*–40* and 243*–5*. However, he does think that there are similarities between the two phenomena that enable one to compare them (cf. 232* and 246*).

36 See Nygren (1953: 563; cf. also 566, 577, 589). The reason I disagree with Nygren will be plain, when my reader gets especially to the chapters on Proclus and Dionysius.

37 As has been already made clear, in line with a major part of recent Dionysian scholarship (to be attested throughout Chapter 3; see e.g. Pupaza (2015) and Garitsis (2002: 9)), I avoid adding to Dionysius' name the denigrating suffix 'pseudo-', without denying of course that we speak of a great Church Father who did not live and act in the first century CE, but contemporaneously with and/or slightly after Proclus, i.e. somewhere between the end of fifth and the beginning of sixth century CE. For the same reason, pace Ritter (2015: 251–2 and n. 2), I will not be calling him 'pseudo-Areopagite' (or 'Pseudo-Areiopagites' [*sic*]), either.

38 See for instance the dialectical relation between transcendence and immanence.

39 Cf. e.g. Gerson (2018: 316 and *passim*) as well as Corrigan (2018: 1, 4; cf., 48 and 51).

40 However, relatively frequently Plotinus uses the verbal adjective of «ἀγαπῶ» (a verb used already from classical antiquity and which comes up many times in Proclus,

as a TLG search shows): «ἀγαπητός» (in its various grammatical forms); see e.g. *Enneads*: III.5.1,39 and VI.8.16,15 (for my system of referencing see n. 1 in Chapter 1). A principal meaning of «ἀγαπῶ» is, of course, 'to love', but the problem is what each culture, tradition, philosophy/philosopher or religion mean by it. NB that the noun «ἀγάπη» does not appear at all either in Plato, or in Plotinus, or Proclus. (The closely related noun «ἀγάπησις» is to be found only once in the pseudo-Platonic *Definitions* 413b10 regarding the Platonic corpus and famously in the beginning of Aristotle's *Metaphysics* A.1,980a22 among else. The sole TLG result for Plotinus: *Enn.* VI.7.28,18 is false, because there we have a verb, whose form is simply identical with the singular dative declination of the noun. For its richer attestation in Dionysius, see n. 8 in Chapter 3.)

41 So, for instance, Marion (2007) is about the erotic phenomenon, while Marion (2002) talks about charity (a common rendering of ἀγάπη). The literature about (Christian) agape is vast and usually within a theological context; see e.g. Knauber (2006), Boyd (2008), Cardenal (2006) (in a poetical spirit), Solovyov (1985), Oravecz (2014), Larchet (2007), various chapters in Jevtic (2012) (with Skliris 2019) and Velimirovich-Popovic-Thaddeus (2013). (Lekkos (2004a, b) is a short, but useful anthology of Patristic texts, while Skliris (2016) is an ingenious film-commentary with theological-philosophical approach and patristic conclusions. The anthology of Zoumboulakis (2017) starts with the Bible and embraces other religious traditions, philosophies and intellectual territories up to the present. Finally, Gontikakis (2012) is oriented towards an orthodox understanding of eschatology through love.) There are also works that have as their single topic friendship; see e.g. Nehamas (2016), Grunebaum (2003), Jollimore (2000), Leichter (2006) and Verkerk (2019) (on Nietzsche). I also note that despite the obvious connections with sexuality (see e.g. Stamoulis 2014) I am not going to dwell much on this correlation (hence a reason I will not be considering the late Mazur 2009), although of course there will be relevant remarks, especially in the chapters on Plotinus and Proclus.

42 This is in general true about ancient Greek philosophy. I have already referred to Price (1989) in n. 1, who examines together love (eros) and friendship in Plato and Aristotle (which is quite a natural thing to do judging from the subject-matter). The same holds both for Joosse (2011) (on Plato and the Stoics), who, despite the title of his thesis (featuring 'friendship'), includes a chapter (4.2) on eros (and erotic virtue: 164–73), and for the short Patristic anthology of Lekkos (2004c). (NB that this very book series has yet another small volume on marriage: Lekkos 2004d). See also Helm (2009) regarding a contemporary philosophical account, as well as the (Anglican) theological approach of Carmichael (2004), who connects friendship specifically with Christian love (agape). What is more, terms like friendship might have a wider scope in their meaning than one would think. For instance, at least

in contexts such as the ancient Greek one, friendship can become an 'umbrella' term to include all or most socio-political relations. Cf. Schramm (2013: 4) (with specific regard to pagan Neoplatonism) and Baltzly-Eliopoulos (2009: 2) (regarding ancient Greek philosophy in general; it is notable that in n. 74 they rebut the alleged Aristotelian basis of Derrida (1997) as a sheer 'misattribution').

1

Plotinus and *Enneads* III.5.[50]: 'On Love'

1.1 The ontological status of Soul's Eros

1.1.1 Synopsis of III.5

Plotinus starts his enquiry concerning Eros,[1] by posing the following question: 'Is it a divinity (god or daimon) or is it an affection of the soul?'[2] The formulation of this problem foreshadows the structure of the whole treatise; hence, III.5 can be divided into two parts. In the first section (§1) Plotinus examines Eros as affection («πάθος») of the human soul. He distinguishes three types: (a) a pure («καθαρός») eros of Beauty without any connection to bodily affairs. People having such appreciation of the beautiful in the world may, or may not, recollect the true intelligible Beauty. (b) Mixed («μικτός») eros is love which embodies the veneration of Beauty via sexual affairs, the aim of which is the generation of offspring, as a path towards immortality. It is noteworthy that for Plotinus *both* instances of love are legitimate, although pure Love, as more self-sufficient, is ranked higher than the mixed. (c) It is the third instance that represents a deviation, since, in this category, eros is a desire contrary to nature («παρὰ φύσιν»).[3]

The remaining chapters (§§2–9) constitute the second section of the treatise, the 'theology' of love. Plotinus has to reconcile two traditions: (a) the idea that Eros is a *god*, son and follower of Aphrodite, a view found not only in 'divine' Plato's *Phaedrus*,[4] but also in 'theologians' such as Hesiod. (b) The other fundamental text is, of course, the *Symposium*, in which Diotima proclaims the *daimonic* nature of Eros. Plotinus succeeds in combining these two notions by exploiting the distinction that Pausanias [*sic*] makes in the *Symposium* between Heavenly («Οὐρανία») and Common («Πάνδημος») Aphrodite.[5] Thus, in his interpretation, Eros-god is the offspring of Heavenly Aphrodite, i.e. of the Undescended Soul, which is pure and free from the interfusion with matter[6] (cf. §2), whereas Eros-daimon is descendant of the World-Soul, which is represented by Common Aphrodite(cf. §3). In other words, both of the divine instances of Eros correspond to the first section's legitimate affections of human souls[7]: pure and mixed eros.

There is, however, another problem. The reconciliation of the two Platonic versions of love is not yet complete, since Plotinus has to account for the different mythical genealogies, too. Whereas according to the tradition expressed in the *Phaedrus* Eros is son of Aphrodite («ἐξ αὐτῆς»),[8] in the *Symposium* he is said to be born by Poverty's («Πενία») intercourse with Plenty («Πόρος») on the day of Aphrodite's birth («σὺν αὐτῇ»).[9] Hence, from §5 and onwards Plotinus' comes to his main exegetical task. This part, which deals with the interpretation of the *Symposium*'s myth, forms the second subdivision of the general theological section. In §5 the Neoplatonist rebuts Plutarch's cosmological interpretation of the same myth, although, interestingly enough, Plotinus himself had subscribed to a similar cosmological allegory in his earlier treatise 'On the impassibility of things without body'.[10] In §6 Plotinus relates Eros' genealogy to a general survey on the nature of daimons. According to §7 what differentiates Eros from the rest of the daimons is that Eros is the desire for the absolute Good, whereas the others crave partial goods.[11] So, after an explanation of Eros' insatiability due to his parents' traits, in §8 Plotinus figures out what 'Zeus' stands for in the myth, and in the first half of the concluding §9 the Neoplatonist elaborates on the identity of Poros with other elements of the myth. Finally, after some succinct, but crucial, methodological remarks on the interpretation of myths (and rational discourses), Plotinus gives us a synopsis of his interpretation, according to which the different mythical elements (e.g. Poros and Penia) are reduced to aspects of Soul. In that way, Plotinus completes his survey by showing the continuity of the aforementioned two parts of his erotic theology: as in the first part Soul was said to be Eros' mother, so too in the second one, since Penia, as well as Poros, represent Soul.

1.1.2 The main issue

As can be seen from the above brief account of III.5, this treatise raises a host of interesting subjects which have preoccupied the commentators. The vindication of sexual love, the complicated psychology depicted in the two Aphrodites, Plotinus' version of 'daimonology' and, most importantly, his attitude towards the interpretation of myths are only some aspects that deserve the reader's attention. I would like, however, to focus on the most crucial issue that arises from this tractate, namely the question of the ontological status of Eros, as depicted in the 'theological' part of the treatise. In §2 Plotinus states that (Heavenly) Aphrodite's, i.e. Soul's, intellectual activity towards her progenitor, Nous,[12] produced «ὑπόστασιν καὶ οὐσίαν»,[13] which is none other than 'the beautiful Eros, he who is born as an ὑπόστασις that is eternally set towards Another that is beautiful'.[14] Ascribing «ὑπόστασις» and/or «οὐσία» to Eros is something frequently met in both parts of the theological section.[15] This fact seems to suggest that Plotinus sees Eros as an entity in its own right, which, despite being dependent upon Soul as source of its existence, is external to Soul, just as Soul is generated but still different to Intellect (Nous). Furthermore, Plotinus ascribes these very substantives to Heavenly Aphrodite-Soul itself, calling her 'a kind of separate ὑπόστασις, that is οὐσία not participating in matter'.[16] Thus, since Heavenly Aphrodite stands for the proper 'Hypostasis' of Undescended Soul, it seems that Plotinus suggests that its offspring is itself a Hypostasis, although a degraded one, just as Soul, being an offspring of Nous, is an 'ousia', albeit inferior to Nous' «ὄντως ὄντα».[17] Indeed, in §3 Plotinus writes: 'That Eros is an Ὑπόστασιν, however – οὐσίαν sprung ἐξ οὐσίας – there is no reason to doubt. It may be inferior to the one that produced it, but οὖσαν nevertheless.'[18] Finally, in the following lines he compares Eros' generation with Soul's emanation from Nous.[19]

Do these straightforward statements suggest 'the emergence of Eros as a separate Hypostasis'[20] and 'the incipient break-up of the "traditional" Plotinian system of hypostases into something more elaborate and scholastic', as some commentators have suggested?[21] If so, we would seem to be faced by two serious difficulties: (a) Plotinus does not seem to embrace such a 'more elaborate' view of reality in his remaining four treatises, written after III.5; (b) in previous treatises, Plotinus has ardently condemned any attempt to introduce more entities outside the austere 'numerus clausus' of the three Principal Hypostases, i.e. One, Nous, Soul.[22] A relatively easy way out of this problem is to emphasize, with many commentators, that, although Plotinus uses in his writings the term 'hypostasis', it never has the technical meaning that was ascribed to it by Porphyry, when the latter was giving the titles to Plotinus' treatises.[23] Hence, when the term «ὑπόστασις» is used by Plotinus, it does not denote any of his three principles («ἀρχαί»), but merely 'existence', i.e. something that exists.[24] An equivalent story could be said about «οὐσία». Strictly speaking, it applies to the realm of «ὄντως ὄντα», i.e. the world of Forms. However, Plotinus can speak qualifiedly about an 'ousia' in the physical world, as a degradation of the 'noetic ousia'.[25] In this flexible use, 'ousia' can have an equivalent meaning to hypostasis.[26]

Still, although this response saves us from the insertion of more Principal Hypostases in the Plotinian system, it leaves Eros as a substantial entity[27] which is distinct from and external to Soul.[28] I think on the contrary that a closer reading of III.5 gets us further than that in making Eros internal to Soul. I am going to argue that eros is the activity that constitutes Soul as a proper entity. In another formulation, eros is Soul itself, seen from the perspective of its upwards orientation. I will defend my proposal by drawing on representative passages from both theological sections of III.5, but in an inverse order, starting from the end, as Plotinus would urge us to do.

1.1.3 Eros and myth

The first passage that will concern us is in §9, the final synopsis of Plotinus' interpretation of the *Symposium*-myth. To this Plotinus applies the hermeneutical principles he has laid down earlier in the same chapter; hence, I need to begin with them[29]:

> Now myths, if they really are such, must do two things: split up temporally the things they refer to, and divide from one another many of the Entities' aspects which, while existing as a unity, are yet distinct as regards rank and functions. After all, even reasoned discourses, like myths, on the one hand assume 'births' of things which are unbegotten,[30] and, on the other, divide things which exist as a unity. When the myths have fulfilled their didactic function to the best of their ability, they make it possible for the perceptive learner to come to a re-integration.[31]

According to our Neoplatonist, two elements are present in the interpretative process. The first one is that of 'διαιρεῖν/διαίρεσις'[32] and has two aspects: a temporal and a systematic. That is, myth and rational discourse describe in a linear-temporal fashion realities that are atemporal and eternal. In fact, division into temporal parts denotes onto-logical relations. This is also what the second aspect tries to elucidate by discriminating things that are not in fact distinct from each other. Such distinctions help discursive thought to see the same reality from different points of view. The hermeneutical approach is completed by the act of 'συναιρεῖν/συναίρεσις'[33]: what the mytho-logical narrations have split in terms of time and structure, the 'synairetic' act of the philosopher-interpreter comes to re-unify, so that we can contemplate the depicted reality in its genuine, pure and complete state, i.e. as a part of the non-discursive, atemporal realm of ὄντως ὄντα, the kingdom of Nous.[34] In other words, mythical allegories and philosophical illustrations come to life in the stage of «διαίρεσις». These narrations analyse a unified reality into various kinds of parts and take place 'for the sake of exposition (/teaching) and clarity'.[35] Still, since every allegory calls for de-allegorization, the crucial hermeneutical step is that of the second level of interpretation, «συναίρεσις», where the philosophical mind brings the separated elements into their primary unity again.[36] Take as an example the issue of *Timaeus*' cosmogony.[37] In Plato's 'diairesis' which depicts the ordering of the cosmos taking place in time, due to a Demiurge who contemplates the Forms, Plotinus responds 'synairetically': the function of the Demiurge (efficient cause) is to be contracted/identified with that of the Forms (formal cause), while this procedure is eternal; that the cosmos has a beginning in time means only that it depends ontologically upon its intelligible pattern.

Let us see now Plotinus' application of this methodology in the synopsis of his mythical exegesis.[38] He synairetically reduces to aspects of the soul all the different elements that the myth has depicted as separated, since in the myth the events of Eros' conception take place contemporaneously with Aphrodite's birth. From this point of view, Πενία comes to represent Soul's indefiniteness, a kind of psychic substrate, before it is informed by the emanated λόγοι from Nous. In an analogous way intelligible matter reverts upon the One and becomes proper Nous,[39] who has been identified with Zeus in §8, contrary to Plotinus' standard identification of it with Kronos.[40] These emanated λόγοι/rational principles are 'extended unfoldings' of the Forms, i.e. the Forms discursively perceived by Soul, which in their subsequent degradation at the level of Nature, Soul's lowest part, are going to form the physical world. Πόρος represents these logoi, insofar as Plotinus calls him also a λόγος (in the singular),[41] which stands for the totality of logoi that fulfil Soul. In other words, Poros is soul's discursive apprehension of Nous. Now, before Penia and Poros are reduced to aspects of Soul, Plotinus has already associated other key features of the myth with the main protagonists. So, Zeus' garden is identified by Plotinus with the 'adornments' (κοσμήματα)[42] that are in the garden, and it is these adornments that form a single representation of Πόρος' plenitude. Furthermore, this plenitude is manifested more properly in Poros' *drunkenness* with nectar, which overflows from Nous' satiety. Thus, we are presented with many subsequent and gradual levels of contraction, before we come to the final identification of Πόρος and Πενία as two (constituting) characteristics of Soul: to the extent that Soul has a desire for the good, this represents its 'Poros-aspect'[43]; yet insofar as it desires, it falls short of the good,[44] 'because desire goes with being needy',[45] and this is its 'Penia-aspect'. In this sense

Eros becomes again directly dependent on Soul as his progenitor. But is this the end of the synairetic procedure?

We still have to see what Plotinus says about Eros, but before that I want to elaborate a bit further on each partner of the Poros–Penia pair. I begin from the top with Logos, who in §9 is called not just an offspring of Nous, but actually: «νοῦ γέννημα καὶ ὑπόστασις μετὰ νοῦν».[46] When formulating the problem of Eros' ontological status, I omitted to mention that this question might arise for Poros, i.e. Logos, too, which is ascribed a 'hypostasis',[47] like Eros. Of course, we have just seen that Poros is reduced to an aspect of Soul, representing Soul's discursive apprehension of Nous' Forms. In this way the 'reality' of Logos is not denied, but is internalized, as a part of Soul's existence, in a way that paves the path for Eros' internalization and *synairesis* with Soul that is to come.[48]

I turn to the bottom both in terms of ontological structure, because Penia is lower than Poros-logos,[49] and in terms of narrative structure, since Plotinus chooses to conclude his treatise, and more specifically the *Symposium*-myth exegesis, not with the polarity of Soul's Poros and Penia, but solely with its feminine member. Let us see, then, what remained for Plotinus to state about Penia, in order to extol its importance: 'Its [sc. Eros'] mother is Penia, because desire goes with being needy'.[50] This assertion is familiar from above. But whereas in the treatise's context the maxim 'desire goes with being needy' refers to Eros from a certain point of view, we have already seen Plotinus ascribing desire, and hence 'need' to Soul. It is actually Soul that is in need and, thus, produces the activity towards the good, which is Eros, as we will see shortly. Hence, Penia is Soul both before its reversion towards Nous and after its self-constitution: the fact that it cannot become the Good, but only good-like makes it remain forever an erotic entity.[51] Furthermore, I have already noted the relational sense of Penia and of its correspondent, 'matter'. They can denote a relational indefiniteness; thus, when Plotinus states that 'Penia is Matter, because matter is completely needy',[52] this need not refer to prime matter, although Plotinus is categorical about the 'complete poverty'. That he need not mean prime matter follows immediately from his next phrase, where he speaks about the 'indetermination of the desire for the good'.[53] As he had formerly stressed, 'that which is utterly without part in the good would never seek the good',[54] and this is indeed prime matter. But, since in our case Penia has the possibility of reversion in itself, it means that we are higher in the hierarchy of being, where the Poros-aspect is much stronger.[55] Nor should the phrase 'for there is no determinate form or Reason in something which desires this [sc. the good]'[56] worry us, if seen from a relational point of view. For the desirer to be in a condition to desire (presumably the good), it must already have the traces of the good. Hence, its indeterminateness is relational to that of its principle of formation.[57] Again this aspect of relationality is stressed further in a following phrase: 'But that which is directed to itself[58] is Form, remaining solitary within itself, but when it also desires to receive, it causes the would-be recipient to be Matter for that which comes upon it.'[59] Here, we are reminded of Nous' case where, as we will see (in Section 1.3), Nous is fulfilled in respect of his nature, but when compared to the One becomes 'needy', hence 'drunk' Nous. As I have repeated, there must already be Poros-traces in Penia-Soul so that it reverts to its progenitor. Consequently, whereas Soul-Penia could be said to be Form, i.e. have a certain level of definiteness, with respect to itself, the realization of its divine origin allows the entity to realize its Penia state in relation to its source, and therefore it is like a 'receptacle' for the reception of higher-level form.[60]

I can return, now, to what Plotinus has to say about Love: 'Thus Eros is eternally and necessarily come into existence out of the longing of Soul for the higher and good, and from the moment there was Soul, there was eternally Eros.'[61] Does Plotinus mean that, although necessarily dependent on Soul, Eros is an external entity to Soul? The tendency towards internalization regarding Plenty and Poverty in the preceding discussion would not favour this reading. Plotinus responds: 'It is therefore out of Poros and Penia that Eros is said to be born, in that Soul's[62] lack and desire, and the memory that constitutes the Reasons,[63] come together into a unity in soul and produce an active orientation (τὴν ἐνέργειαν) towards the good, and this is Eros.'[64] Plotinus does not claim here that the activity of Soul gives rise to another substantial entity. Soul is not mother of Eros in the sense that Nous is father of Soul. Rather, Eros represents Soul's own activity towards the intelligible. Furthermore, this activity, i.e. Eros, is self-constituting of Soul in that it expresses the formation of Soul's inherent Penia by Poros, in other words Soul's discursive apprehension of Nous, in the way that inchoate Intellect erotically reverts upon the One and constitutes itself as the proper Hypostasis of Nous. This is the way to understand how 'Eros is eternally and necessarily come into existence out of the longing of Soul for the higher and good, and from the moment there was Soul, there was eternally Eros'.[65]

If Eros forms a substantial and internal aspect of Soul's being,[66] we can also understand why in his other reference to the myth of the birth of love, in VI.9.[9], Plotinus speaks about Soul's innate («σύμφυτος») love, which explains 'why Eros is coupled with the Psyches in pictures and stories. ... every soul is Aphrodite; and this is symbolized in the story of the birthday of Aphrodite and Eros who is born with her (μετ' αὐτῆς). The soul in her natural state is in love with God and wants to be united with him; it is like the noble love of a girl for her noble father'.[67] A soul can be a proper entity only via the erotic orientation of its activity towards the intelligible, and this bond is exemplified by Eros. Hence, Eros is actually Soul itself seen from the point of view of its self-constitution, via its orientation towards the higher levels of reality. This is the radical *synairesis* to which Plotinus invites us, his readers. It is the synairesis that he himself had done, when in *Ennead* VI.7.[38] he had declared that 'the soul, receiving into itself an outflow from thence [i.e. from the Good], is moved and dances wildly and is all stung with longing and *becomes love* (ἔρως)'.[68] In III.5, after the final exegetical stage, Plotinus urges us to go back and read again the treatise under this synairetic point of view. Upon a second reading we will be prepared to understand that when Soul is said to give birth to the οὐσία and ὑπόστασις of Eros, this substance is nothing else but Soul, as fulfilled by its orientation to the intelligible. By generating this erotic self-constituting activity, Soul generates its authentic self: it is an erotic entity.[69]

I close with a final comment. My synairetic reading of Soul's Eros is supported by a parallel that can be drawn to another, more frequently discussed issue: time's relation to Soul. In some parts of III.7.[45] Plotinus seems to be speaking of time as an entity alongside Soul.[70] However, the whole view of III.7 does not leave any doubt about time's ontological status, as an aspect of Soul's discursive life. Thus, Plotinus underlines that 'one must not conceive time as outside Soul, any more than eternity There as outside real being. It is not an accompaniment of Soul nor something that comes after (any more than eternity There) but something which is seen along with it and exists in it and with it, as eternity does There [with real being]'.[71] Even in that formulation one could assume that time is a hypostasis within Soul, but this is just not the case. Time can be 'seen' along with Soul because it is an expression of Soul's discursive life. What I aim to achieve with my present reflections is to show that this is an example of the interpretative attitude that we should hold towards Plotinus' treatment of Eros in III.5, too.[72]

1.1.4 Eros and vision

I now return to §2 of III.5, where Eros is compared to the eye of a lover:[73] an eye that, like the Eros of the *Symposium*, mediates between («μεταξύ»)[74] the lover, that is, Soul, and the beloved, that is, Nous.[75] I will attempt to show how the first theological part of the treatise facilitates a synairetic reading as was suggested above. I do so because Plotinus' hermeneutical remarks apply to both myths and rational discourses,[76] the *Enneads* falling under the latter genre. Moreover, the old idiom of vision can help us identify philosophical, not only hermeneutical, reasons for the *synairesis* I propose. Finally, in this way the two basic claims I pursue will become clearer: (a) the synairetic interpretive proposal, whereby soul is identified with eros or her eyes; (b) a further ontological claim, supported by the previous one, according to which an entity, soul in the particular case, constitutes itself via its erotic orientation towards its higher principles.

So, what does the lover's eye precisely do?

> To the lover it provides a medium through which to see his beloved, while the eye itself precedes vision, that is: prior to making possible this instrument-mediated vision (τὴν τοῦ ὁρᾶν δι' ὀργάνου δύναμιν), the instrument itself is filled with the image seen. It sees earlier, to be sure, but not in the same way, since the eye does impress the visual image on the seer, but itself only enjoys the vision of the beautiful one as it runs past.[77]

Plotinus has moved from the mythical to the metaphorical language of this double simile,[78] and his 'synairetic' view is notable: Eros is internalized; it is no longer a separate entity, but a substantial aspect of Soul, since the seer cannot see without his eyes. Just as vision is the defining capacity of the seer, so eros is the defining capacity of an entity, like soul.

Yet, the problem is that this eye seems to have some desire of its own, independent from that of its bearer because it 'sees earlier' than the lover. True, Plotinus qualifies by adding 'but not in the same way', since the eye's function is instrumental for the enabling of the lover's seeing, and, hence, in metaphorical terms, what remains for the eye-Eros is the appreciation of 'the vision of the beautiful one as it runs past'.[79] But is it that eros can be specifically located somewhere within soul, and thus be differentiated from it, as an eye or an arm is distinct from the body, although an integral part of it? How can we respond to this diairetic challenge?

For one thing, we have the antecedent of Plato's various statements. Our Neoplatonist must be certainly aware of the *Theaetetus*' claim that the eyes are that "'*through* which" (δι' ὧν) we perceive in each case, rather than "*with* which" (οἷς) … It would be a very strange thing … if there were a number of perceptions sitting inside us as if we were Wooden horses, and there were not some single form, soul or whatever one ought to call it, to which all these converge – something *with* which, *through* those things [sc. eyes and ears], as if they were instruments (οἷον ὀργάνων), we perceive all that is perceptible'.[80] So, it is clear that «νοῦς ὁρῆι καὶ νοῦς ἀκούει»,[81] as Epicharmus could put it, too. Nevertheless, it is again Plato who states that 'dialectic gently pulls … out and leads … upwards' not soul *in abstracto*, but the eye of the soul («τὸ τῆς ψυχῆς ὄμμα»), when it is 'really buried in a sort of barbaric bog'.[82] If the intellectual vision plays the fundamental role in the apprehension of the Good and the Beauty of the intelligible realm, depicted either in the Sun and Cave-analogy of the *Republic* or in the ascent of the *Symposium*, then in cases like our last citation the eye cannot be differentiated from its bearer's actual identity: a soul is a proper, i.e. philosophical soul insofar as it envisages the Good, viz. insofar as it has eyes, or rather, as long as it is an eye. On this Platonic antecedent one can base Plotinus' propensity to 'contract' the seer, i.e. Soul, with her eye, i.e. Eros, and thus support my first interpretive claim.

Going on further to base my ontological claim upon the previous one, as is clear from above, it is not only the eye, but the vision that self-constitutes Soul as such.[83] There are two issues in need of clarification here. Starting with the first: could it be that an unactualized capacity is enough? No, Plotinus is ready to connect the eye, i.e. the agent who has the eye, with the ('image-mediated') vision,[84] emphasizing thus the Aristotelian idea of 'second actuality'. For our Neoplatonist an eye is a 'filled' eye, i.e. an entity is fulfilled, insofar as it actualizes its capacity to see. This is the reason why in the context of his first beautiful ascent towards the Good Plotinus assures us that, when one has 'already ascended', he 'has already become sight ... For this eye alone sees the great beauty'.[85] Thus, from the initial stage of the synairesis between the eye and the agent, we get to the next stage of the intimate connection between the seer-eye and the actuality/activity of seeing.

But now we may move to the second issue in need of clarification: why and how does 'second actuality' tell us anything regarding the fulfilment of the agent (or the eye) itself? It is the time for Aristotle's theory of perception to come to the forefront, since for Plotinus, too, the (vision of the) seer in a way becomes assimilated to the object to which he directs his vision.[86] Plotinus evokes this idea clearly in the second recurrence of the eye-simile in §3, when he states that 'it is ... out of that which is strenuously active towards the visual object, and out of that which "streams off,"[87] so to speak, from the object, that Eros is born, an eye that is filled: like image-mediated vision'.[88] From this fundamental assertion it follows that, in order for the eye to become filled with the images that emanate from the object of its vision, it is the eye, i.e. the agent, that must act first. Hence, although the *Cratylus*' (folk-)etymology relates Eros to the passive aspect of vision – viz. 'because it flows in from outside (ὅτι <εἰσρεῖ ἔξωθεν>), that is to say, the flow doesn't belong to the person who has it, but is introduced into him through his eyes ... it [sc. Eros] was called "esros" ("influx")'[89] – Plotinus here emphasizes the active element of the actuality of seeing, stating that 'it is perhaps rather from this that Eros gets its name, because it comes to Existence out of vision, *horasis*'.[90] In this last citation we get a summary of my proposals so far, starting reversely: (a) Being an eye implies the activity of seeing, since it is the latter that literally shapes the form of the former. (b) Plotinus calls this eye/vision Eros, but we have seen how we can move to a synairesis of the eye with(in) the seer. If so, then Eros himself can be contracted with its bearer, Soul. He is only the persona of the entity that is self-constituted by the activity of seeing or, in metaphorical terms, the 'eye that is filled' itself. Moreover, this fact explains why in the end of the first theological part (§4), as with the second one, Plotinus arrives at the same conclusion: 'Eros is Soul's activity as it strains toward good',[91] by which the 'Poros'-principles of Nous come to form Soul's 'Penia'.

To conclude, from this 'synoptic-synairetic' point of view, the eye-simile combines and unifies the two seemingly conflicting notions of Eros: the internalization of Eros as eye of Soul shows us that (a) the activity of contemplating the intelligible, being an erotic act, stems from and instantiates the passionate love with which Soul is filled for her progenitor 'in the way a girl feels noble[92] love for her noble father'.[93] (b) The actual result (the 'offspring') of this erotic intentionality, however, is again to be found 'within' this subject: soul constitutes itself as a proper Hypostasis by eternally gazing at the intelligible realm, that is, by being in constant erotic reference to its progenitor. In other words, Soul, and every inferior being in relation to its superior, is an erotic entity; it is what it is only with actual reference to the immediate source of its existence, and ultimately to the Good. Furthermore, the expression of this erotic intentionality is the activity of contemplation. This is why Plotinus under the mythological veil states that, after Eros' generation, 'the two of them look upward: both the mother and the beautiful Eros, he who is born as an Existence (ὑπόστασις) that is eternally set towards Another that is beautiful'.[94] It turns out that Eros is like a mirror of the Soul: it reflects Soul after the orientation of her intellectual activity towards the intelligible; or the mirror represents how Soul apprehends the reflection of the intelligible in her eyes/herself, amidst her ceaseless struggle to be(come) good-like.[95] In either case, this substantial Eros is actually nothing else but Soul itself, seen from the point of view of its upwards orientation towards the intelligible (cf. my ontological claim).[96] This is the radical '*synairesis*' that Plotinus invites us to do once more (cf. my interpretive claim). It is the ceaseless intentional activity of contemplation (cf. eros as ἐνέργεια) that self-constitutes Soul as a proper entity (cf. Eros as ὑπόστασις and οὐσία).[97]

1.1.5 Eros and tragedy

Finally, I return to the myth of Poros and Penia once more. One of A. M. Wolters' most insightful remarks concerns the identification of a relation between the eye-simile in §3 and the treatment of Eros as son of Poros-Penia in §7.[98] This relation consists not only of verbal affinities,[99] but also of structural analogies, as will be shown later. The synairetic reading of the myth presented in §9 prompted us to read in this way the eye-similes of the first theological part. Now I will close the (hopefully not vicious) circle by coming back to the *Symposium*-myth in §7, which, on the one hand, presents similarities with the first part of the theology, and, on the other, paves the way towards the final synairesis expounded in the last section (§9) of the second theological part. For a final time, I will try to show how Eros can be contracted with Soul. After all, the methodological principles of diairesis and synairesis in §9 are meant to apply to this myth, even if it precedes them.

In §7 Plotinus chooses to stress the tragic nature of Eros, although the context of the picturesque myth of the *Symposium* would suggest a more cheerful atmosphere.[100] We have already seen (Section 1.1.3) that in §9 Poros, in being logos, represents the totality of logoi that emanate from Nous to Soul. On the other hand, Penia represents the indefinite desire of the intelligible, before it gets the logoi. According to the account of §7, 'since Reason, then, entered that which was not Reason, but an indeterminate desire and attenuated Existence (ὑποστάσει), it caused the resulting offspring to be neither perfect nor self-sufficient, but deficient, being born out of indeterminate desire and self-sufficient reason'.[101] Thus, Love 'is not a pure rational principle, since he has in himself an indefinite, irrational, unbounded impulse; for he will never be satisfied, as he has in him the nature of the indefinite'.[102] So, we see again that for Plotinus the characteristic of Penia is fundamental; what is more, even after the coming of Poros the Penia-element remains. As I will note in the next section (1.1.6), Poros is in a sense Penia in relation to its higher principle, if we are not to ascribe dualities that can be found only in the sensible world. The upshot of Plotinus' description is that

> Eros is like a craving[103] which is by its nature *aporos*: needy and without means or resources. Therefore, even in the act of achieving its goal, it is again needy. For it cannot be fulfilled, because its mixed nature forbids it. For only that truly achieves fulfillment, which also constitutionally possesses fulfillment. But that which craves on account of its inherent deficiency is like a leaky vessel; even if it does achieve fulfillment momentarily, it does not retain it, since its powerlessness[104]

is on account of his deficiency, whereas its 'efficiency' [*poristikon*] is due to the Reason-side of its nature.[105]

A part of Eros' aforementioned tragic nature consists in the fundamental insatiability of his desire, which in fact recalls the eye-simile of the first theological part. In that case, we saw that the eye is not fulfilled 'but itself only enjoys the vision of the beautiful one as it runs past', while it 'does impress the visual image on the seer'. Nonetheless, Plotinus' elaboration of this image in terms of the Penia-Poros myth sharpens even more the tragic aspect of ceaseless desire, and actually brings to our mind the behaviour of the incontinent man, who is compared to a leaky jar in Plato's *Gorgias*.[106] However, while such an incontinent man presumably has desires for bodily pleasures, Eros is confined in insatiableness, whereas he pursues the loftiest object of desire.[107]

Still, the central problem that arises from the description of this tragic figure is its actual identity, while we are confronted with another aforementioned problem, that of ascribing desires to that which is only the instantiation of desire itself. Now, let us not forget that Plotinus' agenda is to capture Eros as activity of Soul, at least in Chapter 9 and 4. Furthermore, the affinity of Eros' tragic description in the present context with the eye-simile of the first part can be a useful guide in our interpretation. To be more precise, the picture of Eros as 'mixture' of Reason-Poros and indefiniteness-Penia is analogous to the image of the filled eye. In the second eye-simile Plotinus spoke of that which is active towards the beloved visual object, and of the latter as 'streaming off' images that fill the eye, which is compared to Eros. This 'streaming off' clearly corresponds to the logoi emanating from Nous, i.e. to logos-Poros, while the active orientation to the visual object is analogous to Penia's indefinite desire for Poros. In the eye-case I proposed that Plotinus, making Eros the eye of a lover/desirer, that is, of Soul, on the one hand he internalizes Eros, and on the other he identifies the medium of vision with the activity of seeing itself. The result is that if a seer is seer *qua* actualizing his capacity to see, then the fulfilled eye of the seer stands for the erotic self-constitution of an entity (lover-Soul) as always being in constant erotic reference to its desired object. Hence, in our present case, too, we can diagnose under the veil of Eros' persona the *self*-constituting activity and desire not of Eros, but of Soul itself. In other words, we are confronted with the radical synairesis of Soul with Eros, the latter being a necessary aspect of the former's (way of) being.

However, it is not only the analogy with the eye-simile, but also other elements from §7 alone that lead us towards this synairetic view. As we saw in the last cited passage, Eros is called «μῖγμα» ('mixture'), a word that has been repeatedly used for Eros since the beginning of §7.[108] We can then wonder regardless of the eye-analogy: who is really the 'mixture'? For one thing, Wolters aptly remarks that 'Plotinus interprets Eros as being not so much the independent offspring of Poros and Penia as their *fusion* ...'[109] As a result, the nature of Penia (insatiability) and the nature of Poros (resourcefulness) are presented in the sequel as simply *ingredients* of the ambivalent nature of Eros'.[110] Nonetheless, according to the descriptions that I gave by using the terms of Poros–Penia myth, we could suggest that the actual fusion of these two 'ingredients' is not Eros, but a substantial entity, e.g. Soul, which in fact, due to its constitution, exists as erotic entity. This point can be made with reference to Plotinus' assertions in §7, too. There, he states that Eros' birth from Penia due to her intercourse with Poros denotes that 'it [sc. Eros' generation] is out of Form and Indetermination – *an Indetermination characterizing Soul* when it has not yet achieved the good, but "presages that there is Something" in an indeterminate and indefinite mental image'.[111] From this it follows that Eros and Soul have many things in common, since, if Eros is a 'mixture' of Penia–Poros, these two ingredients are actually reduced to aspects of Soul itself. It is the Penia-state that makes Soul gaze at the intelligible, by which activity it gets formed by Poros-logoi, that is, by the 'unfolding version' of Nous' forms, i.e. the Forms under the mode of Soul's discursive reasoning. Thus, the result of this procedure is not any other substantial entity, apart from Soul proper; it is Soul *qua* constantly related to its intelligible source of formation. Furthermore, as I had briefly noted during the course of the exegesis of §9 (Section 1.1.3), the roles of Penia and Poros are not so stable. Penia can revert towards Nous, because it already contains traces of Poros; what is more, the fact that after the advent of Poros Soul is said to be able to orientate its activity towards the source of Poros means that there is always an aspect of Penia in Soul that causes to be ceaselessly desiring the intelligible, as if Soul were insatiable.

Therefore, if the real and substantial 'mixture' is Soul, Eros must be mixture in another sense. The contrast is sharp when Plotinus makes the following joint reference: 'And it [sc. Eros] depends on Soul in the sense of [sc. Soul being his] principle, since it has been generated by Soul, although it [sc. Eros] is [sc. at the same time] a mixture.'[112] If Poros and Penia are already reduced to aspect/states of Soul, then their mixture cannot be an independent substantial entity within Soul, as also the eye-simile would suggest prima facie, but a certain state of Soul, being the outcome of the dialectical synthesis of Poros and Penia: exactly this dialectical state is expressed by the upwards orientation of Soul, since it desires (Penia-aspect) the intelligible (Poros-aspect). Finally, the image suggested by the last Plotinian citation is exactly equivalent to the image we have seen him using in the end of §2, where he speaks about the generation of Eros from Aphrodite's activity towards her progenitor Kronos, both of them gazing at Aphrodite's progenitor. There (Section 1.1.3), I proposed that the Eros-offspring is nothing else but Soul itself seen as self-constituted by its eternally gazing at its progenitor, i.e. by ceaselessly being an erotic entity. In the same way, here we can propose that what depends on Soul as its principle of generation is Soul's activity, instantiated in its upwards orientation, which, however, self-constitutes Soul as such, that is, as an erotic entity which always strives towards its source. The synairesis of Eros with Soul is again at the forefront.

Consequently, if this is so, the real tragic figure is actually Soul,[113] which cannot be fulfilled, because 'its mixed nature forbids it', with the result of its ceaseless aspiration of the intelligible. If we take this reference in that sense, i.e. as describing Soul's erotic way of being,[114] then the immediately following comparison in Plotinus' text becomes more intelligible; Plotinus states: 'For only that truly achieves fulfilment, which also constitutionally possesses fulfilment.'[115] This reference seems to be to Nous, who 'always desires and always attains'. Hence, if we establish this,[116] then there would be something quite odd in a comparison between the ontology of Eros and Nous. For example, where would Soul fit into that scheme? What is more, if Eros can be conceived as the instantiation of an activity, why contrast it with a Hypostasis such as Nous?[117] However, we have seen that both Soul and Nous are erotic *entities*. Hence, a comparison between Soul's and Nous' way of being becomes more reasonable.

1.1.6 Eros and vision, again

I want to conclude this chapter by clarifying two aspects concerning the importance and convergence of the Poros–Penia image and the eye-simile. I begin with the issue of the necessity of the (erotic) reversion, or why the eye is to see. In a previous section (Section 1.1.4), in the treatment of the second eye-simile, I noted that contra *Cratylus*' etymology, Plotinus emphasizes the active element of the activity of seeing. Nonetheless, one may justly retort that, contrary to what this image suggests, as well as its apparent differentiation from the *Cratylus*, for Plotinus the reversion of an entity and its subsequent self-constitution are both necessary aspects stemming from the very first emanation of that entity.[118] In other words, the active and the passive elements are just two sides of the same coin: if there is to be direction of the vision towards an object, the latter is going to emanate its images to fill the vision of the eye; conversely, if there is any emanation of images from an object to any eye, this means that the latter has directed its vision upon that object. This is one reason I think that the Penia–Poros interpretation serves better to clarify Plotinus' concrete attitude, since it explains why we have the reversion of an entity in the first place. In other words, it gives us an answer as to why Aphrodite can be «ἐρασθεῖσα» before it gives birth to Eros,[119] i.e. before it is fulfilled by the limit that Poros imposes.

As Plotinus states in §9, 'clearly that which is utterly without part in the good would never seek the good'.[120] This description fits only prime matter, which is the source of evil in the world. Contrary to that, intelligible (or 'psychic') matter apparently has already traces («ἴχνη») of the Good. It is the presence of these good-like elements that enable, e.g. inchoate Intellect to 'feel' its need-'poverty' in relation to the Good. Thus, what is potentially good in intelligible matter, Nous tries to actualize, although it ends up with the best-possible image (cf. «εἴδωλον») of the Good, which is the Forms. In this process we see, indeed, that the reversion towards the superior principle is necessary, since the offspring of an entity carries within it the traces of its progenitor.

Moreover, we have already seen (Section 1.1.4) that the activity of vision/contemplation assimilates the vision with what is seen, although the result within the seer is not the actual object of vision duplicated, but the image of the latter. From that point of view, we can understand why the idea of 'second actuality' has such an importance for Plotinus. In his view, an eye is the potential receptacle of the images of vision, i.e. it is a 'not yet filled eye', as intelligible matter is the potentiality of the World of Forms. For Plotinus, an eye can be actual eye, i.e. 'filled', only *qua* seeing. From this whole procedure, we can really perceive why an eye, representing Penia, strives to see, and why, since it sees, it receives the 'glories' of Poros, i.e. the images of the object seen.

The above description leads us to the issue of the actual 'intercourse' of Poros and Penia, or the nature of the 'filled eye'. All these images could suggest a view close to the Aristotelian notion of physical substance, whereby Penia and eye are the passive elements, and Poros and the fulfilment of the eye are the active-formal elements. However, we have seen that Penia–eye are active in that they do not just receive Form, but this reception is the outcome, even if necessary, of their actuality of seeing. This comes to a strong opposition to the paradigm of sensible world, where matter is really inert, unable for contemplation, and just receives form from Soul-Nature.[121] Hence, whereas in the sensible world we can speak about Aristotelian composites, although for Plotinus matter never fully takes on form, in the intelligible world we do not have such dualities. Rather, Penia-intelligible matter, via the actuality of contemplation, transforms itself becoming Poros(-Nous), viz. Good-like. The same holds in the case of the eye which is filled by the images of the object of contemplation, actually becoming like it, in Aristotelian terms.

Such a synairesis of Poros and Penia is not explicitly suggested by Plotinus in his exegesis, as we saw, but it underlies many of his assertions. However, the aforementioned synairesis is not the only possible interpretation. For, as we have stressed, the offspring remains always inferior to its progenitor, although it is the best-possible image. Even if Poros is what makes e.g. Nous Good-like, it is still not the Good. Poros represents the constant relation of Nous to the One; yet, it is still inferior to its source. Hence, in a way Poros is always Penia in relation to the One, and this fact explains why the gazing at the One is eternal. Besides, in Plotinus' flexible use of several notions, every level of reality is said to be 'matter' (hence, Penia) in relation to its superior, i.e. more infinite in relation to its principle of limit.[122] This is why the eye in order to be filled must be (/is) always in the state of second actuality, i.e. gazing at its object.

In a nutshell, Penia can denote the 'first' moment of the generation of an entity and hence explain the reversion in the first instance, but it can also denote that the result of the reversion remains always inferior to ('in need of') its higher principle and thus in constant relation to its progenitor: this is why a self-constituted entity always remains an erotic entity being orientated to the intelligible. This, then, is the gist of Plotinus' view on the nature of love: for an entity to be(come) erotic must be inferior to another one. In this view, eros, as in the *Symposium*, is the force that leads us only upwards. Most importantly, it has been clear throughout our above discussions that this ascending erotic force cannot be a substantial entity, external and/or independent of the erotic entity to which it corresponds. In other words, the synairesis of Penia with Poros, or the eye itself, actually corresponded to an entity (e.g. Soul), whose nature is erotic; that is, an entity which has an erotic intentionality, i.e. an intellectual activity towards its beloved object (Nous/One).

1.2 Potential objections and answers

I will now consider some potential objections to my proposals. My aim is to strengthen even more the solution I put forward by answering to the challenges. Issues that will concern us in this section are the unity of Plotinus' treatise, its daimonology and a specification regarding the relation of Eros to Soul.

1.2.1 Unity of theme

I start with a note on my methodology. One might object that I gave an answer to our problem by collecting evidence from both theological sections of III.5, although they do not refer to the same entity. The passages from the first theological part I evoked (§§2-3) speak about god Eros, son of Heavenly Aphrodite, whereas the *Symposium*-myth relates to daimonic Eros. To this challenge I respond thus: the first part of Eros' theology does not exclusively refer the Eros-god, but also to daimonic Love.[123] Furthermore, in that very section the characteristics ascribed to Eros-god, e.g. the eye-simile, are explicitly attributed to Eros-daimon, too.[124] Hence, even if the *Symposium*-exegesis analyses only the daimonic Eros, this does not preclude the interpreter from drawing conclusions about the phenomenon of eros in general. Such a view is also corroborated by Wolters' aforementioned insightful remark, according to which the eye-simile, which applies to both Eros-god and daimon, is to be understood better under the light of the Poros and Penia exegesis of the last part of the treatise.

Furthermore, in a treatise which aims at extolling the importance of '*synairesis*' and the unity incurred by love, the Plotinian interpreter needs to respond with the corresponding gesture.[125] For example, it might be the case that the exegesis of the myth comes as an answer to the enquiry into the nature of daimons generally, and specifically daimon-Eros, as proclaimed in §5 and started in §6. Still, one might wonder what connects the two theological parts, not the potential differentiations of Eros-daimon from Eros-god. For this reason I have not stressed the aspect of the mother of daimon-Eros, World-Soul's proximity to matter, and the ramifications that this has for the various daimonic powers employed for the administration of this whole.[126] Nor have I inferred that Penia denotes only the indefiniteness that characterizes the level of being of World-Soul, as being close to matter. In conclusion, for the purposes of my enquiry and for the above reasons I view the accounts of Love given in the two parts of the theological section of III.5 as complementary.[127]

I am not the only interpreter who takes this synairetic stance, although I do not always agree with the synairetic fruits of other scholars. The following is a good example: if we turn to §7, we find a reference to a «λόγος ... οὐ καθαρός».[128] Here, I assumed that Plotinus refers to Eros *qua* the offspring of Poros and Penia. We saw that the Neoplatonist reduces the relation of Eros with his parents to a sort of fusion of Poros and Penia-traits, which characterize Soul. If we can speak about such a fusion, then the straightforward interpretation of 'impure logos' concerns the Soul's Eros, not either of Eros' mythological parents. Although this is the option of the majority of translators–commentators, Wolters disagrees.[129] The latter suggests that this[130] «λόγος οὐ καθαρός», which is identified with the λόγος of 1.9, does not refer to Eros, but solely to Poros-logos, which has emanated from Nous, and which contrasts with another Ἀόγος which *does* remain pure: the one which is self-contained (17) and does not mix with ἀοριστία (18). This pure λόγος belongs to the "pure" Soul which is situated above the "mixed" Soul'. Thus, for Wolters this impure logos gives rise to Eros-daimon, aspect of World-Soul, and is juxtaposed to a pure logos, which emanates from Nous and enforms the Pure Soul (-Penia?), which respectively gives birth to the Eros-god, mentioned only in the first theological part, but not in the part of the *Symposium* exegesis.

The asset of Wolters' interpretation is that it leaves open the possibility that the *Symposium* myth can refer directly, albeit implicitly, to the Heavenly Aphrodite (/pure Soul). In this way, Wolters could once more support my reading, because I have noted my propensity to view the two parts of Plotinus' theology synairetically, i.e. as complementary. However, a problematic implication of Wolters' proposal is that with respect to pure Soul there would be apparently no indefiniteness/Penia element, since its logos does not mix with indefiniteness. How could we, then, explain the desire of Undescended Soul for Nous? In previous sections I explained how by speaking of a synairesis of Poros with Penia, every ontological level can be seen as Poros in relation to its inferiors, but Penia in relation to its superiors. In that way, even if pure Soul did not share in the indefiniteness/Penia referred to in the *Symposium* myth, its Poros aspect would still be Penia in relation to Nous, and hence we can account for Heavenly Aphrodite's longing for its progenitor.

Consequently, although I endorse Wolters' general synairetic stance, due to the aforementioned problem I disagree with the details of his approach,[131] a substantial part of which is his thesis on the referent of 'impure logos' in 1.13. Thus, I will stay with the traditional view: 'impure logos' already refers to Eros.[132] Besides, the abrupt change of subject (of «ἐξήρτηται δὲ ψυχῆς») in the immediately following passage,[133] where the reference is undoubtedly to Eros, as is acknowledged by Wolters, too, would make very difficult the explanation as to how these consequent passages relate to each other.

1.2.2 On daimonology

The reference to the daimonic or divine status of Eros brings me to a second potential objection. Save for the aforementioned ascriptions of 'substance' and 'activity' to Eros, Plotinus underlines Love's divine status throughout the treatise. Especially in the end of both theological parts, after he has made the bold statement about Eros' being Soul's activity, Plotinus concludes that 'the Eros of the upper Soul may be considered a god, which keeps Soul eternally attached to that higher reality, but the daimon is the Eros of mixed Soul'.[134] Regarding this second instance of Eros, in the end of the treatise Plotinus adds that it 'is something matter-like ... which is born from Soul, insofar as Soul lacks the good, yet desires it'.[135] Furthermore, in §6 he gives us an extensive discussion of the nature of daimons in general and of the criteria of their distinction from gods.[136] Does not this material build in the view that Eros can be seen as a specific divine entity,[137] which, although related to Soul, is external to it?

My retort is that if Eros-daimon is an instance within a larger group of daimons and deities, then my previous presentation about Eros' ontological status should modify our conception of Plotinian daimonology as a whole. We should not see daimons as substantial entities in their own right, but rather as powers whose exercise fulfils the being of an entity like World-Soul. This synairetic point of view is verified by Plotinus' various statements in §6 itself. First of all, although he ascribes daimonic status to both World-Soul and the rest of the daimons, including her Eros,[138] Plotinus is not unequivocal. World-Soul is the proper substance/entity from which several activities with respect to the administration of the world emanate. Now, in ll.30–2 he refers to 'the other daimons ... being brought forth from Soul ... but by different powers' («δυνάμεσι δὲ ἑτέραις γεννώμενοι»), whereas two lines below (33–5) he remarks that 'it was necessary for the World-soul to be adequate for the world by bringing forth daimon-powers («γεννήσασαν δυνάμεις δαιμόνων»).' That is, on the one hand Plotinus declares that daimons are generated by powers, whereas, on the other, he claims that they are powers themselves.[139] But then the case is as with Eros: we have seen that in Chapter 4 and 9 Eros is the activity that results from Soul's erotic disposition. We concluded that this activity is also self-constitutional of Soul. The same applies to the daimons: insofar as they serve in the administration of the world,[140] daimons self-constitute World-Soul (the proper entity) as the ruling principle of the world. Hence, we can come to a synairesis of the daimons with World-Soul, asserting that they are necessary aspects of World-Soul's being. It turns out that Plotinus' concept of daimons (and equivalently of gods) is more nuanced than expected and that Eros' ontological status can help us in clarifying these ontological questions.[141]

Moreover, my de-mythologizing reading of Plotinus can be verified by Plotinus' stance in other treatises. When, nowadays, we read the *Symposium*, we do not need to take the references to the daimonic nature of Love as fundamental tenets which reveal the complicated structure of reality between the sensible and the intelligible realm. Instead, such mythological references just pave the way for an understanding of Diotima's 'greatest mysteries'.[142] However, every historical phase sees the past from its own eyes. That we, or Plato, do not seem to ascribe much importance to this kind of reference need not reflect the attitude of other historical periods. The example of the perception of the idea of our 'allotted guardian spirit' in conjunction with Socrates' 'guardian spirit' (δαιμόνιον) is characteristic. Philosophers have been always ready to read allegorical references to human psychology under these ascriptions.[143] However, within the course of time, complications were not avoided.[144] The Middle Platonists seem to have made a lot from such references in their elaborate accounts of daimonologies.[145] Such attitudes led to the elaborate religious-pagan hierarchies of later Neoplatonists.[146] Hence, the position of Plotinus within such a historical context[147] would seem to justify why one could take him as suggesting a hypostatization of Eros. But is Plotinus really committed to that view?

The above mention of 'our allotted guardian spirit' becomes an ally of mine, since it testifies to Plotinus' calm and rational engagement with popular-superstitious beliefs and the various pagan-religious elements found in the philosophical works of his past.[148] That is, according to Plotinus' early treatise III.4.[15], entitled 'On our allotted guardian spirit', the Neoplatonic founder is ready to internalize this belief and incorporate it in his psychological theory. For Plotinus this guardian spirit may not be the leading-reasoning part of our soul, but actually it is identified with the ontological level above that which is dominant in our conscious life. In such a view, even the One can be said to be the guardian spirit of a philosopher, who has attained to the level of Intellect.[149] We should approach other references to gods and daimons throughout the Plotinian corpus in a similar way.[150] Under the veil of such 'traditional' references Plotinus may be entertaining innovative views, absolutely compatible with his whole system and also crucial for a better understanding of his rational stance towards reality.

1.2.3 A daimonic counter-objection from within III.5?

One might claim, however, that there is a serious argument within Plotinus' text which undercuts my proposal of the synairesis of Eros with Soul, i.e. the synairetic view of Eros as an internal and necessary aspect of Soul's being. When Plotinus in §5 rebuts Plutarch's interpretation of the *Symposium*-myth which identified Eros with cosmos, the Neoplatonist gives several arguments against the Middle-Platonist. One of them is that 'if the world is equivalent to its Soul, just as man is equivalent to man's Soul, then it necessarily follows that Aphrodite is Eros'.[151] Nonetheless, this statement leads to many absurdities according to Plotinus, since, e.g. if the cosmos would be a daimon, then we would not be able to account for the rest of the daimons: since they have the same substance as each other, therefore they, too, should be parts of the world (or indeed each of them a world), and then the cosmos would be the mishmash of daimons, something unbearable for Plotinus.[152]

What is more important, though, is his thesis concerning the avoidance of identifying Aphrodite, that is, Soul, with its offspring, that is, Eros. Such an attitude shows why the 'synairesis' I propose is not an unqualified identification, and hence it can clarify my views. It is true that talking about Penia and Poros I came close to the point of identifying them with Soul; Soul is Penia in relation to Nous, but Poros in relation to the physical cosmos. In any case, the myth talked about Eros as the offspring of this pair; hence, I diagnosed the derivative sense in which Eros is connected to Soul. Eros depends on Soul, because it is the outcome of her ontological status; we saw that it was the self-constituting activity that brings Soul in contact with the intelligible. Hence, Eros was an activity stemming from within Soul's own nature, not something external. What is more, a Soul without erotic activity cannot be considered as an existent entity, at all. Hence, my 'synairesis' does not simply identify Soul with Eros. It is as if we claimed that a music conductor is the activity of conducting. However, it is true that insofar as he conducts, he is a conductor; thus, the (intentional) activity gives one his proper identity. It is in this way that Eros is an internal and inseparable aspect of Soul; it stems from Soul's own nature as the aspiration of its self-completion. Hence, the real problem that Plotinus has with Plutarch's interpretation is that Eros is not any more the self-constituting *activity* of an entity, but an independent entity itself. This is what could enable one to identify Aphrodite with Eros. Contrary to that, Plotinus' interpretation preserves the derivative sense between Aphrodite and her Eros; for Plotinus an Aphrodite that has not given birth to an Eros is not a real Aphrodite.[153]

1.2.4 Eros and Soul: Who is first?

I will conclude this chapter with an important detail of Plotinus' account of the generation of Eros that completes the synairetic picture I gave. We have seen that eros is the activity of Soul that constitutes it as a substantial entity. In this formulation eros is at once contemporaneous and posterior to its mother. As Kalligas aptly remarks,[154] Aphrodite's Eros is both «ἐξ αὐτῆς», as causally dependent on Soul, and «σὺν αὐτῇ»,[155] because it is Soul's self-constituting activity. This is what Plotinus wants to bring to the forefront when in §2 he states that 'since Aphrodite [sc. Soul] follows upon Kronos [sc. Nous] ... she directed her activity towards him and felt affinity[156] with him, and filled with passionate love for him brought forth Love, and with this child of hers she looks towards him'.[157] Here, the 'loving passion' found in the activity of Aphrodite to her progenitor is distinct from the Love-Eros, the result of her activity. Hence, one could complain: if Soul can be filled with eros prior to its generation, why do we really need a hypostatized Eros-offspring? My synairetic interpretation has already given an answer to this: the erotic activity of Soul gives rise to its authentic self, i.e. an erotic entity.[158]

Now, if we turn to the description of Eros' birth in the second theological part of the treatise, one might note an inconsistency with the previous citation. I refer to our well-known passage: 'Lack and desire, and the memory that constitutes the reason-principles (τῶν λόγων ἡ μνήμη), come together into a unity in soul and produce (ἐγέννησε) an active orientation (τὴν ἐνέργειαν) towards the good, and this is Eros.'[159] The «ἔλλειψις» ("lack") corresponds to the Penia-aspect of Soul, but «ἔλλειψις» of what? Of the Poros-aspect of Soul, which is «τῶν λόγων ἡ μνήμη». Actually, the Poros-aspect is the 'logoi', whereas their memory denotes again the upwards orientation towards them. Now, «ἔφεσις» ("desire") being in the middle has an ambivalent position, since it clearly corresponds to the Penia-aspect of Soul, but the orientation of the desire is determined by the recollection of the *logoi*. However, in the previous citation from the first theological part it seems that the erotic activity is prior to the constitution of Soul's erotic substance/entity. On the other hand, in the passage from §9 it is the fulfilled substance of Soul that generates a posterior erotic activity. In other words, whereas in the passage from §2 Aphrodite would act towards her progenitor filled with erotic passion for him and then generate Eros, in §9 the erotic activity seems to follow the self-constitution of Soul, which is the result of her separate and unqualified 'desire'. Is Plotinus contradicting himself? Or is he just careless with the details? Neither. To this challenge I have a twofold answer: (a) in his methodological remarks Plotinus has warned us about the distortion that a discursive/diairetic grasp of reality can yield. (b) Eros is the *self-conscious* desire of the intelligible, since, as I have stressed, it is through eros that Soul constitutes itself as a proper entity, which means being orientated towards its source/principle.

Let me now elaborate a bit on these two remarks. My first point, although preliminary, reminds us that all these complications, which relate to the temporal sequences, denote complicated ontological structures. Furthermore, our language is restricted by various aspects of our discursive apprehension of reality. Hence, the fact that sometimes Plotinus mentions things happening prior to others, whereas at other times he makes them posterior, may denote the higher degree of unity within the fundamental function of Hypostasis-Soul. When this reality is put to words, the interpreter must not stop at the diairetic elements which discriminate various accounts of the same thing, but (s)he should proceed to a synairesis that sees these accounts as complementary. Besides, as I just noted with respect to the passages in §2, Plotinus aims at showing that Eros is not only derivative, but also contemporaneous with Soul.

I proceed to my second point which is the most vital. In discussing the eye-simile, I suggested that the constitution of Soul is that of an erotic entity, always being in constant reference to the intelligible. This is why in §9 Plotinus separates the «ἔφεσις» from Eros, *qua* the result of ἔφεσις, since exactly this former desire represents the first moment of inchoate Soul's/Penia's reversion which fills it with logoi. This prior ἔφεσις of §9 clearly corresponds to the prior 'erotic passion' of §2. Yet, as we have seen, the orientation of Soul is ceaseless, because there is the element of insatiability, as was emphasized in the section on §7's tragedy (Section 1.1.5).[160] Soul can sempiternally be what it is, only with constant reference to the intelligible. This is why it is an erotic entity. What is more, I do not contradict myself, either, having stated that the offspring of Aphrodite, which gazes at the *noeton* with its mother, is actually Soul itself from the aspect of its self-constituting orientation towards Nous. I have repeatedly stressed that for an entity to be what it is, it must exist orientating its activity towards the higher realms. This is what the «ἐνέργεια» in the last passage from §9 denotes; it is this eternally self-constituting activity. Furthermore, we can propose that: (a) ἔφεσις is this ἐνέργεια that self-constitutes Soul at its first moment of reversion. Thus, the element of Penia prevails here. (b) On the other hand, ἐνέργεια is also the eternal self-constituting activity of the 'already' fulfilled Soul. Hence, at that time the Poros-aspect is more prominent. But in both cases we have both elements working. In this first reversion/activity, Soul must already have the Poros-traces to be 'filled with passion' and generate Eros. Yet, when it generates Eros, that is, when Soul is self-constituted, it stays forever gazing at Nous; hence, the Penia-aspect is always present. This is why 'Eros is eternally and necessarily come into existence out of the longing of Soul for the higher and good, and from the moment there was Soul, there was eternally Eros'.[161]

Finally, I need to close this section with an additional point on the substantial result of Soul's erotic activity and desire for what lies above it. Although not stressed by Plotinus in III.5, a distinction should be drawn between an (internal) product and an (external) by-product. The former is what I have been showing so far: Soul's self-constitution as a proper entity, i.e. Eros. The latter is the subsequent generation of Soul's lower parts, which – via the ultimate generation of matter – leads to the formation of the physical cosmos.[162] Hence, the substantial, derivative and external result of Soul's erotic activity is not Eros, but what lies beneath Soul,[163] as is the case with Soul's generation from Nous' contemplation of the One.[164]

1.3 Nous and Eros

What I have been showing so far is that the erotic generation of Soul from Nous is equivalent to the erotic relation that Nous has with the One.[165] The reason I am now dealing specifically with Nous is twofold: (a) its erotic generation verifies the synairetic reading I proposed with respect to Soul's Eros in III.5. (b) More generally, it illuminates once more the importance that Eros has in Plotinus' ontology. Let me begin by drawing a general scheme drawn from other treatises, where Plotinus gives a more detailed description of the emanation of Nous from the external activity of the One.[166] There, he speaks of two 'moments':[167] firstly, we have the emanation of an 'inchoate Intellect', or 'intelligible matter', which is simple, but in a degraded-potential sense compared with the One's actual simplicity, and hence can be compared to Penia from III.5's *Symposium*-myth. After this first emanation, inchoate Intellect reverts upon the One. However, this gazing at the One has as immediate effect: Intellect's thinking of itself,[168] with the further result of Nous' *self*-constitution as the World of Forms (cf. its Poros-aspect), i.e. as the proper second Hypostasis. Nous' being the best-possible image of the One's unity-simplicity has introduced unity in multiplicity. It is notable that in this picture, Nous' activity towards the One, expressing again an erotic intentionality, self-constitutes Nous' being, that is, as a self-thinking that produces the «ὄντως ὄντα». Hence, it is this eternal erotic reversion that constitutes Nous' proper being, making Nous an erotic being.[169] Of course, in this 'erotic' description of Nous' generation there arises no question concerning any potential postulation of a separate Eros-entity. Finally, although it is true that Plotinus does not usually describe the dependence of Soul on Nous in terms of Nous' relation to the One, in the erotic-'synairetic' treatise III.5 he urges us to do so; since the present focus is on what it is to be an erotic entity, I hope that the analogies of the erotic reversions, activities and self-constitutions between the two lower Hypostases have become clear enough.[170]

Nonetheless, even if we can couch Intellect's generation in terms of III.5's Poros–Penia myth, in VI.7.[38], when Plotinus explicitly connects Nous' being in relation to the One with the *Symposium*-myth, he does not mention Penia at all. A reason might be that in *Enneads* III.6.[26] Plotinus uses again the same mythical material with respect to the formation of the sensible world, where Penia is prime matter, and, as stated (already in Section 1.1.3), for Plotinus sensible matter never fully gets form. Hence, perhaps to avoid negative connotations, he chooses not to speak in terms of Penia, although he does so with respect to Soul in our treatise, which is later than the other two. The III.5-case may be an indication that in the mediating level of Soul, between the sensible and intelligible worlds, we can speak of an increase of indefiniteness, and hence the symbol of Penia is more apt. It is also notable that Penia in our treatise does have intercourse with Poros, and not with an image of it as in the Plotinian interpretation given in III.6.[171] Of course, the fact that Plotinus is ready to give multiple interpretations of a single source of mythological material in various treatises need not imply any inconsistency. It reveals Plotinus' dynamic way of de-allegorization, where the myths serve as useful tools of the presentation that Plotinus wants to give.

Returning to how he treats the same myth in VI.7, Plotinus implicitly identifies Poros with Nous and stresses the role of Poros' drunkenness, which has already been mentioned. It is worth citing the passage:

> Intellect also, then, has one power for thinking, by which it looks at the things in itself, and one by which it looks at what transcends it by direct awareness and reception, by which also before it saw only, and by seeing acquired intellect and is one. And that first one is the contemplation of Intellect in its right mind, and the other is Intellect in love, when it goes out of its mind 'drunk with the nectar'; then it falls in love, simplified into contentment[172] by having its fill; and it is better for it to be drunk with a drunkenness like this than to be more respectably sober.[173]

We see once more that what constitutes Intellect *qua* Intellect is this passionate-loving gazing at the One, as if the result of a divine drunkenness. If we can identify Poros with Nous here, then we have again a duality of mythological elements: Poros and the nectar that has made him drunk. This pair can correspond to the pair of Penia–(drunken) Poros in the III.5-case. Poros has the traces of the One and reverts upon its source in a way that he becomes mad from love, because he is constituted as an erotic entity, as being in constant relation to the source of his divine madness. Furthermore, as we have seen (again in Section 1.1.3), in the *Symposium* exegesis of III.5, the temporal distinctions are not so clear-cut: it seems that the result of Poros' contemplation is his being drunk with the nectar, but we can also claim that the nectar that has filled him is the traces of the One which make Poros eternally revert upon its source and constitute itself. What is more, if we take the drunkenness to be the result of Poros' reversion, then we can see why sober Poros can be the equivalent of Penia in our case.[174] Neither of them is yet filled with the divine traces/limits which are imposed by the (drunken) Poros in the III.5-case and solely by the nectar in VI.7-case. Finally, it is important to note that what emanates from the One, and any other ontological level in general, transfers the ceaseless ardent passion for reversion towards it. Thus, since in III.5 this overflowing nectar is compared to the Logos-(Drunken) Poros inseminating Penia, Dillon aptly remarks that 'the Way Down and the Way Up, in fact, spring together from this drunkenness'.[175]

A further problem, though, with my approach is how to account for Nous' fulfilment contrary to Soul's insatiability, while both entities are erotic. Remember that in §7 Plotinus states that 'only that truly achieves fulfillment, which also constitutionally possesses fulfillment. But that which craves on account of its inherent deficiency is like a leaky vessel'.[176] Furthermore, as the other above-mentioned passages suggest, if Nous is already fulfilled then, how can he have desire for the Good? To these legitimate questions I have two points in response. The first element I would like to exploit here is the eternity of Nous. One aspect of Nous' way of being is eternity; i.e. a constant now, without any temporal extension/succession that characterizes the sensible realm. This erotic-self-constituting reversion is an eternal now. This is an alternative way to understand the seemingly contradictory idea from *Enneads* III.8, according to which Nous 'always desires [cf. Penia aspect] and always attains [cf. Poros aspect]',[177] where the 'always' denotes atemporal eternity. Furthermore, I have already mentioned (e.g. in n.165) that an element that distinguishes Soul from Nous is the former's discursivity in contrast to the 'concentrated' unity of Nous. Temporality, however, implies extension and succession of different time-units. Besides, this is why time is the 'moving image of eternity'. Within this temporal realm, the realm of Soul, we have seen that Soul, too, is an erotic unity, always being in reference to its intelligible source. Nonetheless, in this case the 'always' must be conceived not as eternal now, but as denoting sempiternity, that is the totality of time (-units). Within this temporal framework, for an entity to be 'always desiring and always attaining' would be a stronger contradiction, since, if at one distinct moment Soul is fulfilled, why should it keep desiring its fulfilment?[178] True, we are not obliged to view Soul's generation from a temporal perspective, although Plotinus' elaboration of the issue is not quite clear.[179] On the other hand, a mild failure of one to attain what he strives for can make him pursue further and further to fully attain his object of desire. Hence, in stressing the insatiability of Soul('s Eros), in contrast to Nous' satiety, Plotinus perhaps focuses on the different way of being for his two entities,[180] and at the same time he tries to block a counter-argument that would attempt to obliterate the position that Soul is sempiternally an erotic entity. It is true that Soul is fulfilled by gazing at the intelligible; but, after its fulfilment, why does it not stop its seeing? If it stopped at some points in time, and then it realized that it must revert again, then there would be times that the sensible realm would be really bereft of its ultimate source, which of course would be quite unacceptable for Plotinus and his anti-Gnostic polemic. Consequently, if we are to account for Soul as desiring the *noeton* for the totality of time, perhaps the best solution is to emphasize the tragic nature of its existence, i.e. that it is (always) orientated towards its source, however never fully attaining it, and hence always desiring it.[181]

Finally, my second point exploits the connection of parallel passages from Chapter 7 and 9. Apart from the above citation from §7, in §9 Plotinus states that 'Intellect ... possesses itself in satiety and it is not "drunk" in its self-possession, for it does not possess anything extraneous'.[182] Moreover, as Kalligas has crucially pointed out, this passage suggests that Nous does not get drunk *from itself*.[183] Nous is instead filled from something higher. As the world of Forms, Nous is complete in relation to itself, not with respect to its source, viz. the Good. From that point of view, then, the §9 passage is perfectly compatible with that from VI.7 on Nous' having love for the One. As that passage had stressed, Nous indeed is sober when it thinks itself, i.e. with respect to its own nature. However, as the same passage makes clear in the following lines, in order for this completeness to exist, Nous must be drunk from the power which stems from the One and arouses his manic love for its source of being. It is because Nous has a manic-loving aspiration for the One, that he can constitute itself and, hence, be filled (with respect to himself). Consequently, Nous, seen from its erotic point of view, is analogically as insatiable as Soul is, and this is why he eternally exists as this erotic intentionality, which enables him to have himself in this complete state. On the other hand, from a bird's-eye view Nous is 'more' fulfilled than Soul, since Nous is the proper 'ousia', whereas Soul is a further degradation of that 'ousia'. Hence, in a contrast between Nous and Soul we could hold that Nous is fulfilled relatively to the unfulfilled Soul. This is also how we are to understand the phrase from III.8 where it is stated that 'Nous always desires and always attains'. Nous always desires because it is inferior to the One, but always attains what it is to be Nous, that is the best-possible image of the One. In this sense, we can see again why when I was using the Poros–Penia terms I claimed that there is flexibility in the use of the various elements of the myths. Nous as the world of Forms is the (drunken) Poros; however, because it is inferior to the One, it can be said to be Penia in relation to its principle of form, and hence desiring it. Alternatively, as we have already seen, we can express the same idea in terms of the two moments of Nous' generation: intelligible matter-Penia gets its formation-Poros (-proper Nous) by eternally gazing at the One.

1.4 Conclusions

Although Plotinus' treatise is entitled 'On Love', our preoccupation in my former discussion has been with the ontology of Soul along with extensive references to the other levels of the Plotinian system. With the proposal of the radical 'synairesis' of Eros with Soul or Nous it turns out that an enquiry into the ontology of Eros cannot be conducted without reference to the entity to which Eros belongs, and vice versa. In that way we have come to realize the quintessential role that Eros plays in the constitution of an entity as such. In a nutshell, approaching the problem of the ontological status of Eros, we have ended up with a better understanding of the ontological structure of Plotinus' system in general, and more precisely, we have come to an answer to the problem 'what is it to be an entity?': being erotic. It is as if Plotinus were telling us that there is no way in which to address the problem of Eros without connecting it with the substantial entities, or even stronger: there is no way in which to speak about the ontology of an entity without addressing the aspect of Eros.

Hence, having completed the above discussion, if we were to give an answer to Plotinus' opening question of the treatise, i.e. whether Eros is an affection of soul, god or daimon, I would respond that, first and foremost, Eros' deepest essence is none of these alternatives: Eros is a self-constituting activity of Soul, or every inferior entity for what transcends it, expressed in its contemplation of the intelligible. Hence, the issue of Eros cannot be examined separately from the fact that it is Eros *of* an entity. This is also the reason why, if we were obliged to select one of Plotinus' alternatives, initially, we would be inclined towards the 'affection' one, qualified as a 'substantial' affection. By that we would show the 'erotic passion' with which Aphrodite is filled so that she gives birth to Eros.

However, although there is no pejorative sense in the notion of 'affection' *qua* 'affection' in §1 of our treatise,[184] we had better be more cautious since the 'passivity' of the affection is most of the time related to the interfusion of soul with matter, i.e. to the composite («συναμφότερον»).[185] Instead, as Plotinus has declared in III.6, the immaterial world, as also prime matter, is totally impassive. Thus, Flamand comes much closer to Plotinus' thought when he states that

> sans doute le propos essentiel de Plotin est-il plutôt de montrer qu'Éros, loin de se réduire à une passion, bonne ou mauvaise, est un dieu ou un démon, une réalité vivante étroitement apparentée à l'âme, capable d'en suivre ou d'en inspirer tous les mouvements, capable de l'orienter vers la beauté qui pour elle ouvre la voie au bien et au bonheur véritable.[186]

Flamand's remark reminds us that III.5.[50] precedes treatise I.8.[51]: 'On what are and whence come evils', in which Plotinus encounters one of the most difficult problems posed against systems like the Neoplatonic one:[187] how to account for the existence of evil in the world. Part of Plotinus' answer to the problem is that vice, connected to matter, is complete opposition to being, the total otherness, i.e. non-being.[188] Contrary to this 'non-real', but existing in a sense, aspect of the world, then, in III.5 we see that Plotinus wants to stress so much the crucial reality-existence of Eros that he comes to the point of referring to it as a divine entity in its own right. As we saw, Plotinus does so in order to account for the substantial self-constitution of an entity as such. Furthermore, then, if Eros corresponds to the self-constituting reversion of an entity, then it is the antidote to the vicious «τόλμα» ('audacity'), which corresponds to the procession.[189] As it seems, Plotinus wants to stress that for an entity to be an entity, i.e. to *exist*, it is not enough to speak about its 'audacity', the 'vicious' will of an entity to belong only to itself.[190] It must strive to come back to its progenitor and be self-constituted as an entity. Hence, by realizing the impossibility of being on its own, the entity becomes erotic. Of course, I, like Plotinus, use here anthropomorphic language. I have already stressed the necessary aspect of Penia's reversion due to her Poros-traces,[191] and respectively I have mentioned that the formation of the lower levels of reality is the necessary outcome of the One's majestic power, expressed in its unintended over-flowing. But even within this scheme Plotinus wants to elevate the erotic-'synairetic' element of the generation of reality, not the 'diairetic' one.[192] What is more, if, after my whole argument, we can assert that beneath the references to the substantial Eros lies Soul's erotic way of being, we could follow Plotinus' language and propose the following: if every level of reality has its specific name due to its 'audacious' procession,[193] from the point of view of reversion there is a sole name for every entity: Eros. Everything is Eros in relation to the One,[194] which «κινεῖ δὴ ὡς ἐρώμενον».[195]

Indeed, Plotinus in VI.8.[39] will call even the One 'lovable and love and love of himself'.[196] In this notable assertion we see Plotinus' flexible language, as with the case of the meaning of 'matter'. One of the pivotal conclusions of III.5 is that love implies deficiency (Penia); hence, it can have meaning only for an inferior in relation to its superior. Furthermore, Plotinus declares that 'the Good is not desiring – for what could it desire? – or attaining, for it did not desire [to attain anything]'.[197] Thus, if there is no Penia in the One, Plotinus, in his optimistic view of Eros, is willing to ascribe to the One Eros, but Eros of itself.[198] Another reason why Plotinus reaches this conclusion is that in this treatise he chooses to be kataphatic regarding the One; hence, he transposes language he usually uses for Nous to the case of the One, but in a more exalted way.[199] Hence, from Aristotle's god who loves himself and forms a basis for Plotinus' doctrine of Nous, we have ended up with a rather Aristotelian picture, like the One-god of VI.8.[200]

Furthermore, the fact that Plotinus chooses in the late III.5 to adopt an optimistic (-erotic) view of the generation of reality, rather than a pessimistic ('audacious') one[201] is very important if one considers the significance that the notion of «τόλμα» had among the Gnostics and the Neo-Pythagoreans. Hence, as various interpreters point out, although Plotinus 'makes use of it in his early treatise "On the Three Primary Hypostases" (V 1 [10].1.4), and, somewhat more reluctantly, a bit later (see III 6 [26].14.8) ... he prefers to steer clear of it in the wake of his anti-Gnostic polemic'.[202] This reference becomes even more relevant if one takes into account that Plotinus in his exegesis of the *Symposium*-myth is quite possibly offering his 'authentic' reading of Plato contra the overly ascetic interpretations of Gnostics, who, as Kalligas notes, conceived Eros 'as the cosmogonic force responsible for the incarceration of the divine light in matter'.[203] With respect to the cosmological aspect, I have already noted that the erotic activity of Soul, apart from its self-constitution, has as a by-product the further emanation of the *logoi* until the level of Nature forms the sensible world. For the anti-Gnostic Plotinus the generation of the sensible world, this visible god, is not in itself the vicious outcome of the failure due to the weakness of higher entities.[204] However, in the initial remarks of our exploration I noted that the daimonic Aphrodite-World-Soul corresponded to the human beings characterized by 'mixed love', and we also saw that Plotinus appreciated them, too, contra to any sort of Gnostic asceticism.[205]

Now, this reference to the ethical point of view of the individual souls' love, which was the central topic of Plotinus' §1, is crucial. It can show us why Plotinus stresses the divine existence of Eros and the important position it occupies in the Plotinian structure of reality. We should not forget that Plotinus' penultimate treatise[206] considers the individual souls and in what sense our true self is not the composite, but is identified with the Undescended Soul.[207] However, if we are in fact Undescended Soul(s), how is it possible that people develop desires/loves 'contrary to nature', as we saw in Plotinus' §1? For one thing, we have stressed the necessity that underlies Soul's and also Nous' erotic reversion towards what is beyond and their subsequent self-constitution. How is it, then, that particular souls[208] deviate from the natural course of this vertical necessity? Plotinus has given the answer very clearly in his relevant treatises (e.g. *Enn.* I.8. and I.1.): it is the interfusion with matter that impedes the function of our true self and distances him from its genuine source. Then, in terms of our treatise the exaggerated engagement with our bodily needs and for the sake of our bodily constitution makes us forget our true self, and hence its deep erotic constitution, as looking towards what is higher, not the opposite direction. These 'contrary to nature', bodily desires cannot form expressions of our erotic aspiration towards the intelligible, but only perverted results of an individual that has 'separated' himself from his erotic constitution.

Now, perhaps it is already apparent that in these observations we are doing nothing else than paraphrasing Plotinus' remarks in §7. It is only now that we have had an onto-logical training that we can appreciate why Plotinus, after his first exegesis of the *Symposium* myth in §7, chooses to refer back to the issue of eros as 'affection' of individual souls. His statements can be also revealing as to the way Eros exists. Hence, Plotinus declares that

> the good men of this world direct the Eros which they have to the non-particular and truly worthwhile good, and do not have a particular Eros. But those who identify with other daimons, identify with one daimon after another, leaving the Eros which they simply 'have' inactive, and instead developing their activity along the lines of another daimon, the one they have 'chosen,' in accordance with the harmonizing part of the activity-principle in them, namely Soul. Those, however, whose longing goes out to evil things, have repressed, by the evil desires which develop within, all the Erotes within them, just as they repress, by the bad opinion which they acquire, their innate right reasons. Now the Erotes which are natural and in accordance with Nature are fair and good: those which belong to an inferior Soul are inferior as far as their worth and power goes; others are superior; all consist in Substance (πάντες ἐν οὐσίᾳ). But the unnatural loves of those who have gone wrong – these are affections, and are in no way Substance or substantial Existences (οἱ δὲ παρὰ φύσιν σφαλέντων πάθη ταῦτα

καὶ οὐδαμῇ οὐσία οὐδὲ ὑποστάσεις οὐσιώδεις). They are no longer brought forth by Soul, but come into existence as concomitants of vice, whereas Soul, for its part, only brings forth – in disposition and attitudes – things similar to itself. For it would seem to be generally true that the true goods are Substance (οὐσία) as long as the Soul acts in accordance with Nature, in limits. The alternatives to the good, however, do not derive their activity from Substance, but are nothing but affections (πάθη).[209]

This crucial passage shows why we should not be justified to see Eros as primarily an affection of Soul. However, it is true that, as Wolters notes, here Plotinus seems 'confusingly' to switch the sense of 'affection' from a neutral one in §1 to a pejorative one. However, according to our approach the problem with affection even in this passage is not that it is a «πάθος», but that it is an affection *without ontological grounding*.[210] This is the reason why in §1 Plotinus begins his discussion talking about the 'affection which we ascribe to Eros'.[211] Of course, after all our discussion it turns out that Soul is in fact responsible, a necessary aspect of Soul being its erotic activity. Hence, the souls that achieve in being coordinate with the Undescended Soul, i.e. their true self, have true-substantial erotic desires, which bring them into relation to Nous. However, souls that are dragged by matter have forgotten who they truly are; hence, their desires do not stem from Soul's erotic desire for Nous. This is why a perverted soul-composite, then, gives rise to perverted desires which lead soul deeper in the 'underworld'. It is also very important that Plotinus has used here the baffling substantial vocabulary about Eros. In so doing, he shows us the real incentives of speaking of Eros' existence as a divine entity. Insofar as the perverted people remain remote from this self-constituting activity, they stop existing in a proper sense; hence, in a vicious circle, their diverse activities do not relate them with the realm above. On the other hand, the loves produced according to nature converge in the function of getting us higher; let us not forget that as Plotinus will state in §4, 'the All-soul has an All-Eros, and … the partial Souls each have their own Eros. But just as the relation of the microcosmic Soul to the All-soul is not one of separation, but of inclusion, so that all Souls constitute a unity, in the same way each microcosmic Eros stands in this relation to the All-Eros'.[212] Insofar as our eros is coordinate with Soul's self-constituting, and hence divine, Eros, then we have become true beings, erotic entities, Undescended Souls.[213]

Now, since I have been giving some reasons as to why Plotinus wants to emphasize so much the importance of the existence of Eros, in a way that called for our careful reading, I want to give a final reason: in speaking about Eros as if it were an entity, Plotinus faithfully follows Plato's example in the *Symposium*, where after Diotima's encomium of love in the abstract, Alcibiades comes to complete it by his encomium to the instantiation of love, Socrates.[214] Socrates personifies exactly the power of love that leads one towards the intelligible. What is more, Diotima's account is surrounded by the references to its particular instantiation, since in the description of the daimonic Eros, the offspring of Poros and Penia, one can find direct allusions to Socrates.[215] Hence, Socrates can claim to know particularly the 'erotic' issues because he is an erotic entity. At the same time, according to a potential Plotinian reading, his classic saying that 'he does know that he does not know anything' can show exactly Socrates' realization that he is Penia in relation to the intelligible.[216] Moreover, it is exactly this realization that Socrates tries to generate in his interlocutors, so that they try to convert their Penia into Poros. Far from numbing them, then, Socrates wants to orientate them towards the intelligible; that is, he wants to make them erotic entities, too. It is, then, perhaps for this reason why from lover, Socrates, the real lover of wisdom, can become the beloved; in making the others to feel Penia in relation to him, he «κινεῖ δὴ [sc. them] ὡς ἐρώμενον». Divine Plotinus' erotic (Neo-)Platonism might turn out to be more (Neo-)Socratic than the interpreters would allow him to be. Let us now turn to an ancient interpreter, Proclus, to see what he makes of all these issues: is eros identified only with an ascending power? Is its paradigmatic instantiation Socrates? Does Socrates' relation with other people, and in particular Alcibiades, tell us anything about Eros in the intelligible realm?

Notes

1   The Plotinian text used is by Henry-Schwyzer (1964–83) (H-S$_2$), along with the 'Addenda et Corrigenda' of Henry-Schwyzer (1964–83: 304–25) (H-S$_4$), and the 'Corrigenda ad Plotini textum' of Schwyzer (1987) (H-S$_5$, H-S$_1$ and H-S$_3$ stand for the 'editio maior' and its 'Addenda et ... ' respectively). The references to Plotinus' text indicate the numbers: of the *Enneads*, of the specific treatise (of the place in the chronological order within square brackets, when needed), of the paragraph and the lines (e.g. III.5.[50].8,16–19). Concerning English translations of Plotinus' text, I use the Loeb edition of Armstrong (1966–88), unless otherwise stated. Specifically, for *Enneads* III.5 I cite Wolters' translation (rarely modified), which accompanies his commentary, in Wolters (1984: xxxv–lii).

2   III.5.1,1–2: «Περὶ ἔρωτος, πότερα θεός τις ἢ δαίμων ἢ πάθος τι τῆς ψυχῆς, ... ».

3   Apparently, Plotinus condemns homosexuality and, generally, every expression of intemperate sexual desire, which does not aim at the generation of a new entity.
4   Cf. Plato, *Phaedrus* 243d9.
5   Cf. idem, *Symposium* 180d7-8. Plotinus does not mention the name «Πάνδημος» explicitly, although he had done so in his early treatise VI.9.[9].9,30. Cf. also Kalligas (2014: 519).
6   Hence, in the mythological language Heavenly Aphrodite, daughter of Ouranos, is «ἀμήτωρ» (without a mother). Cf. III.5.2,17.
7   What is more, Plotinus mentions the daimonic loves of individual souls in §4.
8   Cf. III.5.2,13.
9   Ibid.; see *Symposium* 203b1-c6: the famous myth of the genealogy of Eros enunciated by Diotima in the early stages of her discussion with Socrates.
10 Cf. III.6.[26].14,7-18. Except for a clerical mistake, this is perhaps a reason why Sykoutris in his monumental Modern Greek edition of the *Symposium* (1949: 199*, n.1) ascribes to Plotinus' treatise III.5 the view that Eros is equated with the (physical) cosmos.
11 Furthermore, these distinctions account for the specific desires that human beings develop.
12 Usually, the mythical equivalents for Plotinus' system of three Hypostases are the gods of the Hesiodic *Theogony*: Ouranos (-One), Kronos (-Intellect), Zeus (-Soul). Yet, according to the interpretative strand followed in this treatise, Aphrodite, not Zeus, stands for Soul (see also infra, n.40). Hence, there is a complication as to Aphrodite's superior principle, since, according to Hesiod, Aphrodite sprung from the foam of Ouranos', not Kronos', mutilated genitals. Granted that for Plotinus Soul's superior principle is undoubtedly Nous, in III.5.2,33-4 he concedes that for the purposes of his enquiry either Kronos or Ouranos can be conceived as Aphrodite-Soul's progenitor. Proclus solved the aforementioned problem in his own way in the *Commentary on the Cratylus* 183 (1-54) and 110,5-111,16 (Pasquali).
13 Cf. III.5.2,36. (Armstrong translates 'real substance'; Wolters: 'Existence or Substance'.)
14 Ibid., §2,37-8: «ὁ καλὸς Ἔρως ὁ γεγενημένος *ὑπόστασις* (Existence with Wolters) πρὸς ἄλλο καλὸν ἀεὶ τεταγμένη». (Every emphasis in the ancient Greek texts is mine.)
15 Apart from the references to come, see ibid., §3,15 («... ὑπόστασιν ἔχει» sc. ὁ Ἔρως); §4,2 (ἐν οὐσίᾳ καὶ ὑποστάσει) and 3 (ὑποστατὸν ἔρωτα); §7,9 (ὑπόστασιν), 42 (ἐν οὐσίᾳ) and 43 (ὑποστάσεις οὐσιώδεις); §9,40 (ὑπέστη). Cf. also §9,42, where Eros is called «μικτόν τι χρῆμα». In §9,20 «ὑπόστασις» is ascribed to λόγος.

16 Ibid., §2, ll.23-4: «χωριστὴν οὐσάν τινα ὑπόστασιν (Existence) καὶ ἀμέτοχον ὕλης οὐσίαν (Substance)». (Armstrong renders «τινα ὑπόστασιν» as 'separate reality'.) Cf. also ibid., §9,23 («ἡ Ἀφροδίτη ἐν τοῖς οὖσιν ὑποστῆναι λέγεται») and §9,30 (ψυχὴ … παρὰ νοῦ ὑποστᾶσα).

17 It is a fundamental Plotinian tenet that Nous *is* the world of Forms. Cf. e.g. Schubert (1973: 58ff).

18 III.5.3,1–2: «Ὑπόστασιν (Existence) δὲ εἶναι καὶ οὐσίαν (Substance) ἐξ οὐσίας (from Substance) ἐλάττω μὲν τῆς ποιησαμένης, οὖσαν δὲ ὅμως (but it *exists* nevertheless), ἀπιστεῖν οὐ προσήκει». The «ἐξ οὐσίας» may refer to Aphrodite-Soul, but there is an alternative: Kalligas (2014: 516 ad loc.) ingeniously proposes Nous. His interpretation has the merit of (a) breaking the analogy with Soul's emanation of Nous that suggests 'hypostatization' and (b) the fact that 'ousia' does sound like Nous. Although this view could be helpful for the interpretation I will put forward, it might also complicate things: even from this point of view Eros seems to remain external to Soul, although it 'emanates' not from Soul but from Nous, something that is even more difficult to explain in terms of Plotinus' system.

19 See ibid., §3,3–5. (Wolters' translation needs to be emended in view of Igal's addition of <ζῶσα> adopted by H-S₅.) That Plotinus refers to two Aphrodites, a goddess and a daimonic one, complicates the story even more, but I want to refrain from further confusion.

20 Dillon (1969: 42). Dillon adds 'the emergence … indeed of Logos as another [sc. separate hypostasis]' (Dillon 1969: 42; cf. Dillon 1969 40).

21 Ibid., 43.

22 See Plotinus' anti-Gnostic polemic: II.9.[33].1,12–16; 30–3; 57–63. Cf. also Lacrosse (1994: 124–5). NB that in III.5 Plotinus most probably tries to rebut other overly ascetical interpretations of Platonic myths, put forward by various Gnostic sects. Cf. Kalligas (2014: 503–5). We have already seen that in §1 Plotinus tries to defend the sexual desire as a legitimate kind of appreciating the beautiful, contra to Gnostic outright condemnations of everything pertaining to our sensible world. The same can be said about the *Symposium*-myth.

23 Cf. Kalligas (2014: 229) (comment on I.8.3,20), Dörrie (1976: 45), Wolters (1984: 27 and 247), Hadot (1990: 24–5), Lacrosse (1994: 124), Damaskos (2003: 212, n.112 and 213, n.120). If we want to do justice to Porphyry though, he does not use the term unqualifiedly in the titles. *Enneads* V.1 is entitled: «Περὶ τῶν τριῶν ἀρχικῶν ὑποστάσεων» ('On the three primary hypostases', «ἀρχή» being a term usually used by Plotinus to denote his principal hypostases – cf. once more Wolters 1984: 27, 247); V.3: 'On the knowing hypostases and that which is beyond'. See also (Kalligas 2013: 221–2) (comment on the title of V.1.); in 221 Kalligas stresses an additional sense of the word ('being a product'). According to

Ramelli (2012: 326–37, esp. 330), in so doing, Porphyry was influenced by Origen (of the Christian tradition, while in 332 Ramelli suggests that the latter should be identified with Origen, the Neoplatonist colleague of Plotinus).

24 See Wolters' already-cited translations. Dillon (1969: 40) seems to be aware of this modification and in 44, n.16 Dillon refers to the abovementioned §1 of *Enn.* II.9.
25 See also the notion of «λόγοι» found e.g. in III.8, §§2–3 and 7–8.
26 See also Galen, *De placitis Hippocratis et Platonis* 7.1.22,1–23,6 (De Lacy), esp. §23,6 («ἀκουόντων ἡμῶν τοῦ τῆς οὐσίας ὀνόματος, ὅπερ ἐστὶν οἷον ὕπαρξις»), cited by Chiaradonna (2009: 64 and n.92). For another Plotinian example where the compound of «ὑπόστασις and οὐσία» clearly suggests 'existence' in its context, see VI.4.9,24–5: «Ἡ γὰρ δύναμις ἐκεῖ [sc. in the true All] ὑπόστασις καὶ οὐσία … ». For another use of 'ousia' that denotes only the nature of a thing – in that case: time – see III.7.13,23 (with Armstrong's trans.: 'essential nature').
27 Moreover, it ascribes desire to what is the personification of desire.
28 Hence, Damaskos (2003: 306), referring to Plotinus' innovations against the Platonic interpretation of the *Symposium* myth, states that 'in the Plotinian treatment, Eros arises as a separate entity [/hypostasis: «ὑπόσταση»], in the sense that it is something [κάτι]'. (Every translation from Modern Greek is mine.) He makes this statement although elsewhere he emphasizes that we cannot speak about a new 'hypostasis' in the narrower-technical sense of the term. (Cf. supra, n.23, where I refer to Damaskos (2003: 212 and 213, nn.112 and 120); cf. also, 177, n.10, where he cites a passage by V. Cilento.) In these assertions Damaskos faithfully follows Dillon's aforementioned conclusions (in their moderate sense), especially if one considers Damaskos' whole statement: 'Eros arises as a separate entity …, and Logos [sc. arises] as another entity.' Cf. also de Vogel (1963: 23 but contrast 24).
29 III.5.9,24–9. See also Brisson (2004: 74–5 and 80).
30 Kalligas (2014: 532), seeing an allusion to the *Timaeus*' problem concerning the eternity of the world, follows the minority of the MSS' printing «ἀγενήτων» with one 'ν' (cf. also Kalligas (2014), in the table of 666). NB that all over the treatise Eros is said to be born (γενητός) from Aphrodite or Penia, and the very last word of the treatise is «γεγενημένος», although the spelling with two 'νν' is also present e.g. in §5,3–4: «γεγεννημένος». According to Liddell-Scott-Jones (1940) (henceforth LSJ), the verb «γεννάω» (beget) is the causal of «γίγνομαι» (to be born/produced/come to pass), whose cognates are written with one 'ν'. Hence, Wolters (1984: 30) remarks that, as the critical apparatus of our treatise attests, the confusion between the right spelling of their cognates is reasonable.
31 «Δεῖ δὲ τοὺς μύθους, εἴπερ τοῦτο ἔσονται, καὶ μερίζειν χρόνοις ἃ λέγουσι, καὶ διαιρεῖν ἀπ' ἀλλήλων πολλὰ τῶν ὄντων ὁμοῦ μὲν ὄντα, τάξει δὲ ἢ δυνάμεσι διεστῶτα, ὅπου καὶ οἱ λόγοι καὶ γενέσεις τῶν ἀγεννήτων ποιοῦσι, καὶ τὰ

ὁμοῦ ὄντα καὶ αὐτοὶ διαιροῦσι, καὶ διδάξαντες ὡς δύνανται τῷ νοήσαντι ἤδη συγχωροῦσι συναιρεῖν.»

32 That is, pulling apart/disassociating/dividing/decomposing/disintegrating.

33 That is, pulling together/associating/(re)composing/synthesizing/re-integrating/contracting. (From now onwards I will be using the last rendering, as well as the Greek term transliterated quite often.)

34 Cf. also Vasilakis (2015: 71) (with n.23). For Nous' unity see in III.5.9,3: «Τὸ γὰρ ἐν νῷ *συνεσπειραμένον*, ... » ('For that which is in Intellect is *contracted together*, ... '; Armstrong's trans.), with Armstrong's n.1 ad loc.: 198 (vol.III), and the references of Kalligas (2014: 530).

35 IV.3.9,14–15: ' ... διδασκαλίας καὶ τοῦ σαφοῦς χάριν ... ' (my translation). See also the following lines, ibid., 18–20: 'In discussing these things [e.g. the ordering of matter by soul] one can consider them apart from each other. [When one is reasoning about] any kind of composition, it is always legitimate to analyse it in thought into its parts.' («ἐπινοῆσαι ταῦτα χωρίζοντας αὐτὰ ἀπ' ἀλλήλων τῷ λόγῳ οἷόν τε. ἔξεστι γὰρ *ἀναλύειν* τῷ λόγῳ καὶ τῇ διανοίᾳ πᾶσαν *σύνθεσιν*.» Armstrong's trans.). Cf. also VI.7.35,28–9: 'ὁ δὲ λόγος διδάσκων γινόμενα ποιεῖ, τὸ δὲ [sc. Nous] ἔχει τὸ νοεῖν ἀεί, ... '. In this last case the succinct methodological remark is preceded by a reference to Poros' drunkenness («μεθυσθεὶς τοῦ νέκταρος»), i.e. a familiar to us reference to the *Symposium* myth (203b5) present in *Enn.* III.5, but this time with reference to Nous' relation to the One, expressed in the formula «νοῦς *ἐρῶν*»; cf. VI.7.35,24–7.

36 In another paper (work in progress) I examine the issue of Plotinus' methodological remarks in greater length and present a more detailed story about how they relate with the form and content of III.5 and on which Platonic texts Plotinus founds this approach. Moreover, the characteristics of the lover of *Enn.* I.3 is taken also into account.

37 Cf. also Pépin (1976; 504).

38 See III.5.9,30ff. and an exposition in Pépin (1976: 192–8), although I do not accept the negative part of his assessment of Plotinus' practice in Pépin (1976: 197).

39 Cf., e.g. III.9.5(1–3): 'The soul itself ... is matter (ὕλην) in relation to intellect.'

40 Cf. also Emilsson (2017: 40).

41 See III.5.9,1.

42 Ibid., §9,14. See the context of ll.8–14, where other synonyms for κοσμήματα are: «καλλωπίσματα» ('showpieces'), ἀγλαΐσματα (glories), ἀγάλματα (images).

43 See also ibid., §9,44–5.

44 Cf. ibid., §9,56–7: « ... ἐκ ψυχῆς, καθόσον ἐλλείπει τῷ ἀγαθῷ, ἐφίεται δέ, ... ».

45 Ibid., l.49: «ὅτι ἀεὶ ἡ ἔφεσις ἐνδεοῦς». An exploration of Plotinus' vocabulary of (erotic) desire is offered by Arnou (1967: 59–64). See also Corrigan (2018: 10–11).

46 III.5.9,19–20.
47 Sole occurrence within III.5, whereas the conjunction of 'hypostasis and ousia', so strongly put forward in the first part of the theology of Eros, never appears with respect to logos.
48 Dillon (1969: 40) is once more vacillating between a diairetic and a synairetic reading when he states with respect to Logos that it 'is being made in some way an hypostasis between Nous and Soul. It cannot be regarded as an hypostasis in the same way as the basic three ... but it is being accorded Real Existence, as was Eros, child of Aphrodite Urania'. Dillon's general stance is that these 'innovative' Plotinian theses foreshadow the elaborations of the hierarchical scheme of reality in the later Neoplatonists, notably Iamblichus and Proclus (cf., e.g., Dillon (1969: 24 and *passim*.)). Such an 'anticipating' attitude is criticized by Kalligas (2014: 515), as having misled Dillon. See also the fair criticism of Damaskos (2003: 269 cf. 268 and 270), against Dillon's far-fetched interpretation (cf. Dillon (1969: 40)) of Poros as a kind of Nous' 'part', which receives Logos instantiated by the 'nectar', and which, then, is 'participated' by Soul-Penia, all this conceived by Dillon as foreshadowing Iamblichus' doctrine of «μετεχόμενος νοῦς». After all, what we want to find is a coherent view in Plotinus not just an anticipation of Iamblichus. See also the next note: 49.
49 With respect to the aforementioned problem regarding logos (n. 48), one should add that, at least in this case, Plotinus and his synairetic attitude remain coherent and consistent, even when one cross-examines other works of his, as well: logos features prominently in Plotinus' late and important work 'On Providence': *Enn.* III.2–3.[47–8], *passim*. A relevant comment by Kalligas (2014: 449) on III.2.2,18–33 (cf. also ibid., ll.15–18) is illuminating: 'The Logos constitutes a cosmopoeic formative "ordinance" which, drawing its hypostasis from Intellect, has the capacity to configure matter in accordance with that model, creating thereby a representation of the intelligible in the sensible. The fact that the agent that receives this ordinance and impresses it on the sensible – namely, Soul – is not mentioned in the present passage had once caused Armstrong ... to consider that the Logos here supplants the Soul in its formative role. Yet as will become clear below, at [III.2.]16.12–17, the reality is that the Logos arises from the illumination cast by Intellect on Soul, which in this way has the possibility of acquiring cognizance of this illumination through its reasoning; cf. V 1.7.42–43.' In other words, the logos of III.2 and 3 is the Poros-logos of III.5 interpreted in a synairetic way. See also infra, nn.131 and 162.
50 III.5.9,48–9, cited partly above (in n. 45). The fundamental idea in that eros implies deficiency is initially introduced in Aristophanes' speech in the *Symposium* (e.g. 191a5–6 and d3–5). See also Mortley (1980: 45 and 49).
51 See infra, Section 1.3.

52 III.5.9,49–50: «ὕλη δὲ ἡ Πενία, ὅτι καὶ ἡ ὕλη ἐνδεὴς τὰ πάντα».
53 Ibid., §9,50–1: «τὸ ἀόριστον τῆς τοῦ ἀγαθοῦ ἐπιθυμίας».
54 Ibid., ll.44–5: «οὐ γὰρ δὴ τὸ πάμπαν ἄμοιρον τοῦ ἀγαθοῦ τὸ ἀγαθὸν ἄν ποτε ζητήσειεν.»
55 Hence, I cannot understand why at this point Damaskos (2003: e.g. 304) changes his mind and thinks that Plotinus' treatise concludes with reference to the matter of the sensible world. (Compare his stance in Damaskos (2003: 276–7 and 296), and cf. Arnou (1967: 70–9).) Even if we assume that Plotinus is specifically speaking about the World-Soul, with the restrictions that the kinship with matter might impose on it, 'Penia-matter' could have only an indirect relation to sensible matter, as expressing the increased level of Soul's indefiniteness that enables the interfusion with matter. However, we are not obliged to read in the context only the World-Soul.
56 III.5.9,51–2: «οὐ γὰρ μορφή τις οὐδὲ λόγος ἐν τῷ ἐφιεμένῳ τούτου».
57 The whole surrounding phrase may seem paradoxical: Plotinus states that 'the Indetermination of the desire for the good ... makes the desirer more matter-like the more he desires' (III.5.9,50–1 and 52–3: «τὸ ἀόριστον τῆς τοῦ ἀγαθοῦ ἐπιθυμίας ... ὑλικώτερον τὸ ἐφιέμενον καθόσον ἐφίεται ποιεῖ.»). We are still talking about Soul, not about Eros, which personifies and is the necessary outcome of Soul's desire, and we would expect Plotinus to state that the desire leads to the subsequent formation/self-constitution of the desirer; hence, it leads to a decrease of indefiniteness, not the opposite. Nonetheless, here he wants to emphasize the crucial aspect of Penia. Thus, Plotinus may mean that the realization of an entity that is Penia in relation to its progenitor awakes its desire to get formed by its source; hence, it is disposed as «ὑλικώτερον» towards its progenitor, which makes its desire to be self-constituted as enformed even more ardent.
58 Ad loc. Kalligas (2004) agrees with Wolters in that we should read «αὑτὸ» instead of «αὐτὸ». This is also the reason why Wolters prefers printing «ἐν αὑτῷ» in the same line. Although in this second instance Kalligas does not think necessary to alter the text (cf. Kalligas 2014: 666), he translates following Wolters' proposal.
59 III.5.9,53–5: «τὸ δὲ πρὸς αὐτὸ εἶδός ἐστι μόνον ἐν αὐτῷ μένον· καὶ δέξασθαι δὲ ἐφιέμενον ὕλην τῷ ἐπιόντι τὸ δεξόμενον παρασκευάζει».
60 As I have noted, the form does not actually 'mix' with this receptacle, but rather it is the Penia-receptacle that is transformed into this higher-level Poros.
61 Ibid., §9,39–41: «ἀεὶ δὲ οὕτως ὑπέστη ὅδε ἐξ ἀνάγκης ἐκ τῆς ψυχῆς ἐφέσεως πρὸς τὸ κρεῖττον καὶ ἀγαθόν, καὶ ἦν ἀεί, ἐξ οὗπερ καὶ ψυχή,Ἔρως». In this pivotal passage both (a) the necessity (cf. «ἐξ ἀνάγκης») of eros/reversion and (b) its taking place in an ascending hierarchy (cf. «πρὸς τὸ κρεῖττον») are mentioned.

62 The subjective genitive 'ψυχῆς' is absent from Plotinus' text, but the context supports Wolters' insertion, which is for the sake of clarity of the translation.
63 Kalligas and Armstrong take the genitive «τῶν λόγων» as objective ('and the memory *of* the rational principles … '), while Wolters as appositive. Although I favour Wolters' rendering, in both cases there are clear overtones of the theory of recollection. (Cf. also Kalligas (2014: 533).)
64 §9,45–8: «ἐκ Πόρου οὖν καὶ Πενίας λέγεται εἶναι, ᾗ ἡ ἔλλειψις καὶ ἡ ἔφεσις καὶ τῶν λόγων ἡ μνήμη ὁμοῦ συνελθόντα ἐν ψυχῇ ἐγέννησε τὴν ἐνέργειαν τὴν πρὸς τὸ ἀγαθόν, ἔρωτα τοῦτον ὄντα». Cf. §4,21–3 (penultimate period of the first theological section).
65 Passage cited again supra, n. 61.
66 Cf. also Smith (2007: 238).
67 VI.9.9,24–34: « … ἐρᾷ οὖν κατὰ φύσιν ἔχουσα ψυχὴ θεοῦ ἑνωθῆναι θέλουσα, ὥσπερ παρθένος καλοῦ πατρὸς καλὸν ἔρωτα». Here Plotinus speaks of Soul's love for the One, without the explicit mediation of Nous. This is why Kalligas (2014: 535) objects to Wolters' stubborn remarks that Plotinus in III.5 speaks about love towards Nous, not the Good. If Nous has/is the trace(s) of the One, it follows that an aspiration for Nous is also an aspiration for the One, the ultimate source of everything.
68 VI.7.22,8–10: «καὶ τοίνυν ψυχὴ λαβοῦσα εἰς αὐτὴν τὴν ἐκεῖθεν ἀπορροὴν κινεῖται καὶ ἀναβακχεύεται καὶ οἴστρων πίμπλαται καὶ ἔρως γίνεται».
69 Cf. also Vasilakis (2015: 74).
70 See e.g. III.7.11,17: «ἐκινήθη μὲν αὐτή [sc. Soul], ἐκινήθη δὲ καὶ αὐτός [sc. time]».
71 Ibid., §11,59–62: «Δεῖ δὲ οὐκ ἔξωθεν τῆς ψυχῆς λαμβάνειν τὸν χρόνον, ὥσπερ οὐδὲ τὸν αἰῶνα ἐκεῖ ἔξω τοῦ ὄντος, οὐδ᾽ αὖ παρακολούθημα οὐδ᾽ ὕστερον, ὥσπερ οὐδ᾽ ἐκεῖ, ἀλλ᾽ ἐνορώμενον καὶ ἐνόντα καὶ συνόντα [sc. with Soul], ὥσπερ κἀκεῖ ὁ αἰών».
72 See also a passing remark on III.5.7.12-15 by Armstrong (vol.III, 190, n. 1), who connects Soul's Eros and Time.
73 For a pre-history of the simile see Bartsch (2006: 57–114, esp. 58–84). Regarding Plotinus see also Alexidze (2019).
74 The precise reference is to Eros-god, while the *Symposium* speaks of Eros-daimon.
75 And through Nous the Good, as remarked in n. 67.
76 See supra, in Section 1.1.3.
77 III.5.2,39–46. The last remark reminds us of Eros' insatiability expounded ibid., §7 in the context of the Poros–Penia myth. See infra, Section 1.1.5.
78 Cf. Wolters (1984: 83).
79 III.5.2,45–6: «τὴν θέαν τοῦ καλοῦ αὐτὸν παραθέουσαν».

80 Plato, *Theaetetus* 184c10-d6. (All translations of Plato come from Cooper (1997), unless otherwise stated.)
81 (Ps-)Epicharmus, *Carmen Physicum* 249.1 (Kaibel): 'The mind sees and hears; the rest is deaf and blind'. Cf. idem, Ἀξιοπίστου γνῶμαι 12DK.
82 *Republic* VII.533d1-3.
83 Cf. also the excellent notes on §2,32-8 and 39-46 by Kalligas (2014: 514-16).
84 See for example the close proximity of «ὄμμα ... ὄρασις,Ἔρως ... » in III.5.3,13.
85 Cf. I.6.[1].9,22-5: «εἰ τοῦτο γενόμενον σαυτὸν ἴδοις, ὄψις ἤδη γενόμενος θαρσήσας περὶ σαυτῷ καὶ ἐνταῦθα ἤδη ἀναβεβηκὼς μηκέτι τοῦ δεικνύντος δεηθεὶς ἀτενίσας ἴδε· οὗτος γὰρ μόνος ὁ ὀφθαλμὸς τὸ μέγα κάλλος βλέπει». (Armstrong's trans. heavily modified.)
86 This is how the «ὀφθαλμός» which looks at the sun becomes «ἡλιοειδής». (Cf. also Plato, *Phaedrus* 253a1-5.) Cf. Emilsson (1988: 70-1) and Kalligas (2014: 417); see also Tornau (2005: 281).
87 According to Wolters (1984: 99), 'it is probably no coincidence either that ἀπορρέοντος is similar in sound to πόρος, since both refer to the same "parent" of eros, and especially since Πόρος is identified in chapter 9 with the "images" (9.12 ἀγάλματα, 9.33 εἰκόνας; cf. ῥυέντες, 9.35 ῥυέντος) down from intellect (the beloved object of vision) to Soul.'
88 III.5.3,11-13: «ἐξ οὖν τοῦ ἐνεργοῦντος συντόνως περὶ τὸ ὁρώμενον καὶ ἐκ τοῦ οἷον ἀπορρέοντος ἀπὸ τοῦ ὁρωμένου ὄμμα πληρωθέν, οἷον μετ' εἰδώλου ὅρασις, Ἔρως ἐγένετο».
89 Plato, *Cratylus* 420a9-b2.
90 III.5.3,14-15. Cf. also *Etymologicum Magnum* 379.50 (Gaisford).
91 III.5.4,22-3: « ... ἔρως δὲ ἐνέργεια ψυχῆς ἀγαθοῦ ὀριγνωμένης». Cf. ibid., §9,45-8 and supra, n. 64.
92 Thus, we avoid potentially negative ramifications of the type 'Oedipus-Electra' relation.
93 VI.9.[9].9,34. (Armstrong's trans. modified.)
94 III.5.2,37-8.
95 Both images invoke the picture of a lover seeing himself in the eyes and soul of the beloved, for which see *Alcibiades I* 132e8-133b11, esp. 133b2-10 and *Phaedrus* 255d5-6. Cf. Aristotle, *Magna Moralia* 2.15, esp. 1213a8-27 or 7,4-8,1 (Susemihl-Armstrong).
96 Cf. also Kalligas (2014: esp. 515).
97 Thus, my account supersedes that of Wolters', which suggests that Plotinus is simply equivocal with respect to the identity of Eros, calling it either activity or the result of the activity. Cf. Wolters (1984: 137, note on §4,22); his explanation 'is probably that Soul's ἐνέργεια "constitutes" Eros, the way "acting" constitutes

an "act." Eros is, as it were, the "internal object" of Soul's activity. In the same way, Eros, the desire of Soul, is also said to *result* from that desire; see on 9.40'.

98 See Wolters (1984: 97). For Wolters the eye-simile, applying to both Eros-god and -daimon, is to be understood better under the light of the Poros and Penia exegesis of the last part of the treatise.

99 See supra, n. 87.

100 According to *Symposium* 223d3-6, 'authors should be able to write both comedy and tragedy: the skillful tragic dramatist should also be a comic poet'.

101 III.5.7,9–12: «λόγος οὖν γενόμενος ἐν οὐ λόγῳ, ἀορίστῳ δὲ ἐφέσει καὶ ὑποστάσει ἀμυδρᾷ, ἐποίησε τὸ γενόμενον οὐ τέλεον οὐδὲ ἱκανόν, ἐλλιπὲς δέ, ἅτε ἐξ ἐφέσεως ἀορίστου καὶ λόγου ἱκανοῦ γεγενημένον». It should be noted that Poros (translated also as Resource) and especially Penia play a pivotal role in the interesting exegesis of Plato's *Symposium* offered by Lamascus (2017). Such a reference point is unusual for a contemporary interpreter and, thus, brings Lamascus closer to Plotinus' viewpoint (or makes us better see the modern relevance of Plotinus' account).

102 Ibid., §7,12–15: «καὶ ἔστι λόγος οὗτος οὐ καθαρός, ἅτε ἔχων ἐν αὐτῷ ἔφεσιν ἀόριστον καὶ ἄλογον καὶ ἄπειρον· οὐ γὰρ μήποτε πληρώσεται, ἕως ἂν ἔχῃ ἐν αὐτῷ τὴν τοῦ ἀορίστου φύσιν». Here I choose Armstrong's translation, because Wolters (1984: 179) thinks that the «λόγος οὐ καθαρός», being identified with the λόγος of l.9, does not refer to Eros, as the rest of the interpreters take it.

103 Wolters (1984: 183) renders «οἶστρος» as 'craving', and not as 'gadfly' or 'sting' (so Armstrong), as the rest of the translators do. He evokes Creuzer's note ad loc. (in the latter's Parisien edition of Plotinus from 1855; in this note, inter alia, we find a reference to VI.7.22,9), adding that the sense of 'gadfly' 'is rare after Aristotle, being supplanted by μύωψ (so already in Plato)'. But if Eros bears characteristics of Socrates both in the *Symposium* and in III.5, why not stick with the *Apology*'s 'gadfly'? Cf. also Osborne (1994: 114 and n. 112).

104 I altered Wolters' 'cleverness' into 'powerlessness', since Wolters wants to retain the MSS' reading «εὐμήχανον» (followed by H-S$_2$) instead of «ἀμήχανον», proposed by Kirchhoff (followed by H-S$_4$). Although Wolters' long justification (1984: 187–92) has influenced me, I follow H-S$_4$ and Kalligas' choice (cf. Kalligas 2014: 527 and 665) in retaining Kirchhoff's emendation. The parallel text from Plutarch, *De Is.* 57.374d, given in H-S$_4$ makes the case stronger for the «ἀμήχανον» option. Furthermore, in their 'Fontes Addendi' H-S$_4$ ascribe to our present III.5-passage a reference to Aristophanes, *Ranae* 1429, regarding the opposition of «ἀμήχανον» with «ποριστικόν». Kalligas (2014: 527) supplies more references in order to show the commonplace of the aforementioned opposition. In another paper I will pursue the consequences of Plotinus' affinity with the passages from playwrights in respect of Plotinus' literary engagement with the characters of the *Symposium*.

105 III.5.7.19–25: «καὶ ἔστιν ὁ ἔρως οἷον οἶστρος ἄπορος τῇ ἑαυτοῦ φύσει· διὸ καὶ τυγχάνων ἄπορος πάλιν· οὐ γὰρ ἔχει πληροῦσθαι διὰ τὸ μὴ ἔχειν τὸ μίγμα· μόνον γὰρ πληροῦται ἀληθῶς, ὅτιπερ καὶ πεπλήρωται τῇ ἑαυτοῦ φύσει· ὃ δὲ διὰ τὴν συνοῦσαν ἔνδειαν ἐφίεται, κἂν παραχρῆμα πληρωθῇ, οὐ στέγει· ἐπεὶ καὶ τὸ ἀμήχανον αὐτῷ διὰ τὴν ἔνδειαν, τὸ δὲ ποριστικὸν διὰ τὴν τοῦ λόγου φύσιν». Cf. also ibid., §9,42–4. Thus, borrowing the main title of Delikostantis (2003) (who borrows it from Sophocles' *Antigone* 360 – a famous chorus part praising the human being – albeit ignoring the punctuation and negation), we could give the following alternative and more succinct characterization of Eros (or actually, in the synairetic reading I propose in the present chapters, of soul, for which see also infra, n. 63 in Section 2.1.2): «παντοπόρος ἄπορος» ('resourceful without resources').

106 See *Gorgias* 493a5-b3.

107 This can be an apt example of tragic irony or indeed of Socratic one: the gadfly pursues knowledge constantly without being able to possess it.

108 See l.16; cf.l.17.

109 Wolters (1984: 181) adds that Plotinus 'can do this by exploiting two peculiarities of the Greek word μείγνυμι (and its compounds): the connotation of sexual intercourse which it has (LSJ B 4) alluding thus to the union of Poros and Penia …, and the possibility of construing it with ἐκ (LSJ I)'.

110 Wolters (1984: 181).

111 III.5.7,6–9.

112 III.5.7,15–17. My translation following Kalligas' choices.

113 It seems that instead of tragedy we are confronted with a tragic monologue.

114 Cf. my approach on the eye simile (Section 1.1.4): seer is a seer *qua* actualizing his capacity to see, instantiated in his eyes.

115 Cited supra within n. 105.

116 We should do so due to the parallel and unmistakable reference to Nous from §9: III.5.9,18–19: 'Intellect, however, possesses itself in satiety and it is not "drunk" in its self-possession for it does not possess anything extraneous.' Cf. also Armstrong (1967: 191, n. 3) (on III.5.7.20). Lacrosse (1994: 125–7, esp. 126) neglects this evidence and proposes that in the passage from §7,20–2 we should read Soul, *qua* bearer of Eros, and her Eros. Hence, the contrast he draws is between a fulfilled hypostasis, i.e. Soul (or Nous for that matter) and its Eros, which is unfulfilled. Despite this hermeneutical discrepancy Lacrosse's overall interpretation of the significance of Eros does not really diverge from mine.

117 Of course, in Nous' complete unity in multiplicity the activity of thinking is identified with Nous' essence, viz. the Forms. However, we have seen that Eros is the orientation to what is higher, which in the case of Nous results in Intellect's thinking of himself.

118 It is not up to Nous not to be(come) Nous, and so forth.
119 See III.5.2,34–5.
120 Ibid., 9,44–5.
121 And hence we have all the complications that arise from Soul's second/downwards reversion.
122 Hence, I diverge from Smith (2007: 241), who sees in Poros and Penia the polarity of our undescended and embodied self. In my view the 'duality' of these principles can describe a single entity, e.g. either the Undescended or the embodied soul. For Smith's approach see also Smith (2007: 236), but compare also the end in Smith (2007: 242), which comes closer to my 'unitary' reading. Finally, the relevant note of Gerson (2006: 60, n. 48) is too short to be evaluated.
123 See III.5.3,27ff. and my Synopsis above (Section 1.1.1).
124 Cf. e.g. III.53,29. Hence, my divergence from Brisson (2004: 79), who suggests that Heavenly Aphrodite gives birth to an Eros identified with the higher Soul (because he is a god?), whereas the Soul of the sensible world engenders a daimonic Eros, who is her vision. But why such a 'diairetic'-fragmentary reading? Although Brisson comes partly close to my response, he ignores the aforementioned equivalence between god and daimon-Eros. More specifically, how can the Eros of Undescended Soul be a Soul, whereas that of the World one is not? What does the latter imply about the ontological status of daimonic Eros? Furthermore, if indeed Heavenly Aphrodite is to be identified with Undescended Soul, and the Common one with the World-Soul, what is the actual identity of this 'higher soul'?
125 This aspect is nicely brought out by Smith (2007: *passim*, e.g. 236 and 242), although I do not agree with all of his conclusions.
126 As Kalligas (2014: 524) points out, these partial 'powers' neglect sometimes the overall planning of Soul's administration, being in conflict with it and with each other.
127 In another paper (work in progress) I examine the structure of Plotinus' treatise in more depth; I relate it with the theme of III.5 and will show at greater length why a more synoptic view of the different parts of the treatise is preferable.
128 III.5.7,12–13: 'So Love is not a pure rational principle ... ' (Armstrong's trans.).
129 Cf. Wolters (1984: 179).
130 Cf. III.5.7,13: «οὗτος».
131 See also the case of Dillon (1969), whose attitude is to read the whole treatise, or at least the theology section, as being an exegesis of the *Symposium* myth. Although I am sympathetic to this view, his conflation of the data given in the second section of the theology (logos) with that of the first one (ousia) leads him to results I cannot follow. For instance, when commenting on the second section of the theology, §7,15ff, Dillon (1969: 36) states the following: 'Eros itself

is a *logos*, proceeding from Soul. What seems to be stated here is that it is also a mixture produced from another *logos* (Poros) *proceeding from Nous*, (which is not mentioned), this *logos* descending from Nous to mingle with the soul (as unboundedness).' Yet, the statement that 'Eros itself is a *logos*, proceeding from Soul' does not appear in the passage he comments on, and actually it is not stated, at least explicitly, anywhere in the treatise. See also Kalligas (2014: 516) (note on §3,1–11), who underlines that the reference to «λόγος» is made only in the second part of the theology; hence, another reason to see Dillon's overall conclusion as illegitimate. See also supra, nn. 48–9.

132 See e.g. Kalligas' relevant comments and translation (in Kalligas 2014 and 2004) ad loc.

133 See III.5.7,15ff.

134 Ibid., §4,23–5.

135 Ibid., §9,55–7: «οὕτω τοι ὁ Ἔρως ὑλικός τίς ἐστι, καὶ δαίμων οὗτός ἐστιν ἐκ ψυχῆς, καθόσον ἐλλείπει τῷ ἀγαθῷ, ἐφίεται δέ, γεγενημένος».

136 In this Plotinian context Osborne (1994: 113) notes a literary inversion of the Platonic theme of lack, because now the daimons are said to have «πάθη» whereas the gods lack them (they are «ἀπαθεῖς». See III.5,6,10–11).

137 Cf. also ibid., §9,42: 'This Eros is a mixed thing («μικτόν τι χρῆμα») ... '.

138 Since we are closer to matter, the multiplication-indefiniteness-division increases; thus, Plotinus speaks about daimons in the plural, whereas so far he has referred to only 'one' god: Aphrodite and the necessary aspect of her being: god Eros. This is not to suggest that he does not accept the existence of a plurality of deities, e.g. the stars, the visible gods. It is interesting, however, what he is willing to refer to in this treatise and what not to.

139 Cf. also Wolters (1984: 164).

140 Cf. III.5.6,31–3.

141 Hence, I believe that my approach is more adequate than Hadot's one, when he relates the answer to the problem of the ontological status of Eros with Plotinus' principles of classification concerning (a) intelligences and souls within the intelligible realm and (b) gods, daimons and humans within the realm of Soul. See Hadot (1990: 24–5): 'L' 'Âme' représente ... un ensemble, lui aussi hiérarchisé et unifié ... A l'interieur ..., la moindre distinction réelle est elle-même essence et substance. Si donc, ..., l'Amour est désigné comme une *hupostasis*, cela signifie, selon le sens habituel du terme chez Plotin, une 'production substantielle'. Pour situer exactement l'Amour dans le système plotinien des réalités, il faut remarquer, ..., que, chez Plotin, on constate une interférence entre le principe de classification qui distingue les Esprits et les âmes et un autre principe de classification qui distingue les vivants raisonnables en dieux, demons et hommes (par exemple *38* (VI, 7), 6, 26–34), ... Voulant insister fortement sur le caractère

substantiel, et donc sur la bonté de l Amour, comme désir naturel de l'âme, Plotin n'a donc aucune difficulté à le concevoir comme un dieu ou un démon, comme un être vivant et eternel du même type que l'âme elle-même, ... Mais ce n'est évidemment pas une quatrième hypostase.'

142 Perhaps Plato would seem more committed to the existence of daimons in *Laws* 713c5-e3. Cf. also Kalligas (2014: 482, n. 1) (Introduction to *Enn.* III.4).

143 See Kalligas' references (Kalligas 2014: 484–5) to Xenocrates and the Stoics, notably Chrysippus. From the Pre-Socratic reflections on the theme of 'daimon', let us not forget Heraclitus, B119DK: «ἦθος ἀνθρώπῳ δαίμων», and Democritus, B170 and 171DK.

144 Cf. also Sykoutris (1949: 193*, n. 7).

145 See Plutarch, Περὶ τοῦ Σωκράτους δαιμονίου (e.g. 580d-e); Apuleius, *De deo Socratis* (e.g. 11.145); Μάξιμος Τύριος, Τί τὸ δαιμόνιον Σωκράτους α´ (e.g. VII 5, 90.17-92.4 Hobein) καὶ β´. Cf. Kalligas (2014: 485–6) with notes.

146 See e.g. Proclus' *Commentary on the* First Alcibiades 67,19–83,16, and cf. infra my discussion in 2.2.3. At ibid., 75,11–15, Proclus refers to and criticizes Plotinus' relevant view of the 'guardian-spirit', for which see infra in the next paragraph of my text. (This is also acknowledged in the Introductory Note to III.4 by Armstrong (1967: 140).)

147 See also the informative survey of Timotin (2012).

148 From the present discussion I exclude mentions to Christian 'angelology', which (without having in mind the much later 'Doctor Angelicus', i.e. Thomas Aquinas) I do not intend to denigrate.

149 See especially III.4. §6, *passim*.

150 In III.5 Plotinus refers to the specific issue of the 'guardian spirit' in §4,4–6.

151 Ibid., §5,13–15.

152 See ibid., §5,15–18.

153 Cf. the beginning of Pausanias' speech in the *Symposium* 180d4: « ... οὐκ ἔστιν ἄνευ Ἔρωτος Ἀφροδίτη». What this discussion brings out is that there is an inseparable unity between the entity and its (intentional) activity, between what an entity is and how it exists.

154 Cf. Kalligas (2014: 515).

155 Remember Plotinus' initial questions in III.5.2,11 and 13–14, which I included in my Synopsis (Section 1.1.1).

156 The notion of «οἰκείωσις» is Stoic in origin and its cognates are used more than once in our treatise (see §1: ll.13,18,25,38; §2,34). Cf. Wolters (1984: 10).

157 III.5.2,32–35: «ἐφεπομένη δὴ τῷ Κρόνῳ ... ἐνήργησέ τε πρὸς αὐτὸν καὶ ᾠκειώθη καὶ ἐρασθεῖσα Ἔρωτα ἐγέννησε καὶ μετὰ τούτου πρὸς αὐτὸν βλέπει». (Armstrong's trans.) Wolters translates as follows: 'Being intent ... upon Kronos ... Soul has conceived toward him both an activity and an affinity, and in her

passion for him has given birth to Eros, together with whom she now looks toward him.'

158   See also supra, nn. 69 and 96.
159   III.5.9,46–8.
160   Compare also the view of Rist (1964: 98): 'Desire gives way to adoration, though the word used … is still …'Ἔρως'.
161   See supra (nn. 61 and 65) on this passage.
162   The procedure of the (de-)generation of logoi, which Soul projects to matter, is described in III.8. §§1–7. Ibid., §4,39–40, Plotinus states that 'everywhere we shall find that making and action are either a weakening or a consequence (παρακολούθημα) of contemplation'. My 'by-product' captures the sense of «παρακολούθημα». See also supra, n. 49.
163   This aspect is stressed by Stathopoulou (1999: e.g. 87). In view of the Neoplatonic thesis that the world is eternal, we could paraphrase the aforecited phrase from III.5 in the following way: 'Cosmos has eternally and necessarily come into existence out of the longing of Soul for the higher and good, and from the moment there was Soul, there was eternally cosmos.'
164   See also III.5.3,3–4.
165   However, a complication in the analogy comes from the notion of Undescended Soul. Whereas the One is ungraspable in its hyper-being by the lower hypostases, Soul, *qua* Undescended, partakes in Nous, having the same content as he. However, *qua* Soul, it is external to Nous, as a different Hypostasis, which implies that it reasons on the same content in a different mode than Nous. Thus, what differentiates Soul from Nous is the former's 'discursion' («διά-νοια»); Soul's reasoning is not an intuitive 'all-at-once' procedure as Nous, but it moves in distinct steps, e.g. by separating the cause from its result. As we will see, this is an aspect of what Poros as Logos stands for in the *Symposium*-myth. Hence, the reason why Soul might feel in need of Nous and revert to it is less a matter of lack in respect of content; it is, rather, a matter of lack with respect to the mode of apprehension of the same content. See also the whole text of the reference I cite supra, in n. 57.
166   For specific references see in the following notes. On the whole, I follow Emilsson's excellent account (2007: esp. 80–90), where he gives a detailed commentary on the passage concerning Nous' generation from V.3.10,8–11 and 16.
167   No need to repeat that the discursivity of our human language imposes 'diairetic' restrictions to the description of such a procedure that transcends time, being eternal. If there seems to be any 'splitting' in different 'moments' and temporal relationships, all these are ways to denote only 'synairetic' onto-logical relations.
168   See also Vernant (1990: 475, 477).

169 Cf. VI.7.[38].35,24: «νοῦς ἐρῶν».
170 For a support of the idea that there is an analogy between Soul and Nous despite the fact that Nous is not Undescended as Soul is, see Emilsson (2007: 78 and n. 9).
171 See III.6.14,7–18.
172 Instead of Armstrong's 'happiness', since it is too strong a rendering of «εὐπάθεια». An alternative translation is also 'satisfaction'.
173 VI.7.35,19–27: «Καὶ τὸν νοῦν τοίνυν τὴν μὲν ἔχειν δύναμιν εἰς τὸ νοεῖν, ᾗ τὰ ἐν αὐτῷ βλέπει, τὴν δέ, ᾗ τὰ ἐπέκεινα αὐτοῦ ἐπιβολῇ τινι καὶ παραδοχῇ, καθ' ἣν καὶ πρότερον ἑώρα μόνον καὶ ὁρῶν ὕστερον καὶ νοῦν ἔσχε καὶ ἕν ἐστι. Καὶ ἔστιν ἐκείνη μὲν ἡ θέα νοῦ ἔμφρονος, αὕτη δὲ νοῦς ἐρῶν, ὅταν ἄφρων γένηται μεθυσθεὶς τοῦ νέκταρος· τότε ἐρῶν γίνεται ἁπλωθεὶς εἰς εὐπάθειαν τῷ κόρῳ· καὶ ἔστιν αὐτῷ μεθύειν βέλτιον ἢ σεμνοτέρῳ εἶναι τοιαύτης μέθης».
174 I have already remarked that Plotinus tries to avoid this straightforward connection. This can also be a reason why in VI.7 he does not use the name of Poros, but he restricts himself to using one element from the myth only.
175 Dillon (1969: 38). Cf. an analogous remark (but said of the One and the soul) e.g. in Rist (1970: 168 and 172); cf. also Rist (1999: 382) (on Nous' relation to the One; in Rist (1999: 386) there is connection with the Dionysian ecstasy, for which see infra, Section 3.1.2). Finally, Dillon's statement (for the Heraclitean echoes of which see infra, n. 97 in Section 3.1.2) foreshadows the dialectics of providential and reversive eros in Proclus that we will see in Chapter 2.
176 III.5.7,21–4. Lacrosse avoids the problem by contrasting things in different categories: Soul and her erotic activity. See supra, n. 116.
177 Cf. III.8.11,23–4: «ὥστε ἐν μὲν τῷ νῷ ἡ ἔφεσις καὶ ἐφιέμενος ἀεὶ καὶ ἀεὶ τυγχάνων, ... »
178 For a more general formulation of this dilemma and an answer, see Tornau (2005: 277 with n. 27).
179 See also Moutsopoulos (1978: 170–1).
180 Hence, my train of thought here perhaps is the same as Armstrong's, although coming from the opposite direction; see Armstrong (1967: 190), n. 1: 'The idea that the soul's Love has a radical incompleteness, a permanent incapacity to be satisfied ... has ... something in common with the account of the "restless power" in soul which produces time in III.7 [45] 11.'
181 This is another reason why I believe that the *Symposium*-account in III.5 is more adequate of that of the first part, since seen from a certain perspective it can be applied to Soul's specific way of being in contrast to Nous' one. Furthermore, here one could find a parallel with Gregory of Nyssa's conception of soul's infinite erotic desire for the infinite God. See Blowers 1992: 151 and n. 1 (in 165 for references). Corrigan, though, draws the parallel on the basis of Plotinian Nous; cf. Corrigan (2018: 10), n. 25. More generally, regarding Gregory of Nyssa's

	relation to Plotinus, see among else Pavlos (2017: 9–10, 27) (with bibliography in notes), and for an interesting approach to Gregory's views on love (in relation to virtue epistemology), see Voutsina-Athanasopoulou-Kypriou (2005: esp. 252–4).
182	III.5.9,18–19: «νοῦς δὲ ἑαυτὸν ἔχει ἐν κόρῳ καὶ οὐ μεθύει ἔχων. οὐ γὰρ ἐπακτόν τι ἔχει».
183	Cf. Kalligas (2014: 531, n. ad loc.).
184	Although a negative sense arises in §7 as we will see.
185	Hence, it has also the pejorative sense of something being external to an entity, i.e. not stemming by the entity's own nature.
186	Flamand (2009: 418).
187	Flamand (2009: 418) reminds us also the difficult conditions under which Plotinus spent the last years of his life, i.e. the time when he wrote the aforementioned treatises (cf. Porphyry, *Vita Plotini* 2,10–23). It is notable that the aforementioned treatises are followed by II.3.[52]: 'On whether the stars are causes', which tackles again the problem of evil from its particular point of view.
188	Plotinus' symmetrical system is really a masterpiece: also the One is beyond being, hence non-being, albeit in the opposite direction.
189	Cf. also Vasilakis (2015: 74).
190	The anthropomorphic language used by Plotinus is conspicuous. We should not forget, however, that according to the principles of his system both procession and reversion are necessary aspects of every entity. Exceptions are the first term of the series, the One, which has no prior, and the last term, prime matter, which proceeds from Soul, but is totally unable to revert; hence, matter, the necessary source of evil, and non-being is non-erotic. This is why it does not have real 'existence'. On the other hand, as we will see infra (e.g. n. 196), in his positive assertions about the One Plotinus will be in a position to ascribe Eros to the One.
191	In that context I stressed the notion of non-deliberation. Hence, from such a point of view, a substantial view of Eros, «ψυχοπομπός», who does not deliberate in his upwards striving, and by doing so he spurs 'souls on to the Beauty on high' (III.5.2,4–5), could be a justification for how to account for Plotinus' image of entities 'deliberating' to proceed out of their 'fathers'.
192	Furthermore, it is true that what each entity achieves after its procession is to become the best possible, but still inferior, image of its progenitor. Additionally, the parallel with Empedocles' principles-*forces* of Love and Strife is tempting. However, Plotinus' version is vertical, not horizontal, and eternal. In contrast, in Empedocles we have the circular succession of periods when Love or Strife prevails, the latter being quite unacceptable to Plotinus as a view. See infra in my main text.
193	According to one thesis put forward in the *Cratylus*, there is a substantive connection between the name and the nature/essence of a thing.

194 Lacrosse (1994: 129ff in his Conclusion) speaks of 'the omnipresence of love', but he follows different, though not opposing, paths from mine.
195 Aristotle, *Metaphysics* Λ.7,1072b3: 'it moves by being loved'.
196 VI.8.15,1. Cf. also ibid., §16,12–16. Corrigan (2018: 104 and n. 65) notes the possibility that Plotinus is here influenced by the Valentinian Gnostics; cf. also Corrigan (2018: 124). See, however, a pertinent remark of mine supra, in the Introduction, n. 33, as well as the crucial disambiguations offered infra, nn. 203 and 204.
197 III.8.11,24–5.
198 For an alternative (although not incompatible with my) interpretation, see Tornau (2005: 279–80) with interesting scholarly discussion in n. 36 (of 280–1; cf. also n. 62 in 288). I suspect that Tornau's proposal would not be easily accepted by Corrigan.
199 See e.g. VI.8.7,46–54; ibid., §13,6–8 and §16,27–33, esp. l.32: « ... οἷον ... ἐγρήγορσις καὶ ὑπερνόησις ... ». These are my answers against Pigler (2002), who structures her whole approach on VI.8.§§15 and 16 (i.e. top-down) rather than III.5 (i.e. from bottom-up). However, I am in agreement with much of what she (and Bertozzi 2012 in chapter 3: 154–288) says and this will be revealed in the next chapter (Section 2.1), where I discuss Plotinus' lack of incongruity with Proclus regarding the issue of providential eros. See also the discussion of Rist (1964: 76–85, 96–7, 99), with Rist (1970: 166); de Vogel (1963: 22, with some not very transparent but pertinent remarks in 24; de Vogel (1981: 69–70, 74) (and n. 49 in 79); and Esposito Buckley (1992: 42, 44–7 and 56, esp. 45).
200 Let us not forget that an indication of the power of an entity is the extent and importance of entities dependent on it. We have seen that the by-product of the erotic constitution of an entity is the generation of further entities. Within this framework it is natural that the One, being the ultimate source of reality, would be said to be an erotic entity, too. Still, because it is ultimate, the erotic intentionality cannot be but self-directed. Aspects of this idea are treated by Gerson (2006: 55ff., esp. 66). In Gerson's argumentation the Plotinian relation of Beauty to Goodness plays a central role. For another Neoplatonizing interpretation of the relation of Beauty to the Good in Diotima's speech, see Beierwaltes (1986: 298–9; cf. 305).
201 Although, as we saw, they are two sides of the same coin. Besides, this is another aspect of Eros' tragic nature.
202 Kalligas (2014: 398, note on II.9): 'Against the Gnostics', [33].11,20–3. This interpretive attitude stems from Dodds (1965: 24–6, esp. 25–6); cf. also Atkinson (1983: 5), as well as Vasilakis (2019b: 156, n. 15). In his more recent and elaborate note on V.1.1,3–9 (not yet translated into English), Kalligas (2013: 223–4) does not stress this aspect. In any case, Plotinus' erotic dialogue seems to be a part of his 'recantation'.

203 Cf. Kalligas (2014: 503). It is also interesting that for Kalligas this is a basic reason why Plotinus offers us the exegesis of a myth, a procedure that he perhaps was not very fond of. In any case, Kalligas' remark gives an answer to why the scope of our treatise would appear to be narrower than many interpreters would expect. (See also supra, n. 26 of the Introduction.)

204 It is true, however, that sometimes Plotinus' language reminds of the Gnostics. In any case, we have to stress that the generation of the inferior levels of reality is unintended according to Plotinus. As the myth depicts, Penia has intercourse with Poros when the latter is sleeping, i.e. without his choice to come into contact with Penia. Yet, to be more precise, the Neopythagorean and Gnostic uses of «τόλμα» are not identical. See the lengthy note of Atkinson (1983: 4–6, esp. 4–5). One of the most important differences is that although in both systems the notion is negatively coloured, in the Gnostics (at least the Valentinians) τόλμα represents the *upwards* movement of Sophia, who tries to unite itself with Nous, the 'abortive' result of which is the generation of the demiurge and the material world. Thus, although the product of τόλμα eventually refers to our familiar downwards movement, its cause is found in the opposite direction, something that forms a direct disagreement with the Neoplatonic worldview.

205 See in the 'Synopsis' (Section 1.1.1), nn. 7 and 22.

206 I.1.[53]: 'What is the living being, and what is man?'.

207 Cf. also Gerson (1994: 157–8).

208 An important exception is World-Soul which is never dragged by matter; cf. e.g. IV.3.9,29–34, esp. ll.33–4.

209 III.5.7,30–49.

210 Hence also my complement to the brief remarks of Osborne (1994: 115).

211 III.5.1,10–11.

212 Ibid., §4,9–13. Cf. also ibid., ll.13–18.

213 Of course, there are two side issues here, which could complicate the picture: (a) the existence of individual souls in Nous; (b) the great flexibility of individual souls to not only move deep down to matter, contrary to World-Soul, but also ascend even to the Union with the One, again in contrast with the rest of stable Hypostases-levels of reality. See, however, Edwards' reservations regarding the second part of point (b) in Edwards (2013: 19–23).

214 Cf. Sykoutris (1949: 145*–6*). It is interesting that Sykoutris (1949, e.g. 159*–80*) much before Nussbaum's relevant approach (chapter 6 of Nussbaum 2001: 166–99) was aware of the importance of Alcibiades' speech. However, he never saw the problem of the individual as object of love in Plato, as Vlastos (1973: e.g. 28, 32, 34) famously did, exactly because the Modern Greek philologist thought that Alcibiades' speech completes Diotima's account (cf. e.g. Sykoutris 1949: 151*, 154* and 180*).

215 This identification had already been observed in Antiquity, as Sykoutris (1949: 142, n. 1) notes. See also Osborne (1994: 93ff, esp. 94–5). What is more, Plotinus in our treatise refers to some of these characteristically Socratic features of daimonic Eros in §5,20–21: «ἄστρωτον, ἀνυπόδητον, ἄοικον». Wolters in his comments (e.g. Wolters 1984: 147 and esp. 189, n. 73) seems to ignore the possibility of such a perspective.

216 If Socratic ignorance was supportive of the Academic Skeptics' view of Plato, I believe that it still survives in the Neoplatonic system, i.e. a dogmatic-positive view of Plato, under the guise of the ineffability and unknowability of the One. See also Monrad (1888: 163ff, esp. 174–6 and 184–6). Again, of course, it is via Plato's realization (e.g. of the restrictions of language), and by way of Middle Platonists, like Plutarch, that Socrates can be connected to Plotinus.

2

Proclus on the *First Alcibiades*

In the Introduction to his magisterial edition of the *Elements of Theology*, E. R. Dodds cites the following passage from Proclus' *Commentary on the First Alcibiades* as evidence of Dionysius' 'slavish' imitation of the Platonic Successor[1]: «καὶ θεοὶ τοίνυν θεῶν ἐρῶσιν, οἱ πρεσβύτεροι τῶν καταδεεστέρων, ἀλλὰ προνοητικῶς, καὶ οἱ καταδεέστεροι τῶν ὑπερτέρων, ἀλλ' ἐπιστρεπτικῶς.»[2] For my present purposes I want to suspend any judgement concerning the relation between the acknowledged Church Father and Proclus.[3] Instead, I will go backwards in order to contrast the penultimate head of the Academy with the official founder of Neoplatonism. One central element in my previous discussion of Plotinus was that Love implies deficiency («Πενία»); hence, only an inferior being would aspire to its erotic union with the superior ontological levels, not the other way round. Eros was identified with the self-constituting reversion («ἐπιστροφή») of an entity towards its progenitor.

Now, Proclus in the aforementioned passage seems to violate this fundamental principle glaringly; it is not only the inferior beings (/gods) that can have (reversive) eros towards the superior ones, but also the other way round: eros can also be the descending (-providential) love of the superior orders for the inferior ontological ranks. Does this mean, then, following the Plotinian analysis, that apart from the standard relation of the lower for the higher beings, the superior beings are deficient, too, because in need of their inferiors? However, in that case the boundaries between 'superiority' and 'inferiority' are completely blurred. In what sense is an entity higher in the ontological rank if it needs its descendants? And in that case, why do the 'inferiors' desire the 'superiors'? In response to this difficulty, I have to state from the very beginning that Proclus does not approve of any such compromise.[4] It is a characteristic of all Neoplatonists that they give a hierarchical picture of reality: the existence of each ontological level depends solely upon its superior.

If, then, we cannot accuse Proclus of any blatant inconsistency, does this mean that by his time we have had a fundamental shift in the notion of Eros? Is it that Eros does not imply deficiency anymore, and that he has become, like Aphrodite, «ἀμήτωρ», i.e. the offspring of Πόρος alone, due to his love/provision for Πενία? But how one can really square the notion of ascending eros with that of descending eros? Does Proclus have two completely separate stories about these opposing instances of love? Moreover, is the gap between Proclus' and Plotinus' conception of Eros really unbridgeable? In the following sections I will try to show not only the unity of Proclus' highly systematic thought and the complementarity of his accounts, but also his real attitude towards Plotinus concerning our specific matter: although at first sight it might seem implausible, Proclus in fact explicates what is only implicit in Plotinus.[5] My main focus will be on Proclus' *Alcibiades Commentary* with the aid of the *Elements of Theology*. More specifically, my basic point is that the model of descending and ascending eros maps onto the familiar Neoplatonic scheme of procession and reversion. Descending or providential eros is a species of providence and a by-product of reversive eros.

My discussion of Proclus is divided into two parts. In the first part (Section 2.1) I emphasize the ethical aspect of Proclus' views, while in the second part (Section 2.2) I will dwell on metaphysical questions. Hence, since in the chapter on Plotinus I was basically speaking about reversive eros, in the first part of the chapter on Proclus I will draw more on the nature of providential love. I will give various examples of descending eros, whose illustration will help us understand the complementary relation of ascending and descending eros in Proclus, although for a definite and more elaborate answer the reader needs to wait until the second metaphysical part of my treatment.

2.1 Providential and Reversive Eros: Proclus versus Plotinus?

2.1.1 From Alcibiades' reversive eros to Socratic love

In this section I will establish the existence of reversive eros in Proclus and I will introduce us to Socratic love: although not to be identified with Alcibiades' reversive love for Socrates, Socrates' care for Alcibiades is erotic. Thus, I begin with a passage where Proclus employs a trio known to us –Penia, Poros and Eros – who appear in the Platonic *Symposium* and reappear in Plotinus' exegesis in *Enn.* III.5.[6]

Asking the right questions (τὸ ... καλῶς ἀπορῆσαι) is the cause of facility in solution (εὐπορίας). The poverty (πενία) within us is cause of our lack of resource (ἀπορίας), and love (ἔρως) arouses us to the search for perfect knowledge; but resource (πόρος) lies in the being and <intelligent substance> of the soul, since it is the son of Counsel (Μήτιδος[7]). Our substance proceeds from above, from the divine intellect, but what is potential within us is the poverty and indeterminacy of life. Now when we are aroused to the love of the knowledge of ourselves, we behold the resource within us and the whole ordering of the soul.[8]

This excerpt is not concerned with the genealogy of eros *per se*, and hence it does not give an account of what eros is. Instead, it is posed within the more restrained context of illustrating the form of enquiry («εὕρεσις» on our own) as opposed to learning («μάθησις» by someone else).[9] However, immediately there follows a second round of 'de-allegorizing' references[10] which become much more reminiscent of Plotinus, since poros is associated with our intellectual substance, itself derived from Intellect, as are the λόγοι/λόγος in Plotinus' case. What is more, penia's relation to our intellectual 'potentialities', as well as indefiniteness, recalls the Plotinian approach. Penia is related to the (generation of our) eros for the knowledge (of ourselves), which is equated with contemplation of our own 'poros', i.e. with the (recollection of the) inherent λόγοι in us. All these elements are very close to Plotinus' spirit and we could apply analogous remarks to those I made above concerning Plotinus.[11]

Thus, although the above excerpt does not primarily intend to clarify the nature of love, it does associate the notion of penia (-deficiency) with eros, and it is certainly a deficiency that characterizes Alcibiades, who falls short of Socratic self-knowledge. Although he didn't, Proclus could have used this very simile also in more metaphysically loaded passages, given the preeminent position he ascribes to ἔνδεια in relation to ἔρως/ἔφεσις in both the *Alcibiades Commentary* and the *Elements of Theology*. Starting with the former, Proclus is crystal clear when stating that «ἔστι ... ὁ ἔρως ἔφεσίς τινος ἐρρωμένη καὶ σύντονος,[12] καὶ πᾶν τὸ ἐρῶν ἐφίεταί τινος οὗ ἐστιν ἐνδεές».[13] These lines could have been written by Plotinus, as well as Plato.[14] Granting the intimate relation between desire and love, the same idea is recapitulated in the *Elements*, although the word «ἔρως» and its cognates are absent from this introductory work[15]: «τὸ γὰρ ὀρεγόμενόν του ἐνδεές ἐστιν οὗ ὀρέγεται».[16] Consequently, we see that for Proclus, as for Plotinus, the notion of eros does imply deficiency-penia with reference to the object desired, and the hierarchy still exists: the lover is inferior to the beloved to which it aspires, as in the case of Alcibiades' inferiority to Socrates. Thus, eros is related to the reversion of the lower entity to its higher principle.[17] As Proclus puts it in the *Alcibiades Commentary*, 'the whole order of love is for all beings the cause of reversion to the divine beauty'.[18]

If then we can establish that ἔνδεια/πενία (of the inferior for the superior) continues to play a fundamental role in Proclus' conception of ἔρως, is it not a pleonasm to speak about «ἐπιστρεπτικὸς ἔρως», as in the passage cited in the beginning of Chapter 2? Presumably, the qualification means to distinguish 'reversive' from «προνοητικός» eros, i.e. love of the superior for the inferior. But in light of the Plotinian background this idea appears hard to understand. Could Proclus ever think that there is any kind of 'penia' in superior entities with respect to the lower ones? I have already shown in the introduction that this is not the case. For Proclus «αὐτάρκεια» ('self-sufficiency'), viz. not being in need of anything else external to oneself,[19] is a divine ideal.[20] For example, when speaking about the Good in the *Elements*, he states that 'the unqualified Good lacks nothing, since it has no desire towards another (for desire in it would be a failure of goodness)'.[21] Hence, the nearer an entity is to the Good on the ontological scale, the more self-sufficient it is,[22] and, thus, the more distanced it is from its inferior orders of reality.[23] The same ideas are to be found in the *Alcibiades Commentary*, too.[24]

Therefore, it seems that the Plotinian notion of ἐπιστρεπτικός ἔρως is incompatible with that of a descending love. Does this mean that, if Proclus wants to be consistent, he must totally divorce the providential eros from the reversive one? Or is there any possibility of accommodating the two within his system? The answer is yes and it is well featured in the loving pair of Socrates and Alcibiades, since the complement of Alcibiades' reversive eros is Socrates' erotic care or providential eros. While Socrates does fall short of higher entities, like his guardian-spirit, for which he must have reversive eros, he is not in need of Alcibiades.

Let us see then what providential eros exactly is according to Proclus, because only then will we be able to make a fair comparison with Plotinus. A good place to start is one of the initial substantial references to Eros in the *Commentary*. The Successor, commenting on the opening phrase of the dialogue,[25] states:

> The form of the discussion is most suited to the business of love. For it is the property of divine lovers to turn (ἐπιστρέφειν), recall and rally the beloved to himself; since, positively instituting a middle rank between divine beauty and those who have need of their forethought, these persons, inasmuch as they model themselves on the divine love, gather unto and unite with themselves the lives of their loved ones, and lead them up with themselves to intelligible beauty, pouring, as Socrates in the *Phaedrus*[26] says 'into their souls' whatever they 'draw'

from that source. If, then, the lover is inspired by love, he would be the sort of person who turns back and recalls noble natures to the good, like love itself.[27]

As becomes clear from the continuation of the excerpt, the 'divine lover' described here is Socrates.[28] What is more, this «ἔνθεος ἐραστής» is said to be possessed by the god of Love, i.e. a higher entity in the ontological realm. Furthermore, it is assumed that Socrates patterns himself upon the characteristic activity of that deity, which is to elevate the inferior beings of its rank towards the divine beauty. Consequently, a first conclusion one could draw from this comparison is that for Proclus, Socrates' relationship to Alcibiades allegorically represents the relation between the higher and the lower entities of the ontological realm.[29] By examining aspects of the way Socrates is associated with Alcibiades, we actually deal with the way the ontological hierarchy is structured, as reflected in our intra-mundane reality, and vice versa.[30]

But the connection between ethics and metaphysics[31] is deeper than that. Indeed, Proclus holds that Socrates' relationship to Alcibiades is no mere accidental reflection or 'analogical' mirroring of the intelligible world's hierarchy. He states that Socrates actually bestows divine providence on the young boy, owing to the bestowals of his guardian spirit, which partakes of the erotic order.[32] Consequently, Socrates' relation to Alcibiades is actually an expression of the divine within our intra-mundane reality. The passage cited above also suggests to assume that there is a specific ontological relation between the divine lover and Eros, since the lover receives bestowals which are ultimately derived from that very entity.

As with Plotinus, we will be able to appreciate better what Proclus says about love if we try to locate this entity within the ontological scheme and try to understand its function.[33] Here we may confine ourselves to the following rough sketch[34]: as in the *Symposium*, Eros is a medium/mediator between the beloved, which is the Beautiful, and the lovers of it. Love, due to its aspiration, is the first to try to unite itself with Beauty (reversive love) and constitutes the bond for the lower entities to arrive at that divine level (providential love). What Eros actually does is to bestow on the inferior members of its rank its characteristic property, which is erotic aspiration. In that way Proclus combines the two notions of ascending and descending love into one: it is insofar as Eros has an ascending love that it also enables the inferiors to be elevated, too. If we insist on asking why Eros ever has this descending attitude at all, then the ultimate answer is that he is providential. In other words, Alcibiades can have reversive-ascending eros for Socrates and Socrates can have providential-descending eros for Alcibiades, while also having reversive eros for higher entities, like his guardian-spirit.

Thus, it is an essential feature of the Proclean divine lover, i.e. Socrates, who patterns himself upon the god Eros, to elevate his beloved along with himself towards the intelligible Beauty.[35] The lover's reversive eros does not seem to be incompatible with his providential love.[36] To the contrary, insofar as the lover has a reversive eros, i.e. insofar as he is directed towards the intelligible realm, where Eros, Beauty and the Good lie, he is also providential towards his beloved. Finally, whereas Plotinus drew inspiration especially from the *Symposium*, Proclus follows the path of the *Phaedrus*, where among other things it is stated that

> 'those who belong to … each of the … gods proceed … in accordance with their god and seek that their boy should be of the same nature, and when they acquire him, imitating the god themselves and persuading and disciplining their beloved they draw him into the way of life and pattern of the god, to the extent that each is able, without showing jealousy or mean ill-will towards their beloved; rather they act as they do because they are trying as much as they can, in every way, to draw him into complete resemblance to themselves and to whichever god they honour'.[37]

2.1.2 From eros to the Demiurge and the statesman

In this section I will give further illustrations of providential love by drawing analogies between Socrates as lover, Timaeus' Demiurge and the *Republic*'s statesman. In all cases, the upwards direction does not impede the interaction with Alcibiades, the Receptacle and the ideal city respectively. I begin with the divine lover, whose providential attitude, with respect to both the intelligible and the intra-mundane realm, is a recurrent theme in the *Alcibiades Commentary*. It is worth giving some further illustrations of it:

> The souls that have chosen the life of love are moved by the god who is the 'guardian of beautiful youths' to the care of noble natures, and from apparent beauty they are elevated to the divine, taking up with them their darlings, and turning both themselves and their beloved towards beauty itself. This is just what divine love primarily accomplishes in the intelligible world, both uniting itself to the object of love and elevating to it what shares in the influence that emanates from it and implanting in all a single bond and one indissoluble friendship with each other and with essential beauty. Now the souls that are possessed by love and share in the inspiration therefrom, …, are turned towards intelligible beauty and set that end to their activity; 'kindling a light' for less perfect souls they elevate these also to the divine and dance with them about the one source of all beauty.[38]

There could hardly be a better expression of the way Proclus views, on the one hand, the combination of upwards and downwards eros, and, on the other, the intimate relation between the intelligible erotic pattern and its worldly instantiations.[39] This special and complex relationship is illustrated also by the fact that when 'men's souls receive a share of such [sc. erotic] inspiration, through intimacy with the god [i.e. Eros, they] are moved with regard to the beautiful, and descend to the region of coming-to-be for the benefit of less perfect souls and out of forethought for those in need of salvation'.[40] Note again the 'self-sufficiency' of the lover.[41] It is true that the *Symposium*, and perhaps the *Phaedrus*, too, in some passages, gives us the impression that the lover needs his beloved, because the latter constitutes the means/instrument for the former to recollect the source of real beauty and, thus, ascend to the intelligible,[42] a claim that has led modern Platonic scholars to find 'egocentric' characteristics in Plato's account.[43] Proclus, however, definitely rejects such an interpretation: the beloved cannot constitute – at least such a kind of – means to an end, since the divine lover already has communication with the higher realm.[44] It is precisely this bond with the intelligible world that enables the lover to take providential care of his (potential) beloved, i.e. of a person fitted for that special care,[45] and hence (try to) elevate the latter, too, to the former's object of desire.

According to the strong unitarian Neoplatonic reading of Plato, it becomes clear that for Proclus the relationship of the divine lover with his beloved, both in the *Symposium* and in the *Phaedrus*, is the exact analogue of the Demiurge's relation to the Receptacle and that of the philosopher-king to his own 'political receptacle'.[46] The *Timaeus*' Demiurge mediates – like eros – between the most beautiful intelligible living being and the Χώρα. We could never think that he is assisted in grasping the former due to the existence of the latter. Contrariwise, it is insofar as he contemplates the intelligible, and is also aware of the 'disorderly moving' receptacle, that he projects the Forms into the latter, in order to set it in order, decorate it and fashion it as the best-possible image of the intelligible.[47] Now, if one presses the question more, and asks why the contemplation of Forms is not sufficient for the Demiurge, but he goes on to instantiate them in the receptacle, Timaeus' answer is that the former 'was good (ἀγαθός), and one who is good can never become jealous of anything',[48] whereby it is implied that the Ὑποδοχή was fitted («ἐπιτήδεια») for the Demiurge's action upon it.[49] Actually, the analogy between the divine lover and the divine craftsman is made explicit by Proclus himself. Towards the end of the following passage the Successor makes the receptacle speak to the demiurge, as a beloved would do to its lover. Since I count this instance as the most moving and poetical moment of the whole

Commentary,⁵⁰ and because we have the opportunity to see another remarkable instance of the ontological analogy between Socrates and the intelligible entities with respect to the issue of goodness and providence, it is worth citing the whole passage:

> The young man seems to me⁵¹ to admire above all these two qualities in Socrates, his goodness of will and his power of provision; which qualities indeed are conspicuous in the most primary causes of reality, are especially displayed in the creative order, and initiate the whole world-order. 'For god,' he says, 'having willed all things to be good, according to his⁵² power set the world in order,'⁵³ by his will tendering the good to the whole universe, and by his power prevailing over all things and everywhere extending his own creations. Socrates, therefore, faithfully reproducing these characteristics,⁵⁴ set an ungrudging will and power over his perfection of inferiors, everywhere present to his beloved and leading him from disorder to order. Now the young man wonders at this, 'what on earth is its meaning,'⁵⁵ and how Socrates is everywhere earnestly and providently (for this is the meaning of 'taking great care') to hand. If what 'was in discordant and disorderly movement'⁵⁶ could say something to the creator, it would have uttered these same words: 'in truth I wonder at your beneficent will and power that have reached as far as my level, are everywhere present to me and from all sides arrange me in orderly fashion.' This spirit-like and divine characteristic, then, and this similarity with the realities that have filled all things with themselves, he ascribes to Socrates, viz: the leaving of no suitable time or place void of provision for the beloved.⁵⁷

We can assume that the Receptacle's above-mentioned grateful speech for its decorator could be reiterated by the 'political receptacle', the body of the πόλις, if all classes were united to express with one mouth their gratitude towards their own decorator.⁵⁸ We can assume that, because in the *Commentary* Proclus offers us, apart from the already-mentioned analogies, many others for the relation of the lover with his beloved and that of the philosopher-statesman with its (beloved) state. Furthermore, the Successor's language even in these political contexts clearly echoes the wording used for the demiurgic functions of the *Timaeus*.⁵⁹

These interconnections allow us to give a Proclean answer to the thorny question of the *Republic*: 'why does the philosopher have to become a ruler of the city?'; or in other words: 'why does the philosopher have to return back to the cave?'⁶⁰ Plato (or better Socrates) has always puzzled the commentators with his response that 'we'll be giving just orders to just people,'⁶¹ since in the previous books justice has been defined in the 'internal' terms of the orderly relation of the parts of the soul within the individual.⁶² Proclus might well have responded that Socrates just did not do justice to the readers by not presenting them with the whole picture⁶³; in fact, it is the goodness, in which the philosopher participates, which makes him, like the Demiurge, good, «ἀγαθῷ δὲ οὐδεὶς περὶ οὐδενὸς οὐδέποτε ἐγγίγνεται φθόνος».⁶⁴ As is evident from the passages cited above there is an organic relation between goodness and providence. The 'better' an entity is, i.e. higher in the ontological hierarchy, the more providential it is, i.e. its bestowals reach further down the scale, and hence it has a wider scope. As with the Proclean divine lover, it is insofar as the statesman participates in the intelligible that he goes on to set into order its own 'disorderly moving' receptacle.⁶⁵ Thus, Proclus is in line with the Platonic *Alcibiades*' parallel between the relation of lover and beloved, on the one hand, and that of the statesman and the city, on the other. The way the lover educates and fashions his beloved must be the paradigm of the philosopher-politician's attitude towards the body politic.⁶⁶

And in any case, there is no question that the mature philosopher-king would need the state in order to help him grasp the Forms,⁶⁷ just as in the case of Proclus' divine lover. Now, whether this scheme of universal correspondence between the Demiurge, the philosopher-king and the divine lover⁶⁸ exists in Plato is an open question.⁶⁹ We might also question the ontological elaborations with which Proclus has invested Plato. However, Proclus' insight gives us a Neoplatonic justification not to view Plato as an 'egoist' with respect to erotic matters. If this is so, then Proclus had already given a brave and articulate answer against Plato's modern critics. Finally, let me conclude by noting that in this *Commentary* Proclus spends a considerable amount of time attempting to prove that it was not in vain that the 'daimonion' let the Silenus try to elevate the son of Cleinias.⁷⁰ Unlike Socrates with Alcibiades, I do not suggest that we should necessarily be persuaded by Proclus. Nonetheless, I hope that the present reflections may at least reveal a reason why it would be fruitful for Platonic scholars⁷¹ to consider in their discussions Neoplatonic perspectives, as well.⁷²

2.1.3 From Platonic eros to Aristotelian friendship

Having shown how Proclus' combination of ascending and descending eros works in the same way for various Platonic dialogues, I continue in illustrating providential eros, this time by drawing its connections to «φιλία» (friendship). Again some modern scholars⁷³ have proposed that, in fact, Plato in the *Phaedrus* gives us an account of friendship, whose perfect type, at least, surpasses the problems of ascribing egocentric incentives with regard to the erotic desire (ἔρως), since, even when natural beauty fades out, the friendly, spiritual and non-sexual affection between the members of the ideal pair can still remain.[74] In that, of course, the commentators follow Plato's own text which refers to the erotic relationship between lover and beloved as φιλία.[75] So, for example, towards the end of his recantation, Socrates will state that 'these are the blessings … so great as to be counted divine, which will come to you [sc. the beloved] from the friendship of a lover'.[76] Hence, it is not only the beloved's «ἀντέρως»[77] which is actually thought of as friendship,[78] as one would normally expect under the specific social and spatio-temporal circumstances,[79] but the lover himself is called «ἔνθεος φίλος».[80]

Now, as would be expected, Proclus, too, uses the terms ἔνθεος ἐραστής and ἔρως interchangeably with divine φίλος and φιλία, perhaps in a more systematic manner than Plato does.[81] This is also important because of its consistency with the view of the divine lover as non-egoist and providential towards the beloved.[82] Of course, it is true that the Successor also sometimes praises friendship in a quite Aristotelian manner.[83] However, the above identification allows him to illustrate the lover's positive disposition towards the beloved using the vocabulary of friendship. Consider the following example:

> By addressing the subject of disproof as "dear" (φίλον), he [sc. Socrates] anticipates the wound by his affection (τῇ οἰκειώσει) and at the same time shows that for him a purpose of purification is friendship, because "no god is ill-disposed to men, therefore neither does he [sc. Socrates] do anything of this sort out of ill-humour (δυσνοίᾳ),"[84] as he has observed in the *Theaetetus*,[85] and because among the gods the agent of purification extends its operation to the imperfect out of goodness, not out of estrangement towards them.[86]

What is striking about this passage is that, following the characteristic Proclean strategy of drawing parallels between Socrates–Alcibiades and the ontological hierarchy, it applies the terms of friendship to (higher) godly and (lower) human entities,[87] although famously Aristotle had declared that man cannot be friends with god, since there is no equality between them.[88] Indeed, Proclus will be in a position to ground the thought that 'if … all belongs to the gods, all belongs also to good men (σπουδαίων)'[89] on the assumption of the well-known Pythagorean maxim that 'the possessions of friends are held in common'.[90]

Of course, these differences from Aristotle ultimately stem from Proclus' fundamental ontological equation of Eros with Friendship. I will come back to the ontological issue later (in Section 2.2.5). For now it may suffice to say that when in the *Commentary* the Successor is confronted with two distinct traditions with respect to the god of Friendship («φίλιος»),[91] the one in favour of φίλιος Zeus and the other of god Eros,[92] Proclus characteristically unites/'contracts' the two, claiming that 'Love is contained within Zeus'.[93] Sometimes friendship seems to apply more to instances of a 'horizontal' union within one stratum of reality, hence between quasi-equal entities,[94] whereas eros, denoting the deficiency of an entity, fits better a vertical scheme, in which lower strata of reality desire what lies beyond them.[95] Proclus thinks of friendship when speaking of love and vice versa.[96]

On the other hand, Proclus' divergence from Aristotle, as to the possibility of friendship between gods and humans, is not radical, since the Successor holds that there is an ontological hierarchy. Not only that, but he also thinks that the hierarchical scheme is a condition for the possibility of (productive) love/friendship between entities of different levels. This can be inferred from passages like the following: 'The lover, then, must pay heed to any one fine point in the beloved in order that he may be both more perfect and immediately superior. For in this way one would lead upwards, the other be led upwards, and the former would exercise providence with some fellow-feeling (μετά τινος συμπαθείας).'[97] Hence, Proclus of course does not object to the thought that gods are superior entities, and thus surpass human beings in excellence, but he follows an ontological reading of the *Phaedrus*' type relation, where, as we have seen, (a) the lover and the beloved stand for entities of different ontological strata and (b) they are also called 'friends'.

However, even in that respect Proclus is not very far from Aristotle's perfect type of friendship between good, and hence equal, men. The Stagirite assumes that there is a large gap between mortals and god(s), something which is consistent with his ontology-cosmological philosophy. Nevertheless, a characteristic of especially the late Neoplatonists is the attempt to fill this vertical gap by postulating strata of mediating entities, i.e. levels of reality which can bridge the gap between the One and the material cosmos. Now, what preserves the cohesion of this vertical continuum is the similarity between the entities in different strata.[98] According to the *Elements of Theology*, a principle of the procession, and hence of the complementary reversion, is that it takes place through like terms.[99] The same idea is reiterated and related to the issue of eros (/friendship) in the following passage[100] from the *Alcibiades Commentary*: 'What is completely uncoordinated (ἀσύντακτον) has no communion with its inferior, but love finds its subsistence among those who are able to commune with each other, since it itself is perfected through the likeness of the inferior to the superior, through the uniting (συνδέσεως) of the less perfect with the more perfect and through the reversion of what is made complete to the causes of completion.'

We can deduce from this passage that actual and direct friendship/eros can take place only between adjacent entities, viz. between the cause and its immediate effect; that is, between the most similar possible entities. As far as ascending eros is concerned, it is true that every entity aspires to the Good. Yet it actually approaches it through the former's union to its immediate progenitor, as the *Elements* claim.[101] Furthermore, as far as downwards eros is concerned, we can assume that it directly relates adjacent entities, whereas providential eros for even remoter beings should be thought of as indirect. In other words, an entity can be providential for its offspring, but since the offspring gives rise to further entities, the providential preservation of the former entails providential preservation of the latter, too.[102] Consequently, from Aristotle's ideal case of 'friendly' equality (of good properties), Proclus switches to the idea of 'friendly-erotic' similarity.[103] The divergence is a small one, since equality does not exclude similarity.[104] What constitutes a difference is the Proclean introduction of *hierarchical* similarity as a precondition for the (actual and direct) friendship or love to take place.[105] What we see here is then a Proclean synthesis of Platonic and Aristotelian perspectives, which in itself is the further outcome of Proclus' equation of ἔρως with φιλία.

2.1.4 Limiting the scope: From eros to providential eros

I now move to examine Proclus' composite concept of 'providential eros', and, hence, the relation between eros and providence. I will argue that in Proclus' idea of 'providential eros' the emphasis lies not on 'eros', but on 'providence', whose existence is undeniable by every Neoplatonist.[106] In all the passages I have cited so far, although Socrates is called 'divine lover' (or 'friend'), he is hardly ever explicitly said to be in love («ἐρᾶν») with his beloved. Though this is the only logical inference, Proclus prefers constantly to emphasize Socrates' providence («πρόνοια»)[107] towards Alcibiades. It is this very fact that prompted me to highlight Socrates' parallel with the Demiurge, and further with the statesman, although Plato, like Proclus, never characterizes the divine craftsman's providence for the Receptacle as 'love'. This sheds light on the Successor's approach to 'downwards-providential eros'. Proclus' principal aim is not to furnish us, further to the notion of ascending-reversive love, with a distinct account of eros *per se*, but rather to illustrate a distinctive case of providence which complements reversive love. That Proclean providential eros is not the only instance of (divine) providence becomes plain enough from the following passage:

> As, then, other souls established according to another god visit without defilement the region of mortals and the souls that move about therein – some help (ὠφελοῦσι) the less perfect through prophecy, others through mystic rites and others through divine medicine – so also souls that have chosen the life of love[108] are moved by the god who is the "guardian of beautiful youths"[109] to the care (ἐπιμέλειαν) of noble natures (τῶν εὖ πεφυκότων).[110]

As becomes clear from the *Elements*, as well as from many previous citations, it is an essential attribute of gods to be providential, that is, to extend their bestowals (i.e. their divine characteristics) upon the entities that are dependent on them, and hence are of the same rank. Of course, Proclus' system is not one-dimensional, like Plotinus'. In other words, it does have not only a vertical dimension, but also a horizontal one, or, more accurately, a 'transverse'.[111] Hence, after the ultimate unity of the One (and the Indefinite Dyad), the stratum of the Henads already consists of a multiplicity of ultimate divinities, identified with the gods of ancient Greek mythology, in conjunction with the Chaldean Oracles and Orphic religion, each of them representing certain features which are bestowed upon the orders of their descendants.[112] Nonetheless, also within the transverse dimension there are still relations of the type we see in vertical ranks; thus, the superior entities communicate their characteristic features to their successors/inferior entities in the horizontal stratum.[113] However, if this is true of the divine realm, we should not expect that the more deficient beings of the lower strata of reality, e.g. daimonic souls should preserve the unity in multiplicity of their highest progenitors untouched. Thus, the gifted ones succeed in preserving a sole characteristic, ultimately inherited by vertical procession from a Henad, which is Proclus' understanding of the divine processions in the *Phaedrus* myth.[114] Hence, we saw in the former passage that some souls instantiate their providence for the mundane world via medicine, others via prophecy, via 'erotics' (ἐρωτική), etc. Consequently, we repeat that downwards eros is not a universal characteristic of Proclus' system, but only a particular instance of (the universal fact of) «πρόνοια».[115] Another useful way of putting this is in Aristotelian jargon: eros (or friendship) is only a species of the 'providence'-genus. It is because and insofar as Proclus is interested in providence that he speaks of downwards eros. This alone can already alleviate the apparent contrast between Plotinus' ascending eros and Proclus' descending one.

Now, there are also exceptionally gifted souls which can preserve and combine in their providence more than one way, and one such figure is undoubtedly Socrates. Proclus very early in the *Commentary* stresses that the Athenian gadfly is an expert in at least three 'sciences' («ἐπιστῆμαι»)[116]: that of dialectics (διαλεκτική), of maieutic/midwifery (μαιευτική) and of 'erotic' (ἐρωτική).[117] What are exactly these sciences or ways of Socrates' exercising providence? According to the Successor, a very good illustration of Socrates' midwifery, as a modern student of Plato could reasonably expect, is found in the *Theaetetus*,[118] where Socrates 'proceeds as far as the cleansing away of the false opinions of Theaetetus, but thereafter lets him go as now being capable of discerning the truth by himself, which indeed is the function of the science of elicitation (μαιευτικῆς), as Socrates himself observes in that work'.[119] For Proclus, Socrates' 'elenctic' midwifery does have a definite positive result, since 'through elicitation each one of us is revealed to be wise about subjects in which he is unlearned (ἀμαθής), by realizing the innate notions (λόγους) within himself concerning reality'.[120] In other words, Socrates stirs Theaetetus up 'through the art of elicitation to recollection (ἀνάμνησιν) of the eternal notions of the soul', and hence the result is that his interlocutor is united with 'the very first wisdom'.[121] Proclus draws a parallel with the way the recipients of Socrates' providence are elevated and come to salvation («σωτηρία»)[122] through dialectic and 'erotic'. As we have already seen, through eros Socrates elevates and unites individuals worthy of love 'to essential beauty (αὐτοκάλῳ)',[123] while through dialectic he brings round 'to the vision of reality'[124] those 'who love to contemplate the truth'[125] and can be thus led 'even as far as the Good'.[126]

We can draw some important conclusions from the previous remarks: first of all, it is clear that there are three distinct ways to ascend to the divine realm, namely «καλόν, σοφόν, ἀγαθόν» according to the *Phaedrus*.[127] Via dialectic one is elevated to the Good, via maieutic one attains to Wisdom, and through erotic one is united with the Beautiful. Hence, we are presented with three different methods, which are distinguished on the basis of the divine entity they aspire to, since, as becomes clear in the *Commentary*, the three aforementioned divine characteristics represent divine entities of different strata. The Good even transcends reality, Wisdom should be posited somewhere on the level of Henads, whereas the Beautiful is located in the stratum of Being.[128] Especially in light of the fact that for Proclus, gifted souls can attain to the intelligible on their own, by independent discovery, without the aid of any teacher,[129] it becomes clear that eros is not the only means of ascent. Reversive eros is only one path to the intelligible realm, just as providential eros is only one among various instances of providence. In both cases, what is characteristic of the 'via erotica' is that it denotes the attraction to beauty (either the Form of Beauty in the case of reversion, or beautiful particulars in the case of providence).[130]

A further implication of the above remarks relates to Socrates' capacity to adjust his teaching, by elevating 'each individual to his appropriate object of desire'.[131] Proclus compares Socrates with the divine in a manner already familiar to us: 'As in the godhead all goods preexist in the manner of unity,[132] but different individuals enjoy different goods according to the natural capacity of each, so also Socrates embraces all the forms of knowledge within himself, but uses now one now another, adjusting his own activity to the requirements (ἐπιτηδειότητα) of the recipients.'[133] This is why 'it is through love that perfection comes, in the present work [sc. in the *Alcibiades I*], to those that possess this nature (in view of his possession thereof, Alcibiades seemed to be worthy of love[134] to Socrates)'.[135] This point reminds us again the limited scope of descending eros in contrast to the universality of providence: although Socrates is providential to everyone,[136] he is (providentially) erotic only to those natures that belong to the rank of Beautiful (and hence of eros, too), i.e. those who by possessing and aspiring to beauty can be elevated to Beauty itself.[137]

Here, however, we should make a conceptual distinction with respect to the individuals' being fitted/suitable (ἐπιτήδεια) recipients (of providence) and being of a certain nature. Although the previous passage brings these two notions together, their function is not identical. The specific nature of each individual denotes the ultimate source of its bestowals and thus reveals the entity which is its desired object. That is, Alcibiades, in partaking in the beautiful and erotic bestowals, (can) crave for the Beautiful. On the other hand, ἐπιτηδειότης denotes the capacity of the individual to be elevated to a specific level of the intelligible. In other words, the greater ἐπιτηδειότης a person has, the higher a level he can attain in the intelligible hierarchy.[138] Now we can see why nature (φύσις) and ἐπιτηδειότης come to be identified. The reason is that each different desired object is located within a hierarchical structure, and a particular object of desire entails also a certain level of capability of ascent. This remark can also help us understand more fully what Proclus means by separating individual natures into, for example, philosophical ones, erotic and musical ones.[139] But it is only those already capable of and suitable for ascent that are elevated in the end.[140] More optimistically, one might suppose that each individual has some capacity for elevation, but still, the varying natures of these individuals will still result in a strongly hierarchical picture of their possible destinations.

In any case, as we have noted above, Socrates is particularly gifted in comprising in his own personality all different kinds of identity, so that he can benefit anyone, without exception.[141] Nonetheless, since he is a single and unified personality, when exercising erotic providence he does not cease to be simultaneously dialectical and maieutic. Hence, Proclus notes that, although 'the activities of the science of love prevail throughout the whole composition [i.e. the *Alcibiades I*]', along with this we can also 'find the genre of philosophical discussion (τῆς διαλεκτικῆς) in this dialogue illustrated through the subject-matter itself, and everywhere' one 'may detect the peculiar trait of elicitation contained in Socrates' arguments'.[142] I have already noted that Socrates belongs to this class of rarely gifted souls which have preserved untouched the characteristic 'unity in multiplicity' of the divine entities, and hence can be 'everything, but according to their own proper manner'. Thus, in this advanced manner Socrates, according to Proclus, is in a state of exploiting midwifery and dialectics for achieving the aims of erotic, and even more, in exploiting the two former in an erotic way: 'So in this dialogue he primarily demonstrates the science of love and practices in a loving manner both philosophical argument (διαλεκτικόν) and elicitation.'[143]

Still it remains the case that erotic providence *per se* is of limited application, since it is necessarily directed only towards beautiful and love-worthy recipients. With regard to this restriction of the scope of the notion of eros, some ontological references where Proclus evokes again the ontological and 'hidden' hierarchical triad of Good, Wisdom and Beauty[144] may be helpful here. Since the Beautiful has its counterpart in Eros, we might expect something analogous for the other two members of the triad. According to the Successor, as Eros is dependent on the Beautiful, in an analogous way 'Faith' («πίστις»)[145] is related to the Good, and 'Truth' («ἀλήθεια») to Wisdom, i.e. 'the first founding the universe and establishing it in the good, the second revealing the knowledge that lies in all being'.[146] This means that as Eros is the path for union with the Beautiful, 'faith' is the way to grasp the Good, and 'truth' the window for contemplating the Wisdom of the universe.[147] In other words, faith and truth must exemplify the function of dialectics and midwifery, exercised by Socrates, for elevation to the divine.[148] It follows from the analogy that Socrates is able to exercise them because he partakes in their bestowals, and patterns himself upon them, as he does with Eros, in the case of the consideration of beauty. Consequently, it once again becomes clear that eros is only one of at least three ways to ascend/revert to the divine realm.[149]

Along with the reduction of the scope of both providential and reversive eros, another implication is erotic's relative degradation, since it appears that dialectic/faith and maieutic/truth (for both the agent and the recipients of his providence) are more important ways to ascend to the intelligible hierarchy, since the target-entities are ranked higher than the Beautiful, which is Eros' final end.[150] Of course, things are not so clear-cut, since the appreciation of beauty cannot be neglected in Wisdom and the Good. Recollecting again the fundamental axiom that 'all things are in all things, but in each according to its proper nature', the two higher entities should be seen as 'causally' (κατ' αἰτίαν) beautiful, as also the Good is 'causally' 'wise'. However, it is still true that access to the (essential) Beautiful is marked as inferior to the path towards the (supra-essentially) Good. Nonetheless, Proclus notes the specific importance of beauty for our intra-mundane realm, since, following *Phaedrus*' Socrates, 'there is no lustre in the images here below of justice and moderation: but, as it is, beauty alone has received this prerogative – to be most conspicuous and most lovable'.[151] The revelation of beauty in our world has an immediate and peculiar impact on human souls, so that it becomes easier for them to pursue that target, which may elevate them towards the source of beauty itself.

Thus, it appears that beauty, and hence 'erotic' as the way to ascend to the Beautiful, has a particular privilege in comparison with the other two types of ascent.[152] A soul must be extraordinarily gifted in order to be attracted and elevated to Wisdom, or even the Good itself, both of which transcend Beauty. On the other hand, not only has the erotic person better chances to succeed in his pursuit, but also 'the union ... with divine beauty ... results' in 'intimacy with the *entire* divinity',[153] which is 'beautiful, wise and good', as has been already noted (e.g. n. 127). In other words, even if this divine triad is hierarchical, the ascent to beauty, having 'fed and watered the winged nature of the soul',[154] enables the soul to continue its ascent towards further and higher summits, which are the sources of Beauty. Of course, this soul must be especially gifted/'winged' in order to appreciate the new summits that it has been able to behold from the top of Beauty. However, the very possibility of indirect elevation to the Good via Eros' union with the Beautiful makes the 'via erotica' a much more 'practical' way of ascent to the source of everything, than the labours involved e.g. in dialectics, which by 'imitating' faith forms the direct way to get hold of the Good, as far as possible. This is not to suggest that there is only one way to ascend to the divine[155] (whether directly or indirectly).[156] Although beauty has a privileged position for the souls of our intra-mundane realm particularly, eros does not have the fundamental universality we had observed in Plotinus.[157] Furthermore, this verdict holds for both directions of Proclus' thought: both providential and ascending eros.[158]

2.1.5 Qualifying love: From manic eros to undefiled eros

But what exactly is providence? In this section I will juxtapose manic eros and Proclus' ideal of undefiled providential eros. The characteristic features of the Proclean notion will also provide us with a deeper insight as to the relation between providential and reversive eros – or providence and reversion more generally; that is, how these two notions can be regarded as two complementary aspects of an entity's single activity. Let us, then, go back to the *Elements* and see how the notion of providence is initially introduced with respect to the Henads' existence[159]: 'Every god embraces in his substance the function of exercising providence towards the universe; and the primary providence resides in the gods.'[160]

This proposition confirms our already-formed picture with regard to providence as exemplified in the Platonic Demiurge and his erotic and political counterparts, and is parallel to the familiar issue of procession («πρόοδος») in Neoplatonic metaphysics. But apart from making explicit the relation between god(s), goodness and providence, it tells us nothing more about the precise nature of this (divine) providence. More informative is proposition 122: 'All that is divine both exercises providence towards secondary existences and transcends (ἐξῄρηται) the beings for which it provides: its providence involves no remission of its pure (ἄμικτον) and unitary transcendence (ὑπεροχὴν), neither does its separate unity annul its providence.'[161]

One of the significant contributions of this proposition is its explanation as to how divine providence can be made compatible with the other fundamental Greek assumption about gods, which is their transcendence. Indeed, as also Dodds notes, the gist of the Epicurean criticism against the idea of gods' being providential for what lies beneath them was that it 'credits the gods with an interest in an infinity of petty problems and so abolishes their transcendence and makes their life πραγματειώδη καὶ ἐπίπονον'.[162] However, for the Neoplatonic Successor 'the especial glory of Platonism'[163] consists in the preservation of both divine transcendence and providence.[164] In other words, if the '(hyper-) being' of the gods entails both the fact of their transcendence as well as their providential attitude towards the inferiors, then thinking with the Epicureans that providence 'pollutes' divine transcendence or 'eudaimonia' is not the right way. Rather, there can be a compromise between these two fundamental divine aspects, and this solution is realized in the concept of «ἄσχετος» and «ἀμιγής» πρόνοια, i.e. a providence that assumes 'no relation' with its recipients, making the gods 'undefiled' and 'pure' from anything lower to them.

Thus, the paradox[165] of divine providence emerges since it is a kind of (causal) relation of the divine with the lower reality, without there being any actual relation (or interference) between them at all.[166] We may even contend that while Proclus boasts to have solved this problem, he does not really give a solution just by insisting that the gods' providence does not involve being tainted by involvement with what they care for. Doesn't this sound more like a begging of the question against the Epicureans? The answer is no: the necessity of gods' goodness and providence does not mingle with – but actually explains and is explained by – the necessity of their being transcendent, since both are necessary realizations stemming from a single nature, the super-nature of the gods. Hence, although Proclus in the previous proposition stresses as much as possible the universality of divine providence as a way of confirmation of the existence and nature of divinity, he emphasizes that 'in exercising providence they [sc. the Henads/gods] assume no relation to those for whom they provide, since it is in virtue of being what they are that they make all things good, and what acts in virtue of its being acts without relation (for relation is a qualification of its being, and therefore contrary to its nature)'.[167]

Now, it is exactly this paradox of undefiled and non-relational providence that Proclus stresses when describing the (erotically providential) relation of Socrates and Alcibiades as mirrored in the structure of the intelligible hierarchy, and vice versa. The following passage from the *Alcibiades Commentary* could almost be commentary on the aforementioned proposition of the *Elements*. One should read it with particular attention to the multiple verbs and adjectives that reveal what the pure transcendence («ἄμικτος ὑπεροχή») of proposition 122's non-relational (ἄσχετος) πρόνοια is:

> The more accurate accounts say that there are two principal elements in divine and spiritual providence towards the secondary beings: (1) that it passes through all things from the top to the bottom, leaving nothing, not even the least, without a share in itself, and (2) it neither admits into itself anything it controls nor is it infected (μηδὲ ἀναπίμπλασθαι) with its nature nor is it confused with it (μηδὲ συμφύρεσθαι). It is not mixed up (ἀναμίγνυται) with the objects of its provision just because it preserves and arranges everything (for it is not the nature of the divine or spiritual to experience the emotions of individual souls), nor does it leave any of the inferior beings without order or arrangement[168] because of its distinct superiority over all that is secondary, but[169] it both disposes everything duly and transcends what it disposes; at the same time it has the character of the good and remains undefiled (ἄχραντος), it arranges the universe yet has no relation (ἄσχετος) to what is arranged by it; it passes through everything and mingles with nothing (ἀμιγὴς πρὸς πάντα).[170]

Proclus wants to stress not so much the universality of providence *per se*, but the way in which this very idea is compatible with the fact that it 'transcends' everything in its 'distinct superiority'[171] over the inferior beings. Hence, among other designations, he speaks of divine providence as «ἄχραντος» ('undefiled'), «ἄσχετος» ('without relation') and «ἀμιγὴς» ('mingled with nothing') with respect to its recipients.[172] Proclus' obsession with 'purity' is exemplified and explained by the fact that he assigns to it a distinctive position among the (primary) 'divine attributes'.[173] As he states in the *Elements*, the characteristic of purity («καθαρότητος») is 'to liberate (ἐξαιρεῖν) the higher from the lower' beings.[174] 'For the divine purity isolates (τὸ ἀμιγὲς ἐνδίδωσι) all the gods from inferior existences, and enables them to exercise providence toward secondary beings without contamination (τὸ ἄχραντον); ... Purity,[175] then, being a good, is found primarily among the gods.'[176]

We could imagine an objector claiming that there is no Platonic background for Proclus' emphasis on purity. Still, in terms of vocabulary at least, Proclus has in mind a main Platonic erotic dialogue, the *Symposium*, where Diotima declares that «θεὸς δὲ ἀνθρώπῳ οὐ μείγνυται».[177] Of course, in the Neoplatonists' elaborate theologies there are many other strata which are inferior to the proper gods, but still higher than incarnate human beings. However, Plato's succinct allusion here to an ontological separation between different levels must have had a strong impact on Neoplatonic figures with such 'pure' dispositions, such as Proclus. By maintaining the fundamental tenet of separation, the Neoplatonists were able to generalize it and apply it to more particular, subtle and fine-grained distinctions within the intelligible realm. The same attitude to the aforementioned Platonic citation is revealed in the final stages of Diotima's 'mysteries'. Recapitulating the characteristics of the Form of Beauty, which has just been said to be unaffected by the processes of coming to be pertaining to our worldly realm,[178] the priestess declares that it is 'absolute (εἰλικρινές), pure (καθαρόν), unmixed (ἄμεικτον),[179] not polluted by human flesh or colours or any other great nonsense of mortality'.[180] Certainly a Neoplatonist could make a lot of this recurrent theme of ontological purity in Diotima's teaching, which is verified by the (in)famous episode of Socrates' and Alcibiades' lying on the bed together on a cold winter night,[181] while nothing happened between them.[182] As the Form of Beauty was said to be 'not polluted by human flesh', so was the philosopher Socrates.

Now, we have already seen (in Section 2.1.1), too, that Proclus is (too) faithful to Plato's parallel between the ontological and the mundane praise of eros. So, it is not surprising that immediately after the fundamental passage from the

Alcibiades Commentary cited above, describing the divine-undefiled providence as realized in the metaphysical sphere, Proclus picks up on the *Symposium*'s shift and continues to clarify and confirm the issue of undefiled providence at the level of Socrates' erotic relation to Alcibiades. Besides, this was actually the reason why Proclus invoked the issue of divine providence in the first place; he aimed to explain Socrates' relation to his beloved. This is, then, what the Neoplatonist writes:

> This spiritual and divine providence, then, Plato clearly attributes to the beneficent[183] forethought (προμηθείᾳ) of Socrates for the less perfect, both maintaining its vigilance and stability (as regards the beloved) and its full use of any opportunity for zeal, and at the same time its detached (ἄσχετον), unadulterated (ἀμιγῆ) and undefiled (ἄχραντον) character and its refusal to touch (ἀνέπαφον) what belongs to him ... – let this be evidence to you[184] of his detached (ἀσχέτου) and unentangled (ἀμιγοῦς) solicitude for his inferior. For the first relationship of man to man is to speak to him; so the failure to have even this communication with the object of his provision reveals him as completely transcendent and unrelated to his inferior. So at the same time he is both present to him and not present, he both loves and remains detached (καὶ ἐρᾷ καὶ ἄσχετός ἐστι), observes him from all angles yet in no respect puts himself in the same class.[185] Now if their behaviour assumes this manner even in the case of divine men, what must we say about the gods themselves or the good spirits?[186]

This remarkable passage reiterates and confirms the status of (the possibility of) divine providence in the intra-mundane realm, employing similar or even the same basic terminology to the previous passage about the gods (e.g. ἄσχετος, ἀμιγής, ἄχραντος providence).[187]

However, within these designations of providence Proclus adds one which perhaps would be rather odd if applied to the intelligible realm. This word is the adjective «ἀνέπαφος» (untouch-ed/-ing; sc. forethought – *in Alc*. 54,15), and the oddity would arise, because, as the context makes clear, it implies the existence of (material) bodies, which of course are absent from the immaterial intelligible kingdom. Thus, we can plausibly infer that Proclus alludes to the central episode of Alcibiades' narration in the *Symposium*.[188] Still, there need not be only sexual connotations to the word. For Proclus the fact that, while the vulgar lovers 'pestered' Alcibiades with conversation, Socrates was silent towards Cleinias' son[189] is an undeniable evidence of Socrates' undefiled providence.[190] Hence, the absence of verbal communication presents itself as an alternative, although perhaps weaker,[191] visualization of what detached and non-relational providence is.[192] What the Neoplatonists read in the episode of the *Symposium* was not a condemnation of sex *per se*, but rather an instance of Socrates' (providential) refusal to engage with everything, if possible, that pertains to our worldly, and hence bodily, existence.[193]

One immediate result of the above point of view is that the so much praised erotic madness («μανία») of the *Phaedrus*[194] looks now, perhaps, even more alien to us. For one thing, it cannot be anymore a 'mania' in the way we would conceive and feel it,[195] despite Proclus' reassurance that 'one kind of enthusiasm (μανίας) is superior to moderation (σωφροσύνης), but the other falls short of it',[196] the former corresponding to the divine lover, the latter to the coarse multitude.[197] The re-signification of the former type in the context of detached providence, which in the ideal case would exclude even communication via language, brings to the forefront another dimension noted by critics of Plato, and more generally of ancient Greek philosophy: that of 'disinterested affection'.[198] There are two senses that need to be distinguished here: (a) Socrates, or any providential force, does not actually care about the recipient but just automatically gives forth. This is not how I use the phrase 'disinterested affection', and I have given a negative answer to this contention in Section 2.1.4. (b) The providential force does care in the sense that it needs some recipient or other, but doesn't care which recipient is going to receive its providence since any fitting (say beautiful) recipient will do. This is the sense in which I am interested here[199] and that captures Proclus' ideal type of (manic) loving providence.[200] Thus, the (Neo)-Platonic tradition seems well-armed to avoid the arrows of egoism. Nonetheless, we may question whether 'disinterested affection' can describe the functions of the divine, and whether it should serve as a model for us. In other words, the hierarchical picture of ontological reality on the one hand prevents egoism, because it enables providence to be other-directed, but on the other hand it supports disinterested affection to the extent that undefiled providence explains the way two different ontological levels can relate with each other. Of course, I repeat that from Proclus' viewpoint the above critique launched against Plato would not be received as an accusation at all. Proclus would happily respond that this is exactly what he meant by reducing love to an instance of undefiled, detached and pure providence. However, there are two – rather isolated – instances in the *Commentary* where the explicit implications of his conception may reveal it as problematic, at least for us.

In the context of the discussion as to why Socrates' guardian spirit allowed him to associate with Alcibiades, although it could foresee that the young man would not be finally benefitted by the Athenian gadfly,[201] and having invoked several arguments[202] and examples,[203] Proclus concludes his discussion thus: 'So So<crates also achieved what was fitting (καθήκοντος)>;[204] for all the actions of the serious-minded man (σπουδαίου) have reference to this:[205] if he has acted, then, beneficently and in a divine manner, he achieves his end in his activity (ἐν τῇ ἐνεργείᾳ τὸ τέλος ἔχει), even if that in him[206] which admits of external activity also has not been perfected.'[207] Although the text is not fully clear, it seems safe to say that it is not for the sake of the recipient that providence (i.e. 'external activity') takes place, but rather the other way round: it is for the sake of its taking place, that a (fitted) recipient must be found, since providence is necessarily an intentional activity. This seems to suggest that Socrates might not be so interested in Alcibiades' perfection for the sake of Alcibiades, but only to the extent that the latter is expedient as a receptacle for Socrates' external and overflowing activity. In that way, Socrates' or his divine analogue's 'affection' must be qualified. All the more so, since Alcibiades' or his cosmic equivalent's failure of perfection does not seem to imply anything about Socrates' complete status. After all, as we noted from the very beginning (e.g. Section 2.1.2), Socrates does not need Alcibiades in order for the former to recollect the intelligible. In other words, the lover's affection cannot but be 'disinterested'.[208]

This suggestion can be supported by another excerpt, where Proclus comments on a small phrase abstracted from Socrates' initial exchanges with Alcibiades.[209] Proclus explains why Alcibiades was 'worthy of love' («ἀξιέραστος») and suited («ἐπιτήδειος») for Socrates' care, as well as the importance of the lover's knowing the individual nature of his beloved.[210] This is, then, what Proclus notes:

> The phrase "so I persuade myself", seems to me to show clearly that the divinely-inspired lover, if he sees the beloved suited for conversion to intellect, helps him, in so far as he is able[211]; but if he finds him small-minded and ignoble and concerned with things below, he [sc. the lover] turns back to himself (εἰς ἑαυτὸν) and looks towards himself (πρὸς ἑαυτὸν) alone, taking refuge in the proverbial "I saved myself."[212] For the persuasion and self-directed activity are an indication of this knowledge (sc. τῆς ἐρωτικῆς).[213]

It is noteworthy that in both instances we are dealing with an actual beloved,[214] not a candidate one. The first case, that of Alcibiades, recapitulates what we have been seeing the non-egoist and providential divine lover doing, so we need not dwell on this. The case where the potential beloved turns out to be ignoble is more interesting in that it succinctly illustrates the nature of the lover's self-sufficiency. From this description it turns out not only that the divine lover is not in need of his beloved, but actually that he is not very much troubled about the other person and his/her final perfection either (and an analogous point would hold in the cosmic context).²¹⁵ Of course, we should not lay too much weight on the slightly surprising use of the proverbial 'I saved myself', because the lover is in any case, and regardless of the beloved's fate, already saved. We can exclude the egoistic accusation that the lover has used the beloved for the former's ascent and then stopped caring about his 'ladder': the lover did not need the beloved right from the beginning. The beloved's failure to keep pace with him – or, in the words of the previous citation, the fact that 'even if that in him which admits of external activity also has not been perfected' – does not seem to have any impact on the tranquility²¹⁶ of the lover's internal and self-directed activity.²¹⁷ This, I conclude, is indicative of what disinterested affection would mean.

Perhaps then the lover was not much interested in being providential for the sake of the beloved, but rather for the activity's sake, since providence is necessarily an intentional activity. In this case, although the beloved is not a necessary requirement for the divine lover's self-realization, he is reduced to a means for the manifestation of the lover's self-realization. Moreover, in our passage the lesser importance of this 'instrumentality' is evident in that the divine lover presumably can perfectly do alone with himself, as well. Thus, even if there were affection between the lover and his beloved (in both cases), this must have surely been disinterested, on the lover's behalf. Of course, it is natural enough to turn one's back on someone who does not or cannot follow. Nonetheless, it is a question whether we would like to posit that as an ethical ideal.²¹⁸

To conclude, it seems that Proclus' divine and divine-like entities are closer to Aristotle's non-altruistic god, who 'moves' only 'by being loved',²¹⁹ than the vocabulary of providential eros would allow us to hold. Since for Plotinus, too, the One is a final as well as efficient cause,²²⁰ we find that his position is quite close to that of Proclus in this respect.²²¹ Finally, undefiled providential eros gives us a further hint as to its relation to reversive eros: both are aspects of one entity's activity, because the upwards tendency (which makes the providence undefiled) has as a by-product providence, whether erotic or of a different sort. But as I promised above, we need to move to more abstract metaphysics in order to give a firm solution to this problem.

2.2 Locating Eros in the intelligible hierarchy

When describing the Proclean ideal lover, I noted that a description of the position of the Eros-divinity in the intelligible universe would help us in understanding the phenomenon of providential eros. The time has come. In what follows I will not only situate Eros in the Proclean hierarchy, but I will trace its presence in the lower entities that participate in it and in its ancestors. Furthermore, I will show the ontological connection of Eros with Friendship. One of the upshots of this chapter will be to show that Eros is to be found almost in every corner of Proclus' system. Along the way I will have the opportunity to make constant comparisons with Plotinus.

2.2.1 Divine Eros and its function

One of the important differentiations between Plotinus and Proclus is the complexity of the hierarchy: the Platonic Successor has a much more baroque picture of reality than the Neoplatonic founder.[222] For example, contrary to Plotinus' frugal approach, Time and Eternity are hypostatized in Proclus' system.[223] Thus, we should not be surprised if Eros possesses a distinctive position in the Proclean hierarchy, whereas in my discussion of Plotinus I proposed a 'synairetic' reading which contracted Soul (or Nous) with Eros and hence did away with a separate existence of Love. In this section I will discuss Eros' location according to the *Alcibiades Commentary*, and what this tells us about the metaphysical role that Eros plays.

To begin with we need to go back to Plato, and more specifically to the *Symposium*. Proclus makes special use of two ideas found in Diotima's teaching. The first one is that of 'mediation'. 'Everything spiritual (δαιμόνιον), you see, is in between god and mortal',[224] says the medium from Mantineia and adds that 'being in the middle of the two, they round out (συμπληροῖ) the whole and bind fast the all to all'.[225] Later I will speak more about daimons in Proclus and see that Proclean Eros is first and foremost a god. Still, its divine status does not negate its role as a mediator. Besides, we had asserted the same thing when treating Plotinus' image of divine Eros as the eye of a lover which mediates between the object seen and the image in the lover's mind. Thus, there is a loose and a strict sense in which «δαιμόνιον» can be used, and Proclus opts for the loose here. After all, Diotima speaks of 'a *great* spirit'.[226]

The second idea exploited by Proclus is found in the dialectical interchange between Socrates and Agathon. There the gadfly makes the poet admit that Eros is love *of beauty*.[227] Although for the time being I am not interested in Socrates' conclusion that Eros must be bereft of beauty, we need to keep in mind the particular connection between eros and beauty (and not e.g. justice or goodness). Applying this idea to the former point about mediation, and granting that mortals desire to become like the divine, eros must mediate between Beauty and the admirers of beauty. Moreover, its mediation forms the 'bridge', i.e. the condition that enables the latter group attain to the former.

Indeed, this is what Proclus states when turning to the 'more secret doctrines'[228] about Love:

> This god (θεὸν) one should not think to rank either among the first of the things that are or the last; he is not among the first because the object of love is beyond love, and he would not rightly be ranked among the last because what loves participates in love. One must establish him mid-way (ἐν μέσῳ) between the object of love and lovers: he must be posterior to the beautiful but precede the rest.[229]

In these few lines we have a succinct statement both of the position of Eros in the hierarchy and of its role, but we need to elaborate on these two issues. Let us start with the first one.

If Eros' position is relative to the position of the Beautiful in the hierarchy,[230] then locating the latter will help us stipulate with greater precision the location of the former. So, with relative confidence we can assert that the Beautiful is to be found at the first level of the Intelligible Triad,[231] i.e. Being. One might have the inclination to situate it lower, at the bottom of the Intelligible Triad, i.e. in Nous, based on Proclean passages like the following: 'the beautiful marks off (ἀφορίζει) the intelligent (νοερὰν) substance (for this reason intellect is an object both of love and desire, as Aristotle says; ...) ... '.[232] Elsewhere, he notes that 'the beautiful [is] *in* the intellects (ἐν νοῖς)'.[233] Nevertheless, despite this claim which expresses the presence of beauty on the Intellectual level,[234] just a few lines before Proclus states that the beautiful '[is situated] secretly among (ἐν) the first of the intelligibles (νοητῶν) and more evidently at the lower limit of that order',[235] «νοητόν» being a usual description of Being.[236] In order for beauty to characterize the Intellectual Forms, (the source of) Beauty must be prior to this immanent expression. Besides, when Proclus writes that 'the good delimits (ἀφορίζει) all divine being (οὐσίαν)',[237] regardless of whether we take «θεία οὐσία» to denote Being or the Henads,[238] this cannot mean that the ineffable Primal Unity is immanent in these posterior principles.[239] Furthermore, at another passage he stresses the superiority of Beauty by beautifully calling it 'form of forms and as blooming above all the intelligible forms'.[240]

How much does this help us to locate Eros? For one thing, Love, *qua* mediator of Beauty and lovers of beauty, cannot be found at the secret levels superior to Being. But what about the long scale of beings that reaches the level of the worldly lovers? Where exactly shall we place Eros? Proclus is explicit: Love 'is the primal [entity] dependent (ἐξηρτημένος) on beauty'.[241] Love is immediately tied to the Beautiful, like in the pictorial representations of Eros' being next to his beautiful mother, Aphrodite. It is not difficult to understand the reason for this immediate connection of the two entities. 'Etymologically, whether it is called "beautiful" (καλὸν) because it summons (καλεῖν) unto itself, or because it charms (κηλεῖν) and beguiles whatever is able to gaze upon it, it is by nature an object of love (ἐραστόν).'[242] What is lower than the beautiful falls short of it and thus desires it, irrespective of the desiring entity being placed high, in the intelligible realm or low, in the sensible world. Everywhere in this rank of desirers, desire for the beautiful is presupposed. Therefore, Proclus needs to postulate the primal Erotic desire 'before' these desirers that partake in the desire. Since this desiring continuum starts immediately after the manifestation of Beauty in the hierarchy, Proclus is compelled (a) to place Eros immediately after the Beautiful and thus (b) to make it the first desirer.[243]

More precisely, Proclus calls it a 'Monad',[244] which comes third after two other Monads: Faith (Πίστις) and Truth (Ἀλήθεια). Each of these other entities is attached to a target-entity that precedes Beauty, i.e. to the Good and the Wise, respectively. Hence, the Proclean triad 'faith-truth-eros'[245] is attached to the Phaedrean divine triad of 'beautiful, wise, good',[246] as its necessary complement.[247] One can compare the way that Eros is attached to Beauty to the relation of Faith with Goodness. Because I have dealt with this issue in a previous section (2.1.4), I will not pursue it further here. Besides, I am particularly interested in the third Monad, Eros. What we need to keep in mind, though, is that, as with the other members of these triads, Love is the natural complement and necessary accompaniment[248] of Beauty. Indeed, on these grounds one could draw a further parallel: Aristophanes' speech in the *Symposium* uses the image of a «σύμβολον» ('matching half')[249] in order to express the complementarity of the two lovers, although the analogy goes back to Empedocles.[250] It is likewise appropriate to speak of Proclean Eros as the «σύμβολον»[251] of Beauty, *qua* the latter's natural counterpart and follower. To be sure, the two are not the same level of entity, as in the case of Aristophanes' lovers, and Love does not complete the perfection of Beauty. The latter is Beautiful not because there are entities loving it, but rather the other entities love it because it is Beautiful. Still, even from this one-sided and asymmetrical point of view, the *de facto* existence of the one implies the existence of the other. The specialty in Eros' existence being totally dependent on another entity, namely Beauty, lies in the fact that Eros is not a mere intentional entity, but the hypostatization of intention itself. If in this case the subject and the activity (intention-desire) are conflated, we can define Eros only in terms of the 'external' intended object.

Now, having defined the relative position of Eros, we are confronted with another question: is it directly dependent on Beauty in terms of a transverse or a vertical series? In other words, should Eros be situated next to the Beautiful, albeit at the level of Being, or at a lower level that participates in Being? The answer is the second alternative, and in order to verify it we need to return again to the 'more secret doctrines' about love. Proclus writes that Eros 'has its primary and hidden subsistence in the intelligible intellect (νοητῷ νῷ)'.[252] A few lines below he repeats that 'speaking about the intelligible intellect (νοητοῦ νοῦ) the theologian [sc. Orpheus] mentions "dainty Love and bold Counsel (Μῆτις)," ... ; and concerning the intelligent (νοεροῦ) and unparticipated intellect "and Counsel, first begetter, and much delighting Love"'.[253] These passages show that Eros is an Intellect;[254] hence, its dependence upon the Beautiful is within a vertical rank. Thus, according to Dodds' scheme regarding propositions 108–11,[255] Eros should derive a generic characteristic from the level of Beauty, but a specific characteristic from the antecedent terms in his own stratum.[256]

Nonetheless, these quotations generate further problems, since they speak of both an intelligible and an intellective (/intelligent) intellect, which represent different levels of the Proclean hierarchy. There are various ways to remedy this problem and the easiest is to suggest, as Proclus does, that Eros exists only «κατ' αἰτίαν» in the intelligible intellect, 'for if it "leapt forth" therefrom it is causally established therein'.[257] Hence, «καθ' ὕπαρξιν», i.e. existentially, Eros is an intellective intellect. A further problem, though, is that in the usual accounts of Proclus' system Life mediates between the strata of Being and Nous. If Eros is a *nous*, can we still hold that it is directly dependent on Beauty? Indeed, at one point Proclus does mention Life in such a context, stating that 'among the intelligible (νοητοῖς) and hidden gods it [sc. Love] makes the intelligible (νοητὸν) Intellect one with the primary and hidden beauty according to a certain mode of life (ζωῆς) superior to intellection (νοήσεως)'.[258] As if the aforementioned problem were not enough, the passage also implies that Eros can exercise causation upon an entity which precedes it in the hierarchy – even if in a transverse series – namely by causing unity between intellect and the even higher Beauty. Let me tackle this last problem first. Although I will discuss eros' function shortly after, for my present purposes it suffices to invoke the distinction between «κατ' αἰτίαν» and «καθ' ὕπαρξιν» again. The erotic tendency for Beauty resides already in the intelligible intellect, but causally. This intellect's desire for Beauty not only orientates it towards the object of desire, but has also the further consequence, or 'by-product', of the generation of Eros, i.e. the manifestation of the desire itself. With this picture we come very close to a potential interpretation of Plotinus that I rejected, namely that when Heavenly Aphrodite/Soul is filled with eros for her progenitor (Nous), she also gives birth to Eros. With respect to Proclus' interpretation now, we might suggest that Eros unites his preceding intellect only in virtue of manifesting the inherent erotic tendency in this prior *nous*.[259] What is more, we can connect this answer with the discussion of the previous problem about Life. This term is also a mediator between Being and Intellect and in a way exemplifies the mediating function of Eros.[260] Again the «κατ' αἰτίαν» formula can come to our rescue. Eros manifests Life when bringing into unity different elements. Thus, strictly speaking «καθ' ὕπαρξιν» Eros is not directly dependent upon Beauty, which is on the level of Being, but only in virtue of and through the erotic feature that causally subsists in Life. On the other hand, we might want to go further than that and assert that Life exemplifies not so much a stratum of reality, as the vital force and power that links the activity of Intelligence with its object (Being), or indeed the activity itself. In that way Eros, even «καθ' ὕπαρξιν» and on the level of *nous*, can be both vertically and directly dependent upon Beauty, despite Life's mediation.

Note, though, that whether in vertical or horizontal relation to Beauty, Proclus needs to reconcile his remarks with the *Symposium*: if Eros is closely dependent on Beauty and if it is a fundamental Neoplatonic principle that procession is realized through likeness,[261] then Eros cannot lack beauty, at least to a large degree. After all, to take Agathon's side, Eros *is* a god; how could a god be ugly? A sophistic retort could be that *qua* Eros for Beauty, the former lacks the latter, but *qua* divine entity not. Another more Neoplatonic response might be that Proclus does not disagree with the *Symposium*, but refines it: from absolute lack of beauty, Proclus switches to relative absence; Eros is ugly insofar as he is not as beautiful as the Beautiful itself. Still, in absolute terms he can be called beautiful. We have already seen[262] the importance of the old 'similia similibus' idea. An entity can communicate with another due to the similarity that characterizes them. Of course, one might wonder about the proportion of the intensity of the desire. If I am not very thirsty I am not dying to drink water. After intense physical exercise under the Mediterranean sun, however, I really desire to drink. The intuition says that less affinity with the object of desire implies looser desire. Nonetheless, we should not forget that for the Neoplatonists it is the similarity between object and subject that enables them to come into 'contact'. And when two entities are closer to one another, the inferior can appreciate better the status of the higher entity. In other words, it is because I have studied the ingenious complexities of Bach's fugues that I have a greater desire to listen to them again, while a music fan not steeped in this world might not be dying to listen to *The Art of the Fugue* again. It is not accidental that I have made similar observations on the occasion of the last lines of Plotinus' erotic treatise.[263] And as with Plotinus, Proclus' aforementioned qualification of the *Symposium* presents him as a dynamic reader of Plato, a characteristic often missed by interpreters.

2.2.2 Eros as a mediator

I said before that one of the principal ideas that Neoplatonism owes to the *Symposium* is the idea of eros as mediator. This is a recurrent theme in Proclus' *Commentary*:

> What effects this bond of union (σύνδεσμον) between the inferior and the superior if not love? For this god the Oracles call "the binding (συνδετικὸν) guide of all things,"[264] ... Furthermore, love itself is "a mighty spirit," as Diotima says, in so far as everywhere it fulfils (συμπληροῖ) the mean role (τὴν μεσότητα) between the objects of love and those hastening towards them through love. The object of love holds the first position, what loves it the last, and love fills (συμπληροῖ) the middle (μέσον) between the two, uniting (συνάγων) and binding with (συνδέων) each other the desired object and what desires it.[265]

There is, however, a puzzle here. I suggested before that due to the position ascribed to Eros in the *Symposium*, love was a 'bond' by being a 'bridge' that unites gods with mortals. Still, in the Neoplatonic refinement of Eros' position, we located it immediately after the Beautiful. Even if it is a mediator, Eros is not equally distanced from its object of desire and the rest of desiring entities. The scales lean on the side of Beauty, not of the beautiful particulars. How is Eros an effective bond, then, and of what sort? One might propose that it is a mediator only between Beauty and whichever entity is directly posterior to Eros. What about the entities lower in the complex Neoplatonic hierarchy then? Do they indirectly relate to Eros by depending on the entity/-ies right after him?

These questions, like those of the previous section (2.2.1), reveal the limitations of an intellectual 'topography', i.e. the difficulty of our discursive mind to conceive intelligible structures that transcend it. Still, they also prompt us to think harder about the sense in which Eros is the bond of the universe. We need to step back, then, and reflect on the following: how can an entity desire Beauty? Since Eros is the exemplification of the desire for Beauty, posterior entities must participate in Eros in order to have this erotic appetite. In fact, this is a fundamental characteristic of Proclus' system: entities high in the hierarchy bestow their characteristic feature on the posterior entities.[266] The latter either participate directly in the originators of this feature, or indirectly by participation in entities participating in these originators and so forth. The important conclusion, though, is that before we can think or speak about the possibility of a desiring entity, we need to postulate the immediate cause of desire: as we have seen, this is not the Beautiful, the ultimate cause of erotic desire,[267] but Eros himself. Hence, we need to be careful when speaking of the 'bond' between the object and the subject of desire: prima facie it seems that within such a pair of beloved object and loving subject Eros intervenes subsequently[268] in order to enable the unity of the pair by filling and bridging the gap. Still, this is a misleading oversimplification: rather, it is the necessarily anterior existence of Eros that enables the desiring entity to be what it is in the first instance, i.e. a desirer. We can speak of a 'pair' only due to the 'intervention' of Eros, i.e. because there is a triad, or because the real primal pair is Beauty and Eros (i.e. the desire for Beauty), whereas everything else is secondary. In other words, the idea of 'mediation' is logically posterior to Love. Eros is not Eros because he is a mediator; rather, he is mediator because he is Eros. First and foremost, though, Eros is a bond because he craves *his own* union with Beauty.

Now we are better prepared to understand what Proclus means when writing that Eros 'binds together (συνδετικὸς) what is divided, and unites (συναγωγὸς) what precedes and is subsequent to it, and makes the secondary revert (ἐπιστρεπτικὸς) to the primary and elevates (ἀναγωγὸς) and perfects (τελεσιουργὸς) the less perfect'.[269] The conglomeration of so many «καί» does not denote addition of different functions. Rather, these «καί» are explicative, each adjective making more precise what the previous ones denote: Love is a 'binder' insofar as he is 'reversive', i.e. he reverts the inferiors to the superior.

And what does it actually mean to 'revert the secondary', etc.? This erotic function describes the bestowal of the erotic feature, viz. desire, as was described above.[270] But what does this act of bestowal amount to? To providence, as we have seen in previous sections (e.g. 2.1.4 and 2.1.5). It is ultimately due to providence that Eros does not 'grudgingly keep for himself' his defining characteristic, but necessarily gives an inferior image to his participants. Hence, we should not be misled by the language used when Proclus repeats that Eros reverts the secondary, etc., as if there was any downwards intentionality at play. Strictly speaking, Eros is only oriented upwards insofar as he falls short of Beauty. The downwards orientation is to be explained not in erotic terms, but in terms of providence. After all, as we have seen, to be a god, as Eros is, is to be a 'goodness', and this means to be providential,[271] and more precisely detachedly providential.[272] In other words, it is not that Eros is providential for the inferior beautiful particulars because he loves them; rather, because he loves Beauty, he is also providential towards beautiful particulars, which are fitted for the reception of the erotic desire.[273] Consequently, Eros' being a bond for what comes after him is just a by-product of his own being, which consists in striving for the Beautiful.

With the above remarks I have given another answer as to how Proclus can simultaneously and coherently entertain the idea of providential and reversive love. Now, before I finish, there is one more thing I want to clarify with respect to the function of erotic mediation: in a looser sense of the term, almost all entities in Proclus' system are mediators. Save for the First Principle, the Good, and its polar counterpart, Matter, every entity in the complex hierarchy is between two others, either in horizontal or vertical series. What then makes Eros different, viz. a mediator and a bond in the precise sense? This must be the dynamic element. Eros can be characterized as the movement towards the completion of a target or the fulfilling of an entity. Ironically then, Eros' mediation sows the seed of its own annihilation: if every posterior entity has a desire for Beauty, then this implies a desire to overpass the medium of Eros in order to get to Beauty. Proclus' universal laws governing procession and reversion do not allow this abruption of order, and the hierarchy is preserved in the end.[274] Whatever the final result, however, erotic mediation entails and implies existence within a net of dynamic relations: not a system of inert rest, but of a rest in motion or a motionless motion.[275]

So, there are two elements we have to retain from the preceding discussion: (a) that in a sense Eros is a 'universal' mediator that 'binds together' Beauty and beautiful particulars desiring Beauty; (b) that the insistence on entities that desire their fulfilment via their erotic aspiration to beauty brings us close to Plotinus' synairetic reading. Whatever the scheme of Proclean participation, at least most of the entities that are posterior to Beauty can be seen as lower instantiations of eros, in that they strive for Beauty, with the subsequent result of their self-fulfilment. These thoughts bring us back to my remarks about Plotinian Soul and Nous as being erotic with respect to the One.

To recap, I have expounded Proclus' main points about the location and function of the god Eros. Love is an Intellect that is dependent upon Beauty, which shines at the level of Being. Moreover, what actually Eros does is to implant its own characteristic, i.e. desire for beauty, to the lower entities of his rank. Thus, he becomes a mediator, as Diotima would put it, between Beauty and the lower desiring entities. Among the examinations of these matters, I have raised several particular issues, such as Proclus' affinity to Plotinus, and I have also re-addressed the way that Proclus can combine the formula of providential and reversive eros when characterizing a single entity like Eros.

2.2.3 After Eros

Now I want to address a more particular problem: not whether there are erotic entities posterior to Eros; we have seen that this is possible due to the direct or indirect participation of the former to the latter. Rather, I want to explore whether the divinity of Eros is unique in Proclus' hierarchy. In this way, I will be re-addressing the traditional problem tackled by Plotinus in his erotic treatise: whether Eros is a god or a daimon, the Plotinian solution being that the 'son', i.e. the self-fulfilment, of goddess Aphrodite is god, whereas that of the daimonic one(s) is a daimon. After all, Plotinus was trying to bring into consistency various Platonic statements about the divine or daimonic status of Eros that can be found in the *Symposium* and in the *Phaedrus*. Proclus has exactly the same concern, on the occasion, though, of the presence of both alternative statements within a single work, the *Alcibiades Major*.[276] As we will see, although Proclus has a different agenda than Plotinus, there are affinities between the two.

I asserted before that as with Plotinus, so with Proclus: despite Eros' being a proper god contra the symposiasts Socrates and Diotima, Love is a mediator, with the *Symposium*. In fact, it is exactly this divine feature that has set the example for the class of daimons. Proclus notes: 'It [sc. the erotic series] has pre-established in itself the pattern of the whole order of spirits, possessing that intermediacy among the gods that the spirits (δαίμονες) have been allotted "between" the realities of "gods and mortals."'[277] Of course, the idea of daimonic mediation should be interpreted along the lines that erotic mediation was approached earlier: daimons receive bestowals by the higher gods and 'transfer' them to inferiors such as human souls. Ultimately, the bestowing of these properties arouses the desire in these lower entities for their divine ancestors, a process that results in the self-fulfilment of the desirers.

Fair enough; but even if we do have mediating spirits[278] after Eros, can we have Love(s) after Eros? Proclus has two main points in support of the idea that we can. The first and basic one is an elaboration of the Platonic doctrine of homonymy[279] within the frame of the Proclean emanationist system. He observes that 'every intra-mundane god rules over some order of spirits, on which he immediately bestows his own power, … About (περὶ) each of the gods is an untold multitude of spirits, priding themselves on the same names (ἐπωνυμίαις) as the gods who govern them; for they rejoice in being called "Apollo" and "Zeus" and "Hermes" because they represent (ἀποτυπούμενοι) the peculiar characteristics of their own gods'.[280] Thus, in our case we can have daimons each of which can be called Eros, because they partake in the rank of god Eros and, hence, they feature the erotic identity of recalling noble natures back to Beauty, albeit in a more deficient way when compared with divine Love.

Proclus' second and ancillary point reminds us that if we can have multiple erotic daimons, there is nothing preventing us from having a vertical multiplicity of erotic gods, as well. We have seen that Eros is an Intellect; moreover, there are still levels inferior to Eros, and superior to the daimonic strata, that can be termed divine. Therefore, the entities on these levels that partake in Eros can be termed gods, too. Beyond this standard picture, though, the particular point that Proclus makes, which concerns Socrates' guardian spirit, but can be extended to our case as well, is the following:

> The (guardian) spirits of godlike souls who have chosen an intelligent and elevating life are of a certain godlike (θεῖοι) number superior to the whole class of spirits and participating primarily in the gods. For as there is spirit on the level of gods, so there is god on the level of spirits. But whereas in the former case the substance (ὕπαρξις) is divine and the analogy (ἀναλογία) spiritual, on the level of the spirits, the specific character is instead spiritual, and analogy indicates the divine likeness of the essential nature; for because of their superiority over the rest of the spirits, they often appear even as gods. Naturally, then, Socrates calls his own guardian spirit a god, because it was one of the foremost and highest spirits.[281]

So, Proclus' actual point relates not so much to the various godly strata, but to the clarification of what goes on in the strata near the borderline between godly and daimonic.

To understand what he suggests we need to have in mind a threefold classification he has drawn a bit earlier in the *Commentary*. According to this distinction there are daimons: (a) by analogy («κατ' ἀναλογίαν»), (b) by relation («κατὰ σχέσιν») and (c) substantially («κατ' οὐσίαν»).[282] A substantial daimon (c-type) is an entity properly and literally belonging to this mediating class of spirits within Proclus' hierarchy, and is defined by specific substance and activities. On the other hand, a daimon by analogy (a-type) can also be an entity which is godly in substance. Its providing for its immediately inferior entity, though, makes it analogous to the function of a substantial spirit, hence the «κατ' ἀναλογίαν» label. Now, a daimon by relation (b-type) can be an entity which lies inferior to daimons, e.g. a human soul like Socrates, and is so strongly related to its guardian spirit, that he acts and enjoys the unperturbed blessings of this participation as if he were a substantial daimon himself. With regard to the previous quotation, despite Proclus' double use of «analogy», he is interested in both a- and b-type cases. When he applies the spirit analogy to divine beings, he is reiterating his a-type case of daimon. But when he suggests that there are spirits (with regard to their substance) which have an analogy to the divine, he is characteristically misusing the terminology set out above. This second use of analogy picks up the b-type case ('by relation'). Still, in that case Proclus is not speaking about b-type daimons, but b-type gods. A b-type god must be a spirit whose affinity with the divine realm is so strong that it appears to be as a god when compared with other daimons. Thus, according to the passage, we can have (a) by analogy daimons, *qua* mediators, on the level of gods, i.e. Eros, and (b) also daimons who are found at the summit of the spiritual strata and are by relation gods, due to their close kinship e.g. with Eros.[283]

The conclusion of this discussion is that, unsurprisingly, Proclus can exploit various features of his Neoplatonic edifice in order to maintain both (a) that there is a unique and divine entity called Eros and (b) that there is a multiplicity of entities, either godly or daimonic and ultimately human, that can be called and are Eros, albeit in an inferior degree and by participation. Although this is not exactly what Plotinus did in *Enn.* III.5, he too was able to maintain both the divine and daimonic status of Eros. Plotinus, though, did not draw any direct line between the Erotes of the different levels. Eros owed his status to the entity to which he was attached. Hence, prima facie, the relation of divine and daimonic Eros was indirect. Still, according to my synairetic reading, where eros is unified with his 'mother' Aphrodite, i.e. Soul, the direct dependence can be preserved: Eros becomes the expression of Undescended Soul's and World-Soul's being, both of which are directly related to each other. As so often, Proclus' system turns out to be more baroque, although the basic Neoplatonic idea is the same.

Let me finish with another affinity between the two Neoplatonists. In Plotinus' treatise there is a discussion of the individual daimonic Erotes that are attached to individual souls, and we have already seen Proclus addressing similar issues although in different ways. According to my synairetic reading again, Plotinus' individuals would fulfil their potentials in realizing themselves as Erotes. In Proclus' case I have repeatedly noted that Eros does not have the universality that we find in Plotinus.[284] Nevertheless, in the Proclean case, too, there are entities which can be defined through their erotic function. A paradigmatic example is Socrates, who enjoys a strong bond with his daimon, which is a god by relation and participates in the god Eros.[285] True, I have noted Socrates' exceptionality in that he combines other non-erotic features, as well, exemplifying them at the best-possible degree. But insofar as he maintains a particular connection with Eros, as is implied throughout the *Commentary*, and by extending the abovementioned Proclean theory of homonymy, we could suggest that Socrates, *qua* divine lover, fulfils his existence by being (called) a daimon by relation, and more specifically, (a lesser) Eros. In the end, it seems that the initial qualification of the present section was misleading: to speak of a proper erotic entity, i.e. an entity whose function is erotic, whether it features other characteristics or not, is to speak of a lesser Eros. Moreover, to assert that there are such Proclean individuals is to come close to the aforementioned Plotinian conclusion. In other words, the example of Socrates, Plato's teacher, forms a point of contact between the two Neoplatonists: should we be surprised?

2.2.4 Before Eros

Among the 'more secret doctrines about eros' Proclus states that 'the intelligibles (νοητά) on account of their unutterable union have no need of the mediation of love; but where there exists both unification and separation (διάκρισις) of beings, there too love appears as medium'.[286] After all, there is a separation between Beauty and what desires beauty, and we have already seen that for Proclus 'the object of love is beyond love'.[287] Nevertheless, if the *beloved* object is anterior to Eros, cannot this mean that we can seek for erotic traces in the intelligible hierarchy 'prior' to the actual existence of Eros? The basic presuppositions of the Proclean system allow for a positive answer. First of all, by the already-invoked principle of similarity, according to which 'all procession is accomplished through a likeness of the secondary to the primary',[288] why should we only infer that Eros is beautiful, and not that e.g. the Beautiful is erotic, as well? As to the sense in which Beauty is erotic, we may move to the second and more important Neoplatonic principle of the modes of being. I have already referred to the 'existential' and 'by participation' modes with regard to the two previous sections (2.2.1 and 2.2.3). Now it is the time for the third, but most exalted, mode, the 'causal' one («κατ' αἰτίαν»). According to it 'we see the product as pre-existent in the producer which is its cause (for every cause comprehends [προείληφε] its effect before its emergence, having primitively that character which the latter has by derivation [δευτέρως](prop.18))'.[289] Actually, Proclus himself makes explicit reference to this principle twice regarding the generation of Eros in the *Alcibiades Commentary*. For instance, he notes that 'if it [sc. Eros] "leapt forth" therefrom it is causally (κατ' αἰτίαν) established therein [sc. ἐν τῷ νοητῷ νῷ]'.²⁹⁰ For obvious reasons I was compelled to anticipate this discussion in my first section (2.2.1), where I also tried to show how Eros' direct and vertical relation with the Beautiful can be preserved. Thus, in what follows I will exclude references to the levels of Nous and Life, but I will not stop at the Beautiful. The «κατ' αἰτίαν» mode of being of a characteristic cannot be confined solely to the ontological level immediately prior to the manifestation of this feature.²⁹¹ If gods 'have every [sc. attribute] in a unitary and supra-existential mode (ὑπερουσίως)',²⁹² and if ultimately the Good is the cause of everything – or everything «κατ' αἰτίαν» – it will be relevant to look briefly at the Good and the Henads, too. My criterion for verifying the above assumptions will be the Proclean ascription of characteristics and functions to these entities that are found in or are closely connected with Eros.

Let us start with Beauty, the object of erotic desire. As we noted earlier, Proclus connects this substantial feature of Beauty's nature with the etymology of the word «Καλόν», which 'is called "beautiful" because it summons (καλεῖν) unto itself, or because it charms (κηλεῖν) and beguiles whatever is able to gaze upon it'.²⁹³ At the risk of repeating myself, we need to remember that there are at least two conditions enabling an entity to desire Beauty: the immediate cause of erotic desire, i.e. Eros, and the ultimate cause which is the Beautiful. In the previous sections I emphasized the former cause. Now is time for the latter. When 'calling back' the entities that are fitted for such reversion, i.e. those participating in the rank which originates from Beauty, in fact the Beautiful 'reverts' (viz. ἐπιστρέφει) these entities. In other words, it is not only Eros that 'makes the secondary revert (ἐπιστρεπτικὸς) to the primary and [hence] elevates and perfects the less perfect'.²⁹⁴ It is first and foremost Beauty that supplies the presuppositions to the inferior beautiful entities in order to desire their own source. I will not stress again that this is a clear instance of (undefiled) providence, and should be disconnected from anthropomorphic conceptions and downwards intentionality. On the other hand, instead of noting that within this framework Eros seems to be downgraded into the more instrumental role of just supplying further preconditions for this 'call', I will assert that Eros himself exemplifies the actual («καθ' ὕπαρξιν») return (of himself and hence of his inferiors), whose ultimate cause («αἰτία») and source is to be found in Beauty.²⁹⁵ Besides, as we saw in the beginning of the present section, 'where there exists both unification and separation of beings, there too love appears as medium'.²⁹⁶

This might also be the case why in the still higher realm, where there is only unification of multiplicity, we can have entities that exemplify what Eros does, although without his intervention. More precisely, on the Platonic occasion of the connection between the just («δίκαιον») and the advantageous («συμφέρον»),[297] Proclus writes that

> Socrates united the just with the good via the beautiful, since this is the medium (μέσον) and bond (σύνδεσμος) of union between them. "The fairest of bonds (δεσμὸς)," says Timaeus "is that which unites as closely as possible both itself and whatever is combined with it."[298] Much more, then, than any other bond, the beautiful is itself connective (συναγωγόν) and unitive (ἑνωτικὸν) of these two, the just and the good.[299]

To call specifically the Beautiful 'medium' and 'bond' that is 'connective' of other entities amounts to repeating exactly the same ascriptions with which Proclus, following the *Symposium*, has characterized Eros earlier on in the *Commentary*.[300] Of course, I noted before that almost all entities in Proclus' system are in a way mediators. The explicit mentioning of Beauty in this regard and within this *Commentary*, though, should make us suspicious as to Proclus' motives, which must be to emphasize the bond between Beauty and Eros, and the (κατ' αἰτίαν) foreshadowing of erotic characteristics in Beauty. On the other hand, one might object that even if it is also a mediator, Beauty lacks the dynamic element I had noted above with respect to Eros. Although true, firstly, we should not forget that famously everything, including Beauty, desires the Good;[301] hence, the dynamic element is everywhere present in Proclus' system in various degrees. Secondly, to complete an earlier quotation and connect the end of this paragraph with its beginning, 'the intelligibles on account of their unutterable union have no need of the mediation of love'.[302] Where there is no gap, Beauty's pre-erotic role is enough. Consequently, I hope that the above references enable us to see how Beauty's function anticipates the actual characteristics of Eros, so that we may call the former «κατ' αἰτίαν» Eros.

By means of Beauty then, let us now ascend right to the top. Around the middle of the extant *Commentary* the Successor asserts that 'the good …, if it is lawful to speak of it in this way, proceeds down to the lowest level, and illuminates all things and conserves (σώζει) them, arranges them and turns them back (ἐπιστρέφει) to itself'.[303] Proclus is careful to remind us of the ineffability of the First Principle which is due to its absolute simplicity. Thus, the multiplicity of characteristics given should not be seen as a plurality of predicates, but as different aspects of what it is to be good from our point of view.³⁰⁴ Still, in proposition 13 of the *Elements* Proclus gives a longer list: 'It belongs to the Good to conserve (σωστικὸν) all that exists (and it is for no other reason that all things desire it [ἐφετὸν]); and … likewise that which conserves and holds together (συνεκτικὸν) the being of each several thing is unity … And … it belongs to unity to bring and keep each thing together (συναγωγόν ἐστι καὶ συνεκτικόν), … In this way, then, the state of unification (τὸ ἡνῶσθαι) is good for all things.'³⁰⁵ Combining the gist of the previous two passages we may conclude: by bestowing unity, Goodness is «συναγωγόν, συνεκτικόν» and, thus, «σωστικόν», and this amounts to making things return to it (ἐπιστρεπτικόν), i.e. desire it (ἐφετόν).³⁰⁶ Naturally, all of these attributes, which culminate in the notion of desire *qua* return of the desirers to the Good, are connected with Providence, with which I have dealt elsewhere. What I want to do now is to recall that most of the above characteristics (in this verbal form) are used by Proclus also for Eros, and more specifically for providential eros.³⁰⁷ This is not at all surprising, since I had already observed that providential eros is a species of providence. Now we have come to ascertain the same thing from a different angle: the Good is causally erotic; alternatively, Eros forms a specification of the function of the Good, since he exemplifies a particular desire (ὄρεξις), which is erotic, for an entity lower to the Good, i.e. the Beautiful. Eros implants ἔρωτα (for the Beautiful), while the Good ἔφεσιν (desire) for itself.³⁰⁸ Moreover, regarding the desire for the Beautiful (which is ἐραστόν), I noted both the ultimate and immediate cause of it. In contrast to the Καλόν, which cannot 'call' its desirers back without the mediation of Eros, the Good pre-encompasses the duality of ultimate and immediate cause of desire. It is the ultimate 'caller' and the one that implants this desire for return. Were it not for 'Faith',³⁰⁹ I would propose that the duality of Beautiful-Eros exists causally in the unity of the Good, although it is not very clear in which respects Faith is analogous to Eros. Besides, to my knowledge, nowhere in his system does Proclus hypostatize «Ἔφεσις» (desire for the Good), which, unlike Faith, is the direct analogue of Ἔρως, and this tells in favour of my suggestion that the pair of Beauty and Eros is foreshadowed solely in the Good. Finally, I need to remark that the Good causally exemplifies Eros only in its descending attitude, not the ascending one, although the latter is more basic in that it is the reason for the former. The reason for this, however, is that the Good is so fulfilled that its unity is the archetype of what Eros is eternally striving to do, i.e. to be completely united with its object of love. In this way, there is no ascending attitude in the Good, because the only way for it is self-concentration, the by-product of which is the providential attitude for everything that comes after it. Without surprise again, after convergence in the bottom, Proclus meets Plotinus at the top, too, since according to the Neoplatonic founder the Good is 'love of himself', the explanation and the by-product of this being exactly the same as just noted in the case of Proclus. A discrepancy would be that while Plotinus does not qualify, for Proclus it would be fair to say that the Good is eros (and καλόν) only κατ' αἰτίαν.

Proceeding now to a more severe discontinuity with Plotinus, we can verify my previous remarks concerning the One's causally erotic function by looking at the subsequent level of the Henads. We have descended to a level of reality which mediates between the supreme Good and Being, where the Beautiful lies and shines. Although the exact status of the Henads is still a matter of debate,[310] I will stick with the traditional interpretation according to which the Henads unfold the absolute unity of the One[311]: by being separate entities and unities they bridge the gulf between the utter simplicity of the One and the multiplicity of Being. This unfolding of the Good's unity entails the original and actual manifestation of divine characteristics («ἰδιότητες») each of which might be represented by various Henads, and all of which reappear in successive layers of reality (Henadic[312] or not).[313] There are four main groups of divine attributes each of which contains a generic and a specific form. It is in the third group that I am interested for my present purpose. It is labelled by Dodds as 'conversive causes',[314] because its two members are the 'causes of all divine reversion (ἐπιστροφῆς)'.[315] In other words, the reversive and causally erotic function of the One, which we have been talking about, is 'initially' and existentially («καθ' ὕπαρξιν», or rather super-essentially) manifested at the level of the Henads,[316] and precisely its third group.[317] If the One is causally erotic, then all the more so are the conversive causes which are closer than the One to Eros. Reversely, Love appears now more as an immediate specification of the reversive function of Henads than of the One itself. What is more, in the *Alcibiades Commentary* Proclus explicitly connects Eros and its function with the divine attributes.

The particular way he puts things, however, might be problematic: after having mentioned several of the divine characteristics, all of which fall under three of the four aforementioned groups,[318] and while waiting for the mention of our third-'conversive' group, Proclus actually mentions 'the whole order (τάξις) of love', which 'is for all beings the cause of reversion (ἐπιστροφῆς) to the divine beauty'.[319] So, is it that the 'erotic order' is identified with the conversive causes? Is it another name for them? But then, is the conversive group causally or substantially erotic? We can remedy this anomaly in various ways[320]: first of all, these theological enunciations appear quite early in the *Commentary* and do not belong to the section of the 'more secret doctrines' about love, where one should expect greater precision. After all, the specific *Commentary* itself was the first to be taught in the late Neoplatonic Curriculum and served as an introduction addressed to students not well-versed in Platonic theology. Besides the abovementioned (in Section 2.2.2) limitation of an 'intellectual topography', Proclus is not meticulous about exhaustive consistency across different works, which may have been written in different periods of his life, or even within the same work. In any case, though, it is not necessary to take that particular reference to the erotic order as interchangeable with the reversive causes, which strictly are causally erotic. A good reason for thinking this is that in the above passage Proclus does not omit to mention the end of erotic reversion, viz. the union with divine Beauty, which, as we have also seen, is situated below the Henads. Could it be that Eros reverts his posterior entities only to an entity which is below him? This untenable suggestion would lead us to many difficulties. For instance, what about the exemplification of desire in Eros? What is his own beloved object? To deny the answers I gave to these questions in the previous questions, e.g., that Eros, being an intellect is dependent on Beauty, shining at the level of Being, would unnecessarily make the edifice collapse and present Proclus as inconsistent with what he says some pages later in the *Commentary*. But in fact, if we take the mention of the «θεῶν ἰδιότητες»[321] as referring to Henads, we need not assume the same for Eros.[322] First of all, after the statement of members of the three abovementioned Henadic groups, and before stating the erotic order, Proclus adds the case of 'others [viz. other divine attributes] again in charge of some other function and preserving (σώζουσαι) the universe through the communication of themselves'.[323] This case could refer to one of the conversive causes, especially given the mention of «σωτηρία» (preservation-salvation), which we have seen explicitly connected with the reversive function of the Good. Furthermore, the whole enumeration of the divine attributes forms the first element of a comparison which is completed with the mention of Eros. Proclus writes that 'as (ὥσπερ) the individual natures (θεῶν ἰδιότητες) of different gods have revealed themselves as differing, ..., so (οὕτω) also the whole order of love is ... the cause'. He makes a comparison: referring to the functioning of the divine attributes we are assisted in understanding Eros' own function, and this is highly reasonable if, as I expounded above, a particular group of Henadic attributes anticipates the erotic order. Finally, to the justified question why Proclus did not name any of the two conversive causes then, we might retort that, apart from my initial qualifications, the Neoplatonist might have wanted to give a pre-eminence to the topic of Eros, which is one of the principal themes of the *Alcibiades* according to his *Commentary*.

To conclude: having preserved the causal erotic function of the conversive divine attributes, we have verified the causal erotic aspect of the Good, which, as an object of desire, is imitated by the causally erotic Beauty, *qua* the immediate object of love. Thus, the outcome of the present and the two previous sections is that despite Eros' specificity, we can still find him from the bottom to the top of Proclus' system. Such an erotic omnipresence has been enabled mainly through the exploitation of the three modes of being: «κατ' αἰτίαν, ὕπαρξιν and μέθεξιν». After all, Proclus had already prepared us: «Πάντα ἐν πᾶσιν, οἰκείως δὲ ἐν ἑκάστῳ».[324] Even if Plotinus' would not put things this way, I do not think that he would be disappointed with this outcome of Proclus' erotic approach.

2.2.5 Eros and friendship

Given the omnipresence of eros from top to bottom of the Proclean system, we have so far concentrated largely on the vertical dimension of that system. Yet we should not exclude the horizontal dimension. A distinctive feature of Proclus' system is that it unfolds in both these directions.[325] Again, as I have shown previously (Section 2.1.3), the horizontal dimension itself is not bereft of hierarchization, since every new term in a series manifests in a more deficient way the characteristic of its predecessor. Hence, we should be speaking about transverse rather than horizontal strata. Moreover, that was one of my main points when I was explaining the reasons why Proclus equates love (ἔρως) with friendship (φιλία). I will not repeat this discussion here, but simply recall an example that shows the interchangeability of the two: 'Since the whole order of love proceeds from the intelligible (νοητοῦ) father ("In all things," as the oracles say,[326] the father "has sown the fire-laden bond of love," in order that the whole world may be held together by the indissoluble bonds of friendship, as Plato's Timaeus says).'[327] In describing Love's effects Proclus shifts from the word «ἔρως» in line 4 to «φιλία» in l.5. Furthermore, we should expect that if there are many kinds of attractions and relationships in the present world, their cause in the intelligible realm must be much more unified. It is no surprise that Proclus wants to unify and identify friendship with eros in the intelligible.[328]

The previous passage cited makes use of the characteristic of eros-friendship as 'bond', whether this is of the world or of entities at other levels, and connected to each other either vertically or transversely. I have been talking about Eros' providential bestowal of his characteristic upon lower beings, either in vertical ranks, or transverse strata originating from the participants of the former. I proposed that in both cases, the erotic bestowal is the awakening of desire for and reversion towards the Beautiful in the lower entities that participate directly or indirectly in Eros. It might be that these lower erotic entities cannot attain to the Beautiful, which is strictly the object of Eros' desire, but each of them retains this upwards orientation. However, this image does not reveal very much about the way in which erotic entities are 'bonds'. One of the answers proposed was that each erotic entity imparts to a lower one the desire for erotic union with beauty; in its turn this process leads to the fulfilment of each desiring entity, with the subsequent result of a well-ordered and unified whole. Still, if the desired union is with beauty, what does this tell us about the friendly union with each other? Speaking of 'bonds', do we simply mean a mediating entity that implants desire (for union strictly with beauty), or that actually unites *one another*? The first answer to this is that the erotic desire does indeed give an entity a strong attachment to its immediately higher (and beautiful) entities, either vertically or transversely. The idea of an actual bond is thus preserved, because the continuum has no gaps. A second answer that completes the first is the following: the desire for Beauty leads to attachment to the beautiful object that each entity is able to reach.[329] Analogously, each entity strives for the Good, but the good they end up with is their own good, i.e. their own self-fulfilment. In any case, the erotic self-fulfilment which has been caused by an attraction to Beauty has the by-product of strong unity between adjacent beautiful entities ('the indissoluble bonds of friendship'[330]). Consequently, these entities are erotic and friendly bonds of each other, but indirectly, because the direct aim is the union with Beauty. Imagine a society which is well-ordered not because its citizens primarily respect their friends and enemies, but because everyone obeys the law, i.e. due to a common end. It is the direct relation to the law that results in good, friendly and fine-tuned relations.[331] In other words, erotic entities are actual bonds of friendship for one another, because they aspire to a common beloved object.[332]

Let us ascend now to the friendly ontology of the «καθ' ὕπαρξιν» level. There is a remarkable passage where Proclus engages with the problem of the identity of the «φίλιος» god mentioned by Socrates in *Alcibiades I* 109d7.[333] The consideration is owing to the Proclean answer to an anterior problem: 'From what source then do these benefits accrue to souls, viz. friendship and unity (φιλία καὶ ἕνωσις)?',[334] benefits exemplified in Socrates' treatment of Alcibiades. The response lies in Socrates' call to 'the god of friendship who is their common guardian to witness his words and purpose, considering, as a man of knowledge, that union (ἕνωσις) extends to all beings from god, and, as a lover (ἐρωτικὸς), from the god of friendship (φίλιος)'.[335] In other words, Proclus here verifies my first point about the interchangeability and equivalence between eros and friendship. Secondly, he reminds us of the erotic effects of the One (and the Henads), which I termed causally erotic, and to which I will return in the end of this section. Now, I want to turn to Proclus' desire to be more specific about this god of friendship, i.e. the «καθ' ὕπαρξιν» cause of friendship. While according to my treatment so far we would not hesitate to call this god Eros, Proclus' religious background confronts him with two candidates: not only (a) the well-known tradition found e.g. in the *Phaedrus* which makes Eros the god of friendship, but also (b) the tradition that speaks of Zeus as god of friendship.[336] As we might expect Proclus unites the two accounts: «κάλλιον δὲ συνάπτειν ἀμφοτέρους τοὺς λόγους· ἐν γὰρ τῷ Διῒ καὶ ὁ Ἔρως ἐστί.»[337] Here I want to recall my first discussion of the generation of Eros *qua* intellective intellect from an intelligible intellect (νοητὸς νοῦς). Proclus is actually repeating the same points put now in theological terms. He even cites the same Orphic fragment: '"Counsel is first begetter and much-delighting Love,"[338] and Love both proceeds (πρόεισι) from Zeus and co-exists (συνυπέστη) with Zeus among the intelligibles (νοητοῖς); for in the world above is "all-seeing Zeus" and "delicate Love," as Orpheus says.[339] They are therefore related to, or rather united with, each other, and each of them is concerned with friendship (φίλιος).'[340] As with my earlier discussions, Zeus' relation to Eros is understood in terms of «κατ' αἰτίαν» and «κατ' οὐσίαν» modes of being.[341] Thus, this parallel passage, occasioned by a discussion of friendship, helps us confirm the intelligible location of Eros as put forward in the first section.

But why stop at these two? Aren't there other candidates for the role of a divine Love? Why for example not include Empedocles' account? In fact, Proclus, imitating the generosity of his providential gods, can satisfy the Presocratic desires of his readers too. So, earlier in the *Commentary* he writes:

> Again, true friendship is both of the gods themselves and of the classes superior to us and has also come down as far as souls that are good; ... It is necessary to realize that although friendship is a thing to be revered and honoured, yet it requires a life that is divine (θεοπρεποῦς) and intelligent (νοερᾶς); since it [sc. φιλία] subsists primarily among the gods and intelligent (νοερᾷ) life and the intelligible (νοητῷ) god of Empedocles, whom he is accustomed to term a "sphere".[342]

This passage repeats the familiar elements and adds to the previous list of Zeus and Eros the Empedoclean candidate of the φίλιος god. Exploiting the «κατ' αἰτίαν and ὕπαρξιν» formulas we can also explain how φιλία is connected with νοερὰ life, while the god itself is also νοητός. The former corresponds to Eros on the «καθ' ὕπαρξιν» level, while the latter to Zeus' «κατ' αἰτίαν» one. The constant reference to intelligible and intellective/intelligent layers of reality once again confirms our placing of Eros in the intelligible hierarchy and verifies the ontological identification of Eros with Friendship.

Having exhausted the «καθ' ὕπαρξιν» level, let us finish with the causal mode of erotic/friendly being. At this point we should not be surprised if the One, *qua* causally erotic (super-)entity was found to be the ultimate cause of friendship as well. Indeed, Proclus makes the connection explicit:

> Friendship is between good men of serious purpose, but among villains moral character is not in evidence; the reason is that both friendship and the good have come from the One, and from a single cause (ἀφ' ἑνὸς[343] ἥκει καὶ μιᾶς αἰτίας). To each being the source of good is also the source of unity, and the source of unity is also the source of good.[344]

I have dealt with the Aristotelian (and Pythagorean) flavour of the passage[345] elsewhere.[346] Now, I only want to note how the preceding discussion has helped us to avoid attributing any inconsistency to Proclus with respect to the cause of friendship (and eros). The «κατ' αἰτίαν» formula extends up to the First Principle. If Zeus-Sphere is the immediate «κατ'αἰτίαν» erotic-friendly entity, prior to the existence of Eros, the ultimate cause of Eros/Friendship is the One, as we asserted previously. As the ideal of 'unity-unification' was connected with eros, so too it can relate to friendship.[347] Consequently, the present passage confirms that even the One is causally erotic and «φίλιον».

Notes

1 Dodds ([2]1963: xxviii); here Dodds follows Koch (1900).
2 Proclus, *In Platonis Alcibiadem i* p.56, ll.2–4 Westerink ([2]1962) (henceforth, the citation of this work will be in the following form: *In Alc.* 56,2–4, where the first number denotes the pagination of Westerink's edition, and the rest the lineation): 'So gods too love gods, the superior their inferiors providentially, and the inferior their superiors, reflexively.' (The translation used throughout, although sometimes modified, is by O'Neill (1965).)
3 See infra, Chapter 3. For presentations of Proclus' system, apart from Siorvanes (1996), see Manos (2006: 101–251) and more recently Chlup (2012). See also Terezis (2005), which consists of studies occasioned by *in Alc.* 174,1–186,18, of which Terezis gives a modern Greek translation, too (in 17–53), and Kelessidou-Galanou and Terezis (2018), based on the *Elements of Theology* (introduction, Modern Greek translation and commentary).
4 Cf. also Manos (2006: 230).

5   Hence, I disagree with Manos (2006: 230, 225).
6   These two parallels are noted by O'Neill ad loc. (n. 438, although the reference to Plotinus should rather be to III.5. §§7 and 9, not 8 and 9). O'Neill notes in the 'Preface' to his trans.-comm. (1965: vii of the Prometheus Trust's edition) that he is indebted for his Plotinian references to A. H. Armstrong.
7   The 'personal' reference of πόρος here as the son of Μήτιδος shows clearly that at least the previous mentions of πενία, πόρος and ἔρως could have been printed with their first letter as capital, so that they more clearly denote the literary/ mythological allusion. (On the other hand, the second round of mentions to come in ll.8–10, being a sort of interpretation, would rather be kept as it is.)
8   In Alc. 236,3–10.
9   For Proclus' views on these matters, the supremacy of enquiry against learning, and hence the superiority of those who 'behold the truth of themselves, … while the weaker characters need in addition both instruction and reminders from others who possess perfection', see In Alc. 176,18–177,18.
10 See ibid., 236,6–10.
11 So, as Gersh (2014: 27) informs us, it is no wonder that Ficino in his *Commentary on Plotinus' Ennead III.5: On Love* cites from Proclus' *Alcibiades Commentary* (regarding the issue of self-knowledge). Proclus, too, had composed a now lost *Commentary on the Enneads*. For some extant information, see Bidez (1937) and Westerink (1959).
12 Cf. In Alc. 336,23: «σύντονος γάρ ἐστιν ἔφεσις ὁ ἔρως», and ibid., 329,19–21: «τοῦ γὰρ αὐτοῦ ἐστιν ὁ ἔρως καὶ ἡ ἔφεσις, διαφέρει δὲ ἀλλήλων κατὰ τὴν ἄνεσιν ἢ τὴν συντονίαν τῆς ἐφέσεως».
13 Ibid., 328,15–329,1: 'Love is a powerful and intense desire for something, and everything that loves desires something it lacks.'
14 Cf. Plato, *Symposium* 199e6–200b2: « … ὁ Ἔρως ἔρως ἐστὶν οὐδενὸς ἢ τινός; – Πάνυ μὲν οὖν ἔστι. – … τὸ ἐπιθυμοῦν ἐπιθυμεῖν οὗ ἐνδεές ἐστιν, ἢ μὴ ἐπιθυμεῖν, ἐὰν μὴ ἐνδεὲς ᾖ; ἐμοὶ μὲν γὰρ θαυμαστῶς δοκεῖ, ὦ Ἀγάθων, ὡς ἀνάγκη εἶναι·». Cf. also idem, *Lysis* 221d3–e2: «ἡ ἐπιθυμία τῆς φιλίας αἰτία, καὶ τὸ ἐπιθυμοῦν φίλον ἐστὶν τούτῳ οὗ ἐπιθυμεῖ … τό γε ἐπιθυμοῦν, οὗ ἂν ἐνδεὲς ᾖ, τούτου ἐπιθυμεῖ … Τὸ δ' ἐνδεὲς ἄρα φίλον ἐκείνου οὗ ἂν ἐνδεὲς ᾖ». (Furthermore, cf. *Philebus* 34e13–35a4, although admittedly the context and the purpose of the argumentation are different; cf. the thesis 'pleasure as process (of restoration)'.)
15 Cf. also de Vogel (1963: 29, 31). NB that the formula ἔρως *προνοητικός* is said to be absent from Proclus' *Platonic Theology*, too.
16 *The Elements of Theology* (henceforth ET) 8,1: 'All appetite implies a lack of … the object craved.' (The reference's first number denotes the proposition and the second Dodds' lineation. The translation used throughout, sometimes modified, is by Dodds (1963).) Cf. his note ad loc. (Dodds 1963: 195) with cross-references to Plato, *Phil.* 20D and Aristotle, *EN* 1094a1.

17 Cf. Dodds' note on proposition 31 (1963: 218), which could have been illustrated with the Plotinian-Platonic simile of Poros and Penia.
18 In Alc. 30,14-15. Cf. ibid., 29,1: «διὰ μὲν γὰρ τῆς ἐρωτικῆς πρὸς τὸ καλὸν ἀναγόμεθα», and 129,22-4: 'The phrase "my good friend (ὠγαθὲ), speak on" makes Socrates an object of desire (ἐφετόν) to the young man, and turns the lover (ἐραστὴν) into the beloved (ἐρώμενον); for the good is the object of desire and love (ἔρως) leads lovers (ἐρῶντας) towards the good, according to the account of Diotima [cf. *Symp.* 204e-206a].' Finally, see In Alc. 53,5-6.
19 Cf. In Alc. 107,4-6: «τὸ γὰρ μὴ ἑαυτῷ ἀρκούμενον, ἀλλ' ἑτέρων ἐξηρτημένον, καὶ τούτων παντοδαπῶν καὶ ἀστάτων, οὐκ ἂν εἴη τῆς αὐτάρκους φύσεως.»
20 Cf. ET 9,18-24 with Dodds' n. ad loc. (1963: 196).
21 ET 10,4-5. Cf. Dodds' note ad loc. (1963: 197), with various references as evidence to the traditional Greek idea 'that God is not *ἐνδεής*'. Compare also Plot., *Enn.* III.8.11,9-11 and 23-5. Of course, since the One/Good transcends everything, it is also beyond self-sufficiency, 'for so it would be a principle fulfilled with goodness, not the primal Good' (ET 10,6-7; cf. Plot., V.3.17,14). See also ET 8,9-13 and 115,5: «ἀδύνατον, εἶναι τἀγαθὸν καὶ τὸ πρῶτον ἐνδεές.»
22 Cf. ibid., 9,24: «ὁμοιότερόν ἐστιν αὐτῷ τῷ ἀγαθῷ τὸ αὔταρκες» and ibid., 40,14: «τῷ δὲ ἀγαθῷ συγγενέστερον τὸ αὔταρκες». See also ibid., 28,(10-11): «Πᾶν τὸ παράγον τὰ ὅμοια πρὸς ἑαυτὸ πρὸ τῶν ἀνομοίων ὑφίστησιν.») in conjunction with ibid., 26,22 («ἀνελαττώτων ἄρα τῶν παραγόντων μενόντων, τὰ δεύτερα παράγεται ὑπ' αὐτῶν»). Consequently, with respect e.g. to the Henads, placed immediately below the One in the hierarchy, Proclus, ibid., 127,25-6 and 33-4 declares that 'all that is divine is primordially and supremely simple, and for this reason completely self-sufficient (αὐταρκέστατον) ... Being a pure excellence (prop.119), deity needs nothing extraneous (οὔτε οὖν τῶν ἄλλων δεῖται); being unitary, it is not dependent upon its own elements'. See also Dodds (1963; 268) (note on proposition 127 regarding the issue of degrees of self-sufficiency).
23 However, as Dodds (1963: 196) puts it, '"Self-sufficiency" does not exclude a timeless causal dependence on a higher principle .... This is a particular application of the general doctrine that immanence is unintelligible without transcendence.' Cf. also his note on proposition 40(ff) (Doods 1963: 223ff) on the notion of 'self-constituted' («αὐθυπόστατον»); on the notion of «αὐτοτελὴς ὑπόστασις» ('substance complete in itself') see ET 64,29-31: «τέλειαι γὰρ οὖσαι [sc. αἱ αὐτοτελεῖς ὑποστάσεις] πληροῦσι μὲν ἑαυτῶν ἐκεῖνα [sc. τὰ μετέχοντα] καὶ ἑδράζουσιν ἐν ἑαυταῖς, δέονται δὲ οὐδὲν τῶν καταδεεστέρων εἰς τὴν ὑπόστασιν τὴν ἑαυτῶν», with Dodds' note in 1963: 235: 'In Proclus its meaning [sc. of the term *αὐτοτελὴς*] seems to coincide with that of *αὐτάρκης* and *αὐθυπόστατος*.'
24 See in Alc. 103,22-104,10 revolving around the basic idea that « ... τὸ αὔταρκες πρώτως ἐν αὐτοῖς τοῖς θεοῖς ... », whereas the rest of the entities below are «κατὰ

μέθεξιν αὐτάρκη». Cf. ibid., 182,7–8 («τὸ αὔταρκες … τοῦ ἀγαθοῦ στοιχεῖόν ἐστι») and ibid., 153,10–11. Another motif of the first passage is the intimate relation between εὐδαιμονία and self-sufficiency/«ἀνενδεές» found also in 109,15–16 and 102,22. In 107,13–18 and 152,15–153,1 one can ascertain that «αὐτάρκεια … περὶ τὰ ἔνυλα … οὐκ ἔστιν». Finally, in 35,10 Socrates, being a true lover of Alcibiades, is characterized as «αὐτάρκης», contra the common lovers; see infra on the connection between Socrates–Alcibiades' relation and the ontological hierarchy. On the contrast between divine and common lovers, see also Terezis (2002: 58–68, 69).

25   See [Plato?], *Alc. I* 103a1-3: 'I was the first man to fall in love with you, son of Cleinias, and now that the others have stopped pursuing you I suppose you 're wondering why I'm the only one who hasn't given up.' Regarding the authorship of *Alcibiades I*, I am sympathetic to D. S. Hutchinson (see his Introductory note to the dialogue in Cooper (1997: 558)), pace the Neoplatonists, whose late curriculum ascribed an introductory position to the dialogue. Cf. in Alc. e.g. 1,3–5, Dillon and Gerson (2004: xiv–xv) and Dillon (1994: 391). However, Corrigan (2018: 51, n. 6), who basically disagrees with Hutchinson's stance, strikes a good balance citing bibliography that represents various views. For a background to the Platonic *Alcibiades I* and its readings in antiquity, see Johnson-Tarrant (2012), as well as Renaud-Tarrant (2015).

26   Plato, *Phaedrus* 253a6-7.

27   In Alc. 26,10–27,3: « … Εἰ τοίνυν ὁ ἐρωτικὸς τῷ ἔρωτι κάτοχός ἐστιν, ἐπιστρεπτικός τις ἂν εἴη τῶν εὖ πεφυκότων εἰς τὸ ἀγαθόν, ὥσπερ δὴ καὶ ὁ ἔρως, καὶ ἀνακλητικός.» Hence, precondition for this (erotic) reversion is a reversion to oneself (i.e. the state of self-knowledge), as it is stated in earlier lines of this passage: ibid., 26,12–13. See also Markus (2016: 25 and infra, n. 155).

28   On this and with regard to many of my following points, see relevant essays in Layne-Tarrant (2014) (e.g. the paper of M. Griffin with regard to the present section and that of J. M. Ambury for my Section 2.2.1. G. Roskam's paper deals with Neoplatonic Socratic love in general, having as his main bulk of evidence Hermias' *Commentary on the Phaedrus*, a work that might be recording Syrianus' lectures, although there are also comparisons with Proclus, too).

29   Cf. also Whittaker (1928: 243).

30   One can also suggest that Proclus is faithfully following the *Symposium*, in whose ultimate speech Alcibiades, in giving an encomium of Socrates, concludes the feast of speeches with a last praise to the god of love, as is embodied in Socrates. This is the view of Sykoutris (1949); e.g. 145*–6*. For another more emphatic and elaborate example of Proclus' strategy, see in Alc. 37,16–39,5.

31   See also Terezis (2002: 64, 66) and Baltzly (2017: 258).

32   See for instance in Alc. 63,12–67,18 (in conjunction with e.g. 28,18–29,1 and 50,22–52,2). More on this in the next part (Section 2.2.3).

33 Martijn (2010) does the same thing with nature in Proclus' system, focusing on his *Commentary on the Timaeus*.
34 For an extensive treatment see the next part (Sections 2.2.1 and 2.2.2). See also recently Chlup (2012: 242–3).
35 See also Terezis and Tsakoymaki (2014a).
36 Cf. also Terezis (2002: 56–7).
37 *Phaedrus* 253b3-c2; cf. also Armstrong (1961: 108, 117) (while in 109 he suggests the conformity of the *Phaedrus* with Diotima's account of 'procreation' in the *Symposium*) and Dillon (1994: 392). The translation of the *Phaedrus* is taken from Rowe (1988). NB ll.b7-8 of the cited passage: «οὐ φθόνῳ οὐδ' ἀνελευθέρῳ δυσμενείᾳ χρώμενοι πρὸς τὰ παιδικά», since «φθόνος» is what the Platonic Demiurge lacks. Besides, this is the basic characteristic that distinguishes the real lover from the vulgar one: the latter does not have any genuine eros, is related to what is at the bottom of reality, i.e. matter, and does not care whether in fulfilling his passion he may harm the beloved. See the contrasts drawn in in Alc. 34,11–37,15 and 49,13–50,21.
38 In Alc. 33,3–16. For the Platonic quotations see the apparatus of Westerink (1962: ad loc.).
39 Cf. also in Alc. 53,3–10: 'Where there exists both unification and separation of beings, there too love appears as medium; it binds together what is divided, unites what precedes and is subsequent to it, makes the secondary revert to the primary and elevates and perfects the less perfect. In the same way the divine lover, imitating the particular god by whom he is inspired, detaches and leads upwards those of noble nature, perfects the imperfect and causes those in need of salvation to find the mark.'
40 Ibid., 32,9–13: «Καὶ δὴ καὶ ἀνθρώπων ψυχαὶ μεταλαγχάνουσι τῆς τοιαύτης ἐπιπνοίας καὶ διὰ τὴν πρὸς τὸν θεὸν οἰκειότητα κινοῦνται περὶ τὸ καλὸν καὶ κατίασιν εἰς τὸν τῆς γενέσεως τόπον ἐπ' εὐεργεσίᾳ μὲν τῶν ἀτελεστέρων ψυχῶν, προνοίᾳ δὲ τῶν σωτηρίας δεομένων.»
41 Although Adkins (1963: e.g. 44–5, 40) stresses that the Homeric ideal of self-sufficiency survives, obscures and undermines both Plato's and Aristotle's treatment of friendship.
42 Either on his own, which is the picture illustrated in the *Symposium*, or along with his beloved, as appears in the *Phaedrus*; cf. also Armstrong (1964: 202).
43 See for instance the classic criticisms by Vlastos (1973) and Nygren (1953: *passim* and 166–81). With respect to Proclus' relation to his Platonic past, Nygren (1953: 574) notes that 'the idea of Eros has undergone a very radical transformation'.
44 Proclus is quite explicit about that; cf. in Alc. 43,7–8: «Σωκράτης μὲν γὰρ, ἅτε ἔνθεος ὢν ἐραστὴς καὶ πρὸς αὐτὸ τὸ νοητὸν κάλλος ἀναγόμενος ... » ('Socrates, as being an inspired lover and elevated to intelligible beauty itself'). It is clear from the text that Socrates' position is independent of his relation to Alcibiades.

The same holds for the Stoic sage (although he does not have access to a transcendent realm), whose love is only pedagogical. Cf. Collette-Dučić (2014: 88, 99–101), whose insightful Stoic account has many affinities with my present Neoplatonic discussions – partly due to the common precedence of Plato(nism) for both schools. Cf. also Dillon (1994: 390–1), who notes the influence that Stoic systematic treatments of love should have had upon later Platonism.

45 We should not forget that, as is repeated many times throughout the *Commentary* (see in Alc. 29,15; 98,13; 133, 17 and 20; 135,1; 137,2; 138,7; 139,6), Ἀλκιβιάδης is «ἀξιέραστος», i.e. worthy of love. From that fact we conclude that not any chance person could be the object of Socrates' providential *eros*. See also infra in Section 2.1.4.

46 The relation or structural analogy between politics and cosmology in Plato has not been ignored by contemporary scholarship, at least in recent times. See with reference to late Plato O'Meara (2017: e.g. vii–viii).

47 Hence, we could assume that the Demiurge is confronted with two instances of necessity. The (good) one is the necessity which the intelligible paradigm imposes upon the Demiurge for further instantiations of it. The second type of Necessity, as named in the *Timaeus*, is that presented by the Receptacle, whose constitution raises constraints as to the extent to which the Demiurge can instantiate the paragon-cosmos into the former. The model described here has been fundamental for the shaping of the Neoplatonic picture of reality. With respect to the second kind of necessity see especially Adamson (2011).

48 Plato, *Timaeus* 29e1-2: «Ἀγαθὸς ἦν, ἀγαθῷ δὲ οὐδεὶς περὶ οὐδενὸς οὐδέποτε ἐγγίγνεται φθόνος». Cf. Proclus' *Commentary* ad loc.: *in Timaeum* I. 359,20–365,3 (Diehl) and Dodds' note on proposition 25 of the *Elements* (in Dodds 1963: 213) with parallels in Plotinus as well. See also Baltzly (2017: 271) and Edwards (2009: 205).

49 Did not the receptacle possess the potentiality of becoming our physical cosmos, it is not clear whether the Demiurge would have acted in the way he did. Furthermore: were the Ὑποδοχή not 'disorderly moving' it is not clear that the Demiurge would have noticed its existence, and hence act, at all.

50 For another example of Proclus' moving and poetical images (although not mere metaphors) see his fragment from *De sacrificio et magia* 149,12–18 (Bidez). (I follow Kalligas (2009: 16, 31, n. 1) in deleting the 'according to the Greeks' of the title «Περὶ τῆς [καθ᾽Ἕλληνας] ἱερατικῆς τέχνης».)

51 Proclus begins this important passage by mentioning that it is his view («δοκεῖ δέ μοι»). Does this mean that here we have an instance where Proclus adds from his own view to the Neoplatonic tradition?

52 O'Neill translates the «κατὰ δύναμιν» (not 'κατὰ τὸ δυνατόν') of the Greek text as referring to the Demiurge's capacity to fashion his subject matter upon the

paradigm. Zeyl's neutral rendering (in Cooper 1997: ad loc.): 'so far as that was possible', where it is not obvious whether this is ascribed to the Demiurge or what lies beneath him, is preferable. However, Segonds (1985: 197, n. 5) sees in the background the Proclean triad «βούλησις-δύναμις-πρόνοια» (with further references in the literature) and in this sense O'Neill might be better off.

53 Cf. *Timaeus* 30a2-3.
54 Hence, we could also suggest that here Socrates is an analogue for divine providence, insofar as he allows us to come to know it. Cf. also Vasilakis (2017a: 49, n. 22).
55 Cf. *Alcibiades I* 104d2-5; cf. in Alc. 120,10-13.
56 *Timaeus* 30a4-5.
57 In Alc. 125,2-126,3. Cf. also ibid., 134,16-135,1 and Baltzly (2017: 271, 273).
58 Of course, Plato himself gives us plenty of evidence, e.g., in Socrates' introduction of the *Timaeus*, about the intimate relation between the *Timaeus* and the *Republic*, without implying that there might not be also differences between them.
59 The following is a characteristic example; in Alc. 95,14-19: 'For the lover must begin with knowledge and so end in making provision (πρόνοιαν) for the beloved; he is like the statesman, and it is abundantly clear that the latter too starts with consideration and examination, and then in this way arranges the whole constitution, manifesting the conclusions in his works.' Let me add again that actually Proclus faithfully follows the (sometimes striking) similarity of vocabulary one can find in the Platonic works in question. For instance, see *Republic* VI.506a9-b1 and VII.540a8-b1. Cf. also Baltzly (2017: 271-2).
60 Glaucon puts it succinctly when he asks in *Republic* VII.519d8-9: 'Then are we to do them [sc. the philosophers-rulers] an injustice (ἀδικήσομεν) by making them live a worse life when they could live a better one?' For the Neoplatonic answer to this challenge, see also O'Meara (2003: 73-83, esp. 76-7). O'Meara includes references to Proclus' *Alcibiades* and *Republic Commentaries*. Two further essays from Proclus' *Commentaries on Plato's Republic* which would seem relevant, XI: 'On the speech in the *Republic* that shows what the Good is' (I. 269,1-287,17) and XII: 'On the Cave in the Seventh Book of the *Republic*' (I. 287,18-296,15), are not helpful for my present purposes, because they are preoccupied solely with epistemological (and some metaphysical) questions.
61 *Republic* 520e1-2.
62 This difficulty is another evidence, I suppose, for the circularity of Plato's argumentation as Williams (1999: e.g. 258) has sharply remarked.
63 One could claim that the same holds with respect to Socrates' response to another notoriously thorny question, namely that of Cebes' in the initial pages of the *Phaedo* 61d3-5: 'How do you mean Socrates, that it is not right to do oneself violence, and yet that the philosopher will be willing to follow one who is dying?'

In other words, if philosophy is 'practice of death' («μελέτη θανάτου», ibid., 81a1-2; cf. 67e4-5), then why should we not commit suicide, something that at least the early Stoics hesitantly resorted to? Socrates' answer has not been found quite satisfactory by interpreters. What he suggests in this early stage of the dialogue is that since, according to the language of the mysteries («ἀπορρήτοις», ibid., 62b3), 'the gods are our guardians and that men are one of their possessions' (ibid., 62b7-8: «τὸ θεοὺς εἶναι ἡμῶν τοὺς ἐπιμελουμένους καὶ ἡμᾶς τοὺς ἀνθρώπους ἓν τῶν κτημάτων τοῖς θεοῖς εἶναι»), then 'one should not kill oneself before a god had indicated some necessity to do so' (62c6-7: «μὴ πρότερον αὑτὸν ἀποκτεινύναι δεῖν, πρὶν ἀνάγκην τινὰ θεὸς ἐπιπέμψῃ»), like that put to Socrates in the case of his legal (but illegitimate) conviction. Unfortunately, Proclus' *Commentary on the Phaedo* is lost, while his *Alcibiades Commentary* does not draw any parallel with that specific problem. Still, there are general references to the *Phaedo*, since the latter shares the same principal position of both the *Alcibiades* and Proclus' *Commentary*, i.e. that the man, and a fortiori the philosopher, is identified with his soul, the body being a mere tool of the former (cf. e.g. in Alc. 316,9–10; however, Corrigan (2018: 58, n. 24) offers a more complicated and inclusive story). My main point is that the true Platonic self, i.e. our intelligent soul's relation to its body, is homologous to the relation of the Demiurge with the Receptacle and the cosmos, of the philosopher-king with the state and of the lover with his beloved, or in other words of the (Neo-Platonic) teacher with his student(s). What is more, the parallel helps us to give a more complete answer to *Phaedo*'s aforementioned problem: it is exactly because the philosopher can contemplate the Forms that he does not want to cut the indeed unfortunate relation with his/her body. Cf. also what Socrates states in the *Phaedo* 67a1-b2, and Plotinus' similar position towards suicide in his small treatise devoted to that topic, *Enneads* I.9.[16]: 'On going out [sc. of the body]'. Finally, cf. Corrigan (2018: 8, 45).

64 Cited above (n. 48). Of course, as Proclus notes towards the end of the extant *Commentary*, the Just participates in the Good, the former being inferior to the latter (cf. e.g. in Alc. 319,12ff). Hence, every just instantiation is also good (but not vice versa), and, hence, the philosopher's being just is at the same time good.

65 NB that the word «ἐπιμελεῖσθαι» used in *Republic* 520a6-9 is the same with *Phaedrus* 246b6: «πᾶσα ψυχὴ παντὸς ἐπιμελεῖται τοῦ ἀψύχου», the latter being a principal Neoplatonic source of evidence for the idea that soul(s) are providential for what lies beneath them.

66 In that way we see how the *Alcibiades* provides a viable starting point for the transmutation of the existing political system into the ideal state.

67 It is true, though, that according to the Proclean interpretation the fact that the philosopher returns to the cave is a verification of his having genuinely grasped

the Forms. Therefore, he descends to the 'prison' not because he has any need of its 'prisoners', contra the vulgar lovers in relation to Alcibiades, but exactly because he is self-sufficient, and hence able to free them and elevate them to the truth, as far as possible.

68 In both *Symposium*'s and *Phaedrus*' versions.
69 What is more, I am acutely aware that the primary objective of current scholars, such as MM McCabe (see e.g. McCabe 2008) is not to draw general schemes or doctrines out of the whole Platonic corpus, but rather to engage in lively dialogues with individual works, as Plato himself urges us to do.
70 See in Alc. 85,17–92,2. The problem is that the guardian-spirit could foresee the end of this relationship; hence, why did it allow Socrates to associate with Alcibiades? After presenting some problematic solutions found in the tradition, Proclus focuses on the three following points: (a) Alcibiades did become better; (b) he will also be benefitted in another life; (c) the daimon is good like the sun, since 'he achieves his end in his activity'. (In ibid., 91,10–15 Proclus uses also the example of Laius and the oracle.) Cf. also the same three justifications in Olympiodorus, *in Alc.* 27,2–16 (Westerink) (with the commentary/notes by Griffin 2015 ad loc.; Olympiodorus' order of exposition is 'c-a-b', because he thinks 'b' is the most satisfying explanation).
71 See for instance approaches that in some respects are (unwittingly) akin to the Platonic Successor: Kraut (1973), Kraut (1992: esp. 328–9); Miller (2007: esp. 338–9, n. 28); Mahoney (1996). Even Vlastos (1973: 33), making a contrast with Aristotle's god, acknowledges the providential attitude of *Timaeus'* Demiurge, but he, contra Rist (1964: 30-1 and 28 with 1970: 165–6, despite the right qualification of de Vogel (1981: 65–6, 78, n. 28)), as well as Armstrong (1961: 110), does not seem to imagine that this could have (at least a decisively positive) bearing on Plato's views on inter-personal love.
72 Cf. also Vasilakis (2017a: 52).
73 Most notably Sheffield (2011).
74 Cf. also Proclus, in Alc. 35,11–16, with many overtones from Pausanias' speech in the *Symposium* 183e.
75 What is more, the *Lysis*, a (maieutic) dialogue 'on friendship', brings sometimes ἔρως and φιλία very close to each other in terms of connotation; see e.g. 221b7-8 and e3-4; 222a6-7. It is generally noted that ἔρως denotes a passionate desire for something contra the (calm) loving affection implied in φιλία. Cf. e.g. Aristotle, *EN* IX.10,1171a11-12: 'This is why one cannot love several people; love tends to be a sort of excess friendship, and that can only be felt towards one person.' (Every Aristotelian translation comes from Barnes (1984)). Cf. also *EN* VIII.6,1158a10-13.
76 *Phdr.* 256e3-4.

77 See ibid., 255e1. This word is used by Plato to denote the 'loving response' of the beloved; it is translated as 'backlove' by Nehamas-Woodruff (in Cooper 1997). Proclus uses it twice in in Alc. 127,5 and 7.
78 Cf. ibid., 255d8-e2: « … εἴδωλον (image of) ἔρωτος ἀντέρωτα ἔχων [sc. the beloved]·καλεῖ δὲ αὐτὸν καὶ οἴεται οὐκ ἔρωτα ἀλλὰ φιλίαν εἶναι.»
79 See also Rowe's note ad loc. (Rowe 1988: 188).
80 Cf. *Phdr.* 255b6-7; cf. also b1-2 and 253c5.
81 Cf. the following instances: In Alc. 36,15; 38,8; 40,11; 140,7; 134,12, the last one contrasting the inspired lover («ἐνθέου φίλου») with the common one («πρὸς τὸν πολὺν ἐραστήν»). Cf. also the similar case of Alcinous' *Handbook* with a short prehistory in Dillon (1994: 388 (and 392)). On the other hand, Collette-Dučić (2014: 87, 94–5) stresses that for the Stoics a friendly relation is only between equals (that is the sages), while love is the asymmetrical relation of a sage for a young boy appearing to be beautiful. (Cf. also Collette-Dučić (2014: 91ff) and regarding beauty/aesthetics in Stoicism see Celkyte (2014).) Stoic friendship is the aim and effect of Stoic love. See also the particular case of Epictetus (dissenting, perhaps, in some respects from the ancient Stoa) and Cicero in Stephens (1996: 196).
82 See also Corrigan (2017).
83 See for example in Alc. 109,3–6: 'For friends have the same relationship (λόγος) with each other; … Further, friendship is between good men of serious purpose (ἀγαθῶν καὶ σπουδαίων), but among villains moral character is not in evidence.' Cf. also ibid., 221,16–222,2: 'This is the aim of virtue as a whole, so the Pythagoreans assert and also Aristotle who rightly observed that "when all people are friends we have no need of justice," and "mine" and "thine" are annulled, but "when everyone is just we still have need of friendship" to unite us.' For references to the relevant works, see Westerink's critical apparatus ad loc. and O'Neill's nn. 416 and 417.
84 Cf. also *Phaedrus* 255b4: 'The goodwill (εὔνοια) that he experiences at close quarters from his lover amazes the beloved'; cf. Aristotle, *EN* IX.5,1167a3-4: 'Goodwill (εὔνοια) seems, then, to be a beginning (ἀρχή) of friendship' (almost identical to idem, *EE* VII.7,1241a12 and 14), and *EN* VIII.2,1155b33-4: 'goodwill when it is reciprocal being friendship'.
85 Cf. *Theaetetus* 151d1-2.
86 In Alc. 228,23–229,4.
87 In this light we should interpret the ascriptions of «φιλανθρωπία» (and «φιλάνθρωπον»: 'well-disposition towards man') to Socrates (in Alc. 312,10 and 81,3 respectively; cf. the use of Socrates' «φιλοφροσύνη»-'friendliness' ibid., 25,7 and 26,7). Being a word widely used by Christian authors, e.g. Dionysius (see infra, nn. 127 and 128 in Section 3.2), Plato uses the adjective in the superlative

(«φιλανθρωπότατος») for Eros in Aristophanes' speech in the *Symposium* 189c8-d1, and in its basic form for god Kronos in *Laws* 713d6, whereas the substantive «φιλανθρωπία» is ascribed to Socrates in *Euthyphro* 3d7. What is more, the word is included in the Academic *Definitions* 412e11-13: 'Love of humanity, or kindness; the easy-going character state of being friendly to people; the state of being helpful to people; the trait of gratefulness; memory, together with helpfulness.' Finally, let us not forget that according to the *Symposium* 212a6, the man who has ascended to Beauty becomes «θεοφιλής» ('beloved by gods'; cf. also the use of the same word in *Republic* VI.501c1, *Philebus* 39e11 and a statement from Socrates' exchange with Thrasymachus in *Rep.* I.352b1-2, according to which a just person is friend of the gods).

88 Cf. *EN* VIII.7,1158b35-1159a5: 'Gods ... surpass us most decisively in all good things ... when one party is removed to a great distance (πολὺ δὲ χωρισθέντος), as God is, the possibility of friendship ceases', since 'friendship is said to be equality'(«λέγεται γὰρ φιλότης ἰσότης»: ibid., 1157b36; cf. *EE* VII.6,1240b2 and ibid., VII.9,1241b11-13) and, hence, 'perfect friendship is the friendship of men who are good, and alike in excellence' (*EN* 1156b7-8; cf. ibid., 1160a7-8 and 1161a33-6: 'where there is nothing common to ruler and ruled there is not friendship either, since there is not justice; e.g. between craftsman and tool, soul and body, master and slave'). This Aristotelian conception is consistent with the Stagirite's view of the Unmoved Mover. On the other hand, see *EN* X.8,1179a30-1, where, due to the wise man's intellectual 'assimilation to god', it is declared that 'he, therefore, is the dearest to the gods (θεοφιλέστατος)'. In this case Aristotle uses in the superlative the very adjective used (in the positive) by Diotima/Socrates/Plato, when it is declared that the man who will have ascended to the Beautiful, presumably through the 'Theaetetan assimilation to god', will be 'beloved by the gods' (*Symp.* 212a6; cf. also *Tim.* 53d7). In what way Aristotle is near to the Neoplatonic sense will be clearer in what follows. Finally, it is worth mentioning that, the friendship theory of the *Eudemian Ethics* is interestingly different in some respects from the respective 'Nicomachean' one.

89 In Alc. 165,3 and 2. Of course, this statement should rather be read by way of analogy and to the extent that the σπουδαῖοι partake in/are assimilated to the godly realm. A good guide to understand this is the following passage from ibid., 172,4-11.

90 Ibid., 165,2-3: «κοινὰ γὰρ τὰ φίλων»; cf. O'Neill (1965: n. 327) (and Westerink's apparatus ad loc.) for references to Euripides, *Orestes* 735 and Porphyry, *De Vita Pythagorae* 33. This maxim appears quite a few times in Plato (see *Lysis* 207c10; *Rep.* 424a1-2&449c5; *Laws* 739c2 and most notably at the end of the *Phaedrus* 279c6-7. Cf. also *Gorgias* 507e5-6, although «κοινωνία» might have a more general sense there.) For Aristotle see EN VIII.9,1159b31-2, EE VII.2,1237b33

and ibid., 1238a16. Finally, see the strong resemblance of this Proclean syllogism with one by Diogenes the Cynic apud Diogenes Laertius, *Vitae Philosophorum* 37,5–7 (cf. also ibid., 72,1–3).

91 See in Alc. 232,10–234,5.

92 Cf. ibid., 233,11–12: «τῆς γὰρ φιλίας αἴτιος ὁ"Ερως». See also how Proclus introduces Empedocles' divine principle of φιλία (see B29 Diels) in in Alc. 113,13–21.

93 Ibid., 233,15. I follow Westerink in writing «Ἔρως»/'Love' with the first letter capital, since it refers to the god Eros.

94 See also the Aristotelian flavour (at least in its beginning and end) of ibid., 109,3–10.

95 In fact, one possibility is not mentioned here, i.e. that of vertical-downwards eros. One could propose that Proclus had better use the term eros – implying deficiency and strong aspiration – for an entity's upwards tension, whereas to the providential one he could have applied the sole (and 'calmer') term φιλία. Still, this is a device that Proclus does not choose to exploit, since he calls both the lover and the beloved 'friends'. What is more, it would be at odds with the usual vocabulary of the relevant texts of Plato's era, where we have seen (e.g. nn. 78 and 79) that the lover is supposed to have 'eros' for his beloved, although the latter's affection to the former was termed 'friendship'. Nonetheless, Proclus hardly uses the verb «φιλεῖν» to describe the aspiration of lower entities for the higher realm. In this respect of upwards striving eros has a prominence, although it does not exclude φιλία from its semantic scope, but it just makes it much tenser.

96 See the interweaving of the two notions early in the *Commentary*, in Alc. 26,2–5, alluding to *De Oraculis Chaldaicis* 25 (Kroll; cf. O'Neill's n. 50) and the *Timaeus* 2c1-4 and 43a2.

97 In Alc. 140,17–20. Cf. ibid., 123,8 and 12–13: 'Well then, … the agent (τὸ ποιοῦν) must surpass the patient (τοῦ πάσχοντος) in essential being.' What is more, apart from being a precondition for friendship, the hierarchical scheme still remains after the elevation of both lovers, as the following passage suggests (ibid., 116,20–117,1): 'It is never lawful for effects to escape from their causes and rise superior to the nature of the latter.' Cf. also ibid., 146,1–3 and ET 124,26–8. As to the importance of this qualifying 'some' see infra, Section 2.1.5. 'Sympatheia' is an ontological term as well, correlated with (universal) «φιλία», used by the Stoics and then by the Neoplatonists (cf. infra, n. 103 and Dodds 1963: 216).

98 Cf. *ET* 32,6–7: 'But all things are bound together by likeness (συνδεῖ δὲ πάντα ἡ ὁμοιότης).' Cf. also in Proclus' fragment from *De sacrificio et magia* 148,23–149,1. NB that Proclus does not avoid the hierarchization of even the horizontal strata. Cf. ET 110,11–12: 'For not all things are of equal worth, even though they be of the same cosmic order.' Consequently, it is more faithful to Proclus to go with

Dodds (1963: *passim*), who speaks of the horizontal strata as 'transverse'. Thus, it is perhaps easier to understand why Proclus so easily conflates *eros* with *filia* and that even a horizontal friendship of the Aristotelian ideal type cannot take place in Proclus' system.

99 Cf. ET 28,10–11 and 28–34. Cf. also ibid., 125,10–13 and 32,3–4: 'All reversion is accomplished through a likeness of the reverting terms to the goal of reversion.'
100 In Alc. 140,20–141,4. Cf. also ET 123,7–9.
101 Cf. in Alc. 28,30–2.
102 According to Proclus an entity already contains its descendants κατ' αἰτίαν (as their cause). Cf. ET 65 and in Alc. 146,1–2: 'The superior powers everywhere in a simple manner comprehend (περιειληφέναι) their inferior.' Cf. also ET 144,21 and see in the next part (Section 2.2). Hence, the higher entity 'knows' its inferior(s) in the manner appropriate to the former, not the latter. See ET 124,10–13, with numerous parallels in in Alc. (e.g. 87,12–17); cf. also ET 121,10–12. An interesting consequence, exploited by Medieval and early modern philosophers (cf. Dodds 1963: 266, n. ad loc.), is that it gives an answer (perhaps unacceptable to us) to Vlastos' objection about the individual, *qua* individual, as an object of love in Plato. Vlastos (1973: *passim*, e.g. 24, 26, 28–33) observes that what the lover admires in the beloved is not his particular beauty, but the degraded image of the Form of the Beautiful; hence, the lover does not really appreciate the particularity of the beloved, but aspires to the abstraction of the Form. But a higher entity's more abstract mode of knowing the inferior is inevitable and necessary due to their ontological difference. For the Neoplatonists the fact that the superior does not know the inferior in the mode of being of the lower is not a mark of deficiency, but denotes the superiority of the former. In this way, the Neoplatonists give their answer to *Parmenides*' 'greatest difficulty' (for which see also Trouillard 1973: 13) and can explain why the philosopher-king of the *Republic* can have knowledge, and not mere belief, of matters pertaining to the intra-mundane/political realm. However, for a view (by E. P. Butler) that ascribes (almost) the highest position to individuality in Proclus' system (cf. the Henads), see Hankey (2011: 33–6), Hankey (2009: 122 and esp. 124–5), as well as infra, in n. 310.
103 The history of «ὁμοιότης» and the 'similia similibus' theory starts already from the Presocratics (e.g. Empedocles; cf. also Dodds 1928: 141) and has been evoked by many philosophers since then; (see for instance the relevant sections of Plato's *Lysis*). Cf. also *Rep.* IV.425c2 and *Gorgias* 510b2-4 (with the note ad loc. of Dodds 1959: 344).
104 See also the Aristotelian reverberations in Alc. 230,16–231,2. In EN VIII.7,1156b7-8 Aristotle himself speaks of similarity with respect to virtue between good men: 'Perfect friendship is the friendship of men who are good, and alike in excellence (καὶ κατ' ἀρετὴν ὁμοίων).'

105 As to the aforementioned claim about humans being friends with gods, for Proclus the ascription of 'god' belongs to a wide range of entities. See infra, in the next part (e.g. Section 2.2.3).

106 This remark resembles in form Vlastos' observation about the importance of the first constituent of the *Timaeus*' formula, «εἰκὼς μῦθος» ('likely tale': *Tim.* e.g. 29d2; cf. Vlastos (1965: 382), acknowledged by Brisson (1998: 129, n. 11)).

107 Apart from «πρόνοια» another standard word is «ἐπιμέλεια». Another less commonly used word is «προμήθεια» ('forethought'; the last Greek word has the double meaning that the English 'providence' has; not only having forethought, but also *giving* in advance) met four times in in Alc., 54,12; 132,15; 159,7; 161,8 (cf. the god Prometheus/*Προ-μηθεύς*, who in the *Protagoras*' myth, e.g. 320d6, is contrasted to Ἐπι-μηθεύς, and *Rep.* IV.441e5, where the rational part of the soul is said to exercise «προμήθεια» 'on behalf (ὑπὲρ) of the whole soul').

108 Cf. the eschatological myth of *Republic* X and the allocation of types of lives to the souls, their freedom of choice being preserved.

109 That is, god Eros with *Phaedrus* 265c2-3; cf. Plot., III.5.2,2-3.

110 In Alc. 32,16-33,5.

111 Cf. Dodds (1963: e.g. 255, 270) and ET 110,11-12. See also the framework set out by Van Riel (2001).

112 For this rather general account see Dodds (1963: 257-60).

113 Cf. ET 97,9-10. See also Dodds' helpful diagram on propositions 108 and 109 (in Dodds (1963: 255)), where he shows how an entity derives its generic character horizontally/transversely, but its specific one vertically.

114 See *Phdr.* 246e4-247a4 and cf. also Baltzly (2017: 261-2). For the exegesis of the *Phaedrus* see also the useful, albeit old, *Commentary* by Theodorakopoulos (1971).

115 Cf. also Armstrong (1961: 116). The criticism of Armstrong ad loc. by McGinn (1996: 199, n. 30) seems self-contradictory when contrasted with McGinn (1996: 198), while my Section 2.2.4 will show how both authors can be right in a sense.

116 As has been already clear, for the Neoplatonists there is no actual Socratic ignorance. See also Layne (2009: *passim*). This is a mere ironical device. Socrates is a «φιλόσοφος» to the extent that he has already succeeded in achieving communion with the intelligible realm. If there is any subject that Socrates is unaware of, this is because no one can ever have knowledge of that. A good example of this is the ineffability of the supreme gods, let alone of the super-transcendent One, i.e. the field in which Neoplatonism comes closer than ever to Skepticism.

117 In Alc., 27,13-14. O'Neill translates these three 'sciences' as 'those of philosophical discussion, elicitation and love'.

118 Proclus' *Commentary* on this remarkable dialogue is now lost.

119 In Alc. 28,4–8; cf. *Tht.* 210b11-d1.
120 In Alc. 29,2–3.
121 Ibid., 28,16–17 and 19.
122 Cf. ibid., 29,9.
123 Ibid., 28,18–19; cf. 29,1 and 28,15–16.
124 Ibid., 28,17–18.
125 'τοῖς φιλοθεάμοσι τῆς ἀληθείας': ibid., 29,5; cf. *Rep.* V.475e4. Alternative rendering: 'those who love the sight of truth'.
126 In Alc. 29,4; cf. 29,1 and *Rep.* VII.532a7-b5.
127 *Phdr.* 246d8-e1.: ' … the divine which has beauty, wisdom, goodness … ' (Trans. by Nehamas-Woodruff. It must be a clerical mistake that in Rowe's translation the attribute of 'wisdom' is dropped out ad loc.) Cf. in Alc. 29,8 and ibid., 51,8–9 and 11–12. For a different approach, because of the different context, to the triad «ἀληθές-ἀγαθόν-καλόν», see Vasilakis (2009: 63–75) (and 253, which is the equivalent in the English abstract).
128 As I have already noted in my Introduction (both to the book as a whole and to Section 2; cf. also supra, n. 34), Section 2.1 lays emphasis on ethics, while Section 2.2 deals more with metaphysics. It is unavoidable that ontological issues are discussed here, too; however, for a more nuanced and precise picture one needs to refer to Section 2.2; see for instance infra, nn. 238 and 245–7. Proclus, too, in various parts of his *Commentary* changes registers; sometimes he is more elaborate, while in other places uses more loose (even misleading) language. See for example a caveat (with its remedy) noted infra, n. 155 (with n. 148 and the text of n. 149). Frequently, one gets the same impression, when comparing passages from various Proclean works on a single topic. Cf. Vasilakis (2019b: 154, n. 3). One explanation for this is the quality of the audience for whom Proclus writes each time and the context of his argumentation.
129 Apparently, this is how Socrates came to have access to truth.
130 See also in Alc. 92,8–15.
131 Ibid., 152,11–12; cf. ibid., 28,10–11. Modern Pedagogy would be very proud of seeing already in Proclus an explicit mention of the fundamental tenet of the 'individualization' of the learning process. See also the section 151,16–156,15 of the *Commentary*, e.g. in Alc. 152,1–3 and ibid., 153,3–5 (and, on the whole, the last part of Charrue 2019). This is connected with the way Raphael Woolf has accounted for the different picture of Socrates drawn by his two students, Plato and Xenophon, in Peter Adamson's podcast of the *History of Philosophy without any gaps*, episode 17, available at http://www.historyofphilosophy.net/Woolf-Socrates (accessed 1 November 2011). This part of the podcast to which this episode belongs has been published as Adamson (2014), but it does not contain the interviews.

132 Since to take this utterance as a reference to the One, as O'Neill does, is a considerable step.
133 In Alc. 28,11–15.
134 «ἀξιέραστος»; see supra, n. 45 (in Section 2.1.2) and in Alc. 58,9–59,18, as to why Alcibiades was ἀξιέραστος ('eulogy upon the character of Alcibiades').
135 Ibid., 29,13–15.
136 In the *Apology* Socrates' action claims to be of benefit to the whole city.
137 See also infra in Sections 2.2.1 and 2.2.2.
138 This point becomes clear when Proclus states that 'according, then, to the measure of suitability (ἐπιτηδειότητος) that each person possesses, so he is perfected by Socrates and elevated to the divine according to his own rank (τάξιν)' (in Alc. 29,5–7).
139 See in Alc. 152,3–8.
140 Cf. analogously the elitist attitude of Athenian Democracy.
141 We could parallel Socrates with a teacher who is not only able to adjust his teaching according to the abilities of his/her student, but he can also teach them the subject which his student favours more, whatever that is (e.g. from ethical philosophy to mathematics). Actually, all subsequent Platonists, at least the Heads of the Platonic Academy (the Platonic 'Successors') in its various phases, tried to model themselves upon the teacher-paradigm of Socrates and of his pupil, Plato. See also O'Brien-Klitenic Wear (2017).
142 In Alc. 27,15–28,1.
143 Ibid., 28,8–10. Cf. ibid., 29,16–30,4.
144 See ibid., 51,8–13.
145 For alternative translations, see Tornau (2006: 220).
146 In Alc., 51,16–52,1.
147 Cf. ibid., 52,10–13.
148 I say that it 'must' be so, because it is not explicitly mentioned by Proclus. He only connects dialectics-midwifery-erotic science with the triad of good-wise-beautiful, and the latter with faith-truth-eros. It is a logical entailment that there should hold a direct relation as well between dialectics-midwifery-erotic and faith-truth-eros. However, in the *Platonic Theology*, the 'dialectics-midwifery-erotic' triad is explicitly replaced by θεουργικὴ δύναμις-θεία φιλοσοφία-ἐρωτικὴ μανία, so that the (three) actual (triadic) correspondences are: ἀγαθόν/πίστις/θεουργικὴ δύναμις – σοφόν/ἀλήθεια/θεία φιλοσοφία – καλόν/ἔρως/ἐρωτικὴ μανία. Cf. Tornau (2006: 219 with a helpful table and n. 81 for the Proclean reference. See also supra, n. 128 and infra, nn. 149, 155 and 247).
149 Besides, '"everything," says the oracle "is governed and exists in these three"; and for this reason the gods advise the theurgists to unite themselves to god through this triad.': in Alc. 52,13–53,2; cf. *De Oraculis Chaldaicis* 26 (Kroll).

150 Cf. also Tornau (2006: 208). Tornau thinks this is one of the 'gravierende Unterschiede' between Proclus and Plotinus (where eros, as we have seen, has a universality; cf. Tornau 2006: 203, but see also infra, n. 221).

151 *Phdr.* 250b1-3 and d6-e1 (in O'Neill's trans. because) cited in in Alc. 320,11–14. Cf. ibid., 328,6–14 (the quotation from the *Phdr.* reappearing in ll.10–11).

152 One could use Aristotelian terminology and propose that the erotic ascent is 'prior to us'. True, it seems that Proclus would be happy ascribing a certain priority to eros. However, I am not certain if the analogue could survive after its exposure to closer scrutiny. The main problem is that (descending) eros is a way with which the intelligible communicates with what lies beneath. Contrariwise, in Aristotle's case what is prior to us is not prior in nature. Besides, the Stagirite does not have the elaborate Neoplatonic hierarchies (e.g. of Good, Wisdom and Beauty). Still, it is true that beauty and its correlate eros are among the things that have immediate effects in the human being, and can be exploited for an ascent towards the source of apparent beauty. Consequently, from this point of view speaking of 'erotics' as 'prior to us' has a certain merit.

153 In Alc. 29,15–16.

154 *Phdr.* 246e1-2; cf. in Alc. 29,10–11. Cf. also *Phdr.* ibid., e3-4 and in Alc., ibid., 11–12.

155 Besides, it is not clear whether the elevation from the Beautiful to Wisdom and Goodness necessarily has to be mediated by 'truth' and 'faith', respectively. However, even if the connections can be direct without their mediation, it is not certain that souls whose natural capacity was to attain to the Beautiful may be in a position to go even beyond that. Rather, it seems that this indirect elevation to the Good via the Beautiful is a realistic option for souls with a capacity to be elevated to the source of all. Of course, a further problem is that we can actually attain to such summits (actually till the intelligible level, including even the Beautiful) only via theurgy; cf. again in Alc. 52,13–53,2 (referred to supra in n. 149) and n. 148, with the invaluable explications of van den Berg (2017: esp. 232); see also Corrigan (2018: 110 regarding the fruits of prayer according to Proclus). Markus (2016: 28–9) gives a neat solution to this problem: 'Herein lies the answer to Proclus' confusion: ἐρωτική turned inward [i.e. to our soul, and esp. the beauty or in another case the "one of the soul"/ "the one in us"; cf. Tornau 2006: 208 with n.38 and 210] is a force that powers even τελεστική [art: another name for theurgy] and so becomes indistinguishable from the highest and finest telestic. Τελεστική retains its superiority only over the external manifestation of ἐρωτική.' (Markus 2016: 29 with my explications in brackets.) See also the careful and detailed analysis of Tornau (2006: 220–3, 227–8 with nn. 117–20 and 204), esp. 222: 'Für Proklos ... wäre es eine sinnlose Vorstellung, dass ein Mensch, der den Aufstieg primär durch Vermittlung des Eros sucht, dadurch "nur" bis zum

Schönen vordringen könnte und vom Guten ausgeschlossen bliebe, oder dass es einen neuplatonischen Philosophen geben könnte, der nicht zugleich Theurg und pädagogischer Erotiker wäre.'

156 As for the erotic souls, we have already given another reason why direct connection with Beautiful implies indirect communion, and hence 'kinship/intimacy' with Goodness and Wisdom: Beauty is good and wise 'by participation'. In any case, one could indirectly ascend to the Good (and descend to the Beautiful?) via Wisdom, which mediates between the two.

157 Another consequence of this, because for Proclus only Faith corresponds to «μονή» (from the triad 'immanence-procession-reversion') and the mystical union it implies, is that, according to Tornau (2006: 226), the Proclean character of the relation with the Good has stability and calmness in contrast to Plotinus' conception of the passionate and ceaseless erotic aspiration we saw in Chapter 1 (e.g. n. 181). NB that here only the ascending dimension was touched upon.

158 Cf. also Tornau (2006: 212 and 213).

159 See also Butler (2014: 211–35).

160 ET 120,31–2.

161 Ibid., 122,1–4.

162 Dodds (1963: 264); cf. Epicurus, *Principal doctrines* (94 Bailey, the Greek words cited meaning 'laborious and wearisome'). Cf. also idem, *Letter to Menoeceus* 123,2–7 (Arrighetti). NB the philological caveat noted by Vasilakis (2017b: 409, n. 6). See also Tornau (2006: 212, n. 56) for attestations of the identification of the denial of providence with atheism.

163 Proclus, *Platonic Theology* vol.I, ch.ιε´, 76,10ff (Saffrey-Westerink); cf. Dodds (1963: 265, n. 1).

164 Contra Aristotle and the Stoics. Cf. again Dodds, (1963: 265, n.1).

165 The word is used in the superlative by Proclus in describing this phenomenon; cf. in Alc. 60,7.

166 Cf. also ET proposition 142, p.124,l.33-p.126,l.1 'But whatever is divine keeps the same station (τάξιν) for ever, and is free from all relation (ἄσχετόν) to the lower and all admixture (ἄμικτον) with it (prop.98).'

167 Ibid., 122,13–17.

168 Note the dense usage of words denoting Demiurgic functions (cf. also in Alc. 54,4: «κοσμεῖν», and ibid., l.9: «κοσμητική»), while Proclus paves the way to describing the relation of Socrates and Alcibiades.

169 Following O'Neill's minor deletion of «διὰ ταῦτα» 'as a dittography'. Cf. O'Neill (1965: n. 122 ad loc.).

170 In Alc. 53,17–54,10. These thoughts are introduced on the occasion of some of the opening lines of *Alc. I* 103a,3–4: '-and also [sc. you are wondering] why, when the others pestered you with conversation, I never even spoke to you all these years'. The same idea is reiterated in a more concise form some pages later in the *Commentary*: in Alc. 60,3–11.

171　Cf. also in Alc. 199,9–11 and ET 122,2–3 and ibid., 140,5–7.
172　See also in Alc. 167,18–19 and 251,14–15. As to the strict ontological separation between superiors and inferiors, see ET 124,27–8.
173　For an introduction to the doctrine of divine attributes («θεῶν ἰδιότητες» referred to in in Alc. 30,8ff), see Dodds (1963: 278–9).
174　ET 156,32–3.
175　The topic of purity is also related with the issue of 'purificatory' virtues (cf. e.g. Plot. I.2.3,8, and the interpretation of *Phaedo* 69b8-c3), and the relevant Chaldean and Orphic rituals, which were means towards the reversion to the (undefiled) god(s), as Dodds (1963: 280) points out. He also mentions the information given by Marinus (student and biographer of Proclus; cf. *Vita Procli sive de felicitate* §18), that his master used to bathe at sea 'unshrinkingly' at least once in a month up to an advanced age. While Socrates was not a great friend of bathing or washing (see Aristophanes, *Clouds* 835–7 and idem, *Birds* 1554–5 apud Sykoutris 1949: 10, n. 2), in the beginning of the *Symposium* (174a2), i.e. a dialogue about love, he was 'just bathed' («λελουμένον», even having 'put on his fancy sandals', ibid., a3!). Cf. also Osborne (1994: 98–9, n. 60).
176　ET 156, ll.26–27 and 4–5. Divine purity is seen by Proclus as the 'specific' form of the generic 'protective' («φρουρητικόν») cause or attribute, for which see ibid., 154,1–9.
177　*Symp.* 203a1-2: 'Gods do not mix with men', hence the roots of the *Parmenides*' 'Greatest Difficulty'. I take Corrigan's suggestion to translate as 'god does not have sex with human beings' (in Corrigan 2018: xi with n. 8) to be too narrow; but see also infra, n. 193.
178　See *Symp.* 201e1ff.
179　NB that Anaxagoras' Nous was said to be «ἀμιγής» and «καθαρός», too. Cf. Anaxagoras, A 55,5 and 100,8 DK; cf. also 61,7; 56,3 and 100,11. In A56,1–2 Nous is called both «ἀπαθής» and «ἀμιγής». On the other hand, Plotinus' insistence on Eros being a 'mixture' (cf. supra, Section 1.1.5) is because he treats reversive, not providential eros. It is the inferior entities that desire their union (ἕνωσις) with the superior(s), not the other way round.
180　*Symp.* 211e1-3.
181　See ibid., 217c4ff.
182　Ibid., 219c7-d2.
183　«ἀγαθουργῷ»: cf. ET 122,20–21: 'The highest is not that which has the form of goodness (ἀγαθοειδές) but that which does good (ἀγαθουργόν)', with Dodds' thoughtful n. ad loc. (Dodds 1963: 265): 'This is not … an assertion of the superiority of πρᾶξις to θεωρία. For Neoplatonism divine πρᾶξις *is* θεωρία, or rather perhaps its incidental accompaniment (παρακολούθημα Plot.III.viii.4 …)'.
184　Here (as well as in other instances; see e.g. in Alc. 65,19), Proclus speaks directly to his student or reader. Since Plato never does that directly, while Aristotle hardly ever (see the exception e.g. of *Metaphysics* Λ.5,1071a22 and 28), this

gesture might have been a consequence of the conventions and practicalities served by the literary genre of a Commentary.

185 Again, the paradox of divine providence.
186 In Alc. 54,10–55,7.
187 The peculiarity of Socrates' divine relation to Alcibiades becomes a running theme of the *Commentary*. In the light of confirming what providence among and by the gods is, see for instance in Alc. 36,5-7.
188 O'Neill (1965: n. 123) supports my reading, since he helpfully glosses the idea of in Alc. 54,15 as Socrates' refusal 'to touch Alcibiades physically', and he refers to *Alc. I* 131c, e.g. c5-7. For *Symposium*'s episode see supra, nn. 181–2.
189 Cf. again *Alc. I* 103a3-4.
190 Of course, in the end Socrates did speak with Alcibiades, when he thought that the appropriate time («καιρός»; cf. Proclus' relevant discussion in Alc. 120,14ff) had arrived; otherwise, there would be no Dialogue at all!
191 In in Alc. 55,1–2 Proclus notes that 'the first relationship of man to man is to speak to him'.
192 Proclus pursues further the issue of Socrates' silence immediately after addressing the mythological anthropomorphisms of gods. See in Alc. 56,5–16.
193 This statement captures, I think, what Corrigan means by 'ascetic viewpoint' in Corrigan (2018: 71).
194 See *Phdr.* 244a5ff, esp. 245b1-c1. Since 'the greatest of goods come to us through madness, provided that it is bestowed by divine gift' (ibid., 244a7-8), Socrates' giving four examples of it, among which the erotic species, we could safely infer that divine *mania* is identified with divine providence by Proclus.
195 Perhaps this has a connection with what is noted by Tornau (2006: 226), although there he speaks solely in ascending terms.
196 In Alc. 48,20–21.
197 See the whole context in ibid., 48,16–49,3, where the initial puzzle is that '*all* lovers in so far as they are enthusiastic have suffered somewhat the same experience, although some are distinguished according to the superior kind of enthusiasm, others according to the inferior' (in Alc., 48,18–20). For the negative side of *mania*, relating it to ignorance («ἀμαθία»), because 'just as the madman (μαινόμενος) knows neither himself nor others, so also the doubly ignorant' (ibid., 293,15–16), see ibid., 293,14–22 (on the occasion of *Alc. I* 113c5. Etymologically, both «μανθάνω/μάθησις» and «μαίνομαι/μανία», as well as «μαντεύω-μάντις-μαντεία», stem from the same root: «μαν-»).
198 Vlastos (1973: 6) ascribes 'disinterested affection' to Aristotle, but he is not actually critical there. In Vlastos (1973: 33, n. 100) he applies it to Plato and notes it could be egoistic. Remes (2006), who treats ingeniously Plotinus' ethics, speaks of 'disinterested interest', as her title suggests (see also Remes 2006: 3, 17,

20, 22 and cf. 7). This formula can be seen as alternative, and in some contexts even preferable, to 'disinterested affection'. In the abovementioned article Remes basically explains and shows the merits of a Neoplatonic ethical theory through Plotinus' lenses. My critical approach to come is akin to some of the questionable aspects she mentions in Remes (2006: 23).

199 As will also be clear from the following analysis my critical attitude should not be identified with the thesis of Verdenius, which has some affinities with the concerns of Vlastos (1973) about lack of particularity and is presented and criticized by Armstrong (1964: 205–6).

200 Imagine the situation of a parent who satisfies every financial need her child has (e.g. for clothing, food and education), although she lives in a different place and avoids seeing, let alone hugging, it.

201 See in Alc. 85,17ff. See also supra, n. 70.

202 For example, the classic one by which the failure to receive the divine and good bestowals is attributed to the receiver's inability. See Proclus' related simile with the sun and what can share in its light in in Alc. 90,22–91,6 (with O'Neill 1965: n. 213).

203 See another classic example of Laius, father of Oedipus, and the renowned Delphic oracle, in in Alc. 91,10–15, with O'Neill (1965: n. 214).

204 The content of the angle brackets (except for 'also') is supplied in Greek by Westerink (1962); see his apparatus ad loc.

205 O'Neill accepts the reading «αὐτὸν». However, he regards it as an exceptional case of neuter with enclitic 'ν', thus, being able to refer it to «τοῦ καθήκοντος» of l.15. Cf. his justification in O'Neill (1965: n. 216*).

206 Westerink prints here «αὐτοῦ» with manuscript N(eapolitanus; see Westerink 1962: ii of his Introduction). O'Neill (1965: n. 217*) explicitly agrees and takes the clause ('which admits … activity' = «τὸ ἐνδεχόμενον αὐτοῦ») to be referring to Socrates, noting the dependence of «αὐτοῦ» upon «ἐνδεχόμενον». However, his translation would make more sense if we read with Dodds «αὐτῷ», and this is what Segonds (1985: 75b) prints ad loc. We could also rewrite as follows: 'καὶ εἰ μὴ τὸ [ἐν]δεχόμενον [αὐτοῦ] κατὰ τὴν ἐκτὸς ἐνέργειαν <αὐτοῦ> τετελείωται', deleting 'ἐν-' and transposing the «αὐτοῦ» after «ἐνέργειαν», so that the αὐτοῦ refers to Socrates' activity, whereas the 'δεχόμενον', to the recipient, i.e. Alcibiades, something which perhaps underlies Dodds' choice, too: 'even if the recipient has not been perfected in accordance with his (sc. Socrates') external activity'.

207 In Alc. 91,15–92,1.

208 In other words, Alcibiades assumes the place of a preferred 'indifferent' («ἀδιάφορον») for the Stoic-like sage Socrates. The Neoplatonic sage seems wholeheartedly sympathetic (so to speak, since his own ideal is identified with

the Stoic impassivity) to the view expressed in the Stoic archer analogy (see e.g. Cicero, *De Finibus* III. §22, with n. 12 of Annas 2001 ad loc.: 72): The preferred indifferent forms only a target so that the sage can perform a virtuous action, no matter whether the target is accomplished (e.g. the preservation of his health), the actual target lying within the virtuous activity itself. This is also the gist of Collette-Dučić (2014: 101–9 (despite 94), esp. 103–5).

209 See *Alc. I* 104e8-105a1.
210 See in Alc. 133,17ff.
211 It is not very clear to whom this qualification applies: to the lover or the beloved? It would be more natural for Proclus to be referring to the beloved's deficiency, not the lover's. However, as O'Neill's and Segonds' translations reveal, every other nominative to be found in the passage refers to Socrates with much more certainty. Hence, although somehow odd, it might seem that the present qualification applies to the subject of the other clauses, i.e. Socrates. Still, as the semicolon in l.20 makes clear, we have two parts in ll.19–22: the first dominated by «μέν», the second by «δέ», while our phrase belongs to the first one. The structure of the second part need not reflect in its detail that of the first part; besides there are not specific verbal or syntactical analogies. Thus, if only the 'μέν'-clause refers to the 'worthy of love' (ἀξιέραστος – see e.g. in Alc. 133,17), 'suited' and by no means 'ignoble' or 'small-minded' Alcibiades, who nonetheless we know that finally failed in converting to intellect, then we could still plausibly hold that the subject of «καθ ὅσον ἐστὶ δυνατός» is the 'beloved', not the lover.
212 Cf. Archilochus, frgm.6 (Diehl) with O'Neill (1965: n. 286 ad loc.). Just one page before, Proclus used the adjectives «σμικρᾶς ... καὶ ἀγεννοῦς (φύσεως»; cf. in Alc. 138,4) to describe a young man for whom Socrates 'would have long ago given up his love' (cf. *Alc. I* 104e8 and in Alc. 138,2–4), in contrast to what is proclaimed about Alcibiades in the Platonic dialogue.
213 In Alc. 139,18–140,2.
214 This is plain when reading «αὐτόν» in in Alc. 139,21, which refers to the «τὸν ἐρώμενον» of l.19. In other words, Proclus in both cases speaks about one beloved, whose instantiation however is at least dual, and hence refers to different particulars.
215 Imagine a very good teacher or lecturer who delivers talks without being interested in whether his audience understands or is benefitted by him.
216 Cf. the Hellenistic ideal of «ἀταραξία».
217 I believe, then, to have given an adequate explanation as to why my reading of Proclus in the present context is pessimistic compared to the one offered by Layne (2014: 289–90).
218 We would not do justice to Proclus if I did not mention a 'positive' side effect of disinterested affection. On the occasion of *Alc. I* 114d7, where Alcibiades calls

Socrates 'insolent' («ὑβριστὴν»), Proclus comments: 'The fact, too, that Socrates does not reject the name of "insolent" shows his lofty grandeur and contempt for everything inferior (τὸ περιφρονεῖν ἁπάντων τῶν χειρόνων)' (in Alc. 313,10–12). The case is quasi-analogous to a father who, in not paying any particular respect to his child's existence and needs, would never be accused of exercising e.g. corporal punishment upon it.

219 Cf. *Metaphysics* Λ.7,1072b3. While Moutsopoulos (1998) notes the similarities between Proclus and Aristotle in this respect with reference to the *Platonic Theology*, for Proclus' criticism of the 'Unmoved Mover' see his *Commentary on Tim.* I.267,4–12 (cited up until l.6 by Dodds 1963: 198). Cf. also Proclus' *Comm. on Parm.* 922,1–20 (as a part of exegesis of the Greatest Difficulty; lemma: *Parm.* 133b4-c1/*on Parm.* 919,24–35) and Dodds (1963: 213, n. 1).

220 Some Neoplatonists, in particular, Ammonius, son of Hermias, went that far so as to contend that, after all, that was also Aristotle's position. Cf. Verbeke (1982: 46 and n. 9) (in 242). See also the case of Simplicius' view in Corrigan (2018: 13).

221 Hence, we can apply here what Dodds says on the occasion of ET 130, i.e. that 'this doctrine, like so much else in Pr.[oclus], is but the hardening into an explicit law of what is implicit in Plotinus' (Dodds 1963: 269–70; cf. xxi pace Russi 2009: 147 apud Greig unpublished yet-b: 1, n.2 – I thank J. Greig for permission to cite this penultimate reference from his draft). This is not to say that Proclus and Plotinus do not have various differentiations and disagreements (which I have noted in the previous subchapters, as I will do in the ones to come; see for instance with regard to providence Noble-Powers 2015: 69–70 and cf. n. 6 in 53), some of which Tornau (2006: 203) terms as 'gravierende' (see also supra, n. 150, although contrast Tornau 2006: 225, n. 109). However, the problem which I have dealt with has been a more fundamental one, I would say, and verifies that despite differences there are some overarching agreements which give the sense that we deal with one (pagan) Neoplatonic school of thought (in spite of its various representatives). Cf. also Rist (1964: 215–16), Rist (1970: 168, 172), Gersh (1973: 127), McGinn (1996: 197) (although contrast 198 and 199), Esposito Buckley (1992: 40–1, 44–6, 58) and Armstrong (1961: 113); my treatment, though, can give some answers to the latter's reservations about Plotinus in Armstrong (1961: 114–15 and 117), as well as make clearer what Esposito Buckley (1992: 57) means when speaking of 'the absence of providential *care* on the part of the Plotinian One' (my italics). Finally, cf. Corrigan (2018: esp. 104, 105, 109, 110 with 106 and 124 on Iamblichus), although the way Corrigan treats his material, as well as some of his conclusions, at least in the way they are put, are not identical to mine.

222 Cf. Van Riel (2017: 73–4 with esp. n. 2 in 94).

223 This tendency goes back at least as far as Iamblichus.

224 *Symposium* 202d13-e1.

225 Ibid., 202e6-7.
226 Ibid., 202d13. This verbal formula comes up frequently in Proclus' *Commentary*; see e.g. in Alc. 64,8.
227 Cf. *Symp.* 201a9-10.
228 In Alc. 50,22–51,1: «τῶν ἀπορρητοτέρων ... λόγων». Concerning eros: for the «θεωρία περὶ τὴν λέξιν» ('consideration of style') see ibid., 25,19ff, and for the «ζήτησις τῶν πραγμάτων» ('actual investigation of the realities'; cf. the 'Addenda et Corrigenda' of O'Neill 1965: 460–1) see in Alc. 30,5ff.
229 Ibid., 51,1–6.
230 Cf. also ibid., 329,24–330,1: 'since love is immediately of beauty'; «(προσεχῶς γὰρ ὁ ἔρως κάλλους ἐστί)».
231 See Being-Life-Nous: the threefold unfolding of the Plotinian second Hypostasis.
232 In Alc. 317,22–318,1.
233 Ibid., 320,2, opting for a pedantic translation of «ἐν» instead of O'Neill's 'on the level of', although he might be thinking of Aristotle's «ἐν» in the sense of 'accidental to'.
234 Usually called: «τὸ νοερόν».
235 In Alc. 319,14–15.
236 Being precedes Intellect and thus is only «κατ' αἰτίαν» the object of thought. (I have already referred to this fundamental Neoplatonic principle, e.g. in n. 102 of Section 2.1.3, and will adduce it later as well.) Cf. also in Alc. 221,1-2: 'Since it is beautiful (καλόν), it participates in the intelligibles (νοητῶν) also – for there lies the primary beauty (κάλλος), which proceeds therefrom to all things.'
237 Ibid., 318,4–5, although now O'Neill prefers 'delimit' instead of 'mark off' for «ἀφορίζω».
238 In fact, Proclus makes a distinction between the 'foremost' good («τὸ πρώτιστον ἀγαθόν»), which is 'beyond being' and the derivative form of the 'good itself' («τὸ αὐτοαγαθόν»), which is 'the head of the many goods' and subsists in the level of Being. Cf. Corrigan (2018: 40, 44). (Hence, it is also improbable that the Henads could be here an alternative for stipulating «θεία οὐσία» in my text.)
239 So we could draw an analogy: as the ineffable One stands to 'the good itself' (at the level of Being), so does Beauty (at the level of Being) to the beauty found among Intellects.
240 In Alc. 111,14–15: «εἶδος εἰδῶν καὶ ὡς ἐπανθοῦν ἅπασι τοῖς νοητοῖς εἴδεσι».
241 Ibid., 112,1.
242 Ibid., 328,11–13.
243 A Proclean reminiscence of 'self-predication'.
244 Not a Henad. In the simple scheme of the *Elements of Theology* Dodds (1963: 209) notes that Henads are the tops of vertical series, whereas Monads the first terms of horizontal strata. The use here is a bit more complicated. Still, although not exactly Henads, Good, Wisdom and Beauty, can be viewed as initiating vertical ranks.

245 See e.g. in Alc. 51,15–16. This triad appears in the *Chaldean Oracles*, too; see Hoffmann (2000). Regarding the addition of hope to the triad, see Beierwaltes (1986: 311, n. 6) and Hoffmann (2011).
246 *Phaedrus* 246d8-e1; cf. in Alc. 29,8. For Proclus Plato has put the terms in ascending order. In terms of priority it should be the other way round, hence the verbal order in the complementary triad of Faith, etc.
247 In general cf. the relevant chapter (κε') from Proclus' *Platonic Theology* I.109,3–113,10. See two useful diagrams in Manos (2006: 64, 224 respectively) and (once more) the table in (Tornau 2006: 219, n. 81 with his aforementioned excellent analysis of the Proclean triads in Tornau 2006: 216–23).
248 Or 'by-product'/«παρακολούθημα» in more Plotinian language; cf. supra, nn. 162 and 183 in Sections 1.2.4 and 2.1.5, respectively.
249 Cf. *Symp.* 191d4 and 5.
250 Empedocles, B63 DK; I owe the reference to Sykoutris (1949: 88, n. 1), which is a comment on the aforementioned Platonic passage. Sykoutris explains the social convention after which the expression is taken.
251 I am not using the term in its 'technical' sense it acquired within the theurgical practice (and praxis), for which see van den Berg (2017: 225–6).
252 In Alc. 66,7–8.
253 Ibid., 66,11–67,3. For the quotations, see Orphica frgm.83 and 168,9 (Kern) with Westerink's apparatus. The last quotation reappears in in Alc. 233,16. By referring to Μῆτις in connection to Love, as Plato does in the *Symposium*-myth (203b3: mother of Poros), Proclus would satisfy Lacrosse (1994: 63, n. 185), who notes on the occasion of Plot's III.5.7,24–5, that Plotinus, too, could have referred to Eros' grand-mother in his exegesis of the *Symposium* (rather than simply mentioning her name once in III.5.5,3–4). Scholars have also found another mythological tradition behind the «θαυμαστός» (wondrous) god Eros of Phaedrus' speech in the *Symp.* 178a6, according to which eros is the son of Iris (who is said to be daughter of Thaumas in the *Theaetetus* 155d4, and forms) the female counterpart of Hermes *qua* messenger of the gods, although this connection does not feature (at least in the surface) of either Proclus' or Plotinus' interpretations. Cf. Chrysakopoulou (2013: 96) (based on P. Pinotti's exploitation of material from Plutarch's *Amatorius*; cf. Chrysakopoulou 2013: nn. 21 and 22).
254 See a helpful table given by d'Hoine-Martijn (2017: 323–8, esp. 324–5) (Appendix 1), where he puts together a description of the hierarchies of: Proclus, the Chaldean Oracles and the Orphic Rhapsodies among else. As is noted by Brisson (2017: 215), Φάνης (in the third or fourth Orphic rank/third in the intelligible realm *qua* Intelligible-Intellect) is also known as Eros. See also the remarks of Quispel (1979: 196–201).
255 Dodds (1963: 255).
256 A characteristic that ultimately derives from the Monad, i.e. the Unparticipated first entity of a transverse series. Compare supra, n. 244.

257 In Alc. 66,8–9. For the quotation cf. *De Orac. Chald.* 25 (Kroll), again with Westerink (1962: ad loc.).

258 In Alc. 64,14–16 (although O'Neill renders «νοήσεως» as 'intellectual perception'); in the next few lines (64,16–65,1) Proclus continues thus: '(and therefore the Greek theologian terms such love blind: "Cherishing in his heart blind swift Love") … '. See also O'Neill (1965: n. 145 ad loc.).

259 It might be for this reason that Proclus in the *Platonic Theology* VI.98,17–20 states: «Ἡ δὲ Ἀφροδίτη τῆς δι' ὅλων διηκούσης ἐρωτικῆς ἐπιπνοίας ἐστὶν αἰτία πρωτουργός, καὶ πρὸς τὸ καλὸν οἰκειοῖ τὰς ἀναγομένας ὑφ' ἑαυτῆς ζωάς.» One could expect Proclus to identify the goddess of Beauty with the Beautiful itself, but this is not what he opts to do. Rather, Aphrodite is cause of the erotic inspiration (as intelligible *nous*) that unites the posterior entities with the Beautiful, which is even higher than Aphrodite. For the place of Aphrodite in Proclus' system, see Lankila (2009). In the Hymn Proclus devotes to her, she is called «ἐρωτοτόκος» (Love-bearer). Cf. *Hymns* 2.13 (Vogt) and Lankila (2009: 23 and n. 6). See also supra, n. 12 in Section 1.1.2.

260 Cf. also Segonds (1985: 156, n. 2) (ad prim. loc. cit.).

261 See supra, nn. 98, 99 and 103 in Section 2.1.3 for references and analysis.

262 In Section 2.1.3, n. 103.

263 See infra, Section 1.1.3, e.g. in n. 57.

264 See O'Neill (1965: n. 142 ad loc.).

265 In Alc. 64,3–6 and 8–13.

266 See for the erotic case e.g. ibid., 30,14ff.

267 Cf. e.g. ibid., 31,1. A desire must be desire *for* something. See supra in 2.2.1 (e.g. n. 227).

268 The language used does not indicate temporal, but ontological relations.

269 In Alc. 53,4–7 (with the addition of some 'and' lost in O'Neill's translation).

270 See also Manos (2006: 231 with n. 60 (and n. 57 in 230)).

271 See e.g. ET proposition 120 and supra, Section 2.1.5.

272 See also in Alc. 31,10–12: 'Let us perceive its [sc. the love-series'] … hidden summit ineffably established among the very first orders of the gods and united to the most primary intelligible beauty apart (χωριστῶς) from all beings.'

273 Or 'providentially erotic towards beautiful particulars'. Eros in the downwards sense denotes only its connection with and direction to instantiations of beauty; not that it falls short of this beauty.

274 See also the combination of erotic characteristics with other divine properties (in Alc. 30,8ff).

275 See of course Gersh (1973), who devotes an Appendix (I: 123–7) to eros in order to connect it with the concept of activity as expounded in the main body of his study. His succinct and enlightening remarks would be still clearer, I believe, if

he had stressed eros' particular connection to Beauty, as shown in my discussion, and had exploited the Proclean passage he cites in Gersh (1973: 126). This would also give another dimension to his answer to the issue of eros' absence from other Proclean writings, as was noted by de Vogel (1963: 29, 31; 1981: 71) (while I do not agree with many of the distinctions she makes in de Vogel 1981: 72).

276 See *Alcibiades I* 103a5 «δαιμόνιον ἐναντίωμα»; 105d5, 105e5 and 124c8: «θεός». Proclus formulates this problem explicitly in in Alc. 46,9–12 and 78,10–17, although the specific reference is to Socrates' guardian-spirit.

277 In Alc. 31,5–8 (with O'Neill's 'Corrigenda' in 1965: 464); cf. in Alc. 67,12–13 and *Symp.* 202e1. Hence, the reason why Proclus calls Socrates both a daimonic and an erotic person; see in Alc. 63,12–64,4 and 67,9–18, esp. 63,13 and 67,16.

278 As Plotinus devotes a discussion on daimonology in III.5.6, so too Proclus, although the latter's scheme is much more baroque than Plotinus'. See, for example, the sixfold classification given in in Alc. 71,8–72,14. I am not going to touch this general issue though. Let the reader interested in this subject be sufficed with the following references: 'About the spirits in themselves [: in Alc. 68,4–70,15], further about those that have become our common guardians [: ibid., 71,1–78,6], and thirdly about the spirit of Socrates [: ibid., 78,7–83,16].' (This outline is given in ibid., 67,19–68,1.) Within this stretch of text Proclus refers to Plotinus, critically or not. Further relevant sections from the *Alcibiades Commentary* are: 40,15–42,4; 63,12–64,4 and 67,9–18; 114,1–13; 158,3–159,10; 198,12–199,19; 281,15–282,9.

279 See *Phaedo* 78d1–e5 and 102b1–2.

280 In Alc. 68,16–69,3.

281 Ibid., 79,3–12; see also ll.1–3 and 12–14. Cf. ibid., 158,3–159,10, esp. 158,3–17.

282 See ibid., 73,18–75,1. The distinction appears within the section on guardian-spirits. Cf. also the same classification in Olympiodorus, *in Alc.* 15,6–8(ff) with nn. 133–5 ad loc. by Griffin (2015: 180–1).

283 See also Proclus, in Alc. 158,3–17.

284 See supra (e.g. Section 2.2.1) on Eros' particular attachment to Beauty.

285 See also references in previous notes 261 and 262; e.g. in Alc. 158,20–159,10.

286 In Alc. 53,2–4. Cf. ET 38,22–3, where Proclus notes that if mediation is needed in procession, it will be needed in reversion as well.

287 In Alc. 51,3. See supra, e.g. nn. 229 and 230 in Section 2.2.1.

288 ET 29,3–4.

289 Ibid., 65,15–17. This proposition should be examined in conjunction with the famous proposition 103, which states that 'all things are in all things, but in each according to its proper nature'. Cf. also ibid., 56,(4–6) and proposition 118 (regarding the Henads; see infra).

290 In Alc. 66,8–9. Cf. also ibid., 51,13–14.

291 See also ET propositions 56 and 57.

292 Ibid., 118,7. Cf. also ibid., 158,23. (The allusion is to Henads.)
293 In Alc. 328,12–13. For cross-references to Greek literature that mention either etymologies, starting with *Cratylus* 416b6-d11, see Westerink's apparatus ad loc. and Segonds (1986: 454, nn. 2 and 3 ad loc.). To these add Chrysippus, *Fragmenta Moralia* (III.) 208,6 (Arnim; apud Stobaeus, *Ecl.* II,105 Wachsmuth).
294 In Alc. 53,6–7.
295 Thus Beauty is both providentially and causally erotic.
296 In Alc. ll.3–4.
297 Proclus' lemma is from *Alc. I* 115a1-10.
298 *Tim.* 31c1-3.
299 In Alc. 322,12–17. Cf. also ibid., 318,9 and 320,6–7.
300 See e.g. ibid., 53,4–5; 64,3–6 and 9–12; 67,12–13 and supra (e.g. Section 2.2.2).
301 Cf. e.g. ET 8,31; 12,18; 113,10–12.
302 In Alc. 53,2–3.
303 Ibid., 181,11–13.
304 Compare what I suggested above about the plurality of characteristics ascribed to Eros. The same can be said here.
305 ET 13,26–9 and 32–4.
306 Cf. also in Alc. 317,5: «ἡ τοῦ ἀγαθοῦ ἔφεσις σωστικὴ τῶν ἐφιεμένων ἐστίν.»
307 Apart from passages quoted above, see also ibid., 55,13–14: 'Such love is provident and preservative (σωστικὸς) of the beloved, able to perfect (τελειωτικὸς) and maintain (συνεκτικός) them.'
308 Towards the end of the extant *Commentary* Proclus speaks of the Good as both «ἐραστόν» and «ἐφετόν», and he notes that 'love is an intense desire' (in Alc. 336,23; cf. ibid., 329,17–24 and 328,14–329,2). The main reason for this, however, is that on the level of soul the good, the beautiful and the just are interchangeable in contrast to the divine hierarchy (see ibid., 330,2–14.). Because my interest in this section is in what comes before god Eros I am not dealing with this issue at all.
309 See supra, Section 2.1.4.
310 See, for instance, Van Riel (2017), where he makes a persuasive case for the Henads being immanent characteristics of gods at the level of Being and henceforth. On the other hand, Butler argues that Henads are something like modalities of the One, in other words that 'there really is no "One," there are only Ones, that is, the henads'. Cf. Butler (2014: 45), with the precaution though of 47–8. (Cf. also supra, n. 102.)
311 See also the entries in Vasilakis (2019b: 158, n. 24).
312 A difficult point to understand, indeed. See Dodds (1963: 278, notes on propositions 151–9).
313 This procedure involves also 'interweaving' (συμπλοκή) of characteristics. See an example with particular reference to eros within the triad faith-truth-eros in in Alc. 52,2–10.

314 Dodds (1963: 278). Alternatively: 'reversive causes'.
315 ET 153,34. For the difference between the general cause, 'perfective' («τελεσιουργόν»), and the specific one, 'elevative' («ἀναγωγόν»), see ibid., 158,25–9: the elevative reverts things only to their superior principles, and hence Eros must be connected primarily with it. In fact, Proclus makes the Ἔρωτες responsible for «πόθων ἀναγώγια κέντρα» in his second *Hymn* ll.3 and 5; cf. also Dodds (1963: 281, notes on proposition 158).
316 See also ET 158,23.
317 Cf. also ibid., 144,24–7.
318 See in Alc. 30,8–14.
319 Ibid., ll.14–15.
320 According to the brief exposition of Riggs (2009: 83–5, esp. 84), this is far from an anomaly. However, my treatment so far can allow for agreement with what he focuses on. See also Riggs (2010: 100ff) for a detailed analysis which is based on Butler's understanding of Henadology (for which see supra, nn. 102 and 310).
321 In Alc. 30,8.
322 Actually, with Van Riel's interpretation it would not be a problem if the divine attributes were not positioned at the level of the Henads, and in this way Eros could have been practically identified with them. However, I do not want to complicate the picture so much. (See also supra, nn. 310 and 311.) Let us bear in mind the limitations of our human perspective noted above.
323 In Alc. 30, 12–14.
324 ET 103,13.
325 Another characteristic that must be traced back to Iamblichus.
326 Cf. *De Oraculis Chaldaicis* 25 (Kroll); cf. O'Neill (1965: n. 50 ad loc.).
327 In Alc. 26,2–5. Cf. *Tim.* 32c1-4 and 43a2. Another characteristic instance is in Alc. 33,8–11.
328 The 'inspired humans' of this world, like Socrates, preserve this unity.
329 Remember the Platonic qualification 'as far as possible' (κατὰ τὸ δυνατόν).
330 In Alc. 26,4–5; cf. supra, n. 327 (and n. 38 in Section 2.1.2).
331 As in Plato's ideal *Republic*.
332 The reason I put the clarification here is that the discussion of friendship as a bond between two entities reminds us of the tension of how to combine reversion with providence for the reversion of the others.
333 Cf. in Alc. 231,14.
334 Ibid., 233,2–3.
335 Ibid., ll.4–7.
336 See ibid., 7–14. Segonds (1986: 415, n. 3 ad loc.) indicates that this b-tradition is derived mainly from Platonic texts.
337 In Alc. 233,14–15: 'But it is better to combine both accounts, for love is contained within Zeus.'
338 Cf. supra, n. 253 in Section 2.2.1.

339 See Westerink's apparatus ad loc. for references.
340 In Alc. 233,16–234,2.
341 That is, Zeus is κατ'αἰτίαν Eros. I do not have the space to get into details about the entity represented by Zeus in Proclus' hierarchy. See also the treatment by Kirk-Raven-Schofield (1983: 62) of a passage in Proclus, *in Tim.* II.54,28–55,2 (Diehl), which reports the view of Φερεκύδης, and mentions Eros, Zeus, friendship and union, i.e. the principal notions of our passages. Another god who would be worth examining in conjunction is Hermes, who was ψυχαγωγός, like eros, and like Socrates according to Aristophanes, *Aves* 1555. For references to Hermes in in Alc, see 195,4–196,18; 187,19–188,6 (with O'Neill 1965: n. 359 ad loc.); 258,2 (with n. 475 in 338); 105,2 (and n. 229).
342 In Alc. 113,13–15 and 17–21; cf. Empedocles B29 (Diels) with the references in Segonds (1985: 94, n. 1 ad loc.).
343 Segonds ad loc. agrees in taking this as a reference to the One. See also the more obvious case in Alc. 38,6(ff).
344 Ibid., 109,6–8; see also ibid., ll.3–5 and the corollary in ll.8–10 which concerns Alcibiades.
345 Cf. also ibid., 221,16–222,2.
346 See supra, n. 83 in Section 2.1.3.
347 Cf. also in Alc. 274,21–4. Plotinus, V.1.9,6 connects the One with Empedocles' φιλία (to which he also refers in III.2.2.4 and IV.4.40,6; see also the analogical use for Intellect in VI.7.14,20).

3

Dionysius and the *Divine Names*

As one of the first representatives of a major, albeit old, movement in Dionysian scholarship, Koch supported his view that Dionysius[1] is more or less a plagiarizer of Proclus with a meticulous examination of parallel passages from the two authors.[2] One of them concerns love. It is cited for the same reason by Dodds and was used in the introduction of my chapter on Proclus[3]:

> So the Beautiful and the Good is desired and loved and beloved by everything; and because of it and for its sake the subordinate love the superior reversively, and the entities of the same rank [love] their peers in communion, and the superior [love] the inferior providentially, and each of these [love] themselves[4] summarily[5] ...[6]

In the following sections I will attempt to address all the issues raised in this passage, i.e. I will show in what way Dionysius' system is erotic. During this voyage into Dionysius' ontology of Eros I will locate Love in the world-picture of Dionysius and also define its function, as I did in Proclus' case. Thus, I will have the opportunity to make ample comparisons with Proclus' system but also with Plotinus. Finally, I will examine some consequences of Dionysius' erotic approach within his Christian/non-Neoplatonic framework, offering some glimpses of Dionysius' Eastern reception. In my treatment I will be focusing on the *Divine Names*, because this work devotes a specific section[7] to the revealed name of God as Eros.[8]

I will first give a synopsis of the main points of my following presentation of Dionysius. There are four important stages in Dionysius' treatment. These are the harmonious effects of eros, the archetype of eros as descending power, eros as ecstasy and eros as a circular force. Each step forms an explanation of the one before it and offers a refinement of Dionysian theory. As will be seen, though, the central claim pertains to the third step.

The unifying effects of eros should not be new to a reader of Neoplatonism. We have seen that the mutual love and friendship of the entities in the cosmos make it a harmonious, beautiful and functional whole. It is noteworthy that when Dionysius discusses these relationships he does not omit to mention the love between entities of the same rank, which is an additional possibility to the instances of downwards and upwards eros, familiar to us from Proclus.[9] The reason for this loving synthesis must be traced back to (the) Go(o)d, the efficient as well as final cause of the universe, who imbues love into His creating overflow. I will come back to these puzzling enunciations.

Hence we come to the second stage: due to this love that God exhibits for the cosmos He can be named 'Eros'/'Love', or Lover. In other words, the archetype of Love, which is exemplified by God in His relation to what is external to Him, is descending Eros, i.e. what the Neoplatonists can also term Providence. But if so, then the distance from the deficiency-claim of the *Symposium* is stark. Where is eros as a desire for something one lacks? Does not the creation desire and love God? If so, how does this take place?

To these problems the third stage comes as an answer. To be more precise, what God exemplifies is not only descending Eros, but actually ecstasy, i.e. going out of Himself to give something of Himself, or even Himself to the other(s), i.e. to the cosmos. Ecstasy does not immediately imply desire (for something), which would lead us to examine the *Symposium*'s abovementioned claim. It denotes the movement out of oneself, without specifying a particular reason for this movement. If so, it does not matter anymore whether the recipient of love is an entity higher or lower than the lover, i.e. whether a lover is in lack with respect to his beloved or not. Thus, God's paradigm just calls for our ecstatic response to his erotic ecstasy towards us. What I regard as the most crucial point of Dionysius' treatment is that thus, eros has no specific direction (upwards or downwards). Hence, Dionysius can be more comprehensive when enumerating the various possibilities of eros I mentioned before, where he includes the strictly horizontal dimensions.

The fourth step in this ascent, the image of the circle, concludes Dionysius' picture by confirming the discussion of the orientation of ecstatic eros, and this is why I suggested above that the third rather than the fourth state has prominence. The circle implies that Eros is a unique force in the universe: it starts from God and comes back to God. In this image what goes downwards is simultaneously going upwards and vice versa. The beautiful cosmos is the outcome of God's ecstasy. The sustainment of this cosmos, though, requires the loving response of the universe to God; it is God Himself that enables this erotic dialogue. Consequently, Dionysius speaks of Eros as a single force that unites the cosmos not only with respect to its parts, but also with regard to its Father. Finally, we can ascertain that for the Areopagite being is intimately connected with love; to be and to exist is to love and be erotic, i.e. ecstatic in whatever direction (whether procession or reversion).

The above brief exposition suffices to suggest that even if Eros is only a name among other divine names, Dionysius' metaphysics is essentially erotic. However, specific reasons for some of the previous claims must be traced to God's status as Trinity. What is more, others of the above enunciations are verified with the Incarnation of Logos. Although neither of these issues is explicitly mentioned in Dionysius' section on Eros, in the following pages I will try to find their traces, assess their importance and explain his silence regarding them.[10]

I will end this introductory section with a caveat. Although the following discussion will be most of the time abstract, without specific references to everyday life, we should not think that Dionysius' corpus is obsessed with bare metaphysics. The unifying effects of Eros in our world should also have practical and political applications.[11] Indeed, in one of the longest and in my opinion the most interesting and moving of Dionysian *Epistles*,[12] the Areopagite makes ample references to everyday life and specific sociopolitical structures. So, for instance, in the beginning[13] we are reminded that love for God means love for our neighbours,[14] even for our enemies,[15] and in the end[16] we see Christ being identified with those in need, whether sinners or not.[17]

3.1 Divine Eros and its function

The aim of this section is to show how Dionysius accommodates notions such as providential and reversive love in his system. Our guide in this enquiry will be the stipulation of the actual location and function of eros in the different levels of the Dionysian reality. The result will be that as with Proclus eros is to be found everywhere in Dionysius' universe. However, there are also subtle dissimilarities when contrasting Dionysius with Proclus and Plotinus, as we will see.

3.1.1 God and Eros: Causally or existentially?

I begin with a bold Dionysian statement:

> And we may be so bold as to claim also that the Cause of all things loves (ἐρᾷ) all things in the superabundance of his goodness, that because of this goodness

he makes all things, brings all things to perfection, holds all things together, returns all things. Divine Eros is the Good of the Good and indeed for the sake of the Good.[18]

In the chapter on Proclus we ascertained that divine eros, the entity attached to Beauty, and the erotic rank in general had the same characteristics as those expressed in the above passage, such as the attribute of returning other things towards the divine. So too with respect to Beauty itself, a specific group of Henads (the 'conversive' causes) and the Good. In my exposition I stressed that the plural existence of eros in different ontological levels is explained with the aid of prop. 65 of the *Elements of Theology*. The mode of 'existential (καθ' ὕπαρξιν) subsistence' is preceded by the 'causal' (κατ' αἰτίαν) mode. Eros is existentially erotic, whereas the principles above him are causally erotic. However, not even in this manner does Proclus ever affirm that the Good itself actually *loves* what lies beneath it. Hence, this is the first important differentiation between Proclus and Dionysius.[19] For the latter the First Principle is a καθ' ὕπαρξιν lover of the creation. The distance from Plotinus is also clear enough, since, despite the existence of providence, as we saw, the Neoplatonic founder had used erotic language to describe at best the 'relation' of the One with its own self.[20]

For a more precise view of what it means for the First Principle to love the creation, the following passage is indicative:

> What is signified [sc. by the divine name 'Eros'] is a capacity to effect a unity, an alliance, and a particular commingling in the Beautiful and the Good. It is a capacity which preexists through the Beautiful and the Good. It is dealt out from the Beautiful and the Good through the Beautiful and the Good. It binds the things of the same order in a mutually regarding union. It moves the superior to provide for the subordinate, and it stirs the subordinate in a return toward the superior.[21]

The characteristics of implanting unity and harmony in the universe, as well as bringing each level of reality into communion are familiar to us from Proclus. Nonetheless, although the Good and Eros shared similar features in Proclus, God's effects in the world were not deemed as instances of love, but rather of goodness, i.e. providence. Finally, the reader can find another presentation of the loving effects of God-Eros in our world, but in a lengthier and more elaborate manner, in the not thoroughly explored chapters of the *Divine Names* where Dionysius examines God as 'Peace' («Εἰρήνη»).[22]

Now I want to draw our attention to a reasonable question. An objector might justifiedly claim that Dionysius' language is not consistent in all places. There are passages where Dionysius seems to be advocating that eros subsists causally at the level of God, not existentially. For example, a few lines after the first passage cited Dionysius states that 'that yearning (ἔρως) which creates all the goodness of the world preexisted (προϋπάρχων) superabundantly in the Good'.[23] But the fact that Dionysius employs the «κατ'αἰτίαν» and the «καθ'ὕπαρξιν» formulas even together[24] might make things worse, because it implies that he is confused as to their distinction. Nevertheless, this is an uncharitable reading. In what follows I will show why and will suggest a more adequate approach.

Reading his penultimate *Epistle* we can ascertain that Dionysius is very well aware of *Elements*' prop. 65.[25] At one point he writes that the

> image of fire takes on different meanings, depending on whether it refers to the God who transcends all conceptions, to the providential activities or reasons of God, or indeed to the angels themselves. In one instance one thinks under the heading of 'cause', (κατ' αἰτίαν) in another under the heading of 'subsistence'. (καθ' ὕπαρξιν) in a third instance under the heading of 'participation', (κατὰ μέθεξιν).[26]

Not only do we see here Dionysius' knowledge of the *Elements*, but this passage is also helpful for understanding how he connects this threefold distinction with his own system, which is more frugal and synoptic than Proclus', and even Plotinus' one,[27] consisting of two 'elements': God and the creation. So, starting from the bottom, the mode of being 'by participation' refers to the angels as first members of the created order.[28] The other two modes apply to God, but not in the same respect. The 'causal' mode refers to God in Himself, without external relations, since he transcends the reality of created things, while the 'existential' mode of being characterizes God's providential activities that bring Him into relation with the creation.[29] As for erotic providential activities, we should understand them in light of the passages cited before: they are the unifying and harmonious effects of God in the world, because they bring the cosmos into communion with God. If so, the question now becomes: what does it mean for God to be eros in Himself, or eros beyond any conception, or eros causally? Eros is a relational term which denotes the relationship of God and the cosmos. If we want to transcend any reference to the cosmic level, what would it mean to say that God is Eros in a causal manner?

When treating Proclus on this issue it was the unifying effects of the One that led us to speak of it as causally erotic. However, we saw that Dionysius is more radical in his demand, in that he does not consider external relations at the causal level. Perhaps, then, does Dionysius want to guide us to something closer to the Plotinian One which, as we saw, is love of itself? The answer is yes and no. If we were dealing with other Church Fathers like the Cappadocian Gregory the Theologian[30] and the Medieval Richard of St Victor,[31] or with contemporary philosophers and theologians such as Christos Yannaras[32] and Metropolitan John Zizioulas,[33] the key to our quibbles would undeniably be Trinitarian theology. God is love of Himself, but not by being simply alone or just simple, like the Neoplatonic One, but because He is the loving relation between three Hypostases/Persons[34] which are consubstantial (i.e. share the same substance/nature). The mystery of the Christian Trinity reveals God not only as personal (as e.g. in Judaism and Islam), but also as inter-personal.[35] Without mentioning external relations with created beings, it is the internal relations of the three Divine Persons that show us why God is Love, dialogical and an eternal self-giving.[36] Moreover, they explain why, because of this loving overabundance, God is then Love when seen from the point of view of His communion with the creation.[37] In other words, God as Eros καθ'ὕπαρξιν is explained by the fact that God is Eros κατ'αἰτίαν, i.e. because He is a Trinity. This Christian radical innovation against the ancient background[38] is also revealed in the relational names that the Persons have, e.g. Father (of a Son)[39] and Son (of a Father).

Nonetheless, things unfortunately are not that clear in the case of the Areopagite. To be sure, the Trinity is not absent from his writings,[40] but it does not play the central role that it plays in other Church Fathers and it is not, at least evidently, employed in his section on Eros. What is more, to my knowledge, not a single time does Dionysius explicitly connect Trinity, i.e. the relations of the Persons, with Love. Hence, father Florovsky notes that 'Dionysius speaks briefly and fleetingly of the Trinitarian dogma'.[41] However, we need to do justice to the Areopagite. In the second chapter of the *Divine Names* he makes some distinctions concerning the (a) 'unified' and the (b) 'differentiated theologies' (words of God or divine names). The names related to 'divine unity' express the transcendence of God, i.e. attempt to describe him without relation to his creation (e.g. 'Ineffable'), whereas 'divine differentiation' includes the names that have to do with God's relationship with the cosmic order (e.g. Eros). Each of these categories is divided into two sub-categories on the basis of the applicability to the Persons of the Trinity. That is: (i) 'unity' in each of these categories means that the corresponding divine names refer to the entire Godhead (e.g. a: beyond Being; b: Light). On the other hand, (ii) 'differentiation' means that in each of the two categories there are also names that apply only to one or some of the Persons of the Trinity (a: Son; b: incarnated Logos).[42] Moreover, in the end of this methodological chapter, Dionysius announces the scope of his present work (DN) which pertains to subcategory (b-ii), i.e. the unified names related to divine differentiation.[43] In other words, Dionysius tells us that he is interested only in the names that reveal a particular relation between (the entire) God and the cosmos. If we recall our previous discussion of Eros with respect to prop. 65 of the *Elements*, this means that Dionysius is interested in the «καθ'ὕπαρξιν» mode of Eros' existence, i.e. the one that exemplifies God's relation with the cosmos, not the 'causal' mode. Therefore, it is because Dionysius limits the scope of his treatment that there is no elaborate presentation of the Trinity, and hence, presumably, no connection of Trinity with love either. It is true that in this way Dionysius' enterprise becomes more easily accessible by a Jew or a Muslim, and perhaps more frustrating for a Christian. Nonetheless, we should definitely not complain of the absence of something that the author has warned us that he is not going to deal with.[44]

This might not be, however, the end of the story. As an answer to Florovsky's sort of complaint Siasos wants to remain fully faithful to the details of Dionysius' enunciations.[45] In the same chapter (DN 2) the Areopagite writes that issues concerning the Trinity, as well as the Incarnation (i.e. unified and differentiated names of unified theology: a-i and a-ii, plus differentiated names of differentiated theology: b-ii), have been dealt in another book, the *Theological Representations*.[46] The problem is that the existence of this book is seriously disputed since no manuscript of it exists, nor do other ancient authors cite passages from it.[47] Siasos is convinced of its existence because it makes perfect sense within the programme that Dionysius has set out with the unified and differentiated theologies, as well as the structure of the *Mystical Theology*.[48]

Whether we follow Siasos' line, or we content ourselves with thinking that the Areopagite urges us to do the work that he is not doing in his (extant) corpus, I would rather focus on Trinitarian clues which could be found in passages that do exist. The last Dionysian subchapter on Eros in DN, before the Areopagite supposedly quotes three further subchapters on Love from his teacher Hierotheus, is a very vexed one. It speaks of a sort of erotic universality to which I will return (in Section 3.1.2). What I want to do now is to highlight some phrases relevant for our purposes. Dionysius writes that God 'stirs and moves himself through himself'[49] by 'revealing himself via himself'[50] and being 'the good procession of [his own] transcendent unity'.[51] As I said the context is unclear and one can wonder: is here Dionysius speaking about the Trinitarian God, where the Father begets the Son and the Spirit proceeds from the Father, thus revealing Deity as Trinity, or are we dealing with the providential activities of the Deity which result in the creation and sustainment of the cosmos? Despite the interpretive difficulties, the context of the whole chapter on Eros, as well as hints like the word 'beings' («τοῖς οὖσι»)[52] few lines after the above enunciations reassure us that Dionysius has in mind the relation of God and the cosmos. Still, our dilemma was quite reasonable. In fact, there are places where Dionysius is employing almost identical phrases that apply very clearly to the Trinity. For instance, in the already mentioned methodological chapter 2 of DN, the Areopagite notes that with reference to the Trinity 'divine differentiation applies to the goodlike processions of the divine unity, overflowing and multiplying [itself] due to goodness in a super-unified way'.[53] Taking for granted that the author must have been aware of these verbal similarities, while he makes clear that the Son and the Holy Spirit are not creatures,[54] I propose that in this way he might be giving more hints to the reader in order to connect the Trinity with Love. If, that is, the term 'procession' can be used for both the internal relations of the Trinity and the external relations of God,[55] then we can constantly have in mind that Love might be underlying Dionysius' statements about the Trinity in Chapter 2, while the Trinity might be a helpful model in order to understand God's external relations, too, in the chapter on Eros.[56] What is more, the insistence on this bond between Trinity and Love helps us solve another puzzle. Whereas in some passages we have seen Dionysius identifying God with Eros, in other ones he states that Eros is *in* God.[57] Of course, he does not suggest that Eros is a sort of independent principle within Deity. Our treatment so far can give a neat answer: the 'in' formula applies first and foremost to the internal relations of the Trinity, i.e. to the 'causal' mode,[58] which explains why God can be said to be Eros with respect to both Himself (cf. again causally) and the creation (cf. existentially).[59]

Hence, so far I have shown that Trinity does play a role in Dionysius' system, albeit perhaps not the central one, and that «κατ'αἰτίαν» eros can be taken as a hint towards the Trinity. Nevertheless, we need to take also into account that the Areopagite, like all great Platonic philosophers (Plato, Plotinus, Proclus), does not rigidly stick to a technical vocabulary. My above treatment has shown that Dionysius was aware of Proclus' proposition 65, but still he adapted it to fit his own Christian scheme. Still, this is not the only adaptation of this proposition to be found in the *Divine Names*. At one point within the long section on evil Dionysius notes that 'evil is not to be found in the angels either. For if the goodlike angel brings tidings of the divine goodness, he is by participation, i.e. in a secondary manner, that [sc. which he is announcing, and which exists] causally, i.e. in a primary manner'.[60] A strict Proclean would not endorse the loose Proclean language Dionysius is using here. First of all, here we have a binary relation of a thing participating (cf. δευτέρως: angel) and another one which is participated (cf. πρώτως: God). We should expect that the participation (cf. κατὰ μέθεξιν) is of an entity that exemplifies the characteristic which is participated. But instead of calling this characteristic 'existing' «καθ'ὕπαρξιν», the Areopagite states that it is «κατ'αἰτίαν», i.e. at another stage further above. This is not to suggest that in Proclus' system an entity whose characteristic exists «καθ'ὕπαρξιν» does not participate in an entity having this characteristic 'causally'. However, participation strictly speaking is of an attribute which is exemplified by (i.e. exists καθ'ὕπαρξιν in) the entity participated. Again, a participated entity is a cause of the thing participating, but this is different from saying that a characteristic exists causally in an entity. If the characteristic is not exemplified (καθ'ὕπαρξιν) in the participating entity, then its progenitor is not deemed as a proper cause of this very characteristic.[61] Furthermore, if someone claimed that actually Dionysius is interested in the (indirect) relation between an entity existing «κατ'αἰτίαν» and another one existing «κατὰ μετοχήν», then the Dionysian language still falls short of Proclean standards, because he should have said that the thing «κατὰ μετοχήν» exemplifies its characteristic in a 'tertiary' manner ('τρίτως'), following the trinitarian distinction of proposition 65 of the *Elements*.

What does all this show us? First of all, it shows that Dionysius is not a dull and unimaginative follower of Proclus, uninterested in the latter's meticulous classifications. Rather, Dionysius is very flexible in using Proclean schemes and adapting them to his Christian context, according to the purposes of his particular treatments. In our case, he reduces Proclus' triadic distinction into a simpler binary one.[62] Already in my previous treatment we saw that the 'causal' and the 'existential' mode applied to God (with respect to Himself and to creation), whereas the 'participatory' one to creation (starting with the angels). The same rationale applies to this current instance, although the Areopagite omits to mention the verbal formula «καθ'ὕπαρξιν». Still, we know from the above elaborations that God is not only causally Eros but also 'existentially'. Dionysius implies that to be the first cause and to exemplify a characteristic are one and the same thing.[63] Therefore, for him to be erotic is tantamount to being the cause of eros directly, i.e. being eros causally (as distinct from existentially).[64]

An analogous pattern of thought is exhibited when Dionysius speaks of the names «κάλλος» (beauty) and «καλόν» (beautiful).[65] He mentions that the first is used with regard to the cause of the beautiful (the participated[66] entity), whereas the second with regard to beautiful participants.[67] Nonetheless, he does not refrain from calling God, who is identified with Beauty, as Beautiful, too, i.e.

as exemplifying beauty, albeit in an unprecedented manner; hence, Dionysius adds also the usual prefix of 'super-': God is «ὑπέρκαλος».[68] Hence, we can conclude that the conjunction of something exemplifying a characteristic and being the cause of it means that this characteristic is exemplified καθ'ὕπαρξιν, but in an ultra-cosmic manner,[69] following God's Trinitarian super-existence.[70] Now, the reason that there is no 'super-eros' formula[71] might be that eros is not only a relational term,[72] but also a symmetrical one. As we will shortly see, God's love for cosmos implies the corresponding love of cosmos for God. Thus, since we are speaking about one single phenomenon, it would be better to stay with the name 'eros' without further designations. However, the linguistic fact does not negate the thought that Eros is exemplified in God's super-being (both with respect to Trinity and in relation to the creation). In other words, in order to understand eros we need to search for God (and the other way round).

So, so far I have shown that Dionysius' is flexible in using Proclean notions in order to fit them into his more modest ontological scheme. Now, to go a step further, it is this simpler scheme that enables Dionysius to identify providence with love,[73] something that forms another deviation from Proclus. In Proclus we had underscored that with respect to descending eros, providential love was only a species of providence, determined by its recipients which were beautiful entities. Moreover, we had asserted the correspondence of providence with goodness and of love with beauty, because Beauty stood lower than the Good, which was at the top of the metaphysical pyramid. It is no wonder, then, that the frugal Christian metaphysics of One (i.e. consubstantial) God led Dionysius to call Him Good and Beautiful (ἀγαθὸν καὶ καλόν).[74] There does not exist anymore a hierarchy of principles such as beauty and goodness; hence, love ceases to have a more limited scope than providence.[75] To love is to be providential and vice versa.

Continuing on these lines of Dionysius' divergences from Proclus, we may observe that although in the latter's case Eros was an entity attached to and desiring Beauty, while Beauty was only causally erotic, Dionysius contracts not only the Good and the Beautiful, but also Eros with them. If strictly speaking Proclean Eros exemplified the ascending love and desire, while it had downwards love as a by-product due to providence, now the unqualified archetype of Love is the descending one. Trinitarian God exemplifies Eros for the creation, which is none other than descending Eros. We can see how from Plotinus' emphasis on Eros' deficiency, Proclus' bond with providential eros has enabled Dionysius to pick this notion up in order to express a perhaps similar, but in many respects distinctive Christian vision of reality. It might be that in his 'contractions'[76] of various terms (goodness, beauty, eros) the Areopagite may be coming close to my interpretation of Plotinus, who wants us to contract Eros with the entity that bears it, i.e. Soul or Nous. Nonetheless, in Dionysius the contraction does not take place in lower strata, but at the very top, the Go(o)d. Moreover, because of the identification of providence with love the Areopagite does not stay at Plotinus' Good which loves only itself, but he proceeds to ascribe to God an active love (not only providence) for what exists outside Him.[77]

There remains a last issue before going on to examine eros in beings other than God. For the Platonic background of Proclus, it was obvious that Eros would be a mediator. However, now with Dionysius we see that there is no mediation anymore. Eros has been identified with the outer extreme which itself erotically provides for the cosmos. Does Dionysius deviate also from this Platonic background? The answer is no; Proclus and Dionysius are here close enough. When elaborating on the location of Eros in Proclus' system I emphasized that strictly speaking Eros is a bond, i.e. a mediator, in that it bestows the erotic desire on the rest of reality in order that it attain to the intelligible realm. In this sense this is also what Dionysius' erotic God does. He Himself is the very bond between Him and the cosmos.[78]

To recapitulate, in this section I have shown the mode of existence of Eros at the level of God as well as the 'synairesis' of the latter with the former, and I have tried to explain how the causal mode of eros' existence relates to the existential one. To this end I referred to the Trinity, which forms a major differentiation between Christianity and Neoplatonism and I underlined various other divergences of Dionysius from Proclus and Plotinus, many of which relate to Dionysius' simpler and more synoptic ontological scheme. Now it is time to go downwards.

3.1.2 After God: Eros by participation

When trying to locate Eros in Proclus' system I posed the question whether below proper divine Eros there are other erotic divine entities. Exploiting Proclus' emanationist metaphysics we saw how this was the case, using again the third-'participatory' mode of *Elements* proposition 65. In Dionysian reality, however, there is no vertical or horizontal polytheism, so there are obviously no divinities regarding their essence below God-Eros, although each being is go(o)d-like to the extent that it can participate in God.[79]

Still, now we are facing another problem: according to Greek philosophers and Christians alike the cosmos desires and loves God. But whether we express the cosmos' dependence upon God as God's bringing creation into being after His image,[80] or as creation's participation in God's providential processions,[81] we have just seen that the archetype and source of these participated properties is providential/downwards love. How, then, to account for the existence of reversive love? In other words, if love at the level of God is disconnected from the 'deficiency' claim which the *Symposium* bequeathed to the Neoplatonists, how can we explain the very fact of reversive love? There seem to be two options here: either we should distinguish between desire and love, admitting that created beings desire but do not love God, or we should introduce a new kind of love, the reversive/upwards one, which is disconnected from the providential one and characterizes created beings. The first option is easily denied, taking into account Dionysian passages we have already quoted, where it is plain that creation does love God. My task now is to show why and how reversive love is not separated from providential love.

When speaking of divine love Dionysius adds another important section which starts as follows: 'Divine eros[82] is ecstatic, not allowing the lovers to belong to themselves but to the beloveds. This is shown in the providence lavished by the superior on the subordinate. It is shown in the regard for one another demonstrated by those of the same rank. And it is shown by the subordinates in their divine return toward what is higher.'[83] Again we witness the unifying effects of Eros in the realm of being. What is new here is that the reciprocal relations of the various entities are expressed in terms not only of love, but also of «ἔκστασις» (ecstasy).[84] To love means to be ecstatic, i.e. to get outside one's self in order to meet and unite with the other.[85] Most importantly, the direction of love, whether ascending or descending, does not matter anymore. This is inferred by the fact that Dionysius is speaking about 'divine eros'. Owing to the context, even if he does not mean exclusively God, we have already seen that the paradigm of divine eros is the divinity itself.[86] We cast this archetype as providential love before, but the harmony of the universe shows the reality of both ascending/reversive and descending/providential love. Hence, «ἔκστασις»[87] acquires the role of unifying these two concepts. How does it do this?

Dionysius goes on to substantiate his claim first by giving a salient example from the created realm ('upwards ecstasy'). This is Paul, who wrote that 'it is no longer I who live, but Christ who lives in me'.[88] Then Dionysius comes to the Uncreated love ('downwards ecstasy'), which 'is also carried outside of himself in the providential care he has for everything. He is, as it were, beguiled by goodness, by love, and by eros and is enticed away from his transcendent dwelling place and comes to abide within all things, and he does so by virtue of his supernatural and ecstatic capacity to remain, nevertheless, within himself'.[89] In both cases there is an interchangeability between lover and beloved. As soon as the loving 'ecstasy' takes place the roles cannot be distinguished anymore.[90] One of the originalities of Dionysius here is that, to my knowledge, nowhere does downwards ecstasy feature in Plotinus or even in Proclus.[91] Hence, when connecting the archetype of 'providential love' with ecstasy, whereas the traditional Neoplatonic motive saw ecstasy as ascending,[92] Dionysius must not have been interested in the direction of love or ecstasy,[93] but just in the love and union with another, whether inferior or superior in Neoplatonic/Dionysian terms.[94] In other words, Dionysian providential love becomes the paradigm of ecstasy which does not have determinate (upwards or downwards) direction. As soon as there is something other, love forces us to unite with it,[95] hence the exhaustive possibilities that Dionysius gives above: providential/descending, reversive/ascending and love between entities of the same rank.[96] It is in this sense that Heraclitus' dictum acquires a new relevance with Dionysius: 'The way up and the way down are one and the same.'[97]

If someone pressed us to explain reversive love the ultimate answer would be that it is rooted in the beings' natural response to the loving and ecstatic call that God has already proposed to them.[98] In other words, in a paradoxical way the archetype of reversive love is again the providential one.[99] But we should not forget that it is this reversive love, i.e. participation in God[100] as far as possible, that imbues an entity with divine love, with the subsequent harmonious result of the entity's ecstatic love in every possible direction,[101] both in the vertical axis, i.e. upwards (not only to God, but to the neighbouring entities, too) as well as downwards, and in a horizontal fashion.[102]

Exactly due to this Heraclitean annihilation of the importance of direction, and to the gratification of a reader of Aristotle's *Physics* VIII, Dionysius will pass beyond the linear representation of downwards and upwards eros to speak of a cycle. This move might not be surprising against the Neoplatonic background,[103] but it is not explicitly stated with regard to love in Plotinus or Proclus either. Dionysius makes this move in chapter 4.14, which, as I have already noted (in Section 3.1.1), is a quite dense and obscure chapter. The specific problem it tries to address is why 'theologians sometimes refer to God as Eros and Love[104] and sometimes as the object of love and the Beloved'.[105] After my exposition the answer is easy: insofar as God is ecstatic, i.e. an efficient cause, He is called Love, whereas *qua* final cause,[106] i.e. the ultimate aim of the creation's ecstasy, He is called the Beloved. In order to see however how he introduces the idea of the cycle,[107] I will turn to the much briefer chapter 4.17, which is supposed to be the last quotation from Hierotheus:[108]

> Come, let us gather all these [sc. instances of eros: on God's and on the cosmos' behalf][109] once more together into a unity, and let us say that there is a simple self-moving power directing all things to mingle as one, starting out from the Good, reaching down to the lowliest of the beings, returning then in due order through all the stages back to the Good, thus turning from itself and through itself and upon itself and towards itself in an everlasting circle.[110]

Dionysius here speaks of the existence of a single erotic force in universe that goes forth and comes back eternally. It is true that there is a pantheistic, not to say Hegelian, flavour in the passage.[111] Still, apart from the dangers lurking in anachronistic readings, there are Dionysian passages which extol the gap between the ineffable first cause and its effects[112] and thus can acquit Dionysius from pantheism.[113] Hence, if the passage is seen under the light of our present discussion, what the Areopagite wants to make clear is the universality of eros as a single force that moves the universe into communion with its originator and Father.[114] In this circular scheme,[115] as soon as love is downwards, i.e. it is directed towards the creation (God as Lover/Love), it is already coming back to God and forms the loving response of the creation in the natural course of God's loving providence (God as Beloved).[116] The ideal of love as union (but not confusion) pushes Dionysius to go beyond the already-mentioned identification of the «κατ'αἰτίαν» and «καθ'ὕπαρξιν» modes of existence, and to propose the ultimate kinship of the first two modes with the «κατὰ μετοχήν» one. If this claim be put in the non-pantheistic framework set out before, the result is that, as with Proclus and Plotinus, eros acquires an omnipresence in Dionysius' system. Yet, whereas in Proclus I was austere in the designations of causal, existential and participatory levels of love's existence, now eros is always construed in the way Proclus describes as existential. For example, we saw that Dionysius is ready to ascribe Eros to the First Principle, while Proclus avoided it. What is more, in the end Dionysius went on almost to identify God's eros for the creation with creation's eros for God, i.e. the 'existential' and 'participatory' mode of eros, while in the Platonic Successor the participatory level falls short of the existential one.[117]

Before I end I need to add a last note as a counterpoint to the identification of beauty with goodness and of providence with (descending) love in the previous section. Our examination so far shows that if we want to abstract creation's ascending response to God from the universal erotic scheme, desire and (reversive) love are identified. In Proclus we had seen that eros is related to beauty, whereas desire is attached to the Good. It is very reasonable that since in Dionysius Good and Beauty are the same, then desire and (reversive) love are identified because they have the same intentional object.[118] Moreover, we have seen that, although descending and ascending, the name Eros/Love was the same. Dionysius' extraordinary image of eros as a unique circular force gives the non-Neoplatonic possibility to identify providence with desire, or at least see both of them as aspects of exactly the same movement: Eros.[119]

To conclude, let me give a brief overview of what we achieved in this section. My main focus was the «κατὰ μετοχήν»/'participatory' mode of love's existence. I began addressing the problem of how to account for creation's reversive love given the divine paradigm of providential love. The solution involved referring to the notion of «ἔκστασις», the main characteristic of which is a lack of interest as to whether the direction is upwards or downwards. If for Neoplatonism there is a strong connection between being, love and ecstasy, especially for Dionysius to be is to love, i.e. being ecstatic in whatever direction. Consequently, although at the 'causal' and 'existential' level divine love acts as providential, at the level of participation eros expresses itself as both providential and reversive because both of these are possible instances of ἔκστασις within the hierarchy of beings. The lack of dissection or dichotomy with respect to Eros' function led us to the idea of a single circular erotic force in the universe expressed in chapter 4.14 and synoptically put in chapter 4.17, which forms a testimony to the unifying effects of love that can bridge the gap between the transcendent God and its progeny. A final result of this treatment is that eros acquires an omnipresence in Dionysius' universe. Although we had met this idea in other Neoplatonists, too, in Dionysius it receives a more emphatic and existential, i.e. «καθ'ὕπαρξιν», tone.

3.2 From Christian agape to the Christification of Eros

In my treatment of ecstasy I omitted to mention that Dionysius concludes that section by calling God «ζηλωτής» (zealous),[120] i.e. a manic lover, of His beloved cosmos.[121] We have seen that this manic love is expressed within the unending erotic dialogue of this pair of lovers. But what is its ultimate expression? The short answer is Christ's incarnation: The Uncreated God not only created the cosmos, but finally assumed in Himself the created nature of His beloved. Thus, in this last section I will examine some consequences of Dionysius' teaching on love, and especially how the person of Christ relates to Dionysius' erotic theory.[122] In this context I will also attempt a comparison with Proclus' counterpoint to

Christ, the Platonic Socrates. Again we will see that despite the similarities there are cardinal differences, particularly with regard to the meaning of 'undefiled providence'.

The status of Dionysian Christology is much as with his Trinitarian theology: it exists, but it is not developed.[123] Moreover, explicit reference to Christ is absent from Dionysius' section on Eros. Fr. Meyendorff writes that 'undoubtedly, Dionysius ... mentions the name of Jesus Christ and professes his belief in the incarnation, but the structure of his system is perfectly independent of his profession of faith'.[124] While I believe that here Meyendorff is onto something and we had better look at other Fathers, like Maximus the Confessor,[125] if we wanted a full-fledged and well worked out Christology,[126] I am more optimistic than the (Neo-)Palamite scholar and hold that Christ's traces in Dionysius' corpus can help us complete the Dionysian picture of love.

The particular reason why Christology is relevant for my purposes is that in contrast to the discussion of the Trinity in Dionysius, which although pivotal is not explicitly connected with eros, almost every time that the Areopagite refers to Christ, he connects Him with our topic by extolling His «φιλανθρωπία»[127] ('*love* for mankind').[128] Admittedly, love here is denoted by «φιλία» rather than ἔρως (or ἀγάπη).[129] Still, Dionysius is here referring to God's manic love for mankind, which leads to His self-emptying («κένωσις»)[130] and results in the incarnation. If we ask why the incarnation, the paradigm instantiation of theophany, should take place, the most succinct Patristic answer has been given by Athanasius the Great: "He became man so that we be made God."[131] The Trinitarian God's providential, descending and ecstatic eros not only leads to the unification of the cosmos in itself, but implants an indissoluble bond between God and creation. The erotic effects of this unification are so strong that the 'zealous' God becomes a God-Man. Hence, it is only with Christ in mind (and heart) that one can understand Dionysius' erotic image of the circle.[132] When the erotic force that has proceeded from God returns from the level of creation, it bears the seal of both the divine and the created. Thus, the best exemplification of this return is Christ, who is literally both divine and a created human being. This completes Dionysius' picture of the erotic cycle and ultimately acquits him from any pantheistic accusations. Moreover, it explains and anticipates Maximus' view that the end of God's overflowing creation is the person of Jesus.[133] Finally, Christ's manic φιλανθρωπία should not be conceived as an exclusive love for man as opposed to the cosmos, but as the consummation of God's love for His total creation, because the microcosm of human being encompasses in itself both the spiritual (e.g. angelic) and the material (e.g. soulless) creation.[134]

And now I come to the obvious question: if Christ is so important in completing and verifying the Dionysian erotic doctrine, why does Dionysius avoid mentioning Him in the section on Eros? He seems to be absent both from the passage of ecstatic 'jealousy' (in DN §4.13) and from the picture of the circle (§§4:14 and 17), despite the fact that in the latter case I was able to discover indirect references to the Trinity. The short answer is that both Trinity[135] and Christ's «εἰρηνόχυτος φιλανθρωπία»[136] are present in the climax of the chapters on God as 'Peace',[137] which I have characterized as an enlightening and necessary complement to the section on Eros. Of course, there too we do not find an elaboration on the significance of Christ, but only a brief mention.

There are two ways to answer this problem. On the one hand, if we follow the line of Siasos mentioned with reference to Trinitarian theology, then we would expect that these associations were mentioned in another perhaps lost (or more probably fictitious) Dionysian work, the *Theological Representations*.[138] On the other hand, we can work again on the basis of implicit hints in Dionysius' extant work and employ what I will call 'erotic hermeneutics'.[139] It might not be an accident that the two sole instances of Dionysius' quoting his teacher Hierotheus in the DN are on love and Christ.[140] In the case of love, Hierotheus' chapters form a synopsis of Dionysius' teaching, whose explicit target is to explicate and develop the succinct statements of his teacher's theology,[141] while, as I have noted, Christology is only touched in passing. Still, apart from the Areopagite's relation to his teacher's writings, in the very end of *Divine Names*[142] Dionysius himself notes the human restrictions and difficulties of his enterprise and invites the recipient of the work, i.e. Timothy or us, to take a critical stance,[143] and by loving God and trying to imitate His philanthropy[144] he urges us to attempt to correct or develop his theology, as he did with the teaching of his own divine teacher. If so, then the two key themes of love and Christ must be first in the list of subjects calling for further exploration. Since, while brief, they already form the supposed Dionysian interpretation of Hierotheus, the reader ought to understand that these are two key themes in need of further analysis and interconnection by us, even if love figures as just one name among others. To this end we might also note that the last of Dionysius' *Epistles*,[145] as if the last words of his corpus, is addressed to John, who was the best friend and a disciple of Jesus Christ,[146] and/because he is deemed the Evangelist of Love.[147]

These features hint at the centrality of Christ in Dionysius' erotic universe[148] and invite us to connect ecstasy with Christ's *kenosis*-incarnation, seeing the latter as species and perfection of the former,[149] even if Dionysius does not explicitly do so. This is precisely what we find in interpretations of the text by later Fathers. Authors like Maximus[150] and Palamas[151] do not impose a 'Christological corrective' on Dionysius, but rather develop insights implicitly present in his writings.[152] To sum up, whether we read Dionysius via the later tradition or we take Siasos' way, Dionysius' extant exclamation(s) of Christ's 'self-emptying' φιλανθρωπία provide, for the systematic reasons I explained before, the ultimate proof of and the most adequate explanation for understanding why Dionysius concludes his treatment of erotic 'ecstasy' by calling God «ζηλωτής», i.e. a manic lover of His «καλὴ λίαν»[153] creation.[154]

I come now to a final comparison between Dionysius and Proclus. The topic in question is the juxtaposition between undefiled providence and incarnation. One of my central points of reference while treating Proclus' erotic doctrines was Socrates, whose presence is frequent in Proclus (although not in Plotinus). I stated that Socrates' loving relations helped us to grasp the intelligible divine relations, and that ultimately Socrates was an expression, albeit an attenuated one, of the divine in our world. Dionysius' Christian counterpoint to Socrates is Christ.[155] As we just saw, Christ not only helps us to understand what divine eros is, but is its best exemplification. Hence, the cardinal difference between the two figures is that Christ is not just a micro-expression of the divine in our world, but actually God Himself.[156]

Thus, on a first reading Dionysius differs completely from Proclus in this respect. The incarnate Christ is a clear anomaly not only for the Neoplatonic system of Proclus, but for the whole of ancient Greek philosophy.[157] Furthermore, even if Socrates was said to provide for other souls, as well as for his own body, the Neoplatonic ideal was that of 'undefiled providence', where the divine principle exercises providence without any intermingling with or embodiment in the recipient of providence.[158] Socrates formed a marginal case, where in order to exercise providence he had to descend to the earthly realm,[159] while the 'undefiled' part of his care meant e.g. abstinence from sexual relations. By contrast, the quintessence of Christ's philanthropy, i.e. the loving providence of the Uncreated First Principle, is that He descended to created mankind, 'so that we may be made God', in the abovementioned famous words of Athanasius.[160] Christian God's loving ecstasy or *kenosis* means 'intermingling' with the beloved.[161]

Yet Dionysius' language is very close to Proclus'. First of all, without reference to Incarnation Dionysius uses the Proclean vocabulary of divine transcendence and undefiled providence. I choose the following example taken from outside the section on love, because it connects the two themes: 'The divinity is described as omnipotent because he has power over all, and assists the beings which it administers[162] in an unmixed way («ἀμιγῶς»); because he is the goal of all yearning and because he lays a happy yoke on all who wish it, the sweet toil of that holy, omnipotent, and indestructible yearning for his goodness.'[163] This may seem unremarkable; when trying to capture the nature of the First Principle both Neoplatonism and Christianity are bound to assert the Deity's supertranscendence.[164] But even in the case of the incarnate First Principle, i.e. Christ, who has taken human flesh, Dionysius' language is similar: '[(The divinity of) Jesus] is the Being pervading all beings and remains unaffected thereby.[165] It is the supra-being beyond every being ... In all this he remains what he is – supernatural, transcendent – and he has come to join us in what we are without himself undergoing change or confusion.'[166] A reader who has read Proclus and is unfamiliar with the significance that Church Fathers ascribe to Christ could think that Christ performs undefiled providence just as Proclean Socrates does. If so, these passages would mean that for Dionysius incarnation is a secondary issue, because what primarily counts is God's divine transcendence above His creation. On this reading, God would not intermingle with the objects of its providence. However, due to the Dionysian resources regarding Christ mentioned above, we should not be left thinking that Dionysius reproduces Proclus' ideal of 'undefiled providence', adding to this mixture Christ.[167]

Here we may take note of an ancient comment which can be attributed with certainty to Maximus the Confessor[168] on another paradoxical Dionysian enunciation, reminiscent of undefiled providence. In one of the succinct chapters on Eros, supposedly by Hierotheus, the author speaks of God as the «ἄσχετος αἰτία παντὸς ἔρωτος».[169] The paradox, as with Proclus' undefiled providence, is that if eros is a relational term, how can its bearer be «ἄσχετος», i.e. non-related with its object of love? Maximus answers: «ἄσχετον τὸ ἀπόλυτόν φησιν, οὐ πρὸς τὸ πᾶν οὐδεμία σχέσις ἤτοι οἰκειότης φυσική».[170] The absence of intermingling between lover and beloved means that the two are fundamentally different; not soul and body as in the case of Socrates, but Uncreated and Created.[171] Hence, Dionysius could retain this formula when referring even to Christ, because although He is one Hypostasis which is constituted from two natures,[172] there is no confusion between them.[173] Christ's incarnation is not the same as Socrates' embodiment. The fact that Christ has received the total humanity[174] shows why God is a manic lover, while Socrates' undefiled providence denotes his failure when compared with higher daimons or divinities; were he a higher soul he would not need to be incarnate or to educate Alcibiades. The result is that whereas Socrates can elevate his body or Alcibiades only up to the divine point he has reached, Christ takes the whole man, and hence the whole creation, up to the highest level, i.e. in Himself.[175]

To recap, in this last section I examined an important consequence of Dionysius' erotic doctrines. Dionysius' innovations as well as the deepening of the erotic doctrine are particularly evident when examining the case of Christ's manic philanthropy in contrast to the undefiled providence of Proclus' Socrates. As I have tried to show, although the language is similar, the very fact that Christ is a full God in contrast to Socrates changes radically the Proclean scene. Furthermore, in my general treatment in this section I was forced to employ interconnections not observable in the Dionysian surface, especially when interconnecting Trinity and Christ's philanthropy with Eros. The reader might have realized that there are indeed many ways to interpret Dionysius, as with Plato. As the Areopagite himself 'develops' the teachings of his teacher(s), let this be a hint for us, his readers, to imitate him, and finally let our guide be love.

Notes

1 Henceforth I will be using interchangeably the names 'Dionysius' and 'Areopagite'. See also supra, n. 37 of my Introduction. For a new interesting hypothesis regarding Dionysius' pseudonymity, see Stang (2012: e.g. 2–6, and infra, n. 139). (I have not had the time to consult Kharlamov (2020).) Let us bear in mind (or ear) that the name of Paul's convert (cf. Acts 17.34), who became a saint, has sound similarities to the ancient Greek god of wine, Dionysus as well as Dion (Δίων), the Sicilian close friend of Plato, who, according to Nussbaum (2001: 228–30), lies beneath some names of the *Phaedrus*, a Platonic dialogue on love.
2 A similar attitude is expressed in Koch's contemporary, Stiglmayr (1895).
3 See n. 1 in Chapter 2. Since then, the similarity has also been observed among others by Nygren (1953: 579, n. 2). Cf. also Ivanović (2015: 129).
4 This last possibility, not frequently stated by Dionysius, should be interpreted along the lines of Gospel's 'love your neighbour as yourself' (cf. e.g. Mt. 19.19 and Mk 12.31 citing from Lev. 19.18). De Vogel (1963: 16) refers to possible Stoic and Pythagorean connotations.
5 The not very usual Greek here is «συνεκτικῶς» and I follow the rendering of LSJ ad lem. (II), where they refer to the occurrence of the word in Proclus, in Alc. 52,7. De Vogel (1963: 12) translates 'self-preservingly'.
6 «Πᾶσιν οὖν ἐστι τὸ καλὸν καὶ ἀγαθὸν ἐφετὸν καὶ ἐραστὸν καὶ ἀγαπητόν, καὶ δι᾽ αὐτὸ καὶ αὐτοῦ ἕνεκα καὶ τὰ ἥττω τῶν κρειττόνων ἐπιστρεπτικῶς ἐρῶσι καὶ κοινωνικῶς τὰ ὁμόστοιχα τῶν ὁμοταγῶν καὶ τὰ κρείττω τῶν ἡττόνων

προνοητικῶς καὶ αὐτὰ ἑαυτῶν ἕκαστα συνεκτικῶς, ... »: Dionysius the Areopagite, *The Divine Names* (henceforth: DN) §4.10, 155, 8–11/708A. In my system of referencing I first write the number of chapter and subchapter I will be referring to. Then, I give the page and line numbers of the Greek text in the standard edition of Suchla (1990). The number and letter after the slash denotes the pagination of Migne's edition in the *Patrologia Graeca* (PG, vol.3 – reproducing B. Corderius' text), because it is followed by the standard English translation I am using, i.e. that of Luibheid-Rorem (1987) (most of the times heavily modified though).

7   *DN* (last portions of) §4.10–§4.17 (i.e. before the long treatment of evil starts), 155,8–162,5/708A-713D.

8   Or «ἀγάπη» (agape/charity/love; cf. e.g. 1 Jn 4.8). I will not be dealing with the terminological issue. Dionysius regards the two names as interchangeable, although he prefers the name «ἔρως» (cf. Ignatius, *Rom.* 4.7.2,4 Camelot, cited in DN,4.12,157,11/709B; see also infra, n. 157), which 'accidentally' was the central term in the ancient Greek-pagan discussions on love. See his justification in DN 4.11–12, 156,1–158,12/708C-709C, especially his warning (ibid., 4.11,156,2–3/708C), which forms a self-conscious hermeneutical principle so that we understand Dionysius' relations with various Christian and non-Christian traditions: 'In my opinion, it would be unreasonable and silly to look at words rather than at the power of the meanings.' I am afraid that the prejudices of Nygren (1953: 589–93, esp. n. 1 in 589) do not let him appreciate either the above enunciation, or Dionysius' overall treatment. Cf. also Rist (1966: 236–7, 242), Aertsen (2009: 195) and Ivanović (2015: 123–7) (contra Nygren in 123 and esp. 124–6); see also Tornau (2005: 272, n. 4), who also refers to a similar terminological gesture in Origen, and various entries in nn. 34 and 35 of my Introduction. For well-balanced reasons regarding the adoption of eros-terminology by the Fathers, see Voulgarakis (1989: 8–10; cf. also 11). Specifically for Dionysius see also Osborne (1994: 208–10). Finally, I note that, as a TLG search shows, the alternative noun «ἀγάπησις» comes up a couple of times in Dionysius; see e.g. DN 4.12,158,9/709C (twice: in the context of the discussion mentioned in this note for which see also Molodeț-Jitea (2015: 93)) and DN 4.13,159,12/712B. See also supra, n. 40 in my Introduction for antecedents.

9   Cf. also Ivanović (2015: 130); see also a fourth possibility, rarely found even in Dionysius, supra in n. 4.

10 Regarding the philosophical relation between Proclus and Dionysius my discussion will show that although the latter is indebted to the former, Dionysius has enough subtle deviations from the Platonic Successor and Neoplatonism, so that we need not accuse him of plagiarism, as some scholars have done in the past. (I have already referred to the examples of Koch (1900) and Stiglmayr (1895).) Even when their language is very similar (as is also shown in Saffrey (1982)), the

underlying content of the two philosophers might be less akin. Scholarship has drawn attention to this phenomenon recently and what follows helps to confirm this interpretive trend. Most of the scholars referred to in my following notes to the chapter are more or less sympathetic to the view of Dionysius' creative and critical reception of Proclus. Cf. for instance the balanced approach of Louth (2008a: 581) and see also Terezis (1986: 10, 16–22), Gersh (1978: 1 and n. 1), de Vogel (1981: 75), McGinn (1996: 199–200; cf. also 203) and Florovsky (1987: 210; cf. also, 216–18 and 222), as well as most recently Mainoldi (2018). Stang (2012: 27–39, 5) with notes gives a helpful literature review of modern scholarship (i.e. of the twentieth century, including some decades before and after it); see also Stang (2012: 143–4) for a position of his (and of Schäfer 2006b, too), which is similar to what Sorabji (1987: 165) says about John Philoponus and Boethius of Rome (assigning to them the label of 'Christian Neoplatonist'). On the other hand, Rist (1999: 377–8, 387) notes Dionysius' independence from both Neoplatonism and Christianity, due to the synthesis he offers. As will be shown, and has already been clear even from the top of the present footnote, I am not very sympathetic to either line of proposal. For my part, I more or less follow the precepts of Archbishop Alexander (cf. e.g. Golitzin 1993: 99), whom I regard as one of the most perceptible readers of the Areopagite (rendering to us his experiences from Mount Athos and esp. from the Abbot of the Monastery of Simonos Petras, fr. Aimilianos, who helped fr. Alexander understand and appreciate Dionysius; cf. Golitzin 2003: 163, n. 6).

11 This is exactly what is successfully shown in Riggs (2009) with specific reference to the ecclesiastical hierarchy. Cf. also Rist (1999: 386) and Esposito Buckley (1992: 60–1).
12 See Dionysius, *Epistle* 8:1,1–6,55 (Heil-Ritter)/1048A-1100D (PG).
13 See ibid., §1,19–20/1085B.
14 Many Church Fathers, like John Chrysostom (cf. the magnificent extract from his seventy-sixth homily: *In Matthaeum [homiliae 1–90]* PG, vol.58, 700, 33–45), make the most out of this radical idea to be found e.g. in 1 Jn 4.20–1 and Mt. 25.40 (in the Parable of the Judgement); cf. Mk 3.35 and Lk. 6.27–35 (on love of enemies). See also Bozinis (2019). For the experience of the fact that 'ἀγάπη Θεοῦ=ἀγάπη ἀδελφοῦ' in contemporary saints, monks and spiritual fathers, see Papathanasiou (2011: n. 33).
15 See also Larchet (1996).
16 See Ep. 8.6,49–52/1100C.
17 Another early Father gives a beautiful image in order to explain how love of God entails closer bonds between people: if God is the centre of the circle and we are in the other extreme of its radii, then coming close to the centre we also come closer with those in the other radii. Cf. Dorotheus of Gaza, *Doctrinae diversae*

VI.78,1–25 (Préville and Regnault); the excerpt is also included in the nice anthology of Angelopoulos (2001: 105 and 110).
18 DN 4.10,155,14–20/708A-B. The last sentence is taken from the translation of McGinn (1991: 167), as indicated in Papanikolaou (2006b: 126 and n. 13 in 135). In McGinn (1996: 210 and n. 36) the last 'and (indeed)' is omitted following closely the Greek, which however has twice 'and' in the beginning of the sentence that have been left untranslated.
19 See also Ivanović (2015: 130–1).
20 Cf. also Ivanović (2015: 130 and 127).
21 DN 4.12,158,13–18/709D. Especially regarding the last three lines (16–18) there are many other parallel passages in the DN itself: see 4.2,144,18–145,2/696A-B (although here the reference is particularly to the angels); 4.7,152,16–19/704B-(C); 4.10,155,8–11/708A (cited in the opening of my chapter); 4.13,159,1–3/712A; 4.15,161,2–5/713B (supposedly from Hierotheus). It should be noted that the first two references describe the effects of God as goodness (which we will see is identified with love; hence also n. 160 in Luibheid-Rorem (1987: 83) with general parallel references in the Dionysian corpus about providence/procession and return/reversion. Cf. also Luibheid-Rorem (1987: 79, n. 149), Rorem (1993: 151, 169), and see Schäfer (2006a), comparing Dionysius and Proclus on the basis of the triad μονή-πρόοδος-ἐπιστροφή). Finally, DN 7.3,198,16–20/872B and 12.4,226,1–5/972B are more loosely connected with our main passage in that they denote the unity of the cosmos due to God's Wisdom and the first entities, i.e. first images of God, in the Dionysian hierarchies, respectively, but not in the aforementioned detailed manner.
22 See ibid., 11.1–5:217,5–221,12/948D-953B. Hence, 'Peace', and its subsequent «ἡσυχία» ('tranquility'; cf. ibid., 11.1,218,7/949A), appears as an alternative name for 'Eros' (and ἀγάπη). Another frequent term used in that section is «ὁμόνοια» (*passim*), while friendship («φιλία», unhelpfully rendered as 'yoke' by Luibheid-Rorem (1987 ad loc.)) is used once (DN 11.2,219,17/952A, in a context similar to those of Proclus; for «φιλία» see also infra, n. 129 in Section 3.2). In other words, DN §§11,1–5, which is very close to the final section of the book, forms an enlightening complement to the section on Eros in DN §§4.10–17. This is observed by Louth (1989: 95–6), too, who adds as another 'twin' divine name that of 'Power' (DN §§8.1–6).
23 DN 4.10,155,17–18/708B. (NB the word «ἀγαθοεργός», since the contracted form «ἀγαθουργός», although absent from Plotinus, is used many times by Proclus for the Henads and the divine principles in general; e.g. in Alc. 61,4 it characterizes Eros.) Cf. DN 4.12,158,13–15/709D (« ... προϋφεστώσης ... »); ibid., 4.13,159,18–20/712B (« ... προΐδρυται ... »); ibid., 4.14,160,9–10/712C (« ... προοῦσαν ... »).
24 Cf. also ibid., 5.4,183,5/817D: «ὅλον ἐν ἑαυτῷ τὸ εἶναι συνειληφὼς καὶ προειληφώς.» In ibid., 7.2,196,18–20/896B Dionysius combines the two verbs

into one: «[sc. the divine mind] ἐξ ἑαυτοῦ καὶ ἐν ἑαυτῷ κατ' αἰτίαν τὴν πάντων εἴδησιν καὶ γνῶσιν καὶ οὐσίαν προέχει καὶ προσυνείληφεν» (of itself and in itself it precontains and comprehends the awareness and understanding and being of everything in terms of their cause).

25 This is also observed by Dodds (1963: 236), in his note ad loc.
26 Ep. 9.2,18–22/1108D.
27 Whereas in Plotinus there are three divine principles, in Dionysius there is only one (since the Three Hypostases are consubstantial). NB that the notion of Dionysian hierarchy (a word coined by Dionysius) applies only to the created beings. God is outside the hierarchy because the latter's existence is owed to the varied relation that each of its members has with God. Cf. Perl (2013: 24–5, 29, 32), and see the Dionysian definition in his *Celestial Hierarchy* (CH) 3.1,17,3–5 (Heil-Ritter)/164D (PG) with the comments ad loc. by Louth (2010: 9–10). See also his broader, as well as convincing approach in Louth (1989: 105–10, 132–4), with various Dionysian and bibliographical references in Luibheid-Rorem (1987: 197–8, n. 11); cf. also Zizioulas (1985: 91) referring (in n. 72) to Roques (1954). The most recent treatment of Dionysian hierarchy has been given by Vasilakis (2019a) and Purpura (2018: 19–53). To their bibliographies add von Ivánka (1953), Gould (1989), Ashwin-Siejkowski (2009) (without meaning that I necessarily endorse all or part of the views of each paper) and Marsengill (2020), relating visual arts with Dionysian hierarchy from a historical point of view. Finally, Perl (1994) gives an interesting approach comparing pagan Neoplatonism with Dionysius, bringing in his usual tactic Dionysius on a par with Plotinus and Proclus, and acquitting all of them of the various accusations regarding hierarchical mediations (see, though, infra, n. 175). However, there is an aspect, namely the Christological one (to follow in my approach, too; see e.g. infra, nn. 123 and 148 in Section 3.2), which is absent from Perl's agenda (e.g. his treatment of 'synergy'/«συνεργία» in Perl (1994: 23 in contrast to 29)), but is to be found in Vasilakis (2019a: 189–90, 183 and 185 with n. 45 in 193, and esp. n. 96 in 196).
28 I am explaining the passage cited above. That the specific image of fire is used only for angels, not for say humans, does not exclude the possibility that the 'participation' mode applies to every other created order below the angels.
29 By 'providential activities' («νοηταὶ πρόνοιαι ἢ λόγοι») we should not understand an intermediate level of Being between God and angels. See Dionysius' unusually fervent polemic contra polytheism (hence against pagan Neoplatonism, too) in DN 11.6,222,3–13/953C-D; cf. Siasos (1984: 123–4), Louth (1989: 86–7) and Golitzin (1994: 58). Of course, whether this makes the Areopagite immediately a Palamite (i.e. follower of Saint Gregory Palamas) avant la lettre is another problem: when speaking of these providential activities do we mean 'uncreated energies' (with Palamas; cf. e.g. Russell 2019: 2) or created ones (with Barlaam and Aquinas; see also O'Rourke 1992), or even both of them (as in a way the approach

of Bradshaw (2018: e.g. 35 with n. 134) might allow one to infer)? On the other hand, this issue stirs the further question as to what the substantial difference between Proclus (cf. the Henads) and Palamas (cf. God's uncreated energies) is. (Cf. e.g. Hankey 2009: 125.) Perhaps both problems cannot be solved with the sole aid of philosophy. For instance, regarding the first question, the motivation in Tollefsen (2012: e.g. 2) is that Palamas is quite traditional in his hesychastic distinctions, whereas Meyendorff (e.g. in his introduction to Gendle (1983: 21, but see also 13)) is critical of this view, advocating Palamas' modified reception of the Areopagite. (However, scholars have proven that on this issue Meyendorff was biased due to Western hostile readings of Dionysius; cf. Konstantinovsky 2010). See also Louth (2008b: 585 with the notes in 598). With regard to the second debate, despite its title and the enlightening treatment of the encounter between Christianity and ancient Greek culture-philosophy in other Church Fathers, Begzos (2000) does not deal with Dionysius at all. See also infra, my Epilogue.

30 See e.g. Gregory Nazianzenus, «Λ΄.Ὕμνος πρὸς Θεόν» from *Carmina Dogmatica* 509,10–510,4 (PG).

31 In his *De Trinitate* III, e.g. §§4, 6, 14 and 19. Cf. Ware (1986: 10–11 with notes), where he also mentions and criticizes Aquinas' unjust Aristotelian criticism of Richard in this respect (Ware 1986: 11 with n. 21). Dionysius was one of the greatest authorities for Aquinas, who had written a commentary on the DN. Aertsen (2009: 198ff) compares the two philosophers only in terms of the 'Doppelgestalt' of love, as he calls it: while we have seen (supra in n. 8) that for Dionysius eros and agape are interchangeable, due to the Latin tradition and translations, the relation of the two terms acquires a new character in Aquinas, who imports a fourfold distinction: amor-dilectio-amicitia-caritas (cf. also Aertsen 2009: 203). McGinn (1996: 205ff) gives a broader comparison of Aquinas and Dionysius on love.

32 The most notable work in this respect is Yannaras (2007). However, the fundamentals of his approach are already present in Yannaras (2005) (whose first Modern Greek version appeared in 1967). In this book, under the influence of Vladimir Lossky (see e.g. Lossky 1976, esp. chapter 2: 23–43), Yannaras proposes that Dionysius' unknowability of God is the Eastern Orthodox alternative to the Western absence of God found in Heidegger and Nietzsche. Nihilism is avoided in Dionysius, because his God is Love, i.e. Trinity, and hence comes into loving contact with the creation, via his uncreated energies (where Yannaras employs Palamas' understanding of Dionysius. See esp. the final chapter in Yannaras 2005: 99–110). Regarding the (creative) 'distortions' of Lossky's enterprise and its relation to the Western understandings of Dionysius, as well as developments in twentieth century's Roman-catholic theology, see Coakley (2013: esp. 127–36 and 140–1). For a brief presentation of most of Yannaras' translated books in English (including the ones mentioned), see Louth (2009: esp. 332 and 335–8). A (perhaps

unnecessarily too) critical presentation of Lossky's and Yannaras' enterprise with respect to Dionysius is given in Gavrilyuk (2008: 712–16 and 720). For an apology, as the author calls it, of Dionysius' appropriation by the French phenomenological school, esp. Jean-Luc Marion, see Manoussakis (2008). Finally, see Depraz-Mauriac (2012) and Depraz (2019) on reading Marion through Yannaras, who has anticipated many elements of the French phenomenologist's approach.

33 See Zizioulas (1985: e.g. 36–46 and 49 with n. 42) (drawn from his famous article 'From Mask to Person', first appeared in Greek in 1977 and translated into English by Norman Russell). For a brief introduction to the philosophical and personalist theologians just mentioned, i.e. Lossky, Yannaras and Zizioulas, see Papanikolaou (2008).

34 Although the latter term is not used (in this technical sense) by Dionysius, as is duly acknowledged by Klitenic Wear and Dillon (2007: 44). See also infra, n. 173.

35 For a succinct and lucid presentation of the Orthodox Christian understanding of the Trinity, with many scriptural, liturgical and patristic citations, see the corresponding chapter in Ware (1995: 27–42).

36 Hence, I resist here one of Augustine's Neoplatonizing understandings of the Trinity, where the Holy Spirit, *qua* the relation of the Father with the Son, is their mutual Love ('amor'). See e.g. *De Trinitate* VIII.X.14; cf. also Ware (1986: 9, n. 13), Coffey (1990: 194–201), who makes connections with the issue of 'Filioque' and criticizes Augustine (Coffey 1990: 201) for providing insufficient scriptural grounding, and Tornau (2005: 288). (Tornau discusses Augustine's general views on love in Tornau (2005: 282ff) and he dwells a lot on Augustine's understanding of the scriptural 'deus dilectio est'; cf. Tornau (2005: 283, 285–8 and supra, nn. 8 and 31). On the other hand, Edwards (2009: 207ff) focuses on the centrality of Christ for Augustine's views on love.) For all its Western origin, one can trace this idea also in late Byzantium, presumably via the Greek translation of *De Trinitate* by Maximus Planoudes (accomplished in c. 1280–1). See e.g. Gregory Palamas, *Capita physica, theologica, moralia et practica CL* §36,11–15, and relevant bibliography with an old (and it seems by now outdated) orthodox Christian retort by Sinkewicz in Yangazoglou (1992: 21–2, n. 19). However, in a personal exchange I had with fr. Andrew Louth (at Senate House on 12 June 2012) he suggested that Palamas wants rather to stress the presence of the Spirit in the church, as the Love between God and the church. (On this admittedly complicated issue, see also Palamas, *Capita* ... *CL*, 36,28–31 and Siecienski (2010: 146) as well as Chouliaras (2018) for the state of the art.)

37 Even the creation (again, not a Dionysian term) itself is explained on the basis of God's (passionate) Love (cf. DN 4.10,155,17–20/708B and see Osborne (1994: 194–5) and Esposito Buckley (1992: 55)), whence the differentiation from the lack of envy in Plato's Demiurge. Compare also Klitenic Wear and Dillon (2007: 52, 54, 70–1) and Rist (1966: 240).

38 Klitenic Wear and Dillon (2007: 34) argue convincingly that Dionysius picks up Porphyry's 'heretical' interpretation of the *Parmenides*, whereby both the first two Hypotheses are attributed to the One (cf. Klitenic Wear and Dillon 2007: 33, 47). In particular, the second Hypothesis allows for the connection of multiplicity with unity. Despite Porphyry's prominence, whose influence on Dionysius is detailed in Klitenic Wear and Dillon (2007: 45–8), they conclude that with regard to the Trinity 'Dionysius reproduces the thought of the Cappadocian Fathers, as well as the Platonic concept of the unity of the intelligibles' (esp. Being-Life-Intellect), a claim that is fleshed out in the main body of this illuminating chapter (Klitenic Wear and Dillon 2007: 37–48). A virtue of this reading is that it explains why the processions referred to infra in n. 55 are used in contexts about both the Trinity (internal multiplicity) and the creation (external to the Godhead multiplicity), while it parallels my discussion of how the 'causal' and the 'existential' mode refer to God. I am more resistant to accepting, though, that the Cappadocians, being influential to Dionysius, were eagerly copying Porphyry's trinitarian understanding (see Klitenic Wear and Dillon 2007: 34 and 132; cf. also Dillon 1989: 10–12). On the other hand, Riggs (2011: e.g. 75) reads Dionysius' account of the Trinity through the lens of Proclus' henadology (which, once more, is read through the lens of Butler 2014: see also supra, nn. 102 and 310 in Sections 2.1.3 and 2.2.4, respectively).

39 Rather ironically, such an example about the relationality of Eros is already given in Socrates' interchange with Agathon in the *Symposium* 199d1-8.

40 See, for example, the opening prayer of *The Mystical Theology* (MT) 141,2 (Heil-Ritter)/997A (PG. For an old English translation of this work still reprinted, see Rolt (2007), and for a much fresher one, which seems to, but should not, be neglected, see Blum-Golitzin (1991: 379–87); NB that in 386 the little paragraph before chapter V is an editorial interpolation of the translator, and is not clearly marked off). From DN see e.g. §1.4,112,7–113,12/589D-592B; §1.5,116,7–10/593B; §2: *passim*; §11.5,221,8–10 (pace Migne's edition: PG 953A-B, where there is no reference to the Spirit; cf. also infra, n.135); §13.3,229,6–10/980D-981A. Let me add that the language of 'consubstantiality' («ὁμοούσιον») used before, employed by Fathers like Athanasius the Great and the Cappadocians and included in the Nicene Creed, is not used by Dionysius, and reasonably so, if he would like to pretend that he writes in the Apostolic times. So, in DN 1.5,116,9/593B Dionysius indicates 'consubstantiality' with the adjectives «ὁμόθεος» ('possessing the same divinity') and «ὁμοάγαθος» ('possessing the same goodness') Trinity. On the other hand, this is not the case regarding the advanced Neoplatonic language he uses which is well ahead of the Apostolic/Middle-Platonic era. Finally, Loudovikos (2002: 11) notes that, in contrast to Maximus the Confessor, the notion of consubstantiality is absent from Dionysius' ecclesiology, too.

41 Florovsky (1987: 220); cf. also Golitzin (1994: 54) and Florovsky (1933: 109), cited (in English from Russian) by J. Pelikan in his introduction to Berthold (1985: 7 and n. 27 in 13. For Florovsky as a reader of Dionysius see Golitzin (1999)). Cf. also Pelikan's introduction in Luibheid-Rorem (1987: 19 and n. 38) and Armstrong (1982: 221 with the references though in n. 19 of 292).

42 For the sake of clarity, I have inverted Dionysius' order of exposition. For (i) and (ii) see DN 2.3:125,13–126,2/640B-C. Louth (1989: 89) notes that this distinction is familiar from the Cappadocians. For (a) and (b) and their interweaving with (i) and (ii) see DN 2.4–6:126,3–130,13/640D-644D. See also a very helpful table with these distinctions in Siasos (1984: 115–16).

43 See DN 2.11,137,8–13/652A.

44 Cf. also Golitzin (1994: 54).

45 See Siasos (1984: 117).

46 Cf. DN 2.7,130,14–131,1/644D-645A.

47 See also Rorem's nn. 3 and 10 on DN §1 in Luibheid-Rorem (1987: 49, 52).

48 Cf. Siasos (1984: 117–18). On the brief recapitulation of Dionysius' programme in MT, but outside Siasos' argument, see n. 17 in Luibheid-Rorem (1987: 140). Pallis (2016/2017, but still forthcoming: 3–4 of the final draft) disagrees with Siasos' view, too, and gives an interesting arithmological analysis of the CD (with references to Pythagoreanism, Jewish or Neoplatonic), interpreting the symbolisms regarding the number of books and chapters of the extant corpus, as well of the allegedly lost books (seven in total). A dimension he perceptively brings out (2016/2017, but still forthcoming: 4) is that by referring to 'lost' works Dionysius is performing an 'apophatic game'. See a broader and detailed examination of his in Pallis (2013: 45–64, 172–81, esp. 52–6 with more references), as well as a shorter statement in Pallis (unpublished). (I am grateful to D. Pallis for generously sharing with me bibliographical information and material on Dionysius that I have used in various notes.)

49 DN 4.14,160,4–5/712C: « … ἢ ὅτι αὐτὸς ἑαυτοῦ καὶ ἑαυτῷ ἐστι προαγωγικὸς καὶ κινητικός.»

50 Ibid., 160,8/712C: « … ὥσπερ ἔκφανσιν ὄντα ἑαυτοῦ δι' ἑαυτοῦ».

51 Ibid., 160,8–9/712C: « … τῆς ἐξῃρημένης ἑνώσεως ἀγαθὴν πρόοδον … ». There are many parallel phrases in this dense subchapter.

52 Ibid., 160,10.

53 Ibid., 2.5,128,15–17/641D-644A: « … θεία διάκρισίς ἐστιν ἡ ἀγαθοπρεπὴς πρόοδος τῆς ἑνώσεως τῆς θείας ὑπερηνωμένως ἑαυτὴν ἀγαθότητι πληθυούσης τε καὶ πολλαπλασιαζούσης, … ».

54 For instance, Dionysius speaks of 'theogony' («θεογονίας»; cf. Hesiod's work with this title) in DN 128,10/641D; see also the whole passage: DN 128,10–13 and cf. Klitenic Wear and Dillon (2007: 36). Whether Dionysius is its most faithful

exponent or not, the Christian dialectic of Uncreated (Ἄκτιστον: a word absent from the Corpus Areopagiticum) and created (κτιστόν: appearing through Dionysius' quotations of Paul), characteristic of e.g. Athanasius the Great, seems to be absent from (pagan) Neoplatonism.

55 «Πρόοδος» refers to the internal relations of the Trinity also in: DN 2.11,135,14/649B, while at the very same chapter the instances of 136,5/649B and 137,9/652A refer clearly to God's activities with respect to creation (although the noun «δημιουργία» is not used in DN). To the latter camp belong also the «οὐσιοποιὸς πρόοδος» of ibid., 5.1,180,12–13/816B and 5.9,188,18/825A and the πρόοδος (both in singular and in plural) of: 5.2,181,18/816D; 9.5,211,4 and 12/913A and B; 9.9,213,14 and 17/916C. See also Terezis (2012).

56 See also supra, n. 21.

57 Cf. DN 4.12,158,14/709D and 4.10,155,17–18/708B; 4.13,159,19/712B and 4.14,160,10/712C, where the 'in' formula is combined with the 'causal' one (cf. «προϋπάρχων», «προΐδρυται», «προοῦσαν»).

58 Hence that Eros is in God does not mean that God simply has Eros, but He is Eros Himself.

59 It will have become evident by now that Dionysius' 'causal' mode of being and love is to be disconnected from God's 'causaliter' love as it features in Aquinas (cf. McGinn 1996: 207, n. 51), and which is the origin of love by participation, to be treated infra in Section 3.1.2.

60 «Ἀλλ' οὔτε ἐν ἀγγέλοις ἐστὶ τὸ κακόν. Εἰ γὰρ ἐξαγγέλλει τὴν ἀγαθότητα τὴν θείαν ὁ ἀγαθοειδὴς ἄγγελος ἐκεῖνο ὢν κατὰ μέθεξιν δευτέρως, ὅπερ κατ' αἰτίαν τὸ ἀγγελλόμενον πρώτως, … »: DN 4.22,169,20–2/724B.

61 See the helpful table by Dodds (1963: 232).

62 The Christian tendency not only for triads but also for pairs and dual formulas is revealed in the case of the unmediated relation between God and the cosmos. But this should not be so foreign for a Neoplatonist too: apart from the subscription to the ten Pythagorean pairs, all Neoplatonists, including Iamblichus and his incontinence regarding median terms, contrasted the one with the many (see e.g. Proclus, *ET* prop.1 and the first Pythagorean pair).

63 Hence, we return to a Platonism that is characterized by 'self-predication'. Cf. also Osborne (1994: 192–3), although I disagree with some of the claims she makes on this occasion.

64 This is brought out lucidly in the following phrase from DN 2.8,133,3–4/645D: 'The caused things preexist more fully and more truly in the causes (περισσῶς καὶ οὐσιωδῶς προένεστι τὰ τῶν αἰτιατῶν τοῖς αἰτίοις).'

65 See ibid., 4.7,151,2–17/701C-704A.

66 Cf. ibid., 4.7,151,3 and 5/701C. Dionysius' term for the Proclean participle «μετεχόμενον» is the noun «μετοχή».

67 On Dionysian 'aesthetics', see Ivanovic (2019: 51–76), as well as Garitsis (2002), published almost contemporaneously with Triantari-Mara (2002).
68 Cf. DN 151,11/701D, in the neutral form, where the adjective «πάγκαλον» is used, too. Dionysius also employs the etymology we found in Proclus, in Alc. 328,12 (cf. supra, n. 293 in Section 2.2.4), and which is ultimately derived from the *Cratylus* 416b6-d11, in DN 4.7,151,9–10/701C-D: «καὶ ὡς πάντα πρὸς ἑαυτὸ καλοῦν, ὅθεν καὶ κάλλος λέγεται».
69 Cf. also DN 11.6:221,18–22/953C and 222,13–15/(953D-)956A.
70 In ibid., 4.7,151,16 and 18/704A (for God – cf. ibid., 152,4 – and creation respectively) another feminine noun is introduced: «καλλονή».
71 Cf. also Molodeţ-Jitea (2015: 95 in the end of l.9 an 's' is missing from the word '[s]*uper*'). This happens with the name 'Light', too, etc. Of course, none of Dionysius' 'super'-formulas is idiomatic Greek, and to my knowledge there is no antecedent in Classical or Neoplatonic literature of the composite name 'super-eros'. For other exceptions, see «ὑπερουράνιος» in Plato, *Phaedrus* 247c3; «ὑπεράγαθον» and «ὑπέρκαλος» in Plotinus, *Enn.* VI.9.6,40 and I.8.2,8 respectively (cf. «ὑπέρκαλον» in V.8.8,21 and VI.7.33,20); «ὑπερκόσμιος» in Proclus' *Republic Commentary* vol. 2: 257,23 (one of many entries in TLG's search). See also Klitenic Wear and Dillon (2007: 11).
72 See also the explanation with regard to God's name «ὁ ὤν» (from Exod. 3.14, instead of «ὁ ὑπερών») in DN 5.5,184,2–7/820B.
73 Compare the results of God's providence and of His love in DN 4.7,152,12–153,1/704B-C (esp. 152,16–18 and 19–20) and ibid., 4.10,155,8–11/708A (partly cited in the chapter's beginning) respectively. Cf. also Golitzin (1994: 66).
74 Cf. e.g. DN 4.7,152,6–9/704B, which provides a short explanation for Dionysius' identification, and de Vogel (1963: 11 with nn.1–2). The formula of «καλὸς καὶ ἀγαθός» (or in the inverse order) reappears quite frequently in this subchapter (§4.7), as well as §§4.10 and 12, and brings to our mind the ancient Greek «πολίτης» (citizen), whose Athenian ideal was to become «καλὸς κἀγαθός» (although Dionysius does not use the contraction-«κρᾶσις» of «καί» with «ἀγαθός»). Reasonably enough, since although both Aristotle and Dionysius would agree that man is 'by nature a political animal' (cf. Aristotle, *Politics* I.2,1253a2-3), for – I hope – Dionysius contra Aristotle (cf. ibid., 1253a27-9 and 3–4) God is not solitary (because He is Trinitarian). Finally, there might be also resonances with Plotinus, *Enn.* I.6, where although the main thesis is, with Proclus, that the Good is higher than the Beautiful (e.g. §9,37–9) and is its source (§9,41–2), in the vacillating final words of the treatise (§9,39–40 and 42–3) he leaves open the possibility that the Good could be identified with the Beautiful. See Kalligas' surprise ad loc. and his tentative explanation in Kalligas (2014: 218). See also the wider picture by Corrigan (2018: 33–5, 44).

75 Drawing on the Proclean principle that the higher an entity the deeper its effects. See ET proposition 57. (Thus, in a discussion I had with Jan Opsomer in London quite a few years ago, he spoke of Proclus' 'onion'-image of reality.)
76 See supra in Section 1.1.3 on the issue of erotic «συναίρεσις» in Plotinus, *Enn.* III.5.
77 See also supra, n. 20 (with n. 19). NB the Trinitarian grounding noted above and contrast also Proclus, in Alc. 53,2-3: «τὰ μὲν οὖν νοητὰ διὰ τὴν ἄφραστον ἕνωσιν οὐ δεῖται τῆς ἐρωτικῆς μεσότητος.» ('Now the intelligibles on account of their unutterable union have no need of the mediation of love'.)
78 One might propose that Christ is the proper mediator between humanity and God. Although He exemplifies the bond of humanity and divinity, representing Him as a mediating entity is not helpful. Rather Christ encompasses everything. More on Dionysius' Christ infra in Section 3.2. A more apt case is that of Panagia (Παναγία/Holy Mary), the Mother of God (Θεοτόκος), who according to the hymnography is a «μεσίτρια». Dionysius without addressing this issue and without even mentioning her name seems to be referring to her Dormition in DN 3.2,141,6ff/681Cff (cf. also n. 130 in Luibheid-Rorem (1987: 70)), although this view has been repeatedly challenged; cf. Andreopoulos (2016: e.g. nn. 13-14 with bibliography).
79 For this common Neoplatonic principle, see e.g. DN 2.6,129,14-15/644B.
80 According to the famous enunciation of Gen. 1.26-7, man was made after the 'image and likeness' of God. Dionysius in DN 9.6,211,19-20/913C applies this formula not only to mankind, but to everything that has demiurgically 'proceeded' from God. So, for instance, the half of the formula, i.e. the image of God, is ascribed to angels in DN 4.22,169,22-170,1/724B. (I cannot locate with certainty the other allusion to the abovementioned passage of Genesis indicated by the Index of Luibheid-Rorem (1987: 294a to be CH 15.3,53/329C42), although language of similarity is present there. Due to this language, the context of the passage first referred to in this note clearly reminds the reader of the Platonic *Parmenides*' first part.)
81 On the complementarity of the two alternatives, see DN 9.6,211,18-19/913C.
82 Luibheid-Rorem have 'this divine yearning', in their usual habit of not rendering «ἔρως» as love or plainly 'eros' (cf. Luibheid-Rorem 1987: 80, n. 150). Although for this reason I prefer the rendering 'love for God' found in Ware (1995: 25), I believe that preserving the form of Dionysius' cryptic enunciations (adjective and noun here: «θεῖος ἔρως», as Luibheid-Rorem do) is more efficient. So, in this case does Dionysius mean God (the divine eros par excellence) or the cosmos? Both, as we shall see, and as is indicated from the preceding and following passages, are at stake, but because the source is God I would like to emphasize this aspect. (Hence 'love of God' might have been better than 'love for God', where the

genitive 'of God' can be either objective or subjective.) See also Osborne (1994: 28ff), who discerns a third interpretive possibility, too.

83 DN 4.13,158,19–160,3/712A. Cf. also the parallel references given ad loc. in nn. 156 and 160 by Luibheid-Rorem (1987: 82–3).

84 On this important notion see the old study of Völker (1958), who despite the old trend emphasizes Dionysius' antecedents in previous Patristic literature, e.g. Gregory of Nyssa. Yannaras, presumably following Lossky (1974: 120) (see, however, also Papanikolaou (2006a: 198, n. 5)), connects the Dionysian ecstasy with Heidegger's etymology of existence as 'Ek-sistenz'. (Cf. Yannaras 2005: 106–7, speaking in 106 of the 'ecstatic existence of God'; cf. also 131, nn. 16 and 18, where the bibliographical reference to Heidegger.)

85 Cf. also Golitzin (1994: 48, 67) and Ivanović (2015: 132).

86 See/exploit also the use of «θεῖος ἔρως» in DN 4.10,155,16–17/708B.

87 Dionysius' treatment of ἔκστασις gives solid Patristic background to fr. Loudovikos' criticism of Yannaras and Zizioulas regarding the connection of nature with necessity. It is a different thing to say that a nature or a being is ecstatic (as Dionysius does in our passage) and different to speak of a being's 'ecstasy from (or "for") its nature' as these two important contemporary personalist thinkers seem to do. See Loudovikos (2011: *passim*, e.g. 686), who centres his discussion around Maximus the Confessor and shows the latter's relevance to contemporary anthropological problems; for the ongoing debate, see Loudovikos (2013, 2014). Finally, as an example of Dionysius' having no problem with (a being's) nature, see DN 4.26,173,14–15/728C.

88 Gal. 2:20, cited in DN 4.13,159,5–6/712A: «"Ζῶ ἐγώ," φησίν, 'οὐκ ἔτι, ζῇ δὲ ἐν ἐμοὶ Χριστός'.» See the whole passage ibid., 159,3–8/712A. For a parallel instance of ecstasy, that of Hierotheus, see ibid., 3.2,141,11–12/681D, and for an admonition to do so via apophaticism, see ibid., 7.1,194,12–15/865D-868/A. Ibid., 7.4,199,13–16/872D-873A is an interesting passage in which the first instance of «ἐξεστηκώς» (perfect participle of «ἐξίσταμαι») has a negative sense, while the second instance in the next line has the positive meaning, as it happens with the words «μανία-μαινόμενος» in Proclus, in Alc. (see supra, n. 197 in Section 2.1.5), taking its lead from the famous classifications of the *Phaedrus*. (Incidentally, «μαινόμενος» in the negative sense appears in the last line of the Dionysian passage referred to.) Finally, while the ecstasy of MT 142,9–11/997B-1000A and DN 13.3,230,1–3/981B has the positive sense, it is indirectly connected with God-directedness, and directly related to ecstasy from those that put obstacles to the being's relationship and union with God. In any case, Rist (1999: 385–6) argues against Rorem that this instance, too, should be connected with eros, despite the absence of the word in MT.

89 DN 4.13,159,10–14/712A-B: « … δι' ὑπερβολὴν τῆς ἐρωτικῆς ἀγαθότητος ἔξω ἑαυτοῦ γίνεται ταῖς εἰς τὰ ὄντα πάντα προνοίαις καὶ οἷον ἀγαθότητι καὶ ἀγαπήσει

καὶ ἔρωτι θέλγεται καὶ ἐκ τοῦ ὑπὲρ πάντα καὶ πάντων ἐξῃρημένου πρὸς τὸ ἐν πᾶσι κατάγεται κατ' ἐκστατικὴν ὑπερούσιον δύναμιν ἀνεκφοίτητον ἑαυτοῦ.»

90 This is my qualification to the informative n. 266 of Luibheid-Rorem (1987: 130).
91 Cf. also Golitzin (1994: 67, 68), Rist (1966: 239-40), Louth (1989: 95), Aertsen (2009: 196) and Esposito Buckley (1992: 39, 56). As I indicated before (in Section 3.1.1), the reason for this should be traced in the Trinity.
92 See e.g. Plotinus, *Enn.* VI.9.11,22-5, esp. l.23. For this reason, Aquinas seems to be missing the point once again, since he holds that ecstasy cannot be really ascribed to God except by metaphor; cf. McGinn (1996: 206 and 209).
93 This is not exactly what Klitenic Wear and Dillon (2007: 122-3) say, but compare 128-9. It is strange that, given the aims of their book, in these contexts of loving ecstasy Klitenic Wear and Dillon contrast Dionysius only to Plotinus without mentioning Proclus.
94 Contrast Perl (2007: 45-6).
95 This is consonant with what Osborne (1994: esp. 77-9, 80) says about love being itself a motivation with reference to Gregory of Nyssa and Origen; cf. also Osborne (1994: 219).
96 This is a possibility that we do not find formulated in Neoplatonic texts we have approached so far. Rist (1966: 241) connects it primarily with the love between the Persons of the Trinity and derivatively with the love for one's neighbours. Kupperman (2013) takes issue with Rist in this respect but, in my view at least, his quick and oversimplified presentation do not suffice to convince one of his (not so original) conclusions.
97 Heraclitus B60 DK: «ὁδὸς ἄνω κάτω μία καὶ ὠυτή».
98 Cf. 1 Jn 4.19: «Ἡμεῖς ἀγαπῶμεν αὐτόν [i.e. God], ὅτι αὐτὸς πρῶτος ἠγάπησεν ἡμᾶς.» In Photius, *Fragmenta in epistulam ad Romanos* (in catenis) 493,34 (in Staab 1933; cf. also Zografidis (2009: 19a) and Mavropoulos (2017: 251-2)) the formula has become: «ὅτι αὐτὸς ἡμῶν *ἠράσθη* πρῶτος». Cf. a quite similar phrase in Saint Nectarios (2010: 38) and see an analogous scheme about knowledge in Paul's Gal. 4.9, whence Bulgakov (2012: 127), applying this particularly to Dionysius, speaks of an 'erotic gnoseology'. For Maximus' elaborations on the Dionysian theme of love as ecstasy, see Loudovikos (2010: 172-7); see also Harper (2019: esp. 233-68).
99 Thus, it is in this not quite Neoplatonic sense that we should understand the Neoplatonic similarity principle expressed in the following enunciation of DN 9.6,211,18-19/913C: «Καὶ ἔστιν ἡ τῆς θείας ὁμοιότητος δύναμις ἡ τὰ παραγόμενα πάντα πρὸς τὸ αἴτιον ἐπιστρέφουσα.» ('It is the power of the divine similarity which returns everything toward the cause.')
100 More accurately in God's providential activities (which are uncreated according to Palamas).
101 See also Ramfos (1999: 159), who stresses the freedom of man's loving response to the divine call. Cf. Ramfos (1999: 160 and 167). (This erudite work belongs to

Ramfos' previous, 'Neo-orthodox' phase of his writing career.) Cf. also Manos (1995: 58). (Ivanović (2015: 136–9) treats the problem of God's freedom to create.)

102 Cf. also Manos (2006: 67).

103 See e.g. Perl (2007: 35, 37–40); cf. also Perl (2007: 41, 47–8, 112) and Golitzin (1994: 67, 71). Especially with respect to Proclus, see de Vogel (1963: 28 with n. 1) and Gersh (1973: 124–5, 127 responding in a slightly oversimplified manner to Nygren). Cf. also Florovsky (1987: 214–15) (although he refers to other characteristics of the image of the circle, too).

104 As with my n. 66 (in Section 3.1.1) on Dionysius' term «μετοχή» instead of «μετεχόμενον», so too here Dionysius avoids the active participle «ἐρῶν» and «ἀγαπῶν» for the respective nouns «ἔρως» and «ἀγάπη». Using solely the latter term, this is also what Paul does in 1 Cor. 13.4–8 (as part of the 'Hymn of Love', for which see infra, n. 147). This is called 'Pauline predication' by Vlastos and connected to the alleged problem of self-predication in Plato (for which see also supra, n. 63); cf. Edwards (2009: 203 with the reference in 214, n. 9).

105 DN 4.14,160,1–2/712C. Remember and compare the *Symposium*'s Socrates who transformed his beloveds into his lovers.

106 Cf. also Niarchos (1995: 107).

107 See also Ivanović (2015: 133–5).

108 It is an irony that Dionysius' work serves as the unfolding of Hierotheus' condensed teaching. Cf. DN 3.2,140,6–16, esp. ll.6–10.

109 See ibid., §§4:15 and 16.

110 DN 4.17,162,1–5/713D. In the very dense last clause ('thus turning … circle') the locution (hyperbaton) 'turning … in an everlastic circle' captures the meaning of two participles («ἀνακυκλοῦσα» and «ἀνελιττομένη»), since Dionysius seems to be viewing them as complementary (using more than one similar phrases in order to describe one single phenomenon).

111 Still, modern jargon speaks of the distinct notion of 'panentheism', various sorts of which are detected in the Neoplatonic and the Christian structures of reality. See Culp (2013) and the contributions in Clayton-Peacocke (2004), which include Orthodox Christian perspectives on the issue, too.

112 See e.g. the discussion in DN 11.6, esp. 223,4–14/956A-B.

113 For further bibliography on the question, see Rorem (1993: 177, n. 11). Cf. also Perl (2007: 33).

114 See also Golitzin (1994: 66–7, 69) on the cycle imagery.

115 Movement/motion should not be conceived rigidly and exclusively as locomotion, as exactly with the Peripatetic tradition (cf. e.g. *EE* I.6.5,1222b29). Dionysius examines the kinds of motion that pertain to divine minds (i.e. angels) in DN 4.8,153,4–9/704D-705A. The threefold (dialectical) scheme here is circular motion, straight and finally spiral. The three stages should be

conceived as working not successively, but contemporaneously at different levels. The case of soul is examined in the next chapter, ibid., 4.9,153,10–154,6/705A-B. Here, whereas circular motion is the starting point, the two next stages are inverted: first comes spiral and in the end straight motion. The consecutive chapter (DN §, 4.10) speaks of God as the goal and enabler of all these motions, while He is 'beyond every rest and motion' (ibid., 4,10,154,9–10/705C). Still, beside this Platonic or Aristotelian picture of the ineffable First Principle, God also comes into communion with creation, hence in ibid., 9.9,213,15–20/916C-D Dionysius returns to complete and specify the topic. Now, circular motion is put at the end stage which is preceded by the straight and the spiral motion. NB that the final and the starting point in a cycle are the same. More specifically, straight motion refers to God's generation of the cosmos, whereas spiral motion to the cosmos' providential sustainment by God. Finally, 'the circular movement has to do with his sameness, to the grip he has on the middle range as well as on the outer edges of order, so that all things are one and all things that have gone forth from him may return to him once again' (ibid., 9.9,213,18–20/916D). In other words, circular movement here refers to Eros, as treated in my main text. (Klitenic Wear and Dillon (2007: 30) examine the Neoplatonic antecedents of the above-mentioned types of motion. See also Klitenic Wear and Dillon 2007: 55–6.)

116 Hence, one can claim that although the cycle implies a unique force, the hierarchy is not affected; the earth for instance has a North and a South Pole. However, this thought forgets the presence of Christ who is both God and man, while the North Pole will never meet the South. More on this infra (in Section 3.2), but see also the compelling account of Louth (1989: 108), without invoking, at least explicitly, Christ at this point. I must also add that apart from the abovementioned image of the cycle, there is another one in Dionysius that exploits the relation between the circle, its radii and its centre (which has resemblances but should not be confused with the image given supra, n. 17, too) and has inspired Maximus the Confessor; cf. Cvetkovic (2016: esp. 280–1, where one finds the Dionysian texts and references in nn. 3 and 4). For pagan Neoplatonic antecedents and parallel usages of this version, see Greig (unpublished yet-a. In 11 with n. 28 of this draft Greig refers briefly to Dionysius, too. I thank the author for permitting me to refer to this draft.)

117 So, Corrigan (2018: 112) claims that 'Dionysius turns the whole of pagan thought on its head, while simultaneously remaining faithful to its wellsprings in Plato and Aristotle' (who are of course part and parcel of pagan thought, and from whom the Neoplatonists were inspired, too). See also infra, n. 119.

118 Cf. e.g. DN 4.10,155,8/708A: «Πᾶσιν οὖν ἐστι τὸ καλὸν καὶ ἀγαθὸν ἐφετὸν καὶ ἐραστὸν καὶ ἀγαπητόν, … ».

119 Hence, once more Corrigan (2018: 111) concludes that in Dionysius, despite his Proclean background, we find 'an intimate paradoxical coincidence of opposites – transcendence and immanence – in which the divine [i.e. God's] longing for created things is manifested' (my comments in square brackets). Cf. also Corrigan (2018: 110, 112–13 and 124).

120 Not envious («φθονερός» or jealous) of course. See DN 4.13,159,14–18/712B. For the scriptural basis, see e.g. Exod. 20.5 and 30.14 with further references in the upper apparatus of Suchla (1990: ad loc.).

121 See also in Ivanović (2015: 132–3).

122 Hence my disagreement with Perl's methodology enunciated in Perl (2007: 2). See also supra, n. 27.

123 The most extensive and enlightening Dionysian reference to Christ in DN forms another supposed quotation from Dionysius' «καθηγεμών», Hierotheus' Θεολογικαὶ Στοιχειώσεις (a title suspiciously similar to Proclus' *Elements*) and figures as chapter §2.10. In its first part Hierotheus/Dionysius proclaims Christ's divinity (DN 134,7–135,1/648C-D), while incarnation and the paradoxical conjunction of full divinity and full humanity are extolled in the second part (ibid., 135,2–9/648D-649A). See also Hainthaler (1997) and cf. Louth (2008a: 582, n. 7, 580), Armstrong (1982: n. 20 in 292 with some reservations in 221) and Esposito Buckley (1992: 58–9). Hence, I agree with Riggs (2009: 76 see also, 77, 96 and Riggs (2010: 129–30, n. 163)) and Stang (2012: 14 with n. 7) in not assuming that Dionysius was a monophysite, as Klitenic Wear and Dillon (2007: 4–6, 49–50, 131, 133) do. (Cf. also Pelikan's thesis in the introduction to Luibheid-Rorem (1987: 13–17)). Regarding the «θεανδρικὴ ἐνέργεια» of Ep. 4.(1),19/1072C, which has been taken to suggest 'monenergism' (cf. e.g. Pelikan in Luibheid-Rorem (1987: 19–21) and Klitenic Wear and Dillon (2007: 5–6, 133)), although Maximus the Confessor, the champion of Christ's double activity and will, did not do so (cf. the commentators' perplexity noted by Rorem (1993: 9–11)), Louth (1989: 14) speaks of Dionysius' 'Cyrilline way of speaking of the incarnation'. See also Vasilakis (2019a: n. 96 in 196 with 189).

124 Meyendorff (1969: 81); cf. citation by Pelikan in the introduction to Berthold (1985: 7 and n. 28 in 13). Cf. also Florovsky (1987: 225 but contrast 226). So, for instance, when in the penultimate chapter (IV) of the *MT* Dionysius stresses that the ineffable God transcends every perceptual category, we might wonder why he does not allude to Christ. Apart from the specific aims of the treatise, a response might have been that he is thinking in terms of Christ's resurrected («καινόν») body, and this might underlie Maximus' thought infra, in n. 151. However, Dionysius' scholiast (here Maximus indeed; see next n. 119), despite the fact that Christ is in the context few lines below (DN 1.4,114,7–11, esp. l.8), does not allude to Christ either: *Scholia in Dionysii Areopagitae Librum de* Divinis Nominibus

cum additamentis interpretum aliorum, 139 (Suchla) (in the apparatus criticus for 197,29-31 – pagination and lineation borrowed from *PG*: vol.4 – commenting on DN 1.4,114,6). In any case, Golitzin (2013: 41-50, esp. 41) has persuasively argued that the first five Dionysian Epistles form a (chiastic) unity that serves to complete the content of the MT. He thus brings out the Christological and sacramental/mystical/liturgical dimensions of CD that usually get lost when one reads MT in isolation from the rest of the corpus (cf. e.g. Golitzin 2013: 49-50).

125   See e.g. Pelikan in Berthold (1985: 7): 'Maximus explained the language of Dionysius in such a manner that he achieved the Trinitarian and Christocentric reorientation of the Dionysian system and thus rehabilitated it.' Some lines below Pelikan speaks of Maximus' 'Trinitarian Christocentrism'. See also in Berthold (1985: 6), but contrast infra, n. 152. Despite the long tradition reflected in Migne's *PG*, and followed even today in some modern editions/translations (like Gounelas 2002: e.g. 63 and note in 41), most of the *Commentary* on Dionysius' works attributed to Maximus the Confessor was in fact written by John of Scythopolis. Cf. e.g. Louth (1993: 166-7) with references (in nn. 1 and 2) to the groundwork of von Balthasar (1940), as well as the more recent study of Suchla (1980). For a short intellectual portrait of John of Scythopolis, see Louth (2008a: 575-8). (See also in Vasilakis (2017b: 414, n. 33).) Finally, in the critical edition of Suchla (2011) all questions regarding who has written what in the scholia to Dionysius have been answered.

126   Loudovikos (2003: esp. the first essay (15-42), as well as *passim* in the 'Concluding Summary' in English: 103-14) forms an example of how such a Christology can be of an aid to the psychoanalyst.

127   See also Golitzin (1994: 65-6). On the precedents of this word in Plato and Proclus' *Alcibiades Commentary* see supra, n. 87 in Section 2.1.3. For a succinct archaeology of the word in Stoicism, Middle Platonism, Clement of Alexandria and Origen, see Osborne (1994: 171-6 with relevant bibliography in 171-2, n.24; see also nn. 45 and 48 in 177 and 178, respectively). For the use in Gregory of Nyssa, see Rist (1966: 237-8). The most comprehensive study I have come across, starting with both Jewish and ancient Greek background (first attestation of the noun in Aeschylus), tracking its use and semantic changes among Christian (e.g. the Cappadocians) and pagan authors (e.g. Themistius) in order to culminate as a study of φιλανθρωπία in saint John Chrysostom (in fourth century CE), is Krstić 2012. It would be a worth-while subject of research to compare the use of the word by Dionysius and Chrysostom (for the latter is quite central), but such a project would lead us astray for my present purposes.

128   See already the first appearance of Christ in DN, where the «φιλάνθρωπον» is ascribed to the Trinity 'because in one of its persons it accepted a true share (ἐκοινώνησεν) of what it is we are, and thereby issued a call to man's lowly state

to rise up to it [sc. the Divine Trinity]' (cf. DN 1.4,113,6–9/592A), although some lines below, ibid., 1.4,114,3/592B φιλανθρωπία is related primarily to the Scripture (i.e. the word of God). Again, in ibid., 2.6,130,9–10/644C Dionysius speaks of the «φιλάνθρωπος ὁμοβουλία» ('the identity of will that loves mankind') of the Trinity in the context of making clear that despite this, only the second Person, who has the entirety of Godhead though, was incarnated (see ibid., 130,8–9). See also ibid., 2.3,125,21–126,2/640C (implicit about the incarnation) and 2.10,135,2–3/648D (explicitly connected with the incarnation and supposedly quoted by Hierotheus), with further references in n. 56 (on CH 4.4,22,23–5/181B) by Luibheid-Rorem (1987: 158); cf. also Golitzin (1994: 66, n. 161). Finally, as was indicated above there are also instances where φιλανθρωπία is not directly related with Christ or the incarnation; see DN 6.2,191,16/856D, where «ὑπέρβλυσις φιλανθρωπίας» ('overflowing of love for mankind') is ascribed to the Godhead as (the giver of) Life (and perhaps Ep. 8.4,15/1093D and 21–2/1096A, too). See also Rist (1966: 238, n. 11).

129 Apart from the philosophical preexistence of the word «φιλανθρωπία» noted above (n. 127) and the rareness of Greek compounds with the word ἀγάπη or ἔρως («παιδεραστία» being an exception), the issue is like with «φιλοσοφία» (used by Dionysius e.g. in DN 3.3,142,11/684B): although we do not do this in the case of the noun, we describe philosophers as lovers (ἐρασταί) of e.g. truth. (See the formula «ἀληθείας ... ἐρασταί» in ibid., 1.5,117,8/593C.) In general, there are few usages of the word «φιλία» in the *Divine Names* (while it does not appear in the other Areopagitic writings; see e.g. DN 4.21,169,7–11/724A, ibid., 4.19,164,13–14/717A, and in conjunction with harmony ibid., 4.7,152,20), as also in Plotinus (see some instances supra, in n. 347 of Section 2.2.5). Consequently, I do not refer further to it, as I did in Proclus' case. Finally, in the end of DN Dionysius asks Timothy's benevolence, because the former is «φίλος ἀνήρ» of the latter (cf. DN 13.4,230,22/984A) and hopes that his work is «τῷ θεῷ φίλον» ('dear to God'; cf. ibid., 13.4,231,6/984A. It is also in the end of the *Phaedrus* 279c6-7 that a Pythagorean maxim about friends is mentioned).

130 There is a sole reference to 'self-emptying' («κενώσεως»: DN 2.10,135,6/649A; cf. Paul, Phil. 2.7) in the whole Dionysian corpus. For the importance of kenosis in orthodox Christian theology, spiritual life and asceticism, see Sakharov (2002: 93–116).

131 Cf. Athanasius of Alexandria, *De incarnatione verbi* 54.3.1–2 (Kannengiesser): «Αὐτὸς γὰρ ἐνηνθρώπησεν, ἵνα ἡμεῖς θεοποιηθῶμεν». Cf. a close Dionysian remark in the initial chapters of DN 1.4,113,6–9. For other references, see Vasilakis (2017b: 411, nn. 21–3).

132 Cf. also Golitzin (1994: 63, 64, 66, 69, 75).

133 See Maximus the Confessor, *Quaestiones ad Thalassium* 60, esp. ll.33–40 and 51–5 (Laga and Steel-vol.2; see English translation in Blowers-Wilken (2003: 123–9, esp. 124, 125)). See also Vletsis (1994: 237–49, esp. 243–5). This is an optimistic

view quite different from the one presupposed and envisaged by Osborne (1994: 196–9), although elsewhere (25–6) she seems to be coming close to Maximian eschatological perspectives.

134 This is again the line of thought taken by Maximus the Confessor (contra Osborne 1994: 197); cf. Louth (2004: 192), who gives a helpful diagram. Hence, because man is the crowing point of demiurgy, the possibility of 'transfiguration' is granted to the entire cosmos. Cf. also Riggs (2010: 128).

135 See DN 11.5,221,8–10, contra Migne/Corderius' text ad loc. (953A-B). Suchla's text (referred to also supra in n. 40) is here verified by the recent edition of Lilla-Moreschini (2018: 108, 12–14 (ad loc.)).

136 DN 11.5,221,5/953A: 'Loving-kindness of Christ, bathed as it is in peace', or in Lilla's rendering: 'the love for mankind which spreads peace, in keeping with the teaching of Christ' (Lilla-Moreschini 2018: 167, 19–20).

137 This is consistent with Rist (1966: 243), although he proposes that in the section of Eros in DN Dionysius is interested in 'cosmic theology' (Rist (1966: 237), said for the corpus in general), and hence in 'cosmic Eros' (Rist 1966: 236). I am not sure what the distinction he implies is. Armstrong (1982: 221) writes with regard to Dionysius that the theophany of creation out of love as well as the (redemptive) return 'are cosmic and universal, not strictly tied to a particular human person or historic event'. That is, he proposes that creation could be conceived as 'cosmic incarnation' (Armstrong 1982: 222), and in this respect he must be deviating from Rist's understanding.

138 Incarnation falls under the differentiated names of differentiated theology (b-ii); see supra in Section 3.1.1.

139 I will develop this idea regarding methodology in another paper. In an enticing short essay Kocijančič (2016: 89) speaks of 'agapic hermeneutics', which he relates to an ontology (the problem of personal identity) that is implied in and invited by the question as to the true author of the CD.

140 See §4.15–17 and §2.10 respectively.

141 See ibid., §3.2, esp. 140,6–10/681B.

142 See the methodological chapter ibid., 13.4, esp. 230,11–22/981C-981D.

143 In this respect Dionysius might come close to Plato's attitude towards his readers. As for 'cryptic enunciations' in need of further clarification, these are in abundance in both writers. Let us not forget that if Dionysius is hidden, philosophically and literarily speaking Plato is also absent from his dialogues.

144 A quite independent instance is DN 13.4,230,18/981D, where «φιλανθρωπία» is attributed to Timothy ('the one who honours God'), to whom the *Divine Names* is addressed (see e.g. the title of the work, DN 107,1/985A with the caveat indicated by n. 2 in Luibheid-Rorem (1987: 49)), with view to Timothy's reception of Dionysius' treatise.

145 See Ep. 10,1117Aff.

146 Cf. ibid., §1.2–3/1117A. See also ibid., l.23.
147 Hence, I give another perspective to the one noted by Rorem (in Luibheid-Rorem 1987: 288, n. 152) or Klitenic Wear and Dillon (2007: 10). Cf. also Vasilakis (2017b: 410, n. 13). What is more, the theme of Love that John's presence evokes, as well as the affirmed belief in God which supports Dionysius' hope that John will be released and return from his exile (see Ep. 10,25–8/1120A), bring to mind the cardinal stages (or the Pauline triad: faith, hope, love) of the 'Hymn of Love' (see 1 Cor. 13. esp. 13), written by another beloved theologian of Dionysius, Paul (see e.g. DN 3.2,140,3–4/681B. Paul is central to Stang's understanding of Dionysius; see Stang 2012: e.g. 3).
148 Actually, Stang (2012: 101) has argued that 'contrary to the claims of so many modern scholars, then, there is a robust Dionysian Christology and that Christology is deeply Pauline'.
149 Due to her contemporary theological agenda, which is selective in that she challenges Process Theology and J. Moltmann, my suggestion is denied by Osborne (1994: 198, 195); cf. also 186–9. In the (Einsteinian) jargon of Rist (1999: 378) erotic ecstasy manifested in the creation corresponds to the 'General Theory of Divinity', whereas incarnation belongs to the 'Special Theory of Divinity'. Cf. also Rist (1999: 380 and 383–4).
150 Regarding Maximus' relation to Dionysius, see Vasilakis (2016: *passim*, e.g. 110 with bibliography) which takes some distance both from the (admittedly broader) study of de Andia (2015) and of the really well-informed approach of Constas (2017). See also Crîşmăreanu (2015) and supra, n. 125.
151 See also Louth (2008b: 590–3 and 595–8 respectively). For instance, Louth emphasizes Maximus' usage of Dionysian apophatic and kataphatic theology with specific regard to Christ (Louth 2008b: 590–1), and mentions Palamas' concern with the issue of angelic mediation, since after the Incarnation man does not necessarily need intermediaries in his communion with God (see Louth 2008b: 597).
152 With Louth (2008b: 591) pace Meyendorff (cf. also Louth 2008b: 590 and n. 14 in 598). Cf. also the most illuminating treatment of Golitzin (2002) (with particular evocation of fr. John Romanides' relevant work) and the sound retort of fr. P. Wesche's accusations in Golitzin (1990).
153 Cf. Gen. 1.31, which is used in CH 2.3,13,23/141C.
154 So, if, as I said, the creation is explained on the grounds of God as Trinity, then also kenosis and incarnation should be explained on this basis. It cannot be an accident that in the strictly monotheistic religion of Islam God is not and cannot be incarnate (Christ is just a prophet before Mohamed), hence the absence of divine representations in religious painting, too. The root of iconoclasm in Byzantium should be traced back to this non-Christian Eastern attitude.

155 Cf. also Edwards (2009: 203 in the context of Augustine's distance from Proclus and in general pagan Neoplatonism; see also 211 and 200–1).
156 Christ is perfect God and perfect Man. This is extolled by Dionysius, supposedly quoting Hierotheus, in e.g. DN 2.10,135,2–9/648D-649A.
157 Especially when the death on the cross has been characterized as «Ἰουδαίοις μὲν σκάνδαλον,Ἕλλησι δὲ μωρία» (1 Cor. 1.23; cf. also Edwards 2009: 207–8 despite 209). See also Dionysius' well-known quote from the *Letter to the Romans* by Ignatius (of Antioch, the 'God-Bearer'; late first century CE), *Rom*. 4.7.2,4 in DN 4.12,157,11/709B (cf. also supra, n. 8 and Edwards 2009: 206): «Ὁ ἐμὸς ἔρως ἐσταύρωται». Although Ignatius' exact meaning can be debated (but see the discussion with bibliography in Ivanović 2015: 125, n. 13), in Dionysius' usage of the phrase the pronoun «ἐμός» ('my') could be also read here as an emphasis in that crucified eros, i.e. Christ (*qua* God), is to be found only in Christianity. (The singular form of the pronoun is simply to denote each Christian's personal, as well as passionate, encounter with God, not any individualistic deviations. The same text of Ignatius had been quoted by no less than Origen; cf. Ivanović (2015: 125 and n. 12) for the exact reference to the *Commentary on the Song of Songs*. For the Christological usage by Dionysius, see also the exhaustive threefold enumeration of possible connotations in Stang (2012: 101), as well as Ghiț (2015: 113–15).)
158 Cf. ET 122,2–3 and 13–16 and see supra, Section 2.1.5.
159 Vasilakis (2019b) connects Socrates' care among else with the philosopher-king's providential descent to the *Republic*'s cave and explains their relative inferiority to the providence exercised by higher Neoplatonic deities.
160 Since Adam failed to become Christ (i.e. χριστός: nominated, dubbed) by grace, the New Adam became man by nature.
161 Hence there is no 'disinterested affection' anymore (in the sense I gave in Section 2.1.5).
162 The phrase 'assists the beings which it administers' is directly taken from the translation in Lilla-Moreschini (2018: 164, 22–3). The verb in this phrase translates the Greek «ἐπαρκοῦσα» (also printed in Suchla's edition), while Chatzimichael (2008: 539, n. 456) sides with Migne's text («ἐπάρχουσα»), which would be rendered as 'is in control of'. (Still, this sense is already captured by the immediately preceding locution: «πάντων κρατοῦσα».)
163 DN 10.1,215,3–7/937A. See also the word «ἀνεκφοίτητος» ('not proceeding from [sc. oneself]': either in adjectival or adverbial form) used about the Deity, while accompanying and contrasted with Its πρόνοια, in ibid., 4.13,159,12–14/712B (esp. l.14); 2.11,135,16–136,1/649B and 137,5–7/652A; 9.5,210,7–11/912D (l.9) and 13.2,227,6–7/977C; Ep. 9.3,9–25/1109B-D, esp. l.11. In DN 4.8,153,7–8/(704D)-705A there is specific reference to the divine minds, i.e. angels. Cf. also ibid., 4.4,147,4–8/697C (comparing Deity with the Sun). In ibid., 9.4,209,13/912B

God is called «ἀμιγές» ('unmixed' or 'unalloyed' with Luibheid-Rorem ad loc.) Being. This is used not only with regard to God's relation to the creation (see DN 2.5,129,9–11/644B; cf. ibid., 2.11,136,15–17/649C), but also when illustrating the unconfused unity of the Persons of the Trinity (see ibid., 2.4,127,12/641B; cf. ibid., 127,15–128,1/641C; 2.5,128,9–10/641D). Furthermore, God's loving effects make also the various elements of the creation be unmixed with each other; see e.g. ibid., 11.2,218,18–21/949C, where only the term «ἀσύγχυτος» is used to describe the «ἕνωσις» effected by «αὐτοειρήνη», and cf. ibid., 8.7,204,8–10/896A and 2.4,128,5–6/641C. Finally, in ibid., 11.2,219,3–5/949C, peace is said to effect both the 'unmixed' union of the created beings with one another and with the Deity. For Proclus' use of the word, see supra in Section 2.1.5.

164 Cf. also Golitzin (1994: 47, 61) and Edwards (2013: 26).

165 This is quoted (or rather paraphrased in Greek) by Dodds (1963: 265) on the occasion of proposition 122 (although the parallel is not very successful as I intend to show).

166 DN 2.10,134,12–14/648C and 135,4–5/648D (again from the supposed quotation from Hierotheus): « ... οὐσία ταῖς ὅλαις οὐσίαις ἀχράντως ἐπιβατεύουσα καὶ ὑπερουσίως ἁπάσης οὐσίας ἐξῃρημένη, ... κἂν τούτοις ἔχει τὸ ὑπερφυὲς καὶ ὑπερούσιον, οὐ μόνον ᾗ ἀναλλοιώτως ἡμῖν καὶ ἀσυγχύτως κεκοινώνηκε». Cf. also Dionysius' *Ecclesiastical Hierarchy* (EH) 3.III.13,14–20, esp. ll.16–17 (Heil-Ritter)/444C (PG).

167 Rather in a non-polemical way Dionysius reproduces the Proclean language by radically resignifying it (although his suggestion, following Clement of Alexandria, might be that the Greeks just distorted the language and/or content of theology; cf. Karamanolis 2013: 44–5). On this attitude see his explicit remarks in *Epistle* 7, esp. §1,1–3/1077B and 1,13–2,5/1080A-B. Cf. also his Ep. 6.7–8/1077A-B and Louth (1989: 14).

168 Cf. supra, n. 125 and Vasilakis (2017b: 414 with n. 31).

169 DN 4.16,161,15/713C: 'the unrelated cause of all yearning'.

170 *Scholia in Dionysii Areopagitae* ... 257 (Suchla) (apparatus criticus on 269B, 28–9 Migne): 'By ἄσχετον he means the absolute, of which [sc. absolute] there is no relation with the all, i.e. [there is no] *natural affinity* [of the absolute with the all].' (My translation and my additions in brackets); see also the paraphrase of Pachymeres ad loc., 780B (in PG: vol.3) and cf. Chatzimichael (2008: 518, n. 240 ad loc.) (For a short presentation of doctrines on love and ecstasy from soul's perspective that the thirteenth-century Byzantine intellectual, Georgios Pachymeres, owes primarily to Dionysius, see Baltas 2002: 126–8). On the occasion of God's «ἄσχετοι μεταδόσεις» in DN 2.5,129,1/644A (cf. also His «ἄσχετος περιοχή» in ibid., 9.9,213,13/916C), Chatzimichael (2008: 505,

n. 134) draws attention to a relevant scholion by John of Scythopolis (even if he says Maximus), the text of which I have identified as *Scholia* ... 178,11–179,7/221B18-29.

171 In DN 6.2,192,1–5/856D Dionysius states one of his great differences from ancient Greek philosophy, i.e. that the promise of immortality refers not only to man's soul, but also to his/her body (through resurrection).

172 This is the 'hypostatic union' enunciated in the Fourth Ecumenical Council (Chalcedon, 451 CE). See also from the hymnology of the Church the «Δοξαστικόν» (mode plagal of the fourth): «Εἷς ἐστιν ὁ Υἱός, διπλοῦς τὴν φύσιν, ἀλλ' οὐ τὴν ὑπόστασιν». Whereas communion with body in Neoplatonism implies a degraded soul, in Christianity there is no natural alteration of the Uncreated nature of God when embracing the created nature of man's unity of soul and body.

173 See another hymnographical example from the Γ' στάσις of the «Ἀκάθιστος Ὕμνος»: «Ὅλως ἦν ἐν τοῖς κάτω, καὶ τῶν ἄνω οὐδόλως ἀπῆν, ὁ ἀπερίγραπτος Λόγος». Regarding the 'conventional' theological/dogmatic language that is used in various places of this chapter which does not always map unto Dionysius' vocabulary, see Vasilakis (2017b: n. 36 in 414–15; cf. also 418) and supra, nn. 8, 34 and 54.

174 From a Stoic or Neoplatonic point of view Christ is not a sage. Why mourn for a person we love (see Christ's crying for the dead Lazarus in Jn 11.35-6) or why to feel fear in front of our sacrifice (see Christ's passionate prayer in Gethsemane apud e.g. Mk 14.33-5 and esp. Lk. 22.40-4)? On this issue see the well-balanced position of Gavrilyuk (2004: esp. chapter 2 in 47–63), who focuses on early Church Fathers such as Cyril of Alexandria. I am in complete agreement with his verdict (2004: 15) that 'impassibility was not baptized without conversion' (hence the way to understand also DN 4.21,169,5–6/721D properly and respond to the concerns of Osborne (1994: 195, 197)).

175 A reason for this is that Dionysius' system is not characterized by the Neoplatonic mediations of Proclus' and even Plotinus' one. (See also supra, n. 27 and Vasilakis 2017b: 415, n. 38.) Still, if per impossibile there were such mediations Christ would still come to the lower strata of the cosmos and be incarnate. Besides, the Gospel assures that if we want to be among the firsts we should go with the last ones. See e.g. Mt. 20.16 and 26-7; cf. ibid., 19.30 and Perl (2013: 31).

Epilogue

In this work we have passed through stations in the journey of eros' transformations or 'metamorphoses' (to recall Apuleius' novel that contains the central myth of Cupid and Psyche). From the Platonic theme of deficiency in the *Symposium*, of which Plotinus makes so much, we have arrived at the idea of eros as sacrifice, exactly because Dionysius' God has no need whatsoever. As mediator in this transition stands Proclus, the Platonic Successor and Dionysian predecessor.

Save for Plotinus' nuanced interpretations and systematic exploitations of Platonic themes, as well as Dionysius' representation of the Church Fathers, I regard the chapter I devoted to Proclean eros as particularly important, because Proclus has become a bond between two traditions. For this reason, as well as because it explores previously and relatively untouched material, it was the longest chapter. Furthermore, I dealt with the misguided and rather anachronistic debate[1] regarding egoism versus altruism in ancient Greek philosophy, concluding that Neoplatonism is indeed other-regarding. There remains, however, a problem concerning the *quality* of the relation one (pagan) Neoplatonist may develop with the other.

Trying to pin down what a single name, i.e. love (in its various Greek formulations as ἔρως, φιλία or ἀγάπη)[2] means, reflects another important dimension of this work: the relation between philosophical language and content. Whereas Plotinus obviously uses the mythical vocabulary of Plato, the chapter on Proclus has been a good exercise in unearthing philosophical kinship where vocabulary might suggest otherwise. It might not be that Proclus understood better or developed Plotinus' Neoplatonism, but that Proclus helps us understand Plotinus (and Plato) better. On the other hand, the chapter on Dionysius considers the dilemma of whether Neoplatonic philosophical language is assimilated to Christian belief (and hope) or vice versa, and opts for the former.

Still, this book was concerned with not only the dialogue between Christianity and pagan Hellenism,[3] but also the dialogue that needs to be strengthened between West and East.[4] Dionysius has been a cornerstone for both European traditions, represented by Aquinas and Palamas, respectively; hence in my treatment I have been aided by both Eastern and Western interpreters. If love as well as Dionysius are central to Christianity, then love in Dionysius can form a platform for a loving dialogue between the traditions of Western Europe and Byzantium.[5]

This explains also the relevance of my discussion to the preoccupations of some contemporary thinkers. For instance, regardless of what people think Platonic love is, one might say that the shift from love as neediness to sacrificial love is owed to Romanticism (via its conscious or unconscious borrowing from Christianity). Yannaras would deny this. As I indicated in Chapter 3, Yannaras[6] believes that the absence of God, i.e. nihilism, that characterizes modern Western societies and was observed by Nietzsche and subsequently by Heidegger, as well as Sartre, is in opposition to the unknowability of God that we find in Dionysius (and which is rooted in the 'Penia'-element of Socratic ignorance, we may add).[7] From the time that Scholastic Medieval philosophers transformed God into an abstract notion, approachable, although in the end ungraspable, through reason, God seemed to have stopped playing any active and erotic role in the life of the society. On the other hand, for Yannaras, who is a student of Lossky, the Eastern interpretation of Dionysian apophaticism (starting with Maximus the Confessor[8] and extending to Gregory Palamas through John of Damascus and Symeon the New Theologian) denies that we can fit God into logical and linguistic discourse,[9] although it affirms the possibility of having direct experience of God's presence via the participation in His erotic energies. Thus, Yannaras' conclusion is that by neglecting Palamas' distinction of *uncreated* energies and essence[10] the West (including Modern Greece and Slavonic countries) lost the game, and we should rather go back to the Eastern Fathers to resurrect God and our society[11] (κοινωνία-*sobornost* or *sabornost*) from the tomb that Nietzsche discovered and Dostoyevsky illumined.[12]

Whatever the diagnosis, though, may be, as an antidote to this fallen state, we can turn to what unites all these traditions depicted in the present work: i.e. that philosophy is a way of life (or a kind of 'ars amatoria' if you like). Apart from Plato or Socrates, also Plotinus, Proclus and Saint Dionysius the Areopagite (whoever he is) would be very glad if we transformed our lives into eros.

Notes

1 Cf. also Tornau (2005: 272).
2 See also Koutras and Rellos (1991).

3 See one among many approaches to this dialogue by Siniossoglou (2011: *passim*), although I do not agree with many of his conclusions.
4 See a first step in Bradshaw (2004), although in e.g. 263ff he neglects to mention Yannaras' precedence. See also infra and n. 10. Different approaches are offered by Demacopoulos-Papanikolaou (2008) and Plested (2012).
5 For some presuppositions toward this direction, see also Stamoulis (1999: 56–7) (with notes).
6 See e.g. Yannaras (2005, 2007), referred to in nn. 32 and 84 of Chapter 3.
7 See also the very last paragraph of my Chapter 1.
8 Brown Dewhurst (2019), in a way resuming my discussion of the last part of Section 3.2, gives a very interesting comparison of Proclus and Maximus the Confessor with respect to apophaticism: although quite known to Proclus and embedded in his system (see e.g. Jugrin 2019), apophaticism (due to its Dionysian roots one may add) has a different function and results within a Christian context, owing to Maximus' Christological view of love and providence that is absent from Proclus and pagan Neoplatonism in general.
9 For the difference between (Eastern Orthodox) apophaticism and (Western) negative theology, both of which are rooted in the Dionysian theology of negations, see also Jugrin (2018: esp. 161–2) (and 166, referring among else to fr. Dumitru Stăniloae).
10 See the various approaches in Athanasopoulos and Schneider (2013).
11 It is through such a 'meta-noia' (change of mentality) that Western culture could come into fruitful ecumenical contacts not only within its own broad and multifarious tradition (i.e. Christianity), but globally, too, i.e. with other religions/traditions/cultures (for which see a step on the basis of divine love in Treflé Hidden (2014) – with regard to the so-called Abrahamic religions).
12 For a comparison of these two prophetic figures see among else Berdyaev (1957: 58–66) (part of which is available also online at https://anothercity.org/dostoevsky-or-nietzsche-god-man-or-man-god/-last, accessed 9 September 2019), esp. 62–4; see also Popović (1940).

Bibliography

Adamson, P. (2011), 'Making a Virtue of Necessity: *Anangkê* in Plato, Plotinus and Proclus', *Études platoniciennes*, 8: 9–30.

Adamson, P. (2014), *Classical Philosophy. A History of Philosophy without Any Gaps*, vol.1, Oxford: OUP.

Adkins, A.W.H. (1963), '"Friendship" and "Self-Sufficiency" in Homer and Aristotle', *The Classical Quarterly*, New Series, 13 (1): 30–45.

Aertsen, J.A. (2009), '"Eros" und "Agape". Dionysius Areopagita und Thomas von Aquin über die Doppelgestalt der Liebe', in E. Düsing and H.-D. Klein (eds), *Geist, Eros und Agape. Untersuchungen zu Liebesdarstellungen in Philosophie, Religion und Kunst*, (Band 5 von *Geist und Seele*, ed. E. Düsing and H.-D. Klein), 191–203, Würzburg: Verlag Königshausen & Neumann. The article was first published in T. Boiadjiev, G. Kapriev and A. Speer, eds (2000), *Die Dionysius-Rezeption im Mittelalter*, 373–91, Turnhout: Brepols.

Alexidze, L. (2019), 'Eros as Soul's "Eye" in Plotinus: What Does It See and Not See?', in J.F. Finamore and T. Nejeschleba (eds), *Platonism and Its Legacy: Selected Papers from the Fifteenth Annual Conference of the International Society for Neoplatonic Studies*, 41–58, Lydney: The Prometheus Trust.

Andreopoulos, A. (2016), 'The Dormition of the Theotokos and Dionysios the Areopagite', *Analogia. The Pemptousia Journal for Theological Studies*, 1 (1): 77–86.

Andreopoulos, A and D. Harper, eds (2019), *Christos Yannaras. Philosophy, Theology, Culture*, London and New York: Routledge.

Angelopoulos, I.K. (2001), *Μείζων ἡ ἀγάπη. Δώδεκα Πατέρες τῆς Ἐκκλησίας μιλοῦν γιὰ τὴν Ἀγάπη* [*Love is greater. Twelve Fathers of the Church speak about Love*]. Ἡμερολόγιο μὲ CD, selection of texts and trans. by Ἰ.Κ. Ἀγγελόπουλος, produced by Ἀ.Ε. Καραβάνης and Γ.Ν. Μπιλάλης, Athens: «Λυχνία» and Μελωδικὸ Καράβι.

Annas, J. (2001), *Cicero. On Moral Ends*, ed. J. Annas, trans. Raphael Woolf (repr. 2004), Cambridge: CUP, Cambridge Texts in the History of Philosophy.

Armstrong, A.H. (1961), 'Platonic *Eros* and Christian *Agape*', *The Downside Review*, Bath, 79 (255): 105–21; reprinted as ch. IX in Armstrong, A.H. (1979), *Plotinian and Christian Studies*, London: Variorum Reprints, Collected Studies series; CS102.

Armstrong, A.H. (1964), 'Platonic Love. A Reply to Professor Verdenius', *The Downside Review*, 82 (268): 199–208; reprinted as ch. X in Armstrong, A.H. (1979), *Plotinian and Christian Studies*, London: Variorum Reprints, Collected Studies series; CS102.

Armstrong, A.H. (1966–1988), Plotinus, *Enneads I-VI*, with an English Translation by A.H. Armstrong, vols I–VII (vol.I: 1966, revised 1989; vol.II: 1966; vol.III: 1967;

vol.IV: 1984; vol.V: 1984; vol.VI: 1988; vol.VII: 1988), Cambridge, Massachusetts, London, England: Harvard University Press, Loeb Classical Library.

Armstrong, A.H. (1982), 'Negative Theology, Myth, and Incarnation', in D.J. O'Meara (ed.), *Neoplatonism and Christian Thought*, 213–22 (and 290–2: notes), Albany, NY: SUNY Press, Studies in Neoplatonism, vol.3.

Arnou, R. (²1967), *Le Désir de Dieu dans la Philosophie de Plotin*, deuxième édition revue et corrigée (¹1921), Rome: Presses de l'Université Grégorienne.

Ashwin-Siejkowski, P. (2009), 'The Hierarchy of the Church, Authority and Sacraments and the Neoplatonic Philosophy of Pseudo-Dionysius', in P. Colins, W. Klausnitzer and W. Sparn (eds), *Authority in the Church. Theologische Beiträge aus der Church of England, der Evangelisch-Lutherischen Kirche in Bayern und der katholischen Erzdiözese Bamberg*, 174–91, München: Verlag Sankt Michaelsbund.

Athanasopoulos, C. and C. Schneider, eds (2013), *Divine Essence and Divine Energies. Ecumenical Reflections on the Presence of God in Eastern Orthodoxy*, Cambridge: James Clark & Co.

Atkinson, M. (1983), *Plotinus: Ennead V. 1. On the Three Principal Hypostases*, a commentary with translation by M. Atkinson, Oxford: OUP, Oxford Classical and Philosophical Monographs.

Badiou, A and N. Truong (2009), *Éloge de l'amour*, Paris: Flammarion.

Baltas, D.V. (2002), Ὀντολογικὰ ζητήματα στὸ ἔργο τοῦ Γεωργίου Παχυμέρη' ['Ontological Issues in the Work of Georgios Pachymeres'], PhD diss., University of Athens, Faculty of Philosophy-Pedagogy-Psychology (School of Philosophy), Athens. Available online: http://thesis.ekt.gr/thesisBookReader/id/21887#page/1/mode/1up (accessed 12 March 2020).

Baltzly, D. (2017), 'The Human Life', in P. d'Hoine and M. Martijn (eds), *All from One. A Guide to Proclus*, 258–75, Oxford: OUP.

Baltzly, D. and N. Eliopoulos (2009), 'The Classical Ideals of Friendship', in B. Caine (ed.), *Friendship: A History*, 1–64, London and New York: Routledge, Critical Histories of Subjectivity and Culture; (formerly London, Oakville: Equinox).

Barnes, J. (1984), *The Complete Works of Aristotle. The Revised Oxford Translation*, ed. J. Barnes in 2 vols (⁶1995), Princeton: PUP, Bollingen Series LXXI 2.

Bartsch, S. (2006), *The Mirror of the Self: Sexuality, Self-knowledge, and the Gaze in the Early Roman Empire*, Chicago & London: The University of Chicago Press.

Begzos, M.P. (2000), Διόνυσος καὶ Διονύσιος. Ἑλληνισμός καὶ Χριστιανισμός στη συγκριτική φιλοσοφία της θρησκείας [*Dionysos and Dionysius. Hellenism and Christianity in the comparative philosophy of religion*], Athens: Ἑλληνικά Γράμματα.

Beierwaltes, W. (1986), 'The Love of Beauty and the Love of God', in A.H. Armstrong (ed.), *Classical Mediterranean Spirituality. Egyptian, Greek, Roman*, 293–313, London: Routledge & Kegan Paul, vol.15 of World Spirituality: An Encyclopedic History of the Religious Quest.

Belfiore, E.S. (2012), *Socrates' Daimonic Art. Love for Wisdom in Four Platonic Dialogues*, Cambridge: CUP.

Berdyaev, N. (1957), *Dostoevsky*, trans. D. Attwater, New York: Meridian Books (Living Age Books). The English translation was originally published in 1934, *Dostoevsky: An Interpretation*, London: Sheer & Ward, and was reprinted in 2009: *Dostoievsky: An Interpretation*, with a foreword by B. Jakim, San Rafael CA: Semantron Press.

Bernardete, S. (2001), 'Sokrates und Platon. Die Dialektik des Eros', in H. Meier and G. Neumann (eds), *Über die Liebe. Ein Symposion*, 169–96, München: Piper.

Berthold, G.C. (1985), *Maximus Confessor, Selected Writings*, trans. and notes by G.C. Berthold, introduction by J. Pelikan, preface by I.H. Dalmais, New York, Mahwah: The Classics of Western Spirituality.

Bertozzi, A. (2012), 'On Eros in Plotinus: Attempt at a Systematic Reconstruction (with a preliminary chapter on Plato)', PhD diss., Loyola University, Chicago. Available online: http://ecommons.luc.edu/cgi/viewcontent.cgi?article=1294&context=luc_diss (accessed 18 November 2014).

Bidez, J. (1937), 'Un extrait du Commentaire de Proclus sur les "Ennéades" de Plotin', in *Mélanges offerts a A.-M. Desrousseaux par ses amis et ses élèves …*, 11–18, Paris: Librairie Hachette.

Blowers, P.M. (1992), 'Maximus the Confessor, Gregory of Nyssa, and the Concept of "Perpetual Progress"', *Vigiliae Christianae*, 46: 151–71.

Blowers, P.M. and R.L. Wilken, trans. (2003), *On the Cosmic Mystery of Jesus Christ. Selected Writings from St Maximus the Confessor*, Crestwood, NY: St Vladimir's Seminary Press, Popular Patristic Series, No 25.

Blum, R. and A. Golitzin (1991), *The Sacred Athlete: On the Mystical Experience and Dionysios, Its Westernworld Fountainhead*, Lanham, New York, London: University Press of America.

Boswell, M. (2018), *The Way to Love: Reimagining Christian Spiritual Growth as the Hopeful Path of Virtue*, foreword A.G. Holder, Eugene, Oregon: Cascade Books.

Boyd, C.A., ed. (2008), *Visions of Agapé: Problems and Possibilities in Human and Divine Love*, Ashgate; repr. 2016 in Abingdon and New York: Routledge.

Bozinis, K.A. (2019), *Πολιτική αγάπη. Νέα ερμηνευτική προσέγγιση στον Ιερό Χρυσόστομο* [*Political Love: A New Hermeneutical Approach to Sacred Chrysostomus*], Thessaloniki: A. Stamoulis.

Bradshaw, D. (2004), *Aristotle East and West. Metaphysics and the Division of Christendom*, Cambridge, NY: CUP.

Bradshaw, D. (2008), 'The Christian Baptism of Eros', Addendum to Ch.6: 'Philosophies of Greece, Rome, and the Near East' of N. Smart, in O. Leaman (ed.), *World Philosophies*, 1st edn 1999, 188–90, Abingdon/NY: Routledge.

Bradshaw, D. (2018), 'Essence and Energies: What Kind of Distinction?', *Analogia. The Pemptousia Journal for Theological Studies* ('St Gregory Palamas' Special Series-part 4), 6: 5–35.

Brisson, L. (1998), *Plato the Myth Maker*, trans., ed. with an introduction by G. Naddaf, Chicago and London: The University of Chicago Press.

Brisson, L. (2004), *How Philosophers Saved Myths. Allegorical Interpretation and Classical Mythology*, trans. C. Tihanyi, Chicago & London: The University of Chicago Press.

Brisson, L. (2017), 'Proclus' Theology', in P. d'Hoine and M. Martijn (eds), *All from One. A Guide to Proclus*, 207–22, Oxford: OUP.

Brown Dewhurst, E. (2019), 'Apophaticism in the Search for Knowledge: Love as a Key Difference in Neoplatonic and Christian Epistemology', in P.G. Pavlos, L.F. Janby, E.K. Emilsson and T.T. Tollefsen (eds), *Platonism and Christian Thought in Late Antiquity*, 239–57, London and New York: Routledge.

Bulgakov, S. ([1st Russian edn 1917] 2012), *Unfading Light: Contemplations and Speculations*, trans., ed. and with an intro. Th.A. Smith, Grand Rapids, Michigan and Cambridge: William B. Eerdmans Publishing Company.

Butler, E.P. (2014), *Essays on the Metaphysics of Polytheism in Proclus*, New York: Phaidra Editions.

Cardenal, E. (2006), *Love: A Glimpse of Eternity*, revised edition, preface Th. Merton, trans. D. Livingston, 1st edn 1970, Brewster, MA: Paraclete Press.

Carmichael, E.D.H. (L.) (2004), *Friendship: Interpreting Christian Love* (repr. 2006 and 2007), London and New York: T&T Clark.

Celkyte, A. (2014), 'Chrysippus on the Beautiful: Studies in a Stoic Conception of Aesthetic Properties', PhD diss., University of St Andrews.

Charrue, J.M. (2019), *La philosophie néoplatonicienne de l'éducation: Hypatie, Plotin, Jamblique, Proclus*, Paris: L'Harmattan, Ouverture Philosophique Bibliothèque.

Chartier, G. (2007), *The Analogy of Love: Divine and Human Love at the Center of Christian Theology*, Exeter: Imprint Academic.

Chatzimichael, D.K. (2008), Διονύσιος Ἀρεοπαγίτης, *Περί Θείων Ὀνομάτων - Περί Μυστικῆς Θεολογίας*, preface by Χρ. Τερέζης, introduction by Ἀ.Ὀ. Πολυχρονιάδης, text-trans.-comments by Δ.Κ. Χατζημιχαήλ, Thessaloniki: Ζῆτρος.

Chiaradonna, R. (2009), 'Le traité de Galien *Sur la Demonstration* et sa postérité tardoantique', in R. Chiaradonna and F. Trabattoni (eds), *Physics and Philosophy of Nature in Greek Neoplatonism. Proceedings of the European Science Foundation Exploratory Workshop*, Il Ciocco, Castelvecchio-Pascoli, 22–24 June 2006, 43–77, Netherlands: Brill, Philosophia Antiqua, vol.115.

Chlup, R. (2012), *Proclus. An Introduction*, Cambridge: CUP.

Chouliaras, A. (2018), 'The Notion of Eros (Love) and the Presence of St Augustine in the Works of St Gregory Palamas Revisited', *Analogia: The Pemptousia Journal for Theological Studies*, 5 (3): 19–33.

Christodoulidi-Mazaraki, A. (1980), 'Ψυχολογικές προεκτάσεις τοῦ ἀριστοφανικοῦ μύθου στὸ πλατωνικὸ "Συμπόσιο"' ['Psychological Extensions of the Aristophanic myth in Plato's *Symposium*'], *Ἀνάτυπο ἀπό τήν «Ἐπιστημονική Ἐπετηρίδα» τῆς «Παντείου» Ἀνωτάτης Σχολῆς Πολιτικῶν Ἐπιστημῶν Ἀθηνῶν*, Athens, 367–75.

Christodoulidi-Mazaraki, A. (1983), 'Το ερωτικό στοιχείο στην πλατωνική φιλοσοφία. Πλάτων και Freud' ['The erotic element in Platonic philosophy. Plato and

Freud'], PhD diss., University of Athens. Available online: http://thesis.ekt.gr/thesisBookReader/id/11498#page/1/mode/2up (accessed 13 January 2020).

Chrysakopoulou, S. (2013), 'Wonder and the Beginning of Philosophy in Plato', in S. Vasalou (ed.), *Practices of Wonder. Cross-Disciplinary Perspectives*, 88–120 (1st edn in 2012: arrangement with Pickwick Publications), Cambridge: James Clarke & Co.

Clayton P. and A. Peacocke, eds (2004), *In Whom We Live and Move and Have Our Being: Panentheistic Reflections on God's Presence in a Scientific World*, Grand Rapids, MI: William B. Eerdmans.

Clemente, M. (2020), *Eros Crucified: Death, Desire, and the Divine in Psychoanalysis and Philosophy of Religion*, New York and Abingdon: Routledge.

Coakley, S. (2013), 'Eastern "Mystical Theology" or Western "Nouvelle Theologie"?: On the Comparative Reception of Dionysius the Areopagite in Lossky and de Lubac', in G.E. Demacopoulos and A. Papanikolaou (eds), *Orthodox Constructions of the West*, 125–41 and 308–17, New York: Fordham University Press.

Coakley, S. and C.M. Stang, eds (2009), *Re-thinking Dionysius the Areopagite*, Directions in Modern Theology, MA, Oxford and Chichester: Wiley-Blackwell. [The book appeared first in 2008 as a volume of *Modern Theology*, 24 (4).]

Coffey, D. (1990), 'The Holy Spirit as Mutual Love of the Father and the Son', *Theological Studies*, 51: 193–229.

Collette-Dučić, B. (2014), 'Making Friends: The Stoic Conception of Love and Its Platonic Background', in S. Stern-Gillet and G.M. Gurtler, S.J. (eds), *Ancient and Medieval Concepts of Friendship*, 87–115, Albany: State University of New York Press.

Constas, M. (2017), 'Maximus the Confessor, Dionysius the Areopagite, and the Transformation of Christian Neoplatonism', *Analogia. The Pemptousia Journal for Theological Studies*, 2 (1): 1–12.

Cooper, A.G. (2015), 'The Story of God and *Eros*', in C. Patterson and C. Sweeney (eds), *God and Eros: The Ethos of the Nuptial Mystery*, 91–103, Eugene, Oregon: Wipf and Stock Publishers, Cascasde Books.

Cooper, J.M. (1997), *Plato. Complete Works*, edited, with introduction and notes, by John M. Cooper; associate editor D.S. Hutchinson, Indianapolis/Cambridge: Hackett Publishing Company.

Corrigan, K. (2017), 'The Platonist Friend', in J. Finamore and S. Klitenic Wear (eds), *Defining Platonism: Essays on Plato and Platonism in Honor of the Seventy-Fifth Birthday of John M. Dillon*, 29–43, Washington, DC: Franciscan University Press.

Corrigan, K. (2018), *Love, Friendship, Beauty, and the Good: Plato, Aristotle, and the Later Tradition*, Eugene, Oregon: Cascade Books, Veritas 26.

Crîşmăreanu, F. (2015), 'Maxime le Confesseur lecteur de *Corpus Dionysiacum*', in A. Tat and C. Tuţu (eds), *Saint Dionysius the Areopagite: Sources, Context, Reception*, 136–55, Cluj-Napoca: Napoca Star.

Culp, J. (2013), 'Panentheism', in E.N. Zalta (ed.), *The Stanford Encyclopedia of Philosophy* (Spring 2013 edn). Available online: http://plato.stanford.edu/archives/spr2013/entries/panentheism/ (accessed 11 December 2013).

Cvetkovic, Vl. (2016), 'Maximus the Confessor's Geometrical Analogies Applied to the Relationship between Christ and Creation', in G.D. Dragas, P. Pavlov and St. Tanev (eds), *Orthodox Theology and the Sciences: Glorifying God in His Marvelous Works*, 277–91, Sofia: Sofia University Press "St Kliment Ohridski"; Columbia, MO: New Rome Press.

Damaskos, P.K. (2003),Ἔρωτος παρουσίαση, Δεύτερο μέρος: Ὁ Ἔρως στὸ ἔργο τοῦ Πλωτίνου ['Love in Plotinus' work'], PhD diss., University of Athens.

D'Andres, N. (2010), 'Socrate néoplatonicien: une science de l'amour dans le commentaire de Proclus au prologue de l'Alcibiade', PhD diss., University of Genève. Available online: http://archive-ouverte.unige.ch/unige:14566 (but with private access).

D'Angour, A. (2019), *Socrates in Love: The Making of a Philosopher*, London, New Delhi, New York, Sydney: Bloomsbury.

Darley, A.P. (2018), 'Ritual as Erotic Anagogy in Pseudo-Dionysius: A Reformed Critique', *International Journal of Philosophy and Theology*, 79 (3): 261–78.

De Andia, Y. (2015), 'Pseudo-Dionysius the Areopagite and Maximus the Confessor', in P. Allen and B. Neil (eds), *The Oxford Handbook of Maximus the Confessor*, 177–93, Oxford: OUP.

Delikostantis, K.Z. (2003), Παντοπόρος ἄπορος; Νεωτερικές και μετανεωτερικές περιπέτειες του ανθρωπολογικού στοχασμού [*Resourceful without rescources? Modern and Postmodern Adventures of the Anthropological Thought*], Athens: no publisher indicated.

Demacopoulos, G.E. and A. Papanikolaou, eds (2008), *Orthodox Readings of Augustine*, Crestwood, NY: St Vladimir's Seminary Press.

Depraz, N. (2019), 'Apophaticism and Phenomenology: Christos Yannaras in the Light of Jean-Luc Marion', in A. Andreopoulos and D. Harper (eds), *Christos Yannaras. Philosophy, Theology, Culture*, 19–25, London and New York: Routledge.

Depraz, N. and F. Mauriac (2012), 'Théo-phénoménologie I: l'amour –Jean-Luc Marion et Christos Yannaras', *Revue de Métaphysique et de Morale*, 2 (74): 247–75.

Derrida, J. (1997), *The Politics of Friendship*, trans. G. Collins, London and New York: Verso, Radical Thinkers 5.

De Vogel, C.J. (1963), 'Amor quo caelum regitur', *Vivarium*, 1: 2–34.

De Vogel, C.J. (1981), 'Greek Cosmic Love and the Christian Love of God. Boethius, Dionysius the Areopagite and the Author of the Fourth Gospel', *Vigiliae Christianae*, North-Holl and Publishing Company, 35: 57–81.

D'Hoine, P. and M. Martijn, eds (2017), *All from One. A Guide to Proclus*, Oxford: OUP.

Dillon, J. (1969), '*Enn.* III 5: Plotinus' Exegesis of the *Symposium* Myth', Ἀγών. *Journal of Classical Studies*, Berkeley Association of Classics; Department of Classics, University of California, 3: 24–44.

Dillon, J. (1989), 'Logos and Trinity: Patterns of Platonist Influence on Early Christianity', in *Royal Institute of Philosophy Lecture Series*, 25: 1–13 = in G. Vesey (ed.), *The Philosophy in Christianity*, 1–13, Cambridge: CUP, Royal Institute of Philosophy Supplement; reprinted in J. Dillon, 1997, *The Great Tradition*, study 8, Aldershot: Ashgate.

Dillon, J. (1994), 'A Platonist *Ars Amatoria*', *The Classical Quarterly*, 44 (2): 387–92.

Dillon, J. and C.S. O'Brien, ed. (forthcoming), *A Handbook on Platonic Love from Antiquity to the Renaissance*, Cambridge: CUP.

Dillon, J. and L.P. Gerson, ed. and trans. (2004), *Neoplatonic Philosophy: Introductory Readings*, Indianapolis/Cambridge: Hackett.

Dodds, E.R. (1928), 'The Parmenides of Plato and the Origin of the Neoplatonic "One"', *The Classical Quarterly*, 22 (3/4): 129–42.

Dodds, E.R. (1959), *Plato. Gorgias. A Revised Text with Introduction and Commentary*, Oxford: at the Clarendon Press.

Dodds, E.R. (^{2}1963), Πρόκλου Διαδόχου Στοιχείωσις Θεολογική. *The Elements of Theology*, a revised text with translation, introduction and commentary, 2nd edn (^{1}1933; repr. 2004), Oxford: Clarendon Press.

Dodds, E.R. (1965), *Pagan and Christian in an Age of Anxiety. Some Aspects of Religious Experience from Marcus Aurelius to Constantine* (6th reprint: 2000), Cambridge: CUP.

Dörrie, H. (1976), *Platonica Minora*, München: Wilhelm Fink GmbH & Co. KG ('Studia et testimonia antiqua', vol.8).

Douma, K. (1999), «Η παιδαγωγική του έρωτα από τον Πλάτωνα στον Αρεοπαγίτη» ['The Pedagogy of Eros from Plato to the Areopagite'], Δωδώνη [*Dodoni*], 28 (Γ'): 147–56.

Düsing, E. (2009), 'Geist, Eros und Agape – eine historisch-systematisch Problemskizze', in E. Düsing and H.-D. Klein (eds), *Geist, Eros und Agape. Untersuchungen zu Liebesdarstellungen in Philosophie, Religion und Kunst*, 7–40, Würzburg: Verlag Königshausen & Neumann, Band 5 von *Geist und Seele*, ed. E. Düsing and H.D. Klein.

Edwards, M. (2009), 'The Figure of Love in Augustine and in Proclus the Neoplatonist', *The Downside Review*, 127 (448): 197–214.

Edwards, M. (2013), 'Plotinus: Monist, Theist or Atheist?', in L. Nelstrop and S.D. Podmore (eds), *Christian Mysticism and Incarnational Theology: Between Transcendence and Immanence*, 13–28, Farnham and Burlington: Ashgate, Contemporary Theological Explorations in Christian Mysticism.

Emilsson, E.K. (1988), *Plotinus on Sense-Perception: A Philosophical Study*, Cambridge: CUP.

Emilsson, E.K. (2007), *Plotinus on Intellect*, Oxford: OUP.

Emilsson, E.K. (2017), *Plotinus*, London and New York: Routledge.

Esposito Buckley, L.M. (1992), 'Ecstatic and Emanating, Providential and Unifying: A Study of the Pseudo-Dionysian and Plotinian Concepts of *Eros*', *Journal of Neoplatonic Studies*, 1 (1): 31–61.

Esposito, L.M. (1997), 'Pseudo-Dionysius: A Philosophical Study of Certain Hellenic Sources', PhD diss., University of Toronto.

Filosofein (2018), *Φιλοσοφεῖν: Ἐπιστήμη, Εὔνοια, Παρρησία. Εξαμηνιαία Φιλοσοφική Επιθεώρηση: Ἔρωτας και Φιλοσοφία ή η φιλοσοφία ως έρωτας* [*Eros and Philosophy or Philosophy as Eros*], 18.

Flamand, J.M. (2009), 'Traité 50 (III, 5) *Sur l' amour*', presentation, traduction et notes par J.-M. Flamand in *Plotin, Traités 45–50*, presents, traduits et annotés par M. Guyot, Th. Vidart, R. Dufour, Fr. Fronterotta et J.-M. Flamand, sous la direction de L. Brisson et J.-F. Pradeau, 407–80, Paris: GF Flammarion.

Florovsky, G. (1987), *The Byzantine Ascetic and Spiritual Fathers*, vol.10 in *The Collected Works of Georges Florovsky*, gen. ed. R.S. Haugh, trans. R. Miller and A.M. Döllinger-Labriolle – H.W. Schmiedel, Vaduz (Europa): Büchervertriebsanstalt (Exclusive Sales Agent's 2nd printing in Belmont, MA: Notable & Academic Books).

Florovsky, G.V. (1933), *Vizantijskie otci V-VIII (veka)*, Paris. This work has been translated into English in 1987, *The Collected Works of G. Florovsky* as vol.8: *Byzantine Fathers of the Fifth Century* and vol.9: *Byzantine Fathers of the Sixth to Eighth Centuries*, Vaduz: Büchervertriebsanstalt.

Garitsis, K. (2002), *Ὅρασις Ἀοράτου. Ἡ διδασκαλία τοῦ Ὡραίου στὸν Διονύσιο Ἀρεοπαγίτη* [*Vision of the Invisible. The Teaching regarding the Beautiful in Dionysius the Areopagite*], Thira, ἐκδ. Θεσβίτης.

Gavrilyuk, P.L. (2004), *The Suffering of the Impassible God: The Dialectics of Patristic Thought*, Oxford: OUP, Oxford Early Christian Studies.

Gavrilyuk, P.L. (2008), 'The Reception of Dionysius in Twentieth-century Eastern Orthodoxy', *Modern Theology*, 24 (4): 707–23 = in S. Coakley and C.M. Stang, eds (2009), *Re-thinking Dionysius the Areopagite*, 177–94, MA, Oxford and Chichester: Wiley-Blackwell, Directions in Modern Theology.

Gavrilyuk, P.L. (2012), 'Pseudo-Dionysius', in P.L. Gavrilyuk and S. Coakley (eds), *The Spiritual Senses. Perceiving God in Western Christianity*, 86–103, Cambridge: CUP.

Gendle, N., trans. (1983), Gregory Palamas, *The Triads*, edited with an introduction by J. Meyendorff, preface by J. Pelikan, New York, Mahwah: Paulist Press, The Classics of Western Spirituality.

Gersh, S.E. (1973), *Κίνησις Ἀκίνητος. A Study of Spiritual Motion in the Philosophy of Proclus*, Leiden: E.J. Brill, Philosophia Antiqua. A series of monographs on Ancient Philosophy, ed. W.J. Verdenius and J.H. Waszink, vol.XXVI.

Gersh, S. (1978), *From Iamblichus to Eriugena. An Investigation of the Prehistory and Evolution of the Pseudo-Dionysian Tradition*, Leiden: E.J. Brill, Studien zur Problemgeschichte der Antiken und Mittelalterlichen Philosophie VIII.

Gersh, S. (2014), 'One Thousand Years of Proclus: An Introduction to His Reception', in S. Gersh (ed.), *Interpreting Proclus: From Antiquity to the Renaissance*, 1–30, Cambridge: CUP.

Gerson, L.P. (1994), *Plotinus*, London and New York: Routledge, The Arguments of the Philosophers.

Gerson, L.P. (2006), 'A Platonic Reading of Plato's *Symposium*', in J.H. Lesher, D. Nails and F.C.C. Sheffield (eds), *Plato's* Symposium. *Issues in Interpretation and Reception*,

47–67, Washington, DC: Center for Hellenic Studies, Trustees for Harvard University; distributed by Cambridge, Massachusetts, and London, England: Harvard University Press.

Gerson, L.P. (2018), 'Plotinus and Platonism', in H. Tarrant, D.A. Layne, D. Baltzly and F. Renaud (eds), *Brill's Companion to the Reception of Plato in Antiquity*, 316–35, Leiden: Brill.

Ghiţ, F.-C.G. (2011), 'Ἀγάπη καί ἔρως. Ἡ πρόταση τῶν Πατέρων τῆς Ἀνατολῆς καί ὁ διάλογος μέ τή Δύση. Μέ εἰδική ἀναφορά στό ἔργο *Ἀγάπη καί Ἔρως* τοῦ Anders Nygren καί στήν πατερική παράδοση μέχρι τίς *Ἀρεοπαγιτικές Συγγραφές*' ['Agape and Eros. The Proposal of the Church Fathers and the Dialogue with the West. With special Reference to the Work *Agape and Eros* of Anders Nygren and to the Patristic Tradition up to the *Areopagitic Writings*'], PhD diss., Aristotelian University of Thessaloniki, Faculty of Theology.

Ghiţ, F.-C. (2015), 'Les sources et l'identité de l'"Eros" divin dans les ecrits Areopagitiques', in A. Tat and C. Tuţu (eds), *Saint Dionysius the Areopagite: Sources, Context, Reception*, 98–118, Cluj-Napoca: Napoca Star.

(Golitzin), Alexander (1990), 'On the Other Hand: [A Response to Fr Paul Wesche's Recent Article on Dionysius in *St Vladimir's Theological Quarterly*, Vol. 33, No. 1]', *Saint Vladimir's Theological Quarterly*, 34: 305–23.

Golitzin, A. (1993), 'The Mysticism of Dionysius Areopagita: Platonist or Christian?', *Mystics Quarterly*, 19 (3): 98–114.

Golitzin, A. (1994), *Et introibo ad altare Dei. The Mystagogy of Dionysius Areopagita, with Special Reference to Its Predecessors in the Eastern Christian Tradition*, Thessaloniki: Πατριαρχικὸν Ἵδρυμα Πατερικῶν Μελετῶν, Analecta Vlatadon 59.

Golitzin, A. (1999), '"A Contemplative and a Liturgist": Father Georges Florovsky on the Corpus Dionysiacum', *St Vladimir's Theological Quarterly*, 43 (2): 131–61.

Golitzin, A. (2002), 'Dionysius Areopagites in the Works of Saint Gregory Palamas: On the Question of a "Christological Corrective" and Related Matters', *Saint Vladimir's Theological Quarterly*, 46: 163–90.

Golitzin, A. (2003), 'Dionysius Areopagita: A Christian Mysticism?', *Pro Ecclesia*, 12 (2): 161–212.

Golitzin, A. (2013), *Mystagogy. A Monastic Reading of Dionysius Areopagita*, with the collaboration and ed. by B.G. Bucur, Collegeville, Minnesota: Cistercian Publications, Cistercian Studies Series Number Two Hundred Fifty, Liturgical Press.

(Gontikakis,) Vasileios, Abbot of Iviron (2012), «Ἡ θεία ἀγάπη ἑρμηνεύει τά οὐκ ἐξὸν ἀνθρώπῳ λαλῆσαι» ['Divine Love interprets those things that man cannot utter'], *Σύναξη* [*Synaxis*], 121: 73–9.

Gordon, J. (2012), *Plato's Erotic World: From Cosmic Origins to Human Death*, Cambridge, NY: CUP.

Gould, G. (1989), 'Ecclesiastical Hierarchy in the Thought of Pseudo-Dionysius', *Studies in Church History*, 26: 29–41.

Gould, T. (1963), *Platonic Love*, NY: Free Press of Glencoe, reprint 1981, Greenwood Press Reprint.

Gounelas, S., trans. (2002), Διονυσίου Ἀρεοπαγίτου, *Περὶ μυστικῆς θεολογίας* [*On Mystical Theology*], introduction by Vl. Lossky, Athens: ἐκδ. Ἁρμός, series «Γέφυρες»; reprint from 1983, ἐκδ. Πολύτυπο, ed. N. Γιανναδάκης.

Griffin, M. (2015), Olympiodorus: *Life of Plato* and *on Plato First Alcibiades 1–9*, introduction, translation and notes by M. Griffin, London, New Delhi, New York, Sydney: Bloomsbury Academic, Ancient Commentators on Aristotle (general eds: R. Sorabji and M. Griffin).

Griffin, M. (2016), Olympiodorus, *On Plato First Alcibiades 10–28* (introduction), translation (and notes) by M. Griffin, London, New Delhi, New York, Sydney: Bloomsbury Academic, Ancient Commentators on Aristotle (general eds: R. Sorabji and M. Griffin).

Grunebaum, J.O. (2003), *Friendship: Liberty, Equality, and Utility*, Albany, NY: State University of New York Press.

Hadot, P. (1990), *Plotin, Traité 50 (III 5)*, introduction, traduction, commentaire et notes par Pierre Hadot, Paris: Les Éditions du Cerf.

Hainthaler, Th. (1997), 'Bemerkungen zur Christologie des Ps.-Dionys und ihrer Nachwirkung im 6. Jahrhundert', in Ysabel de Andia (ed.), *Denys l'Aréopagite et sa postérité en orient et en occident*, Paris: Institut d'Études Augustiniennes, Collection des Études Augustiniennes, Série Antiquité 151.

Halperin, D.M. (1985), 'Platonic *Erôs* and What Men Call Love', *Ancient Philosophy*, 5: 161–204.

Hankey, W.J. (2009), 'Neoplatonist Surprises: The Doctrine of Providence of Plotinus and His Followers Both Conscious and Unconscious', *Dionysius*, XXVII: 117–25.

Hankey, W.J. (2011), 'God's Care for Human Individuals; What Neoplatonism Gives to a Christian Doctrine of Providence', *Quaestiones Disputatae*, 2 (1&2): 4–36.

Harper, D. (2019), *The Analogy of Love: St Maximus the Confessor and the Foundation of Ethics*, Crestwood, NY: St Vladimir's Seminary Press.

Heide, D. (2019), 'Divine Eros: The Providential and Perfective Ecstasy of God in Dionysius' *Divine Names* IV', *Dionysius*, 37: 44–59.

Heidl, G. (2008), 'Plótinosz: Szerelemről. Enneasz III.5. (50)', *Katekhón*, 14 (1): 73–91.

Helm, B.W. (2009), *Love, Friendship, and the Self. Intimacy, Identification, and the Social Nature of Persons*, Oxford: OUP.

Henry, P. and H.R. Schwyzer, eds (1964–1983), *Plotini opera*; tomi I–III: *Porphyrii Vita Plotini; Enneades I–VI*, Oxonii: e Typographeo Clarendoniano, OCT ('editio minor').

Hobbs, A. (2017), 'Socrates, Eros and Magic', in V. Harte and R. Woolf (eds), *Rereading Ancient Philosophy. Old Chestnuts and Sacred Cows*, 101–20, Cambridge: CUP.

Hoffmann, Ph. (2000), 'La triade chaldaïque ἔρως, ἀλήθεια, πίστις: de Proclus à Simplicius', in A.Ph. Segonds et C. Steel (eds avec l'assistance de C. Luna et A.F. Mettraux), *Proclus et la Théologie Platonicienne*, Actes du Colloque International de Louvain (13–16 mai 1998) en l'honneur de H.D. Saffrey et L.G. Westerink, 459–89, Paris: Leuven University Press and Les Belles Lettres.

Hoffmann, Ph. (2011), '*Erôs, Alètheia, Pistis* ... et *Elpis*: Tétrade chaldaïque, triade néoplatonicienne (Fr. 46 des Places, P 26 Kroll)', in H. Seng and M. Tardieu (eds), *Die Chaldaeischen Orakel. Kontext, Interpretation, Rezeption* (Actes du Colloque de l'Université de Konstanz, 15-18 Novembre 2006), 255-324, Heidelberg: Universitätsverlag, coll. «Bibliotheca Chaldaica», 2.

Horn, G. (1925), 'Amour et extase d'après Denys l'Aréopagite', *Revue d'ascétique et de mystique*, VI: 278-89; (réédité en 1964 par Culture et Civilisation; réimprimé en Belgique).

Ivanovic, F. (2009), 'Ancient Eros and Medieval Agape: The Concept of Love in Plato and Maximus the Confessor', in K. Boudouris and M. Adam (eds), *Greek Philosophy and the Issues of Our Age*, vol.2, 93-114, Athens: Ionia Publications.

Ivanovic, F. (2014), 'The Erotic-Aesthetic Dimension of Deification: Love and Beauty in Dionysius the Areopagite and Maximus the Confessor', PhD diss., Norwegian University of Science and Technology, Trondheim (NTNU).

Ivanović, F. (2015), 'Eros as a Divine Name According to Dionysius the Areopagite', in M. Knežević (ed.), *The Ways of Byzantine Philosophy*, 123-41, Alhambra, California: Sebastian Press, Western American Diocese of the Serbian Orthodox Church/ Faculty of Philosophy, Kosovska Mitrovica/Contemporary Christian Thought Series, no. 32.

Ivanovic, F. (2019), *Desiring the Beautiful: The Erotic-Aesthetic Dimension of Deification in Dionysius the Areopagite and Maximus the Confessor*, Washington, DC: The Catholic University of America Press.

Jevtic, A. (2012), *Από την ελευθερία στην αγάπη. Οι ομιλίες της Ξάνθης* [*From Freedom to Love. The Talks of Xanthi*], ed. Ε. Σαρρή, Athens: Δόμος [Domos].

Johnson, M. and H. Tarrant, ed. (2012), *Alcibiades and the Socratic Lover-Educator*, London: Bristol Classical Press.

Jollimore, T. (2000), 'Friendship without Partiality?', *Ratio (new series)*, XIII (1): 69-82.

Joosse, A. (2011), *Why a Philosopher Needs Others: Platonic and Stoic Models of Friendship and Self-Understanding* (PhD diss.), Utrecht University: Publications of the Department of Philosophy, Quaestiones Infinitae, vol.LXVII.

Jugrin, D. (2018), 'Negative Theology in Contemporary Interpretations', *European Journal for Philosophy of Religion*, 10 (2): 149-70.

Jugrin, D. (2019), 'The One beyond Silence: The Apophatic Henology of Proclus', *Studia Universitatis Babeș-Bolyai. Philosophia*, 64 (1): 63-87.

Kahn, C.H. (1987), 'Plato's Theory of Desire', *Review of Metaphysics*, 41 (1): 77-103.

Kalfas, V. (2008), 'Ο έρωτας στον Πλάτωνα' ['Eros in Plato'], *Αρχαιολογία και Τέχνες* [*Archaeology and Arts*, issue devoted to «Περί Έρωτος ... »], 109: 10a-15b (with an English abstract in 15b).

Kalligas, P. (2004), *Πλωτίνου Έννεάς Τρίτη*, ancient text, trans., commentary by. Π. Καλλιγᾶς, Athens: Academy of Athens, Βιβλιοθήκη Ἀ. Μανούση 5, Centre for Research of Greek and Latin Literature. For English translation of the *Third Ennead*'s Commentary see Kalligas 2014, 413-656.

Kalligas, P. (2009), Πρόκλου, Ἡ ἱερατικὴ τέχνη – Οἱ ὕμνοι [*The hieratic art – The hymns*], introduction, translation, comments by Π. Καλλιγᾶς, Athens: στιγμή, Library of Ancient Authors, no.50.

Kalligas, P. (2013), *Πλωτίνου Ἐννεὰς Πέμπτη*, ancient text, trans., commentary by Π. Καλλιγᾶς, Athens: Academy of Athens, Βιβλιοθήκη Ἀ. Μανούση 12, Centre for Research of Greek and Latin Literature.

Kalligas, P. (2014), *The Enneads of Plotinus: A Commentary*, vol.1, trans. by E.K. Fowden and N. Pilavachi, Princeton: PUP.

Karamanolis, G. (2013), *The Philosophy of Early Christianity*, Durham: Acumen, Ancient Philosophies.

Karfík, F. (2007), 'Éros et l'Âme', in A. Havlíček and M. Cajthaml (eds), *Plato's Symposium. Proceedings of the Fifth Symposium Platonicum Pragense*, 147–63, Prague: OIKOYMENH.

Kelessidou-Galanos, A. (1972), 'Le voyage erotique de l'âme dans la mystique plotinienne', *Πλάτων. Δελτίον τῆς Ἑταιρείας Ἑλλήνων Φιλολόγων [Plato. Bulletin of the Society of Greek Philologists]*, 24 (47/48): 88–101.

Kelessidou-Galanou, A. and Ch. Terezis (2018), Πρόκλος, Στοιχείωση Θεολογική. *Προς μία Σύνοψη της Αρχαίας Ελληνικής Μεταφυσικής* (vol.2), trans., comments A. Kelessidou-Galanos, foreword E. Moutsopoulos, intro.: «Γενικές κατευθύνσεις του φιλοσοφικού συστήματος του Πρόκλου» [General Guidelines of Proclus' Metaphysical System] by Ch. Terezis, Thessaloniki: Ζήτρος [Zitros].

Kharlamov, V. (2020), *The Authorship of the Pseudo-Dionysian Corpus: A Deliberate Forgery or Clever Literary Ploy?*, London and New York: Routledge.

Kierkegaard, S. (1995), *Works of Love*, ed. and trans. H.V. Hong and E.H. Hong with introduction and notes, Princeton: PUP.

Kirk, G.S., J.E. Raven and M. Schofield (1983), *The Presocratic Philosophers. A Critical History with a Selection of Texts*, 2nd edn (¹1957; last reprint: 2005), Cambridge: CUP.

Klitenic Wear, S. and J. Dillon (2007), *Dionysius the Areopagite and the Neoplatonist Tradition. Despoiling the Hellenes*, Aldershot and Burlington, VT: Ashgate, Ashgate Studies in Philosophy & Theology in Late Antiquity.

Knauber, B. (2006), *Liebe und Sein. Die Agape als fundamentalontologische Kategorie*, Berlin, NY: Walter de Gruyter, Theologische Bibliothek Töpelmann, vol.133.

Koch, H. (1900), *Pseudo-Dionysius Areopagita in seinen Beziehungen zum Neuplatonismus und Mysterienwesen. Eine litterarhistorische Untersuchung*, Mainz: F. Kirchheim.

Kocijančič, G. (2016), 'The Identity of Dionysius the Areopagite: A Philosophical Approach', in V. Snoj (ed.), *Antiquity and Christianity: Conflict or Conciliation? Proceedings from the International Symposium 9–10 May 2007, Ljubljana*, 87–95, Ljubljana: Kud Logos. It is a slightly revised version of idem (2007), 'The identity of Dionysius Areopagita: A Philosophical Approach', *Sobornost*, 29 (2): 75–84, and with same title in F. Ivanovič, ed. (2011), *Dionysius the Areopagite between Orthodoxy and Heresy*, 3–11, Newcastle upon Tyne: Cambridge Scholars Publishing. An even more complete version has appeared as idem (2011), 'The Name of God and the Name of the Author', in L. Karfikova and M. Havrda (eds), *Nomina Divina: Colloquium Dionysiacum Pragense*, 107–17, Fribourg: Academic Press.

(Konstantinovsky), Nun Seraphima (2010), 'Method, Mysticism and Analogy: Father John Meyendorff and the Areopagitica', *Sourozh*, 106: 88(a)–103(b).

Kosman, A.L. (1976), 'Platonic Love', in W.H. Werkmeister (ed.), *Facets of Plato's Philosophy* (*Phronesis*, a journal for ancient philosophy: Supplementary volume), 53–69, Assen/Amsterdam: Van Gorcum.

Koutras, D. and M. Rellos (1991), Ἔρως – Φιλία – Ἀγάπη: η αναζήτηση της ευτυχίας [*Eros – Friendship – Charity: The Quest for Happiness*], Athens: Σύνδεσμος Επιστημονικού Προβληματισμού.

Kranidiotis, G. (2018), «Η οντολογία του έρωτα στον ψευδο-Διονύσιο τον Αρεοπαγίτη» ['The Ontology of Eros in pseudo-Dionysius the Areopagite'], Ἀντίφωνο. Available online: https://antifono.gr/η-οντολογία-του-έρωτα-στον-ψευδο-διονύ/ (accessed 5 August 2019).

Kraut, R. (1973), 'Love, Egoism and Political Office in Plato', *The Philosophical Review*, 82 (3): 330–44.

Kraut, R. (1992), 'The Defense of Justice in Plato's *Republic*', in R. Kraut (ed.), *The Cambridge Companion to Plato* (repr. 1999), 311–37, Cambridge: CUP.

Krstić, Danilo (Bishop) (2012), *On Divine Philanthropy: From Plato to John Chrysostom*, ed. Bishop Maxim Vasiljević, Los Angeles: Sebastian Press. Posthumous publication based on the author's ThD diss. of 1968: 'St. John Chrysostom as the Theologian of Divine Philanthropy', Faculty of Divinity, Harvard University, with the published material appearing in (1982) and (1983), Θεολογία, 53 (1–4): 91–128, 460–75, 612–26, 1050–83 and 54 (1–3): 123–52, 243–9, 568–94.

Kupperman, J.S. (2013), 'Eros and Agape in Dionysius the Areopagite', *Journal of the Western Mystery Tradition*, 25 (3). Available online: http://www.jwmt.org/v3n25/kupperman.html (accessed 18 November 2014).

Lacrosse, J. (1994), *L' amour chez Plotin. Erôs hénologique, Erôs noétique, Erôs psychique*, Bruxelles, Ousia, Cahiers de Philosophie Ancienne No 11.

Lamascus, L.D. (2017), *The Poverty of Eros in Plato's Symposium*, London, New Delhi, New York, Sydney: Bloomsbury Studies in Ancient Philosophy.

Lankila, T. (2009), 'Aphrodite in Proclus' Theology', *Journal for Late Antique Religion and Culture*, 3: 21–43.

Larchet, J.-Cl. (1996), 'L'amour des ennemis selon saint Silouane l'Athonite et dans la tradition patristique', *Buisson Ardent. Cahiers Saint-Silouane L'Athonite* (Diffusion CERF), 2: 66–95.

Larchet, J.-Cl. (2007), *Variations sur la charité*, Paris: Cerf.

Layne, D. (2009), 'Double Ignorance: An Examination of Socratic Moral Wisdom', PhD diss., KU Leuven.

Layne, D.A. (2014), 'A Fatal or Providential Affair? Socrates and Alcibiades in Proclus' Commentary on the *Alcibiades I*', in P. d'Hoine and G. Van Riel (eds),

Fate, Providence and Moral Responsibility in Ancient, Medieval and Early Modern Thought. Studies in Honour of Carlos Steel, 267–90, Leuven: Leuven University Press, De Wulf-Mansion Centre.

Layne, D.A. and H. Tarrant, eds (2014), *The Neoplatonic Socrates*, Philadelphia, Pennsylvania: University of Pennsylvania Press.

Leichter, D. (2006), 'What Is Called Friendship? A Heideggerian Account of Friendship', in E. Chelstrom (ed.), *Being amongst Others: Phenomenological Reflections on the Life-world*, 114–24, Newcastle: Cambridge Scholars Press.

Lekkos, E.P., trans. (2004a), *Αγάπη-Α': Προς τον Θεό και τον Πλησίον. Επιλεγμένα Πατερικά Αποσπάσματα* [*Love-A: Towards God and the Neighbour. Selected Patristics Excerpts*], Athens: εκδ. Λύχνος, Η Σοφία των Πατέρων 12.

Lekkos, E.P., trans. (2004b), *Αγάπη-Β': Τι είναι - Πώς εκδηλώνεται. Επιλεγμένα Πατερικά Αποσπάσματα* [*Love-B: What it is - How it is Manifested. Selected Patristics Excerpts*], Athens: εκδ. Λύχνος (The Wisdom of the Fathers 13).

Lekkos, E.P., trans. (2004c), *Φιλία και Έρωτας. Επιλεγμένα Πατερικά Αποσπάσματα* [*Friendship and Eros. Selected Patristics Excerpts*], Athens: εκδ. Λύχνος, Η Σοφία των Πατέρων 15.

Lekkos, E.P., trans. (2004d), *Ο Γάμος. Επιλεγμένα Πατερικά Αποσπάσματα* [*Marriage. Selected Patristics Excerpts*], Athens: εκδ. Λύχνος, Η Σοφία των Πατέρων 14.

Lentakis, A. (1992), *Sacred Prostitution* [*Ιερά Πορνεία*], 3rd edn, Athens: Dorikos.

Liddell, H.G., R. Scott (1940), *A Greek-English Lexicon*, revised and augmented throughout by Sir H. Stuart Jones with the assistance of R. McKenzie, 9th edn, Oxford: Clarendon Press.

Lilla, S. and C. Moreschini, eds (2018), Dionysii Areopagitae, *De divinis nominibus*, praefationem, textum, apparatus, Anglicam versionem instruxit Salvator Lilla; edenda curavit Claudius Moreschini, Alessandria: Edizononi dell'Orso, Hellenica 71.

Lossky, Vl. (1974), *In the Image and Likeness of God*, trans. T.E. Bird et al., Crestwood, NY: St Vladimir's Seminary Press.

Lossky, Vl. (1976), *The Mystical Theology of the Eastern Church*, 2nd edn, Crestwood, NY: St Vladimir's Seminary Press. Translated from French by members of the 'Fellowship of St Alban and St Sergius', first published in English in 1957, Cambridge: J. Clarke & Co.

Loudovikos, N. (2002), 'Eucharist and Salvation: An Apophatic Theology of Consubstantiality. A Commentary on St. Maximus the Confessor', relazionne presentata al Convegno internazionale di dialogo con l'Ortodossia 'Salvezza in Cristo o salvezza dal peccato? Le prospettive teologiche sulla salvezza e sull'uomo nell'Ortodossia e nelle tradizioni cristiane occidentali', Torino, 23 e 24 Maggio 2002. Available online: http://www.fga.it/fileadmin/storico/UPLOAD/ALL/CEA/30.pdf (accessed 19 November 2013). This paper, trans. Dn. Chrys. Nassis, is a chapter from fr. N. Loudovikos (2002), *Η αποφατική εκκλησιολογία του ομοουσίου. Η αρχέγονη Εκκλησία σήμερα*, Athens: Αρμός. The whole book appeared recently in English: Loudovikos, N. (2016), *Church in the Making: An Apophatic Ecclesiology of*

Consubstantiality, Yonkers, NY: St Vladimir's Seminary Press, Series: 21st Century Greek Theologians, vol.1.

Loudovikos, N. (2003), *Ψυχανάλυση και Ορθόδοξη Θεολογία. Περί επιθυμίας, καθολικότητας και εσχατολογίας* [Psychoanalysis and Orthodox Theology. On desire, catholicity and eschatology] (²2006), Athens, εκδ. Ἁρμός.

Loudovikos, N. (2010), *A Eucharistic Ontology. Maximus the Confessor's Eschatological Ontology of Being as Dialogical Reciprocity*, trans. E. Theokritoff, Brookline, MA: Holy Cross Orthodox Press.

Loudovikos, N. (2011), 'Person Instead of Grace and Dictated Otherness: John Zizioulas' Final Theological Position', *The Heythrop Journal*, 52: 684–99. The article was already available online in *The Heythrop Journal*, 48 (2009): 1–16; doi: 10.1111/j.1468-2265.2009.00547.x.

Loudovikos, N. (2013), 'Possession or Wholeness? St Maximus the Confessor and John Zizioulas on Person, Nature and Will', *Participatio. Journal of the Thomas F. Torrance Theological Fellowship*, 4: 'T.F. Torrance and Orthodoxy': 258–86. Available online: www.tftorrance.org/journal/participatio_vol_4_2013.pdf (accessed 17 June 2014).

Loudovikos, N. (2014), 'Hell and Heaven, Nature and Person. Chr. Yannaras, D. Stăniloae and Maximus the Confessor', *International Journal of Orthodox Theology*, 5 (1): 9–32.

Louth, A. (1989), *Denys the Areopagite* (reissued in 2001), London, NY: Continuum, series Outstanding Christian Thinkers.

Louth, A. (1993), 'St. Denys the Areopagite and St. Maximus the Confessor: A Question of Influence', *Studia Patristica*, 27: 166–74.

Louth, A. (2004), 'The Cosmic Vision of Saint Maximos the Confessor', in P. Clayton and A. Peacocke (eds), *In Whom We Live and Move and Have Our Being: Panentheistic Reflections on God's Presence in a Scientific World*, 184–96, Grand Rapids, MI: William B. Eerdmans.

Louth, A. (2008a), 'The Reception of Dionysius up to Maximus the Confessor', *Modern Theology*, 24 (4): 573–83 = in S. Coakley and C.M. Stang, eds (2009), *Re-thinking Dionysius the Areopagite*, 43–54, MA, Oxford and Chichester: Wiley-Blackwell, Directions in Modern Theology.

Louth, A. (2008b), 'The Reception of Dionysius in the Byzantine World: Maximus to Palamas', *Modern Theology*, 24 (4): 585–99 = in S. Coakley and C.M. Stang, eds (2009), *Re-thinking Dionysius the Areopagite*, 55–70, MA, Oxford and Chichester: Wiley-Blackwell, Directions in Modern Theology.

Louth, A. (2009), 'Some Recent Works by Christos Yannaras in English Translation', *Modern Theology*, 25 (2): 329–40. This article has also appeared in *Sobornost Incorporating Eastern Churches Review*, 30 (2) (2008): 81–90.

Louth, A. (2010), 'The Nature of Eastern Orthodox Theology', Lecture at the opening of the Amsterdam Centre for Eastern Orthodox Theology (ACEOT), on 28 May 2010 at VU University Amsterdam. Available online: http://www.aceot.nl/files/The%20 Nature%20of%20Eastern%20Orthodox%20Theology.pdf (accessed 16 October 2013).

Luibheid, C. and P. Rorem (1987), Pseudo-Dionysius, *The Complete Works*, trans. C. Luibheid, foreword, notes and trans. collaboration P. Rorem, preface R. Roques, introductions J. Pelikan, J. Leclercq and K. Froehlich, New York, Mahwah: Paulist Press, The Classics of Western Spirituality.

Mahoney, T.A. (1996), 'Is Socratic *erōs* in the *Symposium* Egoistic?', *Apeiron. A Journal for Ancient Philosophy and Science*, 29 (1): 1–18.

Mainoldi, E.S. (2018), *Dietro 'Dionigi l'Areopagita'. La genesi e gli scopi del Corpus Dionysiacum*, Roma: Città Nuova, Series Institutiones. Saggi, ricerche e sintesidi pensiero tardo-antico, medievale e umanistico, 6.

Manos, A. (1995), 'The Neoplatonic Interpretation as to the Teaching of Divine Love in Dionysius Areopagite', *Diotima*, 23: 55–9.

Manos, A. (2006), *Πρόκλος, ὁ Πλατωνικὸς Διάδοχος. Ἡ ἐπιστήμη τῶν ὄντων μυσταγωγὸς πρὸς τὴν θέα τοῦ Ἑνός* [*Proclus, the Platonic Successor. The science of beings as initiator to the vision of the One*], Athens: ἐκδ. Ἰρηγόρη.

Manos, A.Ch. (2015), *Μιὰ τετρακτὺς λόγων περὶ ἔρωτος* [*A Tetractys of Logoi about Love*], Athens: Ἡρόδοτος.

Manoussakis, J.P. (2008), 'The Revelation of the Phenomena and the Phenomenon of Revelation: An Apology for Dionysius's Phenomenological Appropriation', *American Catholic Philosophical Quarterly*, 82 (4): 705–19.

Maraguianou, E. (1990), *L'amour et la mort chez Platon et ses interpretes*, thèse de Doctorat d'Etat, Universite François Rabelais, Tours, Atelier National de Reproduction des Theses, Universite de Lille III. Available online: http://thesis.ekt.gr/thesisBookReader/id/2621#page/1/mode/2up (accessed 15 January 2020).

Maraguianou-Dermousi, E. (1994), *Πλατωνικὰ Θέματα* [*Platonic Themes*], Athens: ἐκδ. Καρδαμίτσα-Ἰνστιτοῦτο τοῦ Βιβλίου.

Marica, M.A. (2015), 'Eros in the First Century's Christian Theology: Pseudo-Dionysius the Areopagite', *Dialogo*, 2 (1): 179a–86a.

Marion, J.-L. (2002), *Prolegomena to Charity*, trans. S.E. Lewis, New York: Fordham University Press.

Marion, J.-L. (2007), *The Erotic Phenomenon*, trans. S.E. Lewis, Chicago and London: The University of Chicago Press.

Markus, D. (2016), 'Anagogic Love between Neoplatonic Philosophers and Their Disciples in Late Antiquity', *The International Journal of the Platonic Tradition*, 10 (1): 1–39.

Marsengill, K. (2020), 'Images of Holy Men in Late Antiquity in Light of Pseudo-Dionysius the Areopagite: Framing Spiritual Ascent and Visualising Spiritual Hierarchy', in F. Dell'Acqua and E.S. Mainoldi (eds), *Pseudo-Dionysius and Christian Visual Culture, c.500–900*, 133–76, New York: Palgrave Macmillan.

Martijn, M. (2010), *Proclus on Nature: Philosophy of Nature and Its Methods in Proclus' Commentary on Plato's Timaeus*, Leiden, The Netherlands: Koninklijke Brill NV, Philosophia antiqua, vol.121.

Martin, A.M., ed. (2019), *The Routledge Handbook of Love in Philosophy*, Abingdon/NY: Routledge.

Mavropoulos, D. (2017), 'Ἡ διαλεκτικὴ θείου καὶ ἀνθρώπινου ἔρωτα' ['The Dialectics of Divine and Human Eros'], *Ἀνθίβολα. Ἐτήσια Ἔκδοση Χριστιανικοῦ Διαλόγου καί Πολιτισμοῦ* [*Yearly Publication of Christian Dialogue and Culture*] (publishing house: Ἐν πλῷ), 1: 245–58.

May, S. (2011), *Love: A History*, New Haven: Yale University Press.

May, S. (2019), *Love: A New Understanding of an Ancient Emotion*, Oxford: OUP.

Mazur, Z. (2009), 'Having Sex with the One: Erotic Mysticism in Plotinus and the Problem of Metaphor', in P. Vassilopoulou and S.R.L. Clark (eds), *Late Antique Epistemology: Other Ways to Truth*, Houndmills, 67–83, Basingstoke Palgrave Macmillan.

McCabe, M.M. (2008), 'Plato's Ways of Writing', in G. Fine (ed.), *The Oxford Handbook of Plato*, 88–113, Oxford: OUP.

McGinn, B. (1991), *The Foundations of Mysticism. Origins to the Fifth Century*, vol. 1 of *The Presence of God. A History of Western Christian Mysticism*, New York: Crossroad.

McGinn, B. (1996), 'God as Eros: Metaphysical Foundations of Christian Mysticism', in B. Nassif (ed.), *New Perspectives on Historical Theology. Essays in Memory of John Meyendorff*, 189–209, Michigan/Cambridge, UK: William B. Eerdmans Publishing Company, Grand Rapids.

Meyendorff, J. (1969), *Christ in Eastern Christian Thought*, trans. Y. Dubois, Washington, DC: Corpus Books.

Michaelides, P.E. (2018), 'Plotinus' Philosophical Eros for the One: His Unio Mystica, Ethos and Legendary Life', *International Journal of Multidisciplinary Thought*, 7 (1): 59–94.

Miller, M. (2007), 'Beginning the "Longer Way"', in G.R.F. Ferrari (ed.), *The Cambridge Companion to Plato's Republic*, 310–44, Cambridge: CUP.

Miller, P.C. (1992), '"Plenty Sleeps There": The Myth of Eros and Psyche in Plotinus and Gnosticism', in R.T. Wallis (ed.) and J. Bergman (associate ed.), *Neoplatonism and Gnosticism*, 223–38, Albany: State University of NY Press, International Society for Neoplatonic Studies, vol.6 in 'Studies in Neoplatonism: Ancient and Modern' (R. Baine Harris general ed.).

Mitralexis, S., ed. (2018), *Polis, Ontology, Ecclesial Event: Engaging with Christos Yannaras' Thought*, preface J. Milbank, Cambridge: James Clark & Co.

Molodeţ-Jitea, P. (2015), 'Platonic Eros and Christian Eros in the *Corpus Areopagiticum*. A Commentary on *De divinis nominibus*, Chapter IV: 12,13', in A. Tat and C. Tuţu (eds), *Saint Dionysius the Areopagite: Sources, Context, Reception*, 88–97, Cluj-Napoca: Napoca Star.

Monrad, M.J. (1888), 'Ueber den sachlichen Zusammenhang der Neuplatonischen Philosophie mit vorhergehenden Denkrichtungen, besonders mit dem Skepticismus', in *Philosophische Monatshefte*, 156–93, Heidelberg: Verlag von Georg Weiss, 24.

Mortley, R. (1980), 'Love in Plato and Plotinus', *Antichthon*, Australian Society for Classical Studies, 14: 45–52.

Moutsopoulos, E. (1978), «Ὀντολογία καὶ τέχνη παρὰ Πλωτίνῳ» ['Ontology and art in Plotinus'], in E. Moutsopoulos, *Φιλοσοφικοὶ Προβληματισμοί* [*Philosophical Reflections*], vol.2, *Ἀναδρομαὶ καὶ Ἀναδομήσεις*, 169–71, Athens: University of Athens.

Moutsopoulos, E. (1998), 'D'Aristote à Proclus. Mouvement et désir de l'Un dans la *Théologie Platonicienne*', in E. Moutsopoulos (eds), *Philosophie de la Culture Grecque*, 257–62, Athens: Academie d'Athènes.

St Nectarios, Metropolitan of Pentapolis (2010), *Λόγοι Τρεῖς: Περί ἀγάπης Θεοῦ, Περί τῆς θείας ἀγάπης, Περί θείου ἔρωτος*, Modern Greek rendering by fr. Ἡ.Γ. Διακουμάκος, prologue Θ.Ν. Παπαθανασίου, Athens: Παρρησία. The three orations appeared originally in 1904; there exists also an edition of the book with both Greek text and English translation: St Nectarios (2011), *Three Homilies: On the Love of God. On Divine Love. On Divine Eros*, trans. fr. Ἡ.Γ. Διακουμάκος and Caroline Makropoulos, Athens, Παρρησία.

Nehamas, A. (2016), *On Friendship*, New York: Basic Books (A Member of the Perseus Books Group).

Niarchos, C.G. (1995), 'Good, Beauty, and Eros in Dionysius' Doctrine of Divine Causality', *Diotima*, 23: 106–8.

Noble, C.I. and N.M. Powers (2015), 'Creation and Divine Providence in Plotinus', in A. Marmodoro and B. Prince (eds.), *Causation and Creation in Late Antiquity*, 51–70, Cambridge: CUP.

Nussbaum, M.C. (2001), *The Fragility of Goodness. Luck and Ethics in Greek Tragedy and Philosophy*, 2nd revised edn (1st edn 1986), Cambridge: CUP.

Nygren, A. (1953), *Agape and Eros. Part I. A Study of the Christian Idea of Love* (^{1}1932). *Part II. The History of the Christian Idea of Love* (^{1}1938–'39), trans. in one vol. Ph. S. Watson, Philadelphia: The Westminster Press.

O'Brien, C. and S. Klitenic Wear (2017), 'The Figure of the Diadochos from Socrates to the Late Antique Athenian School', in J. Finamore and S. Klitenic Wear (eds), *Defining Platonism: Essays on Plato and Platonism in Honor of the Seventy-Fifth Birthday of John M. Dillon*, 253–70, Washington, DC: Franciscan University Press.

O'Connell, R.J. S.J. (1981), '*Erōs* and *Philia* in Plato's Moral Cosmos', in H.J. Blumenthal and R.A. Markus (eds), *Neoplatonism and Christian Thought. Essays in Honour of A.H. Armstrong*, 3–19, Great Britain: Variorum Publications Ltd.

O'Meara, D.J. (2003), *Platonopolis: Platonic Political Philosophy in Late Antiquity*, Oxford: OUP.

O'Meara, D.J. (2017), *Cosmology and Politics in Plato's Later Works*, Cambridge: CUP.

O'Neill, W. (1965), *Proclus: Commentary on the First Alcibiades*, translation and Commentary by W. O'Neill (2nd edn 1971), The Hague: Martinus Nijhoff. Reprinted, along with Westerink's edition of the text in 2011, Westbury: The Prometheus Trust, 'Platonic Texts and Translations Series', vol. VI.

Oravecz, J.M. (2014), *God as Love: The Concept and Spiritual Aspects of Agape in Modern Russian Religious Thought*, foreword by P. Valliere, Grand Rapids, Michigan and Cambridge: William B. Eerdmans Publishing Company.

O'Rourke, F. (1992), *Pseudo-Dionysius and the Metaphysics of Aquinas*, Leiden: E.J. Brill; (reprinted in 2005, Indiana: University of Notre Dame Press).

Ortega Y Gasset, J. (1957), *On Love. Aspects of a Single Theme*, trans. T. Talbot (^{7}1972; most recent reprint in 2012), New York: A Meridian Book, The World Publishing Company.

Osborne, C. (1994), *Eros Unveiled. Plato and the God of Love* (repr. 2002), Oxford: Clarendon Press.

Pallis, D. (unpublished), '*Pythagoras Redivivus*: Pythagorean Elements of Philosophical Structure and Theology of Numbers in the "Epistles" of Dionysius the Areopagite', paper (in English) that was delivered at the 'Greek National Conference of Philosophy' organized by the *Philosophein* Journal (19 March 2016).

Pallis, D. (2013), 'The Liturgical Theology of Dionysios the Areopagite: A Liturgical Reading of the Areopagitic Writings in the Context of the Christian and Neoplatonist Tradition', MA thesis in Philosophy and Theology, Winchester: University of Winchester.

Pallis, D. (2016/2017, but still forthcoming), «Ένα βυζαντινό υπόδειγμα αποφατικής χριστιανικής σκέψης: Διονύσιος ο Αρεοπαγίτης προς τον ιερέα Σωσίπατρο, με κάποιες συμπληρωματικές σημειώσεις» ['A Byzantine Model of Apophatic Christian Thought: Dionysius the Areopagite to Priest Sosipater, with Some Complementary Notes'], *Κληρονομία*, 39 (1/2).

Papanikolaou, A. (2006a), *Being with God. Trinity, Apophaticism, and Divine-Human Communion* (reprinted in 2008), Notre Dame, Indiana: University of Notre Dame Press.

Papanikolaou, A. (2006b), 'Liberating Eros: Confession and Desire', *Journal of the Society of Christian Ethics*, 26 (1): 115–36. An abridged version of this article has been published as: idem (2008), 'Honest to God: Confession and Desire', in A. Papanikolaou and E.H. Prodromou (eds), *Thinking through Faith: New Perspectives from Orthodox Christian Scholars*, 219–45, Crestwood, NY: St Vladimir's Seminary Press, The Zacchaeus Venture Series: vol.1.

Papanikolaou, A. (2008), 'Personhood and Its Exponents in Twentieth-century Orthodox Theology', in M.B. Cunningham and E. Theokritoff (eds), *The Cambridge Companion to Orthodox Christian Theology*, 232–45, Cambridge: CUP.

Papathanasiou, Th. (2011), «Ένας ησυχαστής του Αγίου όρους στην καρδιά της πόλης: π. Πορφύριος Καυσοκαλυβίτης» ['A hesychast of the Holy Mountain in the heart of the city: fr. Porphyrios of Kavsokalyvia'], *Σύναξη*, 117: 50–67. Available online: http://www.antifono.gr/portal/κατηγορίες/θεολογία-θρησκειολογία/γραπτός-λόγος/4661-ένας-ησυχαστής-του-αγίου-όρους-στην-καρδιά-της-πόλης-π-πορφύριος-καυσοκαλυβίτης-1906-1991.html (accessed 20 January 2014).

Pavlos, P. (2017), 'Christian Insights into Plotinus' Metaphysics and His Concept of Aptitude (Ἐπιτηδειότης)', *Akropolis: Journal of Hellenic Studies*, 1: 5–32.

Pépin, J. (²1976), *Mythe et Allégorie. Les origines grecques et les contestations judéo-chrétiennes* (nouvelle édition, revue et augmentée; ¹1958, Aubier), Paris: Études Augustiniennes.

Perl, E. (1994), 'Hierarchy and Participation in Dionysius the Areopagite and Greek Neoplatonism', *American Catholic Philosophical Quarterly*, LXVIII (1): 15–30.

Perl, E.D. (1998), 'The Metaphysics of Love in Dionysius the Areopagite', *The Journal of Neoplatonic Studies*, VI (1): 45–73.

Perl, E.D. (2007), *Theophany. The Neoplatonic Philosophy of Dionysius the Areopagite*, Albany, NY: State University of New York Press, SUNY series in ancient Greek philosophy (ed. A. Preus).

Perl, E.D. (2013), 'Hierarchy and Love in St. Dionysius the Areopagite', in J. Chryssavgis and B.V. Foltz (eds), *Toward an Ecology of Transfiguration. Orthodox Christian Perspectives on Environment, Nature, and Creation*, with a Prefatory Letter from Ecumenical Patriarch Bartholomew and a Foreword by B. McKibben, 23–33 (and 419: notes), New York: Fordham University Press, Orthodox Christianity and Contemporary Thought.

Pigler, A. (2002), *Plotin. Une Métaphysique de l'Amour. L'amour comme structure du monde intelligible*, Paris: Libraire Philosophique J. Vrin, Tradition de la Pensée Classique.

Plested, M. (2012), *Orthodox Readings of Aquinas*, Oxford: OUP, Changing Paradigms in Historical and Systematic Theology.

Popović, J. (1940), *Dostojevski o Evropi i slovenstvu* [*Dostoevsky on Europe and the Slavs*], Belgrade: Izdavačko-prosvetna zadruga; repr. in 1999, Belgrade: Monastery Celije.

Price, A.W. (1989), *Love and Friendship in Plato and Aristotle* (reprint: 2004), Oxford: Clarendon Press.

Pupaza, Δ. (2015), *Ἡ Θεολογία τοῦ Καλοῦ καὶ τοῦ Ἀγαθοῦ στὸν Ἅγιο Διονύσιο τὸν Ἀρεοπαγίτη* [*The Theology of the Beautiful and the Good in Saint Dionysius the Areopagite*], prologue Δ. Τσελεγγίδης, ed. Ν. Ἀγνάντος, Holy Mountain: Ἱερὰ Μεγίστη Μονὴ Βατοπαιδίου.

Purpura, A.M. (2018), *God, Hierarchy, and Power: Orthodox Theologies of Authority from Byzantium*, New York: Fordham University Press, Orthodox Christianity and Contemporary Thought.

Quispel, G. (1979), 'God Is Eros', in W.R. Schoedel and R.L. Wilken (eds), *Early Christian Literature and the Classical Intellectual Tradition in Honorem Robert M. Grant*, 189–205, Paris: éditions Beauchesne (Théologie Historique, collection fondée par J. Daniélou, dirigée par C. Kannengiesser, no 54).

Ramelli, I.L.E. (2012), 'Origen, Greek Philosophy, and the Birth of the Trinitarian Meaning of *Hypostasis*', *Harvard Theological Review*, 105 (3): 302–50.

Ramfos, S. (²1999), Φιλόσοφος καὶ Θεῖος Ἔρως. Ἀπὸ τὸ Συμπόσιον τοῦ Πλάτωνος στοὺς Ὕμνους θείων ἐρώτων τοῦ ἁγίου Συμεών, τὸ ἐπίκλην Νέου Θεολόγου [*Philosophical and Divine Eros. From Plato's Symposium to St Symeon, the so-called New Theologian's Hymns of divine eros*] (¹1989), Athens: Ἁρμός.

Rapport, N. (2019), *Cosmopolitan Love and Individuality: Ethical Engagement beyond Culture*, Lanham, Boulder, New York, London: Lexington Books.

Reeve, C.D.C. (2006), *Plato on Love*. Lysis, Symposium, Phaedrus, Alcibiades *and Selections from* Republic *and* Laws, edited with introductions and notes (and part of trans.) by C.D.C. Reeve (²2007), Indianapolis: Hackett.

Remes, P. (2006), 'Plotinus's Ethics of Disinterested Interest', *Journal of the History of Philosophy* (published by The Johns Hopkins University Press), 44 (1): 1–23.

Renaud, F. and H. Tarrant, eds (2015), *The Platonic Alcibiades I. The Dialogue and Its Ancient Reception*, Cambridge: CUP.

Rhodes, J.M. (2003), *Eros, Wisdom, and Silence. Plato's Erotic Dialogues*, Columbia: University of Missouri Press.

Ricoeur, P. (1995), 'Love and Justice', *Philosophy & Social Criticism*, 21 (5–6): 23–39.

Riggs, T. (2009), '*Eros* as Hierarchical Principle: A Re-evaluation of Dionysius' Neoplatonism', *Dionysius*, XXVII: 71–96.

Riggs, T. (2010), '*Erôs*, the Son, and the Gods as Metaphysical Principles in Proclus and Dionysius', *Dionysius*, XXVIII: 97–130.

Riggs, T. (2011), 'How to Speak of the Trinity: Henadology, Dionysius and Modern Commentary', in M. Roberts, J. Sanford and S. Wear (eds), *Quaestiones Disputatae. Selected Papers on the Legacy of Neoplatonism*, 2 (2011): 70–82.

Rinne, P. (2018), *Kant on Love*, Berlin/Boston: Walter de Gruyter, Kantstudien-Ergänzungshefte.

Rist, J.M. (1964), *Eros and Psyche* (*Phoenix*, Journal of the Classical Association of Canada, Supplementary Volume VI), University of Toronto Press.

Rist, J.M. (1966), 'A Note on Eros and Agape in Pseudo-Dionysius', *Vigiliae Christianae*, 20: 235–43; (Amsterdam: North-Holland Publishing Co.) The article has been reprinted as ch. XVI in J.M. Rist (1985), *Platonism and Its Christian Heritage*, London: Variorum Reprints.

Rist, J.M. (1970), 'Some Interpretations of Agape and Eros', in C.W. Kegley (ed.), *The Philosophy and Theology of Anders Nygren*, 156–73 and (notes in) 406–9, Carbondale, Illinois: Southern Illinois University Press. Reprinted as ch. I in J.M. Rist (1985), *Platonism and Its Christian Heritage*, London: Variorum Reprints.

Rist, J.M. (1999), 'Love, Knowledge and Incarnation in Pseudo-Dionysius', in J.J. Cleary (ed.), *Traditions of Platonism. Essays in Honour of John Dillon*, 375–88, Aldershot, Brookfield USA, Singapore, Sydney: Ashgate.

Ritter, A.M. (2015), 'Dionysios ps.-Areiopagites im heutigen Forschungsgespräch', *Phasis*, 18: 251–71.

Robin, L. (1933), *La théorie platonicienne de l'Amour*, 2nd edn (¹1908), Paris: F. Alcan.

Rolt, C.E. (2007), *Dionysius the Areopagite on the Divine Names and the Mystical Theology*, New York: Cosimo Classics. Originally published in 1920, Grand Rapids, MI: Christian Classics Ethereal Library.

Romano, F. (1984), 'La passione amorosa in Plotino', *Discorsi*, 4 (2): 7–21.

Roques, R. (1954), *L'univers dionysien. Structure hiérarchique du monde selon le Pseudo-Denys*, Paris: Les Éditions du Cerf.

Rorem, P. (1993), *Pseudo-Dionysius. A Commentary on the Texts and an Introduction to Their Influence*, New York, Oxford: OUP.

Rowe, C.J. (²1988), *Plato. Phaedrus*, trans. and comm. C.J. Rowe, 2nd edn (¹1986), Oxford: Aris & Phillips Classical Texts.

Rozanis, S. (2012), Λόγος αποσπασματικός περί του θείου έρωτος [*Fragmentary Discourse on Divine Eros*], Athens: εκδ. Ψυχογιός, Επιστήμες του Ανθρώπου.

Russell, N. (2019), *Gregory Palamas and the Making of Palamism in the Modern Age*, Oxford: OUP.

Russi, Ch. (2009), 'Causality and Sensible Objects: A Comparison between Plotinus and Proclus', in R. Chiaradonna and Fr. Trabattoni (eds), *Physics and Philosophy of Nature in Greek Neoplatonism*, 145–71, Leiden: Brill.

Saffrey, H.-D. (1982), 'New Objective Links between the Pseudo-Dionysius and Proclus' (trans. M. Brennan), in D.J. O'Meara (ed.), *Neoplatonism and Christian Thought*, 64–74 (and 246–8: notes), Albany, NY: SUNY Press, Studies in Neoplatonism, vol.3.

Sakharov, N.V. (2002), *I Love, Therefore I Am: The Theological Legacy of Archimandrite Sophrony* (revised edn of *Amo ergo sum*), Crestwood, NY: St Vladimir's Seminary Press.

Santas, G. (1988), *Plato & Freud. Two Theories of Love*, Oxford: Basil Blackwell.

Schäfer, C. (2006a), 'Μονή, πρόοδος und ἐπιστροφή in der Philosophie des Proklos und des Areopagiten Dionysius', in M. Perkams and R.M. Piccione (eds), *Proklos. Methode, Seelenlehre, Metaphysik*. Akten der Konferenz in Jena am 18.-20. September 2003, 340–62, Leiden, Boston: Brill, Philosophia Antiqua, vol.XCVIII.

Schäfer, C. (2006b), *The Philosophy of Dionysius the Areopagite. An Introduction to the Structure and the Content of the Treatise* On the Divine Names, Leiden, Boston: Brill.

Schindler, D.C. (2018), *Love and the Postmodern Predicament: Rediscovering the Real in Beauty, Goodness, and Truth*, Eugene, Oregon: Cascade Books.

Schramm, M. (2013), *Freundschaft im Neuplatonismus: Politisches Denken und Sozialphilosophie von Plotin bis Kaiser Julian*, Berlin/Boston: Walter de Gruyter.

Schubert, V. (1973), *Plotin. Einführung in sein Philosophieren*, Freiburg/München: Verlag Karl Alber Kolleg Philosophie.

Schwyzer, R.T. (1987), 'Corrigenda ad Plotini Textum', *Museum Helveticum. Schweizerizche Zeitschrift für klassische Altertumwswissenschaft*, Basel: Schwabe & Co AG Verlag, vol.44, facs.3: 127–233.

Segonds, A.Ph. (1985–1986), Proclus, *Sur le Premier Alcibiade de Platon*, texte établi et traduit par A.Ph. Segonds, 2 vols, Paris: Les Belles Lettres, Coll. des Un. de France, sous le patronage de Assoc. G. Budé.

Sheffield, F.C.C. (2011), 'Beyond *eros*: Plato on Friendship in the *Phaedrus*', *Proceedings of the Aristotelian Society*, CXI part 2: 251–73.
Siasos, L.Ch. (1984), *Εραστές της Αλήθειας. Έρευνα στις αφετηρίες και στη συγκρότηση της θεολογικής γνωσιολογίας κατά τον Πρόκλο και το Διονύσιο Αρεοπαγίτη* ['Lovers of Truth. An Investigation into the Origins and the Composition of the Theological Gnosiology according to Proclus and Dionysius the Areopagite'], PhD diss., Aristotelian University of Thessaloniki, *Επιστημονική Επετηρίδα Θεολογικής Σχολής*, παράρτημα no.45 of vol.28, Thessaloniki.
Siecienski, A.E. (2010), *The Filioque: History of a Doctrinal Controversy*, Oxford: OUP, Oxford Studies in Historical Theology.
Siniossoglou, N. (2011), *Radical Platonism in Byzantium. Illumination and Utopia in Gemistos Plethon*, Cambridge: CUP.
Siorvanes, L. (1996), *Proclus: Neo-Platonic Philosophy and Science*, New Haven: Yale University Press/Gr. Britain: Edinburgh University Press.
Skliris, D. (2016), «Τί είναι αὐτὸ ποὺ τὸ λένε ἀγάπη;» ['What's this thing called love?'], *Σύναξη*, 137: 5–12. Available online: https://antifono.gr/τι-είναι-αυτό-που-το-λένε-αγάπη/ (accessed 27 August 2019).
Skliris, D. (2019), «Homo ludens: Ελευθερία και Αγάπη στη σκέψη του επισκόπου Αθανασίου Γιέφτιτς» ['Homo ludens: Freedom and Love in the thought of bishop Athanasije Jevtic'], Available online: https://antifono.gr/20486-2/ (accessed 7 September 2019).
Smith, A. (2007), 'Plotinus and the Myth of Love', in J.H.D. Scourfield (ed.), *Texts and Culture in Late Antiquity. Inheritance, Authority, and Change*, 233–45, Swansea: The Classical Press of Wales.
Solovyov, V. (1985), *The Meaning of Love*, ed. with a substantially revised trans. T.R. Beyer, Jr., introduction O. Barfield, Hudson NY: Lindisfarne Books.
Sorabji, R. (1987), 'Infinity and the Creation', in R. Sorabji, *Philoponus and the Rejection of Aristotelian Science*, 164–78, London: Duckworth.
Staab, K. (1933), *Pauluskommentar aus der griechischen Kirche aus Katenenhandschriften gesammelt*, Münster: Aschendorff.
Stamoulis, Ch.A. (1999), *Φύση καὶ Ἀγάπη καὶ ἄλλα μελετήματα* [*Nature and Love and other studies*], Thessaloniki, ἐκδ. «Τὸ Παλίμψηστον», Λειμὼν Ἀμφιλαφὴς 3.
Stamoulis, Ch.A. (2009), *Ἔρως καὶ Θάνατος* [*Eros and Death*], Athens: Ἀκρίτας.
Stamoulis, Ch.A., ed. (2014), *Ἔρωτας και Σεξουαλικότητα. Αφήγηση διεπιστημονική. Από την αρχαιότητα στο σήμερα. Από τους μικροοργανισμούς στον άνθρωπο* [*Eros and Sexuality. Interdisciplinary Narrative. From Antiquity to the Present-day. From the Microorganisms to the Human*], Athens: Ἁρμός.
Stang, Ch.M. (2012), *Apophasis and Pseudonymity in Dionysius the Areopagite. 'No Longer I'*, Oxford: OUP, Oxford Early Christian Studies.
Stathopoulou, G.M. (1999), 'Eros in Plotinus', *Φιλοσοφία. Yearbook of the Research Centre for Greek Philosophy* (Academy of Athens), 29: 83–8.
Stephens, W.O. (1996), 'Epictetus on How the Stoic Sage Loves', *Oxford Studies in Ancient Philosophy*, 14: 193–210.

Stiglmayr, J. (1895), 'Der Neuplatoniker Proklus als Vorlage des sogenannten Dionysius Areopagita in der Lehre vom Übel', *Historisches Jahrbuch*, 16: 253–73 and 721–48.

Suchla, B.R. (1980), *Die sogenannten Maximus-Scholien des Corpus Dionysiacum Areopagiticum*, Göttingen: Nachrichten der Akademie der Wissenschaften in Göttingen, philol.-hist. Kl. 3.

Suchla, B.R., ed. (1990), *Corpus Dionysiacum*, vol.I, Pseudo-Dionysius Areopagita, *De Divinis Nominibus*, Berlin, NY: Walter de Gruyter, Patristische Texte und Studien, Band 33.

Suchla, B.R., ed. (2011), *Corpus Dionysiacum IV/1*, Ioannis Scythopolitani Prologus et Scholia in Dionysii Areopagitae *Librum* De Divinis Nominibus *cum Additamentis Interpretum Aliorum*, Berlin/Boston: Walter de Gruyter, Patristische Texte und Studien, Band 62.

Sykoutris, I. (²1949), Πλάτωνος Συμπόσιον, text, trans. and interpretation by Ἰωάννης Συκουτρῆς, 2nd edn (¹1934, ⁶1976, ¹²1994), Athens: Academy of Athens, Hellenic Library no.1, Bookshop of 'Hestia', I.D. Kollaros & ΣΙΑ Α.Ε.

Terezis, Ch. (1986), 'Διάμεσα-Ἀρχέτυπα στὸν Πρόκλο καὶ τὸν Ψευδο-Διονύσιο Ἀρεοπαγίτη. Ἀπὸ τὸν ὕστερο Νεοπλατωνισμὸ στὶς ἀπαρχὲς τῆς Βυζαντινῆς φιλοσοφίας' ['Intermediaries-Archetypes in Proclus and pseudo-Dionysius the Areopagite. From late Neoplatonism to the beginnings of Byzantine philosophy'], PhD diss. (University of) Ioannina. Available online: http://thesis.ekt.gr/thesisBookReader/id/0579#page/1/mode/2up (accessed 16 January 2020).

Terezis, Ch. (2002), 'Οἱ θεολογικοὶ καὶ οἱ ἀνθρωπολογικοὶ ὅροι τοῦ ἔρωτα στὸν Νεοπλατωνικὸ Πρόκλο' ['The theological and anthropological conditions of eros in the Neoplatonic Proclus'], in L.Ch. Siasos (ed.), Ἱμάτια Φωτὸς Ἀρρήτου. Διεπιστημονικὴ προσέγγιση τοῦ προσώπου [*Garments of Ineffable Light. Inter-scholarly approach to the person*], 43–70, Thessaloniki: ἐκδ. Π.Σ. Πουρναρᾶ.

Terezis, Ch. (2005), Πρόκλος. Διαλεκτικὴ καὶ θεωρία στὸν νεοπλατωνικὸ Πρόκλο. Ἕνα σχόλιο στὸν πλατωνικὸ διάλογο Ἀλκιβιάδης [*Proclus. Dialectics and contemplation in the Neoplatonic Proclus. A comment on the Platonic dialogue Alcibiades*], intro.-trans.-interpretive comments Χρ. Τερέζης, Thessaloniki: ἐκδ. Ζῆτρος.

Terezis, Ch. (2012), 'Aspects of the Theory of Dionysius the Areopagite Concerning the Divine Processions as Generating Principles of the Cosmos', *Augustinianum*, 52 (2): 441–57.

Terezis, Ch. and P. Vgenopoulou (1999), «Ὁ ἔρως στὶς ἀρεοπαγιτικὲς συγγραφές. Μία μεθοδολογικὴ πρόταση» ['Eros in the Areopagitic Writings. A Methodological Proposal'], *Γρηγόριος Παλαμᾶς*, 776: 21–36.

Terezis, Ch.A. and S.P. Panagopoulos (2009), 'Ἀγάπη καὶ ἐκκλησιαστικὴ ἱεραρχία στὸν Διονύσιο Ἀρεοπαγίτη', *Θεολογία*, 3: 5–35.

Terezis, Ch. and M. Tsakoymaki (2014a), «Ὁ διδάσκαλος ὡς θεῖος ἐραστής» ['The Teacher as Divine Lover'], in V.E. Pantazis and M. Stork (eds), Ὄμμασιν ἄλλοις. *Ommasin allois: Festschrift für Professor Ioannis E. Theodoropoulos zum 65. Geburtstag*, 327–48, Essen: Oldib-Verlag.

Terezis, Ch. and M. Tsakoymaki (2014b), 'Divine Eros and Divine Providence in Proclus' Educational System', *Peitho: Examina Antiqua*, 1 (5): 163–76.

Theodorakopoulos, I.N. (1971), *Πλάτωνος Φαῖδρος*, introduction, ancient and Modern Greek text with commentary (reprinted 2000), Athens: (Βιβλιοπωλεῖον τῆς Ἑστίας).

Timotin, A. (2012), *La démonologie platonicienne: histoire de la notion de* daimōn *de Platon aux derniers néoplatoniciens*, the Netherlands: Brill, Philosophia Antiqua, vol.128.

Tollefsen, T.T. (2012), *Activity and Participation in Late Antique and Early Christian Thought*, Oxford: OUP.

Tornau, C. (2005), 'Eros versus Agape? Von Plotins Eros zum Liebesbegriff Augustins', *Philosophisches Jahrbuch*, 112: 271–91.

Tornau, C. (2006), 'Der Eros und das Gute bei Plotin und Proklos', in M. Perkams and R.M. Piccione (eds), *Proklos. Methode, Seelenlehre, Metaphysik*. Akten der Konferenz in Jena am 18.-20. September 2003, 201–29, Leiden, Boston: Brill, Philosophia Antiqua. A series of Studies on Ancient Philosophy, vol.XCVIII.

Treflé Hidden, S., ed. (2014), *Jewish, Christian, and Islamic Mystical Perspectives on the Love of God*, New York: Palgrave Macmillan.

Triantari-Mara, S. (2002), *Ἡ ἔννοια τοῦ κάλλους στὸ Διονύσιο Ἀρεοπαγίτη. Θεωρητική προσέγγιση τῆς βυζαντινῆς τέχνης. Συμβολή στήν αἰσθητική φιλοσοφία* [*The Concept of Beauty in Dionysius the Areopagite. Theoretical Approach of Byzantine Art. Contribution to Aesthetics*], Athens: Ἡρόδοτος (Βυζάντιο/Ἱστορία).

Trouillard, J. (1973), 'Le "Parménide" de Platon et son interprétation néoplatonicienne', in J. Trouillard, *Études Néoplatoniciennes*, 9–26, Neuchatel: A La Baconnière (Langages; *Revue de Théologie et de Philosophie*, Lausanne).

Tzavaras, G.G. (1993), *Ἔρωτας-Πόλεμος. Δοκίμιο Κοσμοθεωρίας* [*Eros-War. An Essay on Worldview*], Athens: Δωδώνη.

Ucciani, L. (1998), *Sur Plotin: la Gnose et l' Amour*, Paris: editions Kimé.

Van den Berg, R.M. (2017), 'Theurgy in the Context of Proclus' Philosophy', in P. d'Hoine and M. Martijn (eds), *All from One. A Guide to Proclus*, 223–39, Oxford: OUP.

Van Riel, G. (2001), 'Horizontalism or Verticalism? Proclus vs Plotinus on the Procession of Matter', *Phronesis*, 46 (2): 129–53.

Van Riel, G. (2017), 'The One, the Henads, and the Principles', in P. d'Hoine and M. Martijn (eds), *All from One. A Guide to Proclus*, 73–97, Oxford: OUP.

Vasilakis, A.D. (2009), *Ἡ ὀντολογία τοῦ ὡραίου στὸ ἔργο τοῦ Πέτρου Βράιλα-Ἀρμένη* [*The Ontology of the Beautiful in Petros Brailas-Armenis' Work*], Athens: Σύλλογος πρὸς Διάδοσιν Ὠφελίμων Βιβλίων' ['Society for Spread of Beneficial Books'] (with an English Synopsis in 350–8).

Vasilakis, D. (2015), 'Love and Myth in Plotinus' *Enneads* III.5', *Diotima. Review of Philosophical Research*, 43: 68–75.

Vasilakis, D.A. (2014), 'Neoplatonic Love: The Metaphysics of Eros in Plotinus, Proclus and the Pseudo-Dionysius', PhD diss., King's College London.

Vasilakis, D.A. (2016), 'Maximus as a Philosophical Interpreter of Dionysius: The Case of Christ as Manic Lover', Θεολογία, 87 (2): 103–12.

Vasilakis, D.A. (2017a), 'Platonic *Eros*, Moral Egoism, and Proclus', in D.D. Butorac and D.A. Layne (eds), *Proclus and His Legacy*, 45–52, Berlin/Boston: Walter de Gruyter, 'Millennium Studies' series, vol.65.

Vasilakis, D.A. (2017b), 'Dionysius *versus* Proclus on Undefiled Providence and Its Byzantine Echoes in Nicholas of Methone', *Studia Patristica*, XCVI (22): 407–18.

Vasilakis, D.A. (2018), 'Aspects of the Erotic Way of Life in Proclus', in K. Boudouris et al. (eds), *Proceedings of the XXIII World Congress of Philosophy* (in collaboration with the Greek Philosophical Society and the Fédération Internationale des Sociétés de Philosophie), vol.2, Section 4, 33–6, Charlottesville: Philosophy Documentation Centre.

Vasilakis, D.A. (2019a), 'On the Meaning of Hierarchy in Dionysius the Areopagite', in P.G. Pavlos, L.F. Janby, E.K. Emilsson and T.T. Tollefsen (eds), *Platonism and Christian Thought in Late Antiquity*, 181–200, London and New York: Routledge.

Vasilakis, D.A. (2019b), 'Neoplatonic Providence and Descent: A Test-Case from Proclus' *Alcibiades Commentary*', *The International Journal of the Platonic Tradition*, 13 (2): 153–71.

Vasilakis, D.A. (2019c), 'Proclus on the *First Alcibiades*: From Platonic Eros to Aristotelian Friendship', *Dia-noesis: A Journal of Philosophy*, 7: 123–34.

Velimirovich, Saint Nikolai, St Justin Popovic and Elder Thaddeus (of Vitovnica) (2013), Περί Ἀγάπης Λόγοι [*Speeches on Love*], Modern Greek trans. Σ. Πέτσιν and Ἡ. Σαραγούδας, Athens: ἐκδ. Χρόες, Σύγχρονοι Γέροντες (also from 2016, Athens: ἐκδ. Παρρησία).

Verbeke, G. (1982), 'Some Later Neoplatonic Views on Divine Creation and the Eternity of the World', in D.J. O'Meara (ed.), *Neoplatonism and Christian Thought*, 45–53 (and 241–4: notes), Albany, NY: SUNY Press, Studies in Neoplatonism, vol.3.

Verkerk, W. (2019), *Nietzsche and Friendship*, London, New Delhi, New York, Sydney: Bloomsbury Academic.

Vernant, J.-P. (1990), 'One ... Two ... Three: *Erōs*' (trans. D. Lyons), in D.M. Halperin, J.J. Winkler and F.I. Zeitlin (eds), *Before Sexuality. The Construction of Erotic Experience in the Ancient Greek World*, 465–78, Princeton, NJ: PUP.

Vlastos, G. (1965), 'The Disorderly Motion in the *Timaeus*', in R.E. Allen (ed.), *Studies in Plato's Metaphysics*, 379–420, London/New York: Routledge & Kegan Paul Humanities Press; (reprinted in 2013 by 'Routledge Library Editions: Plato').

Vlastos, G. (1973), 'The Individual as an Object of Love in Plato', in G. Vlastos, *Platonic Studies*, 3–34, Princeton: PUP.

Vletsis, A.V. (1994), Ὀντολογία τῆς πτώσης στή θεολογία Μαξίμου τοῦ Ὁμολογητοῦ' ['Ontology of the Fall in Maximus the Confessor's Theology'], PhD diss., Aristotelian University of Thessaloniki. Available online: http://thesis.ekt.gr/thesisBookReader/id/3709#page/1/mode/2up (accessed 28 June 2014). This work has been published as: idem (1998), *Τό προπατορικό ἁμάρτημα στή θεολογία Μαξίμου τοῦ Ὁμολογητοῦ*.

Ἔρευνα στίς ἀπαρχές μιᾶς ὀντολογίας τῶν κτιστῶν [*The Original Sin in Maximus the Confessor's Theology. Study in the Beginnings of an Ontology of the Creatures*], Katerini: ἐκδ. Τέρτιος.

Völker, W. (1958), *Kontemplation und Ekstase bei Pseudo-Dionysius Areopagita*, Wiesbaden: F. Steiner.

Von Balthasar, H.U. (1940), 'Das Scholienwerk des Johannes von Scythopolis', *Scholastik*, 15: 16–38. English translation in the Appendix of idem (2003), *Cosmic Liturgy. The Universe According to Maximus the Confessor*, trans. B.E. Daley, 359–87, San Francisco: Ignatius Press, Communio.

Von Hildebrand, D. (2009), *The Nature of Love*, trans. J.F. Crosby with J.H. Crosby, introductory study J.F. Crosby, preface K.L. Schmitz, South Bend, Indiana: St. Augustine's Press.

Von Ivánka, E. (1953), '"Teilhaben," "Hervorgang," und "Hierarchie" bei Pseudo-Dionysius und bei Proklos (Der "Neuplatonismus" des Pseudo-Dionysius)', *Actes du Xième Congrès International de Philosophie*, 12: 153–8.

Voulgarakis, I. (1989), «Γιὰ τὸν ἔρωτα στοὺς Πατέρες» ['On eros in the Fathers'], *Σύναξη*, 32: 7–25.

Voulgarakis, I. (2004), *Σχεδίασμα για την αγάπη* [*A Sketch about Love*], ed. E. Βουλγαράκη-Πισίνα, Athens: Μαΐστρος.

Voutsina, P. and S. Athanasopoulou-Kypriou (2005), 'The "Illuminating" Value of Love: Gregory of Nyssa's Understanding of Love as Epistemically Valuable and Love's Contribution to Virtue Epistemology', *Philotheos*, 5: 248–54.

(Ware,) Kallistos (Metropolitan) of Diokleia (1986), 'The Human Person as an Icon of the Trinity', *Sobornost incorporating Eastern Churches Review*, 8 (2): 6–23.

Ware, Kallistos (²1995), *The Orthodox Way*, 2nd revised edn, Crestwood, NY: St Vladimir's Seminary Press; (first published in 1979 by A.R. Mowbray & Co.).

Wasmuth, E. (2016), 'Self-knowledge in *Alcibiades I*', PhD diss., University of Cambridge, Newnham College.

Westerink, L.G. (1959), 'Exzerpte aus Proklos' *Enneaden-Kommentar* bei Psellos', *Byzantinishe Zeitschrift*, 52: 1–10.

Westerink, L.G., ed. (²1962), *Proclus: Commentary on the First Alcibiades*, 2nd edn (¹1954), Amsterdam: North Holland Publishing. Reprinted along with O'Neill's translation and commentary in 2011, Westbury: The Prometheus Trust, 'Platonic Texts and Translations Series', vol. VI.

Whittaker Th. (1928), *The Neo-Platonists. A Study in the History of Hellenism*, 4th edn with a supplement on the *Commentaries* of Proclus (1st edn 1901; repr. 1961), Hildesheim: Georg Olms Verlagsbuchhandlung.

Williams, B. (1999), 'The Analogy of City and Soul in Plato's *Republic*', in G. Fine (ed.), *Plato*, vol.2: *Ethics, Politics, Religion, and the Soul*, 255–64, Oxford: The Clarendon Press.

Williams, B. (2007), 'Pagan Justice and Christian Love', in B. Williams, *The Sense of the Past. Essays in the History of Philosophy*, ed. with an introduction by M. Burnyeat, Princeton: PUP.

Wolters, A.M. (1984), *Plotinus 'On Eros'. A Detailed Exegetical Study of* Enneads *III.5*, Toronto: Wedge Publishing Foundation; (based on his 1972 PhD diss., Amsterdam).

Woolf, R. (2017), 'Love and Knowledge', in V. Harte and R. Woolf (eds), *Rereading Ancient Philosophy. Old Chestnuts and Sacred Cows*, 80–100, Cambridge: CUP.

Wurm, A. (2008), *Platonicus amor: Lesarten der Liebe bei Platon, Plotin und Ficino*, Berlin, NY: Walter de Gruyter, Beiträge zur Altertumskunde, Band 261.

Yangazoglou, S. (1992), *Προλεγόμενα στή θεολογία τῶν ἀκτίστων ἐνεργειῶν. Σπουδή στόν Ἅγιο Γρηγόριο Παλαμᾶ* [*Introduction to the Theology of Uncreated Energies. Study on Saint Gregory Palamas*], Katerini: ἐκδ. Τέρτιος.

Yannaras, Chr. (2005), *On the Absence and Unknowability of God. Heidegger and the Areopagite*, trans. H. Ventis, ed. with an introduction by A. Louth, London: T&T Clark.

Yannaras, Chr. (2007), *Person and Eros*, trans. Norman Russell, Brookline, MA: Holy Cross Orthodox Press.

Zizioulas, John D. (1985), *Being as Communion. Studies in Personhood and the Church*, with a Foreword by J. Meyendorff (reprints in ³2000/1997), Crestwood, NY: St Vladimir's Seminary Press, Contemporary Greek Theologians Series, No 4.

Zografidis, G. (2009), 'Βυζαντινοί έρωτες, θεϊκοί και ανθρώπινοι ... Η διαλεκτική της επιθυμίας και της απάθειας' ['Byzantine Erotes, Divine and Human: The Dialectic of Desire and Impassivity'], *Αρχαιολογία και Τέχνες*, [*Archaeology and Arts*, issue devoted to «Περί Έρωτος και Αγάπης»], 110: 12a–21b (with an English abstract in 21b).

Zoumboulakis, S., ed. (2017), *About Love* [*Γιά τήν ἀγάπη*], Athens: Artos Zois.

Index*

A

activity 22, 23, 26, 27
   erotic 25, 145
   external 37
   intellectual 15, 29
   intentional 90, 94
   providential 145, 147
   self-constituting 19, 20, 25, 34, 35, 36, 41, 45
actuality
   second 22, 28
Adamson, P. ix, 116 n.47, 125 n.131
Aeschylus 177 n.127
affection 44, 45
   disinterested 88–90
agape 4 and *passim*
Agathon (tragic poet) 91, 95, 167 n.39
Aimilianos, Elder (Abbot of Simonos Petras, Mount Athos: Γέρων Αἰμιλιανός) 162 n.10
Alcibiades (son of Cleinias) 46, 159 and *passim* in Chapter 2
Alcinous (Alcinoos/Albinus) 2, 120 n.81
allegory 17
altruism 184
Ambury, J.M. 114 n.28
Ammonius (son of Hermias) 133 n.220
Anaxagoras 129 n.179
Andreopoulos, A. (π. Ἀνδρέας Ἀνδρεόπουλος) 171 n.78
Angelopoulos, J.K. (Ἀγγελόπουλος, I.K.) 163 n.17
St Antony (the Great) 10 n.35
Aphrodite 68, 93, 95, 99, 101
   Heavenly *passim* in Chapter 1
   Common *passim* in Chapter 1
Apollo 100
Apuleius 59 n.145, 184
Aquinas. *See* Thomas Aquinas
Archilochus 132 n.212
Areopagite. *See* Dionysius the Areopagite
Aristophanes 51 n.50, 55 n.104, 93, 121 n.87, 129 n.175, 140 n.341
Aristotle 2, 4, 22, 43, 76–8, 90, 92, 153
Armstrong, A.H. 2, 112 n.6
Aspasia (of Miletus) 5 n.1
Athanasius the Great (of Alexandria) 156, 158, 169 n.54
Athanasopoulos, C. (Ἀθανασόπουλος, K.) 186 n.10
Athanasopoulou-Kypriou, S. (Ἀθανασοπούλου-Κυπρίου, Σ.) 62 n.181
audacity (tolma) 42, 43
Augustine (of Hippo) 6 n.10, 9 n.34, 166 n.36, 181 n.155

B

Baltas, D.V. (Μπαλτάς, Δ.B.) 182 n.170
Barlaam (the Calabrian) 164 n.29
[B]eautiful/[B]eauty *passim* in Chapters 2–3
Begzos, M. (Μπέγζος, Μ.Π.) 165 n.29
Berdyaev, N. 186 n.12
Bertozzi, A. 1
Blowers, P.M. 61 n.181, 178 n.133
Blum, R. 167 n.40
Boethius (of Rome) 6 n.11, 162 n.10
Bozinis, K.A. (Μποζίνης, K.A.) 162 n.14
Bradshaw, D. 5 n.3, 165 n.29, 186 n.4
Bulgakov, fr. S. 173 n.98

C

Cebes 117 n.63
Chatzimichael, D.K. (Χατζημιχαήλ, Δ.K.) 181 n.162, 182 n.170
Chouliaras, A. (Χουλιαράς, π. Αλ.) 166 n.36

---

* All Greek names are transliterated, as they appear in my text and notes. Only for the Modern Greek names I supply the reader with the original in parenthesis.

Christology 156-7
Christodoulidi-Mazaraki, A.
    (Χριστοδουλίδη-Μαζαράκη, Α.)
    5 n.1
Chrysakopoulou, S. (Χρυσακοπούλου, Σ.)
    135 n.253
Chrysippus 59 n.143, 138 n.293
Cicero 120 n.81, 132 n.208
Clement of Alexandria 177 n.127,
    182 n.167
Constas, Maximos (π. Μάξιμος: Κώνστας,
    Ν.) 180 n.150
contemplation 23
Corrigan, K. 2
Counsel (Μῆτις) 69, 94, 110
Creuzer, G.F. 55 n.103
Cupid 185
Cyril of Alexandria 176 n.123, 183 n.174

D

daimon 34, 44, 99-101. *See* also eros
    daimon
Damascius 7 n.16
Damaskos, P.K. (Δαμάσκος, Π.Κ.) *passim*
    in nn. of Chapter 1
D'Andres, N. 1
De Lacy, P.H. 49 n.26
Delikostantis, K.Z. (Δεληκωσταντής,
    K.Z.) 56 n.105
Demacopoulos, G.E. (Δημακόπουλος, Γ.)
    186 n.4
Democritus 59 n.143
desire 24, 25, 35, 39, 69, 91-3, 95-9,
    103-5, 107-10, 150, 152, 154
Dillon, J. ix, 39
Diogenes Laertius 122 n.90
Diogenes the Cynic 122 n.90
Dion 160 n.1
Dionysus 160 n.1
Dionysius the Areopagite 67, 120 n.87,
    passim in Chapter 3
Diotima (of Mantineia) 5 n.1, 13, 33, 46,
    47 n.9, 63 n.200, 64 n.214, 86, 91,
    96, 98, 99, 113 n.18, 115 n.37, 121
    n.88
Dodds, E.R. 67, 84, 94, 106, 141
Dorotheus of Gaza 162 n.17
Dostoyevsky, F.M. 185
Douma, K. (Δούμα, Κ.) 6 n.9

E

ecstasy 4, 141-2, 152-4, 158
egoism 73, 75-6, 88, 90, 184
Electra 54 n.92
Eliopoulos, N. (Ηλιόπουλος, Ν.) 12 n.42
Empedocles 62 n.192, 93, 110, 122 n.92,
    123 n.103, 135 n.250, 140 n.342 and
    n.347
Epicharmus 21, 54 n.81
Epictetus 120 n.81
Epicurean(ism) 84-5
[E]ros 4 and *passim*. *See also* Cupid, love,
    friendship & agape
    ascending/upwards/reversive 3 and
        passim in Chapters 2-3
    daimon 13, 14, 30, 32, 91, 99, 102
    descending/downwards/providential 3
        passim in Chapters 2-3
eternity 20, 39, 91
Euripides 121 n.90

F

[F]aith 82-3, 93, 105
Ficino, Marsilio 2, 8 n.27, 112 n.11
Flamand, J.-M. 42
Florovsky, fr. Georges V. 10 n.35, 146, 147,
    162 n.10, 168 n.41, 174 n.103, 177
    n.124
Freud, S. 5 n.1
friendship 4 and *passim*

G

Galen 49 n.26
Garitsis, K. (Γαρίτσης, Κ.) 10 n.37, 170 n.67
Ghiţ, F.-C.G. 9 n.34
Gnostic(ism) 3, 43
God *passim* and 151
    consubstantial 146, 150, 164 n.27, 167
        n.40
    and the Mother of God 171 n.78
    as Trinity 146-8, 150-1, 160
Golitzin, A. (Archbishop Alexander)
    passim in Chapter 3
Gontikakis, Vasileios (Abbot of Iviron,
    Mt Athos: Βασίλειος Γοντικάκης)
    11 n.41
Gounelas, S. (Γουνελάς, Σ.) 177 n.125
Gregory of Nyssa 10 n.35, 61 n.181, 172
    n.84, 173 n.95, 177 n.127

Gregory Palamas 158, 164–5 n.29, 165 n.32, 166 n.36, 173 n.100, 180 n.151, 184, 185
Gregory the Theologian (Nazianzene/Nazianzenus) 146, 165 n.30
Griffin, M. 7 n.16, 114 n.28, 119 n.70, 137 n.282

H
Harper, D. (π. Δημήτριος) 7 n.15, 173 n.98
Heidegger, M. 185
Heraclitus 59 n.143, 153, 173 n.97
Hermes 100, 135 n.253, 140 n.341
Hermias 114 n.28
Hesiod 13, 47 n.12, 168 n.54
Hierocles (the Neoplatonist) 2
Hierotheus *passim* in Chapter 3
Horn, G. 1
Hutchinson, D. S. 114 n.25
[h]ypostasis 15, 18, 20, 23, 27, 146, 159 and *passim*

I
Iamblichus 2, 51 n.48, 133 n.221 and n.223, 139 n.325, 169 n.62
Igal, J. 48 n.19
Ignatius (of Antioch) 161 n.8, 181 n.157
Incarnation
  of Christ (Jesus) 155–7, 159
Ioannidis, A. (Ιωαννίδης, Γ.) x

J
Jevtic, A. (Bishop Athanase) 11 n.41
John Chrysostom 162 n.14, 177 n.127
John Climacus 10 n.35
John of Damascus 185
John of Scythopolis 177 n.125, 183 n.170
John Philoponus 162 n.10
John the Evangelist (the Theologian) 157, 180 n.147

K
Kalfas, V. (Κάλφας, Β.) 5 n.1
Kalligas, P. (Καλλιγάς, Π.) *passim* in Introduction and Chapter 1, 116 n.50, 170 n.74
Karamanolis, G. (Καραμανώλης, Γ.) 182 n.167
Kelessidou-Galanos, A. (Κελεσίδου-Γαλανού, Α.) 6 n.5, 111 n.3
kenosis (self-emptying) 156–8

Kirchhoff, A. 55 n.104
Koch, H. 141
Koutras, D. (Κούτρας, Δ.) 185 n.2
Kranidiotis, G. (Κρανιδιώτης, Γ.) 6 n.9
Kroll, W. 122 n.96, 126 n.149, 136 n.257, 139 n.326
Kronos 17, 27, 35, 47 n.12, 59 n.157, 121 n.87

L
Lacrosse, J. 1
Laius 119 n.70, 131 n.203
Lekkos, E.P. (Λέκκος, Ε.Π.) 11 nn.41–2
Lentakis, A. (Λεντάκης, Α.) ix
Lentakis, V. (Λεντάκης, Β.) ix
[L]ife 94–5
[L]ogos (logoi) 30, 31, 35, 43, 69, 80, 146
Longo, A. 6 n.7
Lossky, Vl. 165 n.32, 166 nn.32–3, 172 n.84, 185
Loudovikos, N. (Λουδοβίκος, π. Νικόλαος) 167 n.40, 172 n.87, 173 n.98, 177 n.126
Louth, fr. A. *passim* in Chapter 3
[L]ove 4 and *passim*
  Platonic 1

M
Mainoldi, E. fr. S. 162 n.10
Manos, A. (Μάνος, Α.) 5 n.2, 111–12 nn.3–5, 135 n.247, 136 n.270, 174 nn.101–2
Manoussakis, J.P. (Μανουσάκης, π. Παντελεήμων) 166 n.32
Maraguianou, E. (Μαραγγιανού-Δερμούση, Ε.) 5 n.1
Martijn, M. 6 n.7, 115 n.33
matter 29
  intelligible 37, 41
  prime 38, 42
Mavropoulos, D. (Μαυρόπουλος, Δ.) 5 n.2, 173 n.98
Maximus of Tyre 59 n.145
Maximus Planoudes (Μάξιμος Πλανούδης) 166 n.36
Maximus the Confessor 6 n.9, 183 and *passim* in Chapter 3
McCabe, M.M. ix, 119 n.69
Meyendorff, fr. J. 156, 165 n.29, 176 n.124, 180 n.152

Michaelides, P.E. (Μιχαηλίδης, Π.Ε.) 6 n.5
Mitralexis, S. (Μητραλέξης, Σ.) 7 n.15
Moltmann, J. 180 n.149
Moustakas, P. (Μουστάκας, Π.) ix
Moutsopoulos, E. (Μουτσόπουλος, Ε.) 61 n.179, 133 n.219

N
St Nectarios (Metropolitan of Pentapolis: ὁ Αἰγίνης Ἅγιος Νεκτάριος Κεφαλᾶς) 173 n.98
Nehamas, A. (Νεχαμάς, Α.) 11 n.41, 120 n.77, 125 n.127
(Neo-)Pythagorean(ism) 43, 76, 111, 169 n.62
Niarchos, C.G. (Νιάρχος, Κ.) 174 n.106
Nicolaidou-Kyrianidou, V. (Νικολαΐδου-Κυριανίδου, Βάνα) ix
Nietzsche, Fr. 11 n.41, 165 n.32, 185
Nygren, A. 4, 6-7 n.11, 9-10 nn.33-6, 115 nn.42-3, 160 n.3, 161 n.8, 174 n.103

O
Oedipus 54 n.92, 131 n.203
Olympiodorus 2, 7 n.16, 119 n.70, 137 n.282
Opsomer, J. 171 n.75
Origen (Adamantius of Alexandria) 2, 6 n.11, 49 n.23, 161 n.8, 173 n.95, 177 n.127, 181 n.157
Orpheus 94, 110
Ouranos 47 nn.6 and 12

P
Pachymeres, G. (Γεώργιος Παχυμέρης) 182 n.170
Palamas. *See* Gregory Palamas
Pallis, D. (Πάλλης, Δ.) 168 n.48
Panagopoulos, S. (Παναγόπουλος, Σπ.) 6 n.9
Papanikolaou, A. (Παπανικολάου, Α.) 163 n.18, 166 n.33, 172 n.84, 186 n.4
Papathanasiou, Ath. (Παπαθανασίου, Θ.Ν.) 162 n.14
participation 149 and *passim*
Paul (the Apostle) 152, 160 n.1, 169 n.54, 173 n.98, 174 n.104, 178 n.130, 180 n.147, 181 n.157

Pausanias (interlocutor in the *Symposium*) 13, 59 n.153, 119 n.74
Pavlos, P. (Παύλος, Π.Γ.) 62 n.181
[P]eace 144, 157
Penia (Poverty) *passim* in Chapter 1 and 67-70, 185
Pericles 5 n.1
[P]erson 146
philanthropy (φιλανθρωπία: love for mankind) 156-8, 160
Philoponus. *See* John Philoponus
Pigler, A. 1
Pinotti, P. 135 n.253
Plato 1, 2, 3, 4, 13, 17, 21, 25, 33, 43, 45, 69, 73-6, 78, 80, 86-8, 91, 96, 102, 108, 148, 160, 184-5
Plotinus *passim* in Chapter 1 and 67-72, 79, 83, 90-1, 95-6, 98-9, 106, 108, 141, 143-5, 148, 150-1, 153-4, 158, 184-5
Plutarch (Middle-Platonist) 14, 33-4, 55 n.104, 59 n.145, 65 n.216, 135 n.253
Popović, J. (St Justin of Celije) 11 n.41, 186 n.12, 62 n.187, 121 n.90, 167 n.38
Poros (Plenty/Resource) *passim* in Chapter 1 and 68-9
Porphyry 15, 48-9 n.23, 167 n.38
Presocratic 110
Proclus *passim* in Chapter 2 and 46, 47 n.12, 51 n.48, 59 n.146, 61 n.175, 63 n.199, 141-4, 149-51, 153-5, 158-60, 184-5
Prometheus 124 n.107
providence 3, 105
  and procession 3
  undefiled (/unmixed/detached) 84, 88, 98, 103, 158-9
Pupaza, D. (π. Δανιήλ) 10 n.37

R
Ramfos, S. (Ράμφος, Σ.) 9 n.34, 173-4 n.101
Rasmussen, W. ix
Rellos, M. (Ρέλλος, Μ.) 185 n.2
Richard of St Victor 146, 165 n.31
Riggs, T. 1, 2
Romanides, fr. John (π. Ιωάννης Ρωμανίδης) 180 n.152
Roskam, G. 114 n.28

Rozanis, S. (Ροζάνης, Σ.) 5 n.2
Russell, N. 164 n.29, 166 n.33

S
Santas, G. (Σάντας, Γ.) 5 n.1
Sartre, J.-P. 185
self-constitution 20, 35
self-knowledge 69
self-sufficiency 70, 73
Siasos, L. (Σιάσος, Λ.Χρ.) 147, 157–8, 164 n.29, 168 n.42, 45 and 48
Siniossoglou, N. (Σινιόσογλου, N.) 186 n.3
Sinkewicz, R.E. 166 n.36
Siorvanes, L. (Σιορβάνης, Λ.) 111 n.3
Skliris, D. (Σκλήρης, Δ.) 11 n.41
Socrates *passim* in Chapter 2 and 4, 33, 46, 156, 158–60, 185
Sophocles v, 56 n.105
[S]oul
  Undescended 44, 45, 101
Stamoulis, Ch.A. (Σταμούλης, Χ.Α.) 5 n.2, 11 n.41, 186 n.5
Stăniloae, fr. Dumitru 186 n.9
Stathopoulou, G.M. (Σταθοπούλου, Γ.Μ.) 60 n.163
Steiris, G. (Στείρης, Γ.) ix
Stobaeus 138 n.293
Stoic(ism) 11 n.42, 59 n.143 and 156, 116 n.44, 118 n.63, 120 n.81, 122 n.97, 128 n.164, 131–2 n.208, 160 n.4, 177 n.127, 183 n.174
Sykoutris, I. (Συκουτρής, I.) 10 n.35, 47 n.10, 59 n.144, 64 n.214, 65 n.215, 114 n.30, 129 n.175, 135 n.250
Symeon the New Theologian 185

T
Terezis, Ch. (Τερέζης, Χρ.) 1
Themistius 177 n.127
Theodorakopoulos, I.N. (Θεοδωρακόπουλος, I.N.) 124 n.114
Thomas Aquinas 165 n.31, 169 n.59, 173 n.92, 184
Thrasymachus 121 n.87
time 17, 20, 91
Timothy (addressee of Dionysius) 157, 178 n.129, 179 n.144
Tor, Shaul (Sol) ix

Tornau, C. 2
Triantari-Mara, S. (Τριαντάρη-Μαρά, Σ.) 170 n.67
Tsakoymaki, M. (Τσακουμάκη, M.) 6 n.6, 115 n.35
Tzavaras, G.G. (Τζαβάρας, Γ.Γ.) 5 n.2

V
Van Riel, G. 124 n.111, 133 n.222, 138 n.310, 139 n.322
Vasilakis, A.D. (Βασιλάκης, Αντώνιος ιερέως Δημητρίου) ix, 125 n.127
Verdenius, W.J. 10 n.35, 131 n.199
Vgenopoulou, P. (Βγενοπούλου, Π.) 6 n.9
Vlastos, G. (Βλαστός, Γρ.) 3
Vletsis, A.V. (Βλέτσης, Αθ. Β.) 178 n.133
Voulgarakis, I. (Βουλγαράκης, Η.) 5 n.2, 161 n.8
Voutsina, P. (Βουτσινά, Π.) 62 n.181
Vrettakos, N. (Βρεττάκος, Νικηφόρος) v

W
Ware, Kallistos (Metropolitan of Diokleia; formerly Timothy Ware) 165 n.31, 166 nn.35–6, 171 n.82
Wesche, fr. P. 180 n.152
Wolters, A.M. 1 and *passim* in Chapter 1
Woolf, R. ix, 5 n.1, 125 n.131

X
Xenocrates 59 n.143
Xenophon 125 n.131

Y
Yangazoglou, S. (Γιαγκάζογλου, Στ.) 166 n.36
Yannaras, Chr. (Γιανναράς, Χρήστος) 2, 146, 185

Z
Zeus 14, 17, 77, 100, 110–11
Zeyl, D.J. 117 n.52
Zizioulas, John D. (Μητροπολίτης Περγάμου, Ιωάννης Ζηζιούλας) 146
Zografidis, G. (Ζωγραφίδης, Γ.) 173 n.98
Zoumboulakis, S. (Ζουμπουλάκης, Στ.) 11 n.41

www.ingramcontent.com/pod-product-compliance
Lightning Source LLC
Chambersburg PA
CBHW072232290426
44111CB00012B/2059